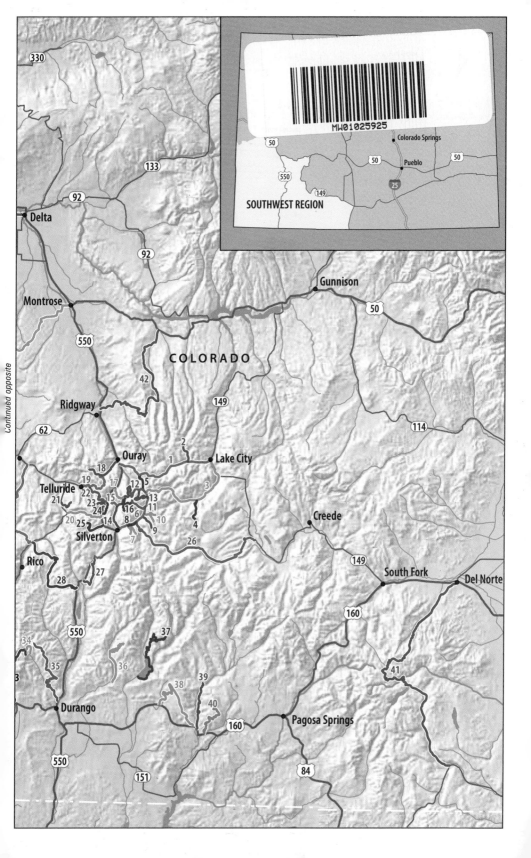

330

133

92

Delta

92

Montrose

550

COLORADO

42

Ridgway

149

Gunnison

50

62

114

2

18

1

Lake City

Ouray

19

17

12   5

3

Telluride

22

15

13

21

23

11

24

16   6

Creede

20   25

8   10

14

9

Silverton

4

7

26

Rico

27

149

South Fork

28

Del Norte

550

160

34

37

41

35

36

3

38   39

Durango

40

550

160

Pagosa Springs

151

84

SOUTHWEST REGION

50

Colorado Springs

550

50

Pueblo

50

149

25

Continued opposite

COLORADO TRAILS
SOUTHWEST REGION

Warning: While every effort has been made to make the 4WD trail descriptions in this book as accurate as possible, some discrepancies may exist between the text and the actual trail. Hazards may have changed since the research and publication of this edition. Adler Publishing Company, Inc., and the authors accept no responsibility for the safety of users of this guide. Individuals are liable for all costs incurred if rescue is necessary.

Printed in the United States of America

Cover photos
Clockwise from bottom left: Silverton to Animas Forks Ghost Town, Black Bear Pass Trail, Carson Ghost Town Trail

Back cover photos
From left: Silverton to Animas Forks Ghost Town, Black Bear Pass Trail

COLORADO TRAILS

SOUTHWEST REGION

PETER MASSEY
JEANNE WILSON
ANGELA TITUS

ADLER
PUBLISHING

Acknowledgements

Many people and organizations have made major contributions to the research and production of this book. We owe them all special thanks for their assistance.

We would like to express gratitude to the staff at the Silverton Chamber of Commerce, the U.S. Forest Service, the Denver Public Library, the Colorado Historical Society, and the various other Chambers of Commerce in southwest Colorado who have given us guidance in our research.

Trail map images from the Benchmark *Colorado Road & Recreation Atlas*. Produced by and copyright ©Benchmark Maps, Medford, Oregon. All rights reserved. Used with permission. Benchmarkmaps.com.

Publisher's Note: Every effort has been taken to ensure that the information in this book is accurate at press time. Please visit our website to advise us of any changes or corrections you find. We also welcome recommendations for new trails or other suggestions to improve the information in this book.

Adler Publishing Company, Inc.
P.O. Box 519
Castle Rock, CO 80104
Toll-free: 800-660-5107
Fax: 303-688-4388
AdlerPublishing.com

ADLER
PUBLISHING

Contents

Before You Go   9

Trails

Trail #1:   Engineer Pass Trail   26
Trail #2:   Nellie Creek Trail   39
Trail #3:   Cinnamon Pass Trail   41
Trail #4:   Carson Ghost Town Trail   47
Trail #5:   North Fork Cutoff   52
Trail #6:   Silverton to Animas Forks Ghost Town   54
Trail #7:   Arrastra Gulch Trail   66
Trail #8:   Silverton Northern Railroad Grade   75
Trail #9:   Maggie Gulch Trail   79
Trail #10: Minnie Gulch Trail   82
Trail #11: Eureka Gulch Trail   86
Trail #12: California Gulch Trail   91
Trail #13: Picayne Gulch and Placer Gulch Trail   97
Trail #14: Silverton to Lake Como Trail   102
Trail #15: Prospect Gulch Trail   107
Trail #16: Gladstone Network   108
Trail #17: Corkscrew Gulch Trail   115
Trail #18: Yankee Boy Basin Trail   120
Trail #19: Imogene Pass Trail   131
Trail #20: Ophir Pass Trail   142
Trail #21: Alta Ghost Town Trail   153
Trail #22: Black Bear Pass Trail   160
Trail #23: Bullion King Lake Trail   166
Trail #24: Brown's Gulch Trail   168
Trail #25: Bandora Mine and Clear Lake Trail   171
Trail #26: Cunningham Gulch and Stony Pass Trail   177
Trail #27: Old Lime Creek Road   184
Trail #28: Bolam Pass Trail   191
Trail #29: Fall Creek Trail   195

Trail #30:   Jersey Jim Lookout Loop   199
Trail #31:   Turkey Creek Trail   209
Trail #32:   Gold Run Loop   213
Trail #33:   Columbus Mine Trail   217
Trail #34:   Kennebec Pass Trail   225
Trail #35:   Junction Creek Trail   232
Trail #36:   Transfer Park Road   238
Trail #37:   Middle Mountain Trail   245
Trail #38:   First Notch Trail   252
Trail #39:   First Fork Road   257
Trail #40:   Devil Mountain Trail   260
Trail #41:   Summitville Ghost Town Trail   268
Trail #42:   Owl Creek and Chimney Rock Trail   276
Trail #43:   Uncompahgre Plateau Trail   282
Trail #44:   Far Pond Trail   288
Trail #45:   Dominguez Ridge Loop   292
Trail #46:   Escalante Canyon Road   297
Trail #47:   Dry Mesa Jeep Road   310
Trail #48:   Escalante Rim Trail   318

Sidebars

The Ute and Chief Ouray   36
The Cannibalism of Alferd Packer   45
Silverton   56
Animas Forks   62
Eureka   72
Ouray   122
The Silver Crash of 1893   141
Otto Mears, The Pathfinder of the San Juans   144
Telluride   150
Mining Operations   158
Elk   224
Aspen   237
Mountain Lion   269
Ridgway   281

Selected Further Reading   324

Before You Go

Why a 4WD Does It Better

The design and engineering of 4WD vehicles provide them with many advantages over normal cars when you head off the paved road:

- improved distribution of power to all four wheels;
- a transmission transfer case, which provides low-range gear selection for greater pulling power and for crawling over difficult terrain;
- high ground clearance;
- less overhang of the vehicle's body past the wheels, which provides better front- and rear-clearance when crossing gullies and ridges;
- large-lug, wide-tread tires;
- rugged construction (including underbody skid plates on many models).

If you plan to do off-highway touring, all of these considerations are important whether you are evaluating the capabilities of your current 4WD or are looking to buy one; each is considered in detail in this chapter.

To explore the most difficult trails described in this book, you will need a 4WD vehicle that is well rated in each of the above features. If you own a 2WD sport utility vehicle, a lighter car-type SUV, or a pickup truck, your ability to explore the more difficult trails will depend on conditions and your level of experience.

A word of caution: Whatever type of 4WD vehicle you drive, understand that it is not invincible or indestructible. Nor can it go everywhere. A 4WD has a much higher center of gravity and weighs more than a car, and so has its own consequent limitations.

Experience is the only way to learn what your vehicle can and cannot do. Therefore, if you are inexperienced, we strongly recommend that you start with trails that have lower difficulty ratings. As you develop an understanding of your vehicle and of your own taste for adventure, you can safely tackle the more challenging trails.

One way to beef up your knowledge quickly, while avoiding the costly and sometimes dangerous lessons learned from on-the-road mistakes, is to undertake a 4WD course taught by a professional. Look in the Yellow Pages for courses in your area.

Using This Book

Route Planning

The regional map inside the front cover provides a convenient overview of the trails in the Southwest Region of Colorado. Each trail is shown, as are major highways and towns, in order to help you plan various routes by connecting a series of 4WD trails and paved roads.

As you plan your overall route, you will probably want to utilize as many 4WD trails as possible. However, check the difficulty rating and time required for each trail before finalizing your plans. You don't want to be stuck 50 miles from the highway—at sunset and without camping gear, since your trip was supposed to be over hours ago—when you discover that your vehicle can't handle a certain difficult passage.

Difficulty Ratings

We use a point system to rate the difficulty of each trail. Any such system is subjective, and your experience of the trails will vary depending on your skill and the road conditions at the time. Indeed, any amount of rain may make the trails much more difficult, if not completely impassable.

We have rated the 4WD trails on a scale of 1 to 10—1 being passable for a normal passenger vehicle in good conditions and 10 requiring a heavily modified vehicle and an experienced driver who expects to encounter vehicle damage. Because this book is designed for owners of unmodified 4WD vehicles—who we assume do not want to damage their vehicles—most of the trails are rated 5 or lower. A few trails are included that rate as high as 7, while those rated 8 to 10 are beyond the scope of this book.

This is not to say that the moderate-rated trails are easy. We strongly recommend that inexperienced drivers not tackle trails rated at 4 or higher until they have undertaken a number of the lower-rated ones, so that they can gauge their skill level and prepare for the difficulty of the higher-rated trails.

In assessing the trails, we have always assumed good road conditions (dry road surface, good visibility, and so on). The factors influencing our ratings are as follows:

■ obstacles such as rocks, mud, ruts, sand, slickrock, and stream crossings;

■ the stability of the road surface;

■ the width of the road and the vehicle clearance between trees or rocks;

■ the steepness of the road;

■ the margin for driver error (for example, a very high, open shelf road would be rated more difficult even if it was not very steep and had a stable surface).

The following is a guide to the ratings.

Rating 1: The trail is graded dirt but suitable for a normal passenger vehicle. It usually has gentle grades, is fairly wide, and has very shallow water crossings (if any).

Rating 2: High-clearance vehicles are preferred but not necessary. These trails are dirt roads, but they may have rocks, grades, water crossings, or ruts that make clearance a concern in a normal passenger vehicle. The trails are fairly wide, making passing possible at almost any point along the trail. Mud is not a concern under normal weather conditions.

Rating 3: High-clearance 4WDs are preferred, but any high-clearance vehicle is acceptable. Expect a rough road surface; mud and sand are possible but will be easily passable. You may encounter rocks up to 6 inches in diameter, a loose road surface, and shelf roads, though these will be wide enough for passing or will have adequate pull-offs.

Rating 4: High-clearance is required, 4WD is preferred, though some stock SUVs are acceptable. Expect a rough road surface with rocks larger than 6 inches, but there will be a reasonable driving line available. Patches

of mud are possible but can be readily negotiated; sand may be deep and require lower tire pressures. There may be stream crossings up to 12 inches deep, substantial sections of single-lane shelf road, moderate grades, and sections of moderately loose road surface.

Rating 5: High-clearance 4WDs are required. These trails have either a rough, rutted surface, rocks up to 9 inches, mud and deep sand that may be impassable for inexperienced drivers, or stream crossings up to 18 inches deep. Certain sections may be steep enough to cause traction problems, and you may encounter very narrow shelf roads with steep drop-offs and tight clearance between rocks or trees.

Rating 6: These trails are for experienced four-wheel drivers only. They are potentially dangerous, with large rocks, ruts, or terraces that may need to be negotiated. They may also have stream crossings at least 18 inches deep, involve rapid currents, unstable stream bottoms, or difficult access; steep slopes, loose surfaces, and narrow clearances; or very narrow sections of shelf road with steep drop-offs and possibly challenging road surfaces.

Rating 7: Skilled, experienced four-wheel drivers only. These trails include very challenging sections with extremely steep grades, loose surfaces, large rocks, deep ruts, and/or tight clearances. Mud or sand may necessitate winching.

Rating 8 and above: Stock vehicles are likely to be damaged, and drivers may find the trail impassable. Highly skilled, experienced four-wheel drivers only.

Scenic Ratings

If rating the degree of difficulty is subjective, rating scenic beauty is guaranteed to lead to arguments. Colorado contains a spectacular variety of scenery—from its sky-scraping mountains and alpine meadows to its ghost towns and mining camps. Despite the subjectivity of attempting a comparative rating of diverse scenery, we have tried to provide a guide to the relative scenic quality of the various trails. The ratings are based on a scale of 1 to 10, with 10 being the most attractive.

Estimated Driving Times

In calculating driving times, we have not allowed for stops. Your actual driving time may be considerably longer depending on the number and duration of the stops you make. Add more time if you prefer to drive more slowly than good conditions allow.

Current Road Information

All the 4WD trails described in this book may become impassable in poor weather conditions. Storms can alter roads, remove tracks, and create impassable washes. Most of the trails described, even easy 2WD trails, can quickly become impassable even to 4WD vehicles after only a small amount of rain. For each trail, we have provided a phone number for obtaining current information about conditions.

Abbreviations

The route directions for the 4WD trails use a series of abbreviations as follows:

SO	CONTINUE STRAIGHT ON
TL	TURN LEFT
TR	TURN RIGHT
BL	BEAR LEFT
BR	BEAR RIGHT
UT	U-TURN

Using Route Directions

For every trail, we describe and pinpoint (by odometer reading) nearly every significant feature along the route—such as intersections, streams, washes, gates, cattle guards, and so on—and provide directions from these landmarks. Odometer readings will vary from vehicle to vehicle, so you should allow for slight variations. Be aware that trails can quickly change. A new trail may be cut around a washout, a faint trail can be graded by the county, or a well-used trail may fall into disuse. All these factors will affect the accuracy of the given directions.

If you diverge from the route, zero your trip meter upon your return and continue along the route, making the necessary adjustment to the point-to-point odometer readings. In the directions, we regularly reset

the odometer readings—at significant landmarks or popular lookouts and spur trails—so that you won't have to recalculate for too long.

Most of the trails can be started from either end, and the route directions include both directions of travel; reverse directions are printed in red below the main directions. When traveling in reverse, read from the bottom of the table and work up.

Route directions include cross-references whenever two 4WD trails included in this book connect; these cross-references allow for an easy change of route or destination.

Each trail includes periodic latitude and longitude readings to facilitate using a global positioning system (GPS) receiver. These readings may also assist you in finding your location on the maps. The GPS coordinates are given in the format dd°mm.mm'. To save time when loading coordinates into your GPS receiver, you may wish to include only one decimal place, since in Colorado, the third decimal place equals about two yards and the second less than 20 yards.

Map References

We recommend that you supplement the information in this book with more-detailed maps. For each trail, we list the sheet maps and road atlases that provide the best detail for the area. Typically, the following references are given:

- Bureau of Land Management Maps
- U.S. Forest Service Maps
- *Colorado Atlas & Gazetteer*, 7th ed. (Yarmouth, Maine: DeLorme Mapping, 2004)—Scale 1:250,000
- *Colorado Road and Recreation Atlas*, 1st ed. (Medford, Oregon: Benchmark Maps, 2007)—Scale 1:200,000
- *The Roads of Colorado* (Addison, Texas: Mapsco, Inc., 2007)—Scale 1:160,000
- Maptech-Terrain Navigator Topo Maps—Scale 1:100,000 and 1:24,000,
- *Trails Illustrated* Topo Maps; National Geographic Maps—Various scales, but all contain good detail.

We recommend Benchmark's *Road and*

Recreation Atlas series. The maps have page-to-page overlap, large type, show topographical relief, and they are field-checked for accuracy. These atlases provide United States, regional, and state maps for orientation, as well as enlarged "Metro Maps" for navigating urban areas. The Recreation Guide section, which provides information on local attractions, recreation, and much more, is also handy for trip research and planning. When looking for maps for this book we chose the Benchmark atlas.

The *Trails Illustrated* series of maps are also good for navigating these trails. They are reliable, easy to read, and printed on nearly indestructible plastic paper. However, this series covers a limited number of the 4WD trails described in this book.

The Mapsco and DeLorme atlases are useful maps at a reasonable price if you wish to explore the hundreds of side roads not covered in this book.

U.S. Forest Service maps lack the topographic detail of the other sheet maps and, in our experience, are occasionally out of date. They have the advantage of covering a broad area and are useful in identifying land use and travel restrictions. These maps are most useful for the longer trails.

Another option, albeit more expensive, that has unique advantages is the Terrain Navigator Pro series of maps published on CD-ROM by Maptech. These CD-ROMs include the entire set of 1,941 U.S. Geological Survey topographical maps of Colorado at the 1:24,000 scale and all 71 maps at the 1:100,000 scale. These maps offer many advantages over normal maps:

- GPS coordinates for any location can be found and loaded into your GPS receiver. Conversely, if you have your GPS coordinates, your location on the map can be pinpointed instantly.
- Towns, rivers, passes, mountains, and many other sites are indexed by name so that they can be located quickly.
- 4WD trails can be marked and profiled for elevation changes and distances from point to point.
- Customized maps can be printed out.

- The CD-ROMs can be used with a laptop computer and a GPS receiver in your vehicle to monitor your location on the map and navigate directly from the display.

All these maps should be available through good map stores.

Backcountry Driving Rules and Permits

Four-wheel driving involves special driving techniques and road rules. This section is an introduction for 4WD beginners.

4WD Road Rules

To help ensure that these trails remain open and available for all four-wheel drivers to enjoy, it is important to minimize your impact on the environment and not be a safety risk to yourself or anyone else. Remember that the 4WD clubs in Colorado fight a constant battle with the government and various lobby groups to retain the access that currently exists.

The fundamental rule when traversing the 4WD trails described in this book is to use common sense. In addition, special road rules for 4WD trails apply:

- Vehicles traveling uphill have the right of way.
- If you are moving more slowly than the vehicle behind you, pull over to let the other vehicle pass.
- Park out of the way in a safe place. Blocking a track may restrict access for emergency vehicles as well as for other recreationalists. Set the parking brake—don't rely on leaving the transmission in park. Manual transmissions should be left in the lowest gear.

Tread Lightly!

Remember the rules of the Tread Lightly! program:

- Be informed. Obtain maps, regulations, and other information from the forest service or from other public land agencies. Learn the rules and follow them.
- Resist the urge to pioneer a new road or trail or to cut across a switchback. Stay on constructed tracks and avoid running over

young trees, shrubs, and grasses, damaging or killing them. Don't drive across alpine tundra; this fragile environment can take years to recover.

■ Stay off soft, wet roads and 4WD trails readily torn up by vehicles. Repairing the damage is expensive, and quite often authorities find it easier to close the road rather than repair it.

■ Travel around meadows, steep hillsides, stream banks, and lake shores that are easily scarred by churning wheels.

■ Stay away from wild animals that are rearing young or suffering from a food shortage. Do not camp close to the water sources of domestic or wild animals.

■ Obey gate closures and regulatory signs.

■ Preserve America's heritage by not disturbing old mining camps, ghost towns, or other historical features. Leave historic sites, Native American rock art, ruins, and artifacts in place and untouched.

■ Carry out all your trash, even that of others.

■ Stay out of designated wilderness areas. They are closed to all vehicles. It is your responsibility to know where the boundaries are.

■ Get permission to cross private land. Leave livestock alone. Respect landowners' rights.

■ Report violations of these rules to help keep these 4WD trails open and to ensure that others will have the opportunity to visit these backcountry sites. Many groups are actively seeking to close these public lands to vehicles, thereby denying access to those who are unable, or perhaps merely unwilling, to hike long distances. This magnificent countryside is owned by, and should be available to, all Americans.

Special Preparations for Remote Travel

Due to the remoteness of some areas in Colorado backcountry and the very high summer temperatures, you should take some special precautions to ensure that you don't end up in a life-threatening situation:

■ When planning a trip into the desert, always inform someone as to where you are going, your route, and when you expect to return. Stick to your plan.

■ Carry and drink at least one gallon of water per person per day of your trip. (Plastic gallon jugs are handy and portable.)

■ Be sure your vehicle is in good condition with a sound battery, good hoses, spare tire, spare fan belts, necessary tools, and reserve gasoline and oil. Other spare parts and extra radiator water are also valuable. If traveling in pairs, share the common spares and carry a greater variety.

■ Keep an eye on the sky. Flash floods can occur in a wash any time you see thunderheads—even when it's not raining a drop where you are.

■ If you are caught in a dust storm while driving, get off the road and turn off your lights. Turn on the emergency flashers and back into the wind to reduce windshield pitting by sand particles.

■ Test trails on foot before driving through washes and sandy areas. One minute of walking may save hours of hard work getting your vehicle unstuck.

■ If your vehicle breaks down, stay near it. Your emergency supplies are there. Your car has many other items useful in an emergency. Raise your hood and trunk lid to denote "help needed." Remember, a vehicle can be seen for miles, but a person on foot is very difficult to spot from a distance.

■ When you're not moving, use available shade or erect shade from tarps, blankets, or seat covers—anything to reduce the direct rays of the sun.

■ Do not sit or lie directly on the ground. It may be 30 degrees hotter than the air.

■ Leave a disabled vehicle only if you are positive of the route and the distance to help. Leave a note for rescuers that gives the time you left and the direction you are taking.

■ If you must walk, rest for at least 10 minutes out of each hour. If you are not normally physically active, rest up to 30 minutes out of each hour. Find shade, sit down, and prop up your feet. Adjust your shoes and socks, but do not remove your shoes—you may not be able to get them back on swollen feet.

■ If you have water, drink it. Do not ration it.

■ If water is limited, keep your mouth closed. Do not talk, eat, smoke, drink alcohol, or take salt.

■ Keep your clothing on despite the heat. It helps to keep your body temperature down and reduces your body's dehydration rate. Cover your head. If you don't have a hat, improvise a head covering.

■ If you are stalled or lost, set signal fires. Set smoky fires in the daytime and bright ones at night. Three fires in a triangle denote "help needed."

■ A roadway is a sign of civilization. If you find a road, stay on it.

■ When hiking, equip each person, especially children, with a police-type whistle. It makes a distinctive noise with little effort. Three blasts denote "help needed."

■ To avoid poisonous creatures, put your hands or feet only where your eyes can see. One insect to be aware of in southwest Colorado is the Africanized honeybee. Though indistinguishable from its European counterpart, these bees are far more aggressive and can be a threat. They have been known to give chase of up to a mile and even wait for people who have escaped into the water to come up for air. The best thing to do if attacked is to cover your face and head with clothing and run to the nearest enclosed shelter. Keep an eye on your pet if you notice a number of bees in the area, as many pets have been killed by Africanized honeybees.

■ Avoid unnecessary contact with wildlife. Some mice in Colorado carry the deadly hantavirus, a pulmonary syndrome fatal in 60 to 70 percent of human cases. Fortunately the disease is very rare—as of March 2007, only 55 cases had been reported in Colorado and 465 nationwide—but caution is still advised. Other rodents may transmit bubonic plague, the same epidemic that killed one-third of Europe's population in the 1300s. Be especially wary near sick animals and keep pets, especially cats, away from wildlife and their fleas. Another creature to watch for is the western black-legged tick, the carrier of Lyme disease. Wearing clothing that covers legs and arms,

tucking pants into boots, and using insect repellent are good ways to avoid fleas and ticks.

Obtaining Permits

Backcountry permits, which usually cost a fee, are required for certain activities on public lands in Colorado, whether the area is a national park, state park, national monument, Indian reservation, or BLM land.

Restrictions may require a permit for all overnight stays, which can include backpacking and 4WD or bicycle camping. Permits may also be required for day use by vehicles, horses, hikers, or bikes in some areas.

When possible, we include information about fees and permit requirements and where permits may be obtained, but these regulations change constantly. If in doubt, check with the most likely governing agency.

Assessing Your Vehicle's Off-Road Ability

Many issues come into play when evaluating your 4WD vehicle, although some of the 4WDs on the market (excluding "crossover" SUVs) are suitable for even the roughest trails described in this book. Engine power will be adequate in even the least-powerful modern vehicle. However, some vehicles are less suited to off-highway driving than others, and some of the newest, carlike sport utility vehicles simply are not designed for off-highway touring. The following information should enable you to identify the good, the bad, and the ugly.

Differing 4WD Systems

All 4WD systems have one thing in common: The engine provides power to all four wheels rather than to only two, as is typical in most standard cars. However, there are a number of differences in the way power is applied to the wheels.

The other feature that distinguishes nearly all 4WDs from normal passenger vehicles is that the gearboxes have high and low ratios that effectively double the number of gears. The high range is comparable to the range on a passenger car. The low range provides lower speed and more power, which is useful when towing heavy loads, driving up steep hills, or crawling over rocks. When driving downhill, the 4WD's low range increases engine braking.

Various makes and models of SUVs offer different drive systems, but these differences center on two issues: the way power is applied to the other wheels if one or more wheels slip, and the ability to select between 2WD and 4WD.

Normal driving requires that all four wheels be able to turn at different speeds; this allows the vehicle to turn without scrubbing its tires. In a 2WD vehicle, the front wheels (or rear wheels in a front-wheel-drive vehicle) are not powered by the engine and thus are free to turn individually at any speed. The rear wheels, powered by the engine, are only able to turn at different speeds because of the differential, which applies power to the faster-turning wheel.

This standard method of applying traction has certain weaknesses. First, when power is applied to only one set of wheels, the other set cannot help the vehicle gain traction. Second, when one powered wheel loses traction, it spins, but the other powered wheel doesn't turn. This happens because the differential applies all the engine power to the faster-turning wheel and no power to the other wheels, which still have traction. All 4WD systems are designed to overcome these two weaknesses. However, different 4WDs address this common objective in different ways.

Full-Time 4WD. For a vehicle to remain in 4WD all the time without scrubbing the tires, all the wheels must be able to rotate at different speeds. A full-time 4WD system allows this to happen by using three differentials. One is located between the rear wheels, as in a normal passenger car, to allow the rear wheels to rotate at different speeds. The second is located between the front wheels in exactly the same way. The third differential is located between the front and rear wheels to allow different rota-

tional speeds between the front and rear sets of wheels. In nearly all vehicles with full-time 4WD, the center differential operates only in high range. In low range, it is completely locked. This is not a disadvantage because when using low range the additional traction is normally desired and the deterioration of steering response will be less noticeable due to the vehicle traveling at a slower speed.

Part-Time 4WD. A part-time 4WD system does not have the center differential located between the front and rear wheels. Consequently, the front and rear drive shafts are both driven at the same speed and with the same power at all times when in 4WD.

This system provides improved traction because when one or both of the front or rear wheels slips, the engine continues to provide power to the other set. However, because such a system doesn't allow a difference in speed between the front and rear sets of wheels, the tires scrub when turning, placing additional strain on the whole drive system. Therefore, such a system can be used only in slippery conditions; otherwise, the ability to steer the vehicle will deteriorate and the tires will quickly wear out.

These days, a substantial number of SUVs offer both full-time and part-time 4WD in high range.

Manual Systems to Switch Between 2WD and 4WD. There are three manual systems for switching between 2WD and 4WD. The most basic requires stopping and getting out of the vehicle to lock the front hubs manually before selecting 4WD. The second requires you to stop, but you change to 4WD by merely throwing a lever inside the vehicle (the hubs lock automatically). The third allows shifting between 2WD and 4WD high range while the vehicle is moving. Any 4WD that does not offer the option of driving in 2WD must have a full-time 4WD system.

Automated Switching Between 2WD and 4WD. Advances in technology are leading to greater automation in the selection of two- or four-wheel drive. When operating in high range, these high-tech systems use sensors to monitor the rotation of each wheel. When any slippage is detected, the vehicle switches the proportion of power from the wheel(s) that is slipping to the wheels that retain grip. The proportion of power supplied to each wheel is therefore infinitely variable as opposed to the original systems where the vehicle was either in two-wheel drive or four-wheel drive.

In recent years, this process has been spurred on by many of the manufacturers of luxury vehicles entering the SUV market—Mercedes, BMW, Cadillac, Lincoln, and Lexus have joined Range Rover in this segment.

Manufacturers of these higher-priced vehicles have led the way in introducing sophisticated computer-controlled 4WD systems. Although each of the manufacturers has its own approach to this issue, all the systems automatically vary the allocation of power between the wheels within milliseconds of the sensors' detecting wheel slippage.

Limiting Wheel Slippage

All 4WDs employ various systems to limit wheel slippage and transfer power to the wheels that still have traction. These systems may completely lock the differentials or they may allow limited slippage before transferring power back to the wheels that retain traction.

Lockers completely eliminate the operation of one or more differentials. A locker on the center differential switches between full-time and part-time 4WD. Lockers on the front or rear differentials ensure that power remains equally applied to each set of wheels regardless of whether both have traction. Lockers may be controlled manually, by a switch or a lever in the vehicle, or they may be automatic.

The Toyota Land Cruiser offers the option of having manual lockers on all three differentials, while other brands such as the Mitsubishi Montero offer manual lockers on the center and rear differential. Manual lockers are the most controllable and effective devices for ensuring that power is provided to the wheels with traction. However, because they allow absolutely no slippage, they must be used only on slippery surfaces.

An alternative method for getting power to the wheels that have traction is to allow limited wheel slippage. Systems that work this way may be called limited-slip differentials, posi-traction systems, or in the center differential, viscous couplings. The advantage of these systems is that the limited difference they allow in rotational speed between wheels enables such systems to be used when driving on a dry surface. All full-time 4WD systems allow limited slippage in the center differential.

For off-highway use, a manually locking differential is the best of the above systems, but it is the most expensive. Limited-slip differentials are the cheapest but also the least satisfactory, as they require one wheel to be slipping at 2 to 3 mph before power is transferred to the other wheel. For the center differential, the best system combines a locking differential and, to enable full-time use, a viscous coupling.

Tires

The tires that came with your 4WD vehicle may be satisfactory, but many 4WDs are fitted with passenger-car tires. These are unlikely to be the best choice because they are less rugged and more likely to puncture on rocky trails. They are particularly prone to sidewall damage as well. Passenger vehicle tires also have a less aggressive tread pattern than specialized 4WD tires, and provide less traction in mud.

For information on purchasing tires better suited to off-highway conditions, see Special 4WD Equipment, page 22.

Clearance

Road clearances vary considerably among different 4WD vehicles—from less than 7 inches to more than 10 inches. Special vehicles may have far greater clearance. For instance, the Hummer has a 16-inch ground clearance. High ground clearance is particularly advantageous on the rockier or more rutted 4WD trails in this book.

When evaluating the ground clearance of your vehicle, you need to take into account the clearance of the bodywork between the wheels on each side of the vehicle. This is particularly relevant for crawling over larger rocks. Vehicles with sidesteps have significantly lower clearance than those without.

Another factor affecting clearance is the approach and departure angles of your vehicle—that is, the maximum angle the ground can slope without the front of the vehicle hitting the ridge on approach or the rear of the vehicle hitting on departure. Mounting a winch or tow hitch to your vehicle is likely to reduce your angle of approach or departure.

If you do a lot of driving on rocky trails, you will inevitably hit the bottom of the vehicle sooner or later. When this happens, you will be far less likely to damage vulnerable areas such as the oil pan and gas tank if your vehicle is fitted with skid plates. Most manufacturers offer skid plates as an option. They are worth every penny.

Maneuverability

When you tackle tight switchbacks, you will quickly appreciate that maneuverability is an important criterion when assessing 4WD vehicles. Where a full-size vehicle may be forced to go back and forth a number of times to get around a sharp turn, a small 4WD might go straight around. This is not only easier, it's safer.

If you have a full-size vehicle, all is not lost. We have traveled many of the trails in this book in a Suburban. That is not to say that some of these trails wouldn't have been easier to negotiate in a smaller vehicle! We have noted in the route descriptions if a trail is not suitable for larger vehicles.

In Summary

Using the criteria above, you can evaluate how well your 4WD will handle off-road touring, and if you haven't yet purchased your vehicle, you can use these criteria to help select one. Choosing the best 4WD system is, at least partly, subjective. It is also a matter of your budget. However, for the type of off-highway driving covered in this book, we make the following recommendations:

- Select a 4WD system that offers low range and, at a minimum, has some form of limited slip differential on the rear axle.
- Use light truck, all-terrain tires as the standard tires on your vehicle. For sand and slickrock, these will be the ideal choice. If conditions are likely to be muddy, or if traction will be improved by a tread pattern that will give more bite, consider an additional set of mud tires.
- For maximum clearance, select a vehicle with 16-inch wheels or at least choose the tallest tires that your vehicle can accommodate. Note that if you install tires with a diameter greater than standard, the odometer will under calculate the distance you have traveled. Your engine braking and gear ratios will also be affected.
- If you are going to try the rockier 4WD trails, don't install a sidestep or low-hanging front bar. If you have the option, have underbody skid plates mounted.
- Remember that many of the obstacles you encounter on backcountry trails are more difficult to navigate in a full-size vehicle than in a compact 4WD.

Four-Wheel Driving Techniques

Safe four-wheel driving requires that you observe certain golden rules:

- Size up the situation in advance.
- Be careful and take your time.
- Maintain smooth, steady power and momentum.
- Engage 4WD and low-range gears before you get into a tight situation.
- Steer toward high spots, trying to put the wheel over large rocks.
- Straddle ruts.
- Use gears and not just the brakes to hold the vehicle when driving downhill. On very steep slopes, chock the wheels if you park your vehicle.
- Watch for logging and mining trucks and smaller recreational vehicles, such as all-terrain vehicles (ATVs).
- Wear your seat belt and secure all luggage, especially heavy items such as tool

boxes or coolers. Heavy items should be secured by ratchet tie-down straps rather than elastic-type straps, which are not strong enough to hold heavy items if the vehicle rolls.

Colorado's 4WD trails have a number of common obstacles, and the following provides an introduction to the techniques required to surmount them.

Rocks. Tire selection is important in negotiating rocks. Select a multiple-ply, tough sidewall, light-truck tire with a large-lug tread.

As you approach a rocky stretch, get into 4WD low range to give yourself maximum slow-speed control. Speed is rarely necessary, since traction on a rocky surface is usually good. Plan ahead and select the line you wish to take. If a rock appears to be larger than the clearance of your vehicle, don't try to straddle it. Check to see that it is not higher than the frame of your vehicle once you get a wheel over it. Put a wheel up on the rock and slowly climb it, then gently drop over the other side using the brake to ensure a smooth landing. Bouncing the car over rocks increases the likelihood of damage, because the body's clearance is reduced by the suspension compressing. Running boards also significantly reduce your clearance in this respect. It is often helpful to use a "spotter" outside the vehicle to assist you with the best wheel placement.

Steep Uphill Grades. Consider walking the trail to ensure that the steep hill before you is passable, especially if it is clear that backtracking is going to be a problem.

Select 4WD low range to ensure that you have adequate power to pull up the hill. If the wheels begin to lose traction, turn the steering wheel gently from side to side to give the wheels a chance to regain traction.

If you lose momentum, but the car is not in danger of sliding, use the foot brake, switch off the ignition, leave the vehicle in gear (if manual transmission) or park (if automatic), engage the parking brake, and get out to examine the situation. See if you can remove any obstacles, and figure out the line you need to take. Reversing a couple of

yards and starting again may allow you to get better traction and momentum.

If halfway up, you decide a stretch of road is impassably steep, back down the trail. Trying to turn the vehicle around on a steep hill is extremely dangerous; you will very likely cause it to roll over.

Steep Downhill Grades. Again, consider walking the trail to ensure that a steep downhill is passable, especially if it is clear that backtracking uphill is going to be a problem.

Select 4WD low range and use first gear to maximize braking assistance from the engine. If the surface is loose and you are losing traction, change up to second or third gear. Do not use the brakes if you can avoid it, but don't let the vehicle's speed get out of control. Feather (lightly pump) the brakes if you slip while braking. For vehicles fitted with an antilock breaking system, apply even pressure if you start to slip; the ABS helps keep vehicles on line.

Travel very slowly over rock ledges or ruts. Attempt to tackle these diagonally, letting one wheel down at a time.

If the back of the vehicle begins to slide around, gently apply the throttle and correct the steering. If the rear of the vehicle starts to slide sideways, do not apply the brakes.

Sand. As with most off-highway situations, your tires are the key to your ability to cross sand. It is difficult to tell how well a particular tire will handle in sand just by looking at it, so be guided by the manufacturer and your dealer.

The key to driving in soft sand is floatation, which is achieved by a combination of low tire pressure and momentum. Before crossing a stretch of sand, reduce your tire pressure to between 15 and 20 pounds. If necessary, you can safely go to as low as 12 pounds. As you cross, maintain momentum so that your vehicle rides on the top of the soft sand without digging in or stalling. This may require plenty of engine power. Avoid using the brakes if possible; removing your foot from the accelerator alone is normally enough to slow or stop. Using the brakes digs the vehicle deep in the sand.

Pump the tires back up as soon as you are

out of the sand to avoid damaging the tires and the rims. Pumping the tires back up requires a high-quality air compressor. Even then, it is a slow process.

Slickrock. When you encounter slickrock, first assess the correct direction of the trail. It is easy to lose sight of the trail on slickrock, because there are seldom any developed edges. Often the way is marked with small rock cairns, which are simply rocks stacked high enough to make a landmark.

All-terrain tires with tighter tread are more suited to slickrock than the more open, luggier type tires. As with rocks, a multiple-ply sidewall is important. In dry conditions, slickrock offers pavement-type grip. In rain or snow, you will soon learn how it got its name. Even the best tires may not get an adequate grip. Walk steep sections first; if you are slipping on foot, chances are your vehicle will slip, too.

Slickrock is characterized by ledges and long sections of "pavement." Follow the guidelines for travel over rocks. Refrain from speeding over flat-looking sections, because you may hit an unexpected crevice or water pocket, and vehicles bend easier than slickrock! Turns and ledges can be tight, and vehicles with smaller overhangs and better maneuverability are at a distinct advantage.

On the steepest sections, engage low range and pick a straight line up or down the slope. Do not attempt to traverse a steep slope sideways.

Mud. Muddy trails are easily damaged, so they should be avoided if possible. But if you must traverse a section of mud, your success will depend heavily on whether you have open-lugged mud tires or chains. Thick mud fills the tighter tread on normal tires, leaving the tire with no more grip than if it were bald. If the muddy stretch is only a few yards long, the momentum of your vehicle may allow you to get through regardless.

If the muddy track is very steep, uphill or downhill, or off camber, do not attempt it. Your vehicle is likely to skid in such conditions, and you may roll or slip off the edge

of the road. Also, check to see that the mud has a reasonably firm base. Tackling deep mud is definitely not recommended unless you have a vehicle-mounted winch—and even then—be cautious, because the winch may not get you out. Finally, check to see that no ruts are too deep for the ground clearance of your vehicle.

When you decide you can get through and have selected the best route, use the following techniques to cross through mud:

■ Avoid making detours off existing tracks to minimize environmental damage.

■ Select 4WD low range and a suitable gear; momentum is the key to success, so use a high enough gear to build up sufficient speed.

■ Avoid accelerating heavily, so as to minimize wheel spinning and to provide maximum traction.

■ Follow existing wheel ruts, unless they are too deep for the clearance of your vehicle.

■ To correct slides, turn the steering wheel in the direction that the rear wheels are skidding, but don't be too aggressive or you'll overcorrect and lose control again.

■ If the vehicle comes to a stop, don't continue to accelerate, as you will only spin your wheels and dig yourself into a rut. Try backing out and having another go.

■ Be prepared to turn back before reaching the point of no return.

Stream Crossings. By crossing a stream that is too deep, drivers risk far more than water flowing in and ruining the interior of their vehicles. Water sucked into the engine's air intake will seriously damage the engine. Likewise, water that seeps into the air vent on the transmission or differential will mix with the lubricant and may lead to serious problems in due course.

Even worse, if the water is deep or fast flowing, it could easily carry your vehicle downstream, endangering the lives of everyone in the vehicle.

Some 4WD manuals tell you what fording depth the vehicle can negotiate safely. If your vehicle's owner's manual does not include this information, your local dealer may be able to assist. If you don't know, then avoid crossing through water that is more than a foot or so deep.

The first rule for crossing a stream is to know what you are getting into. You need to ascertain how deep the water is, whether there are any large rocks or holes, if the bottom is solid enough to avoid bogging down the vehicle, and whether the entry and exit points are negotiable. This may take some time and involve getting wet, but you take a great risk by crossing a stream without first properly assessing the situation.

The secret to water crossings is to keep moving, but not too fast. If you go too fast, you may drown the electrics, causing the vehicle to stall midstream. In shallow water (where the surface of the water is below the bumper), your primary concern is to safely negotiate the bottom of the stream, to avoid any rock damage, and to maintain momentum if there is a danger of getting stuck or of slipping on the exit.

In deeper water (between 18 and 30 inches), the objective is to create a small bow wave in front of the moving vehicle. This requires a speed that is approximately walking pace. The bow wave reduces the depth of the water around the engine compartment. If the water's surface reaches your tailpipe, select a gear that will maintain moderate engine revs to avoid water backing up into the exhaust; and do not change gears midstream.

Crossing water deeper than 25 to 30 inches requires more extensive preparation of the vehicle and should be attempted only by experienced drivers.

Snow. The trails in this book that receive heavy snowfall are closed in winter. Therefore, the snow conditions that you are most likely to encounter are an occasional snowdrift that has not yet melted or fresh snow from an unexpected storm. Getting through such conditions depends on the depth of the snow, its consistency, the stability of the underlying surface, and your vehicle.

If the snow is no deeper than about 9

inches and there is solid ground beneath it, crossing the snow should not be a problem. In deeper snow that seems solid enough to support your vehicle, be extremely cautious: If you break through a drift, you are likely to be stuck, and if conditions are bad, you may have a long wait.

The tires you use for off-highway driving, with a wide tread pattern, are probably suitable for these snow conditions. Nonetheless, it is wise to carry chains (preferably for all four wheels), and if you have a vehicle-mounted winch, even better.

Vehicle Recovery Methods

If you do enough four-wheel driving, you are sure to get stuck sooner or later. The following techniques will help you get back on the go. The most suitable method will depend on the equipment available and the situation you are in—whether you are stuck in sand, mud, or snow, or are high-centered or unable to negotiate a hill.

Towing. Use a nylon yank strap of the type discussed in the Special 4WD Equipment section on page 22. This type of strap will stretch 15 to 25 percent, and the elasticity will assist in extracting the vehicle.

Attach the strap only to a frame-mounted tow point. Ensure that the driver of the stuck vehicle is ready, take up all but about 6 feet of slack, then move the towing vehicle away at a moderate speed (in most circumstances this means using 4WD low range in second gear) so that the elasticity of the strap is employed in the way it is meant to be. Don't take off like a bat out of hell or you risk breaking the strap or damaging a vehicle.

Never join two yank straps together with a shackle. If one strap breaks, the shackle will become a lethal missile aimed at one of the vehicles (and anyone inside). For the same reason, never attach a yank strap to the tow ball on either vehicle.

Jacking. Jacking the vehicle allows you to pack rocks, dirt, or logs under the wheel or to use your shovel to remove an obstacle. However, the standard vehicle jack is unlikely to be of as much assistance as a high-lift jack.

We highly recommend purchasing a good high-lift jack as a basic accessory if you decide that you are going to do a lot of serious, off-highway four-wheel driving. Remember a high-lift jack is of limited use if your vehicle does not have an appropriate jacking point. Some brush bars have two built-in forward jacking points.

Tire Chains. Tire chains can be of assistance in both mud and snow. Cable-type chains provide much less grip than link-type chains. There are also dedicated mud chains with larger, heavier links than on normal snow chains. It is best to have chains fitted to all four wheels.

Once you are bogged down is not the best time to try to fit the chains; if at all possible, try to predict their need and have them on the tires before trouble arises. An easy way to affix chains is to place two small cubes of wood under the center of the stretched-out chain. When you drive your tires up on the blocks of wood, it is easier to stretch the chains over the tires because the pressure is off of them.

Winching. Most recreational four-wheel drivers do not have a winch. But if you get serious about four-wheel driving, this is probably the first major accessory you should consider buying.

Under normal circumstances, a winch would be warranted only for the more difficult 4WD trails in this book. Having a winch is certainly comforting when you see a difficult section of road ahead and have to decide whether to risk it or turn back. Also, major obstacles can appear when you least expect them, even on trails that are otherwise easy.

Owning a winch is not a panacea to all your recovery problems. Winching depends on the availability of a good anchor point, and electric winches may not work if they are submerged in a stream. Despite these constraints, no accessory is more useful than a high-quality, powerful winch when you get into a difficult situation.

If you acquire a winch, learn to use it properly; take the time to study your owner's manual. Incorrect operation can be extremely dangerous and may cause damage to the winch or to your anchor points, which are usually trees.

Navigation by the Global Positioning System (GPS)

Although this book is designed so that each trail can be navigated simply by following the detailed directions provided, nothing makes navigation easier than a GPS receiver.

Each satellite is constantly transmitting data, including its identification number, its operational health, and the date and time. It also transmits its location and the location of every other satellite in the network.

By comparing the time the signal was transmitted to the time it is received, a GPS receiver calculates how far away each satellite is. With a sufficient number of signals, the receiver can then triangulate its location. With three or more satellites, the receiver can determine latitude and longitude coordinates. With four or more, it can calculate elevation. By constantly making these calculations, it can determine speed and direction. To facilitate these calculations, the time data broadcast by GPS is accurate to within 40 billionths of a second.

The U.S. military uses the system to provide positions accurate to within half an inch. When the system was first established, civilian receivers were deliberately fed slightly erroneous information in order to effectively deny military applications to hostile countries or terrorists—a practice called selective availability (SA). However on May 1, 2000, in response to the growing importance of the system for civilian applications, the U.S. government stopped intentionally downgrading GPS data. The military gave its support to this change once new technology made it possible to selectively degrade the system within any defined geographical area on demand. This new feature of the system has made it safe to have higher-quality signals available for civilian use. Now, instead of the civilian-use signal having a margin of error between 20 and 70 yards, it is only about one-tenth of that.

A GPS receiver offers the four-wheeler

numerous benefits:

■ You can track to any point for which you know the longitude and latitude coordinates with no chance of heading in the wrong direction or getting lost. Most receivers provide an extremely easy-to-understand graphic display to keep you on track.

■ It works in all weather conditions.

■ It automatically records your route for easy backtracking.

■ You can record and name any location, so that you can relocate it with ease. This may include your campsite, a fishing spot, or even a silver mine you discover!

■ It displays your position, enabling you to pinpoint your location on a map.

■ By interfacing the GPS receiver directly to a portable computer, you can monitor and record your location as you travel (using the appropriate map software) or print the route you took.

However, remember that GPS units can fail, batteries can go flat, and tree cover and tight canyons can block the signals. Never rely entirely on GPS for navigation. Always carry a compass for backup.

Special 4WD Equipment

Tires

When 4WD touring, you will likely encounter a variety of terrain: rocks, mud, talus, slickrock, sand, gravel, dirt, and bitumen. The immense array of tires on the market includes many specifically targeted at one or another of these types of terrain, as well as tires designed to adequately handle a range of terrain.

Every four-wheel driver seems to have a preference when it comes to tire selection, but most people undertaking the 4WD trails in this book will need tires that can handle all of the above types of terrain adequately.

The first requirement is to select rugged, light-truck tires rather than passenger-vehicle tires. Check the size data on the sidewall: it should have "LT" rather than "P" before the number. Among light-truck tires, you must choose between tires that are designated "all-terrain" and more-aggressive, wider-tread mud tires. Either type will be adequate, especially on rocks, gravel, talus, or dirt. Although mud tires have an advantage in muddy conditions and soft snow, all-terrain tires perform better on slickrock, in sand, and particularly on ice and paved roads.

When selecting tires, remember that they affect not just traction but also cornering ability, braking distances, fuel consumption, and noise levels. It pays to get good advice before making your decision.

Global Positioning System Receivers

GPS receivers have come down in price considerably in the past few years and are rapidly becoming indispensable navigational tools. Many higher-priced cars now offer integrated GPS receivers, and within the next few years, receivers will become available on most models.

Battery-powered, hand-held units that meet the needs of off-highway driving currently range from approximately $150 to a little over $300 and continue to come down in price. Some high-end units feature maps that are incorporated in the display, either from a built-in database or from interchangeable memory cards. Currently, only a few of these maps include 4WD trails.

If you are considering purchasing a GPS unit, keep the following in mind:

■ Price. The very cheapest units are likely outdated and very limited in their display features. Expect to pay from $175 to $400.

■ The display. Compare the graphic display of one unit with another. Some are much easier to decipher or offer more alternative displays.

■ The controls. GPS receivers have many functions, and they need to have good, simple controls.

■ Vehicle mounting. To be useful, the unit needs to be placed where it can be read easily by both the driver and the navigator. Check that the unit can be conveniently located in your vehicle. Different units have different shapes and different mounting systems.

■ Map data. More and more units have

map data built in. Some have the ability to download maps from a computer. Such maps are normally sold on a CD-ROM. GPS units have a finite storage capacity and having the ability to download maps covering a narrower geographical region means that the amount of data relating to that specific region can be greater.

■ The number of routes and the number of sites (or "waypoints") per route that can be stored in memory. For off-highway use, it is important to be able to store plenty of waypoints so that you do not have to load coordinates into the machine as frequently. Having plenty of memory also ensures that you can automatically store your present location without fear that the memory is full.

■ Waypoint storage. The better units store up to 500 waypoints and 20 reversible routes of up to 30 waypoints each. Also consider the number of characters a GPS receiver allows you to use to name waypoints. When you try to recall a waypoint, you may have difficulty recognizing names restricted to only a few characters.

■ Automatic route storing. Most units automatically store your route as you go along and enable you to display it in reverse to make backtracking easy.

After you have selected a unit, a number of optional extras are also worth considering:

■ A cigarette lighter electrical adapter. Despite GPS units becoming more power efficient, protracted in-vehicle use still makes this accessory a necessity.

■ A vehicle-mounted antenna, which will improve reception under difficult conditions. (The GPS unit can only "see" through the windows of your vehicle; it cannot monitor satellites through a metal roof.) Having a vehicle-mounted antenna also means that you do not have to consider reception when locating the receiver in your vehicle.

■ An in-car mounting system. If you are going to do a lot of touring using the GPS, consider attaching a bracket on the dash rather than relying on a Velcro mount.

■ A computer-link cable and digital maps. Data from your GPS receiver can be downloaded to your PC; maps and waypoints can be downloaded from your PC; or if you have a laptop computer, you can monitor your route as you go along, using one of a number of inexpensive map software products on the market.

Yank Straps

Yank straps are industrial-strength versions of the flimsy tow straps carried by the local discount store. They are 20 to 30 feet long and 2 to 3 inches wide, made of heavy nylon, rated to at least 20,000 pounds, and have looped ends.

Do not use tow straps with metal hooks in the ends (the hooks can become missiles in the event the strap breaks free). Likewise, never join two yank straps together using a shackle.

CB Radios

If you are stuck, injured, or just want to know the conditions up ahead, a citizen's band (CB) radio can be invaluable. CB radios are relatively inexpensive and do not require a Federal Communications Commission license. Their range is limited, especially in very hilly country, as their transmission patterns basically follow lines of sight. Range can be improved using single sideband (SSB) transmission, an option on more expensive units. Range is even better on vehicle-mounted units that have been professionally fitted to ensure that the antenna and cabling are matched appropriately.

Winches

There are three main options when it comes to winches: manual winches, removable electric winches, and vehicle-mounted electric winches.

If you have a full-size 4WD vehicle—which can weigh in excess of 7,000 pounds when loaded—a manual winch is of limited use without a lot of effort and considerable time. However, a manual winch is a very handy and inexpensive accessory if you have a small 4WD. Typically, manual winches are rated to pull about 5,500 pounds.

An electric winch can be mounted to your vehicle's trailer hitch to enable it to be removed, relocated to the front of your vehicle (if you have a hitch installed), or moved to another vehicle. Although this is a very useful feature, a winch is heavy, so relocating one can be a two-person job. Consider that 5,000-pound-rated winches weigh only about 55 pounds, while 12,000-pound-rated models weigh around 140 pounds. Therefore, the larger models are best permanently front-mounted. Unfortunately, this position limits their ability to winch the vehicle backward.

When choosing among electric winches, be aware that they are rated for their maximum capacity on the first wind of the cable around the drum. As layers of cable wind onto the drum, they increase its diameter and thus decrease the maximum load the winch can handle. This decrease is significant: A winch rated to pull 8,000 pounds on a bare drum may only handle 6,500 pounds on the second layer, 5,750 pounds on the third layer, and 5,000 pounds on the fourth. Electric winches also draw a high level of current and may necessitate upgrading the battery in your 4WD or adding a second battery.

There is a wide range of mounting options—from a simple, body-mounted frame that holds the winch to heavy-duty winch bars that replace the original bumper and incorporate brush bars and mounts for auxiliary lights.

If you buy a winch, either electric or manual, you will also need quite a range of additional equipment so that you can operate it correctly:

- at least one choker chain with hooks on each end,
- winch extension straps or cables,
- shackles,
- a receiver shackle,
- a snatch block,
- a tree protector,
- gloves.

Grill/Brush Bars and Winch Bars

Brush bars protect the front of the vehicle from scratches and minor bumps; they also provide a solid mount for auxiliary lights and often high-lift jacking points. The level of protection they provide depends on how solid they are and whether they are securely mounted onto the frame of the vehicle. Lighter models attach in front of the standard bumper, but the more substantial units replace the bumper. Prices range from about $150 to $450.

Winch bars replace the bumper and usually integrate a solid brush bar with a heavy-duty winch mount. Some have the brush bar as an optional extra to the winch bar component. Manufacturers such as Warn, ARB, and TJM offer a wide range of integrated winch bars. These are significantly more expensive, starting at about $650.

Remember that installing heavy equipment on the front of the vehicle may necessitate increasing the front suspension rating to cope with the additional weight.

Portable Air Compressors

Most portable air compressors on the market are flimsy models that plug into the cigarette lighter and are sold at the local discount store. These are of very limited use for four-wheel driving. They are very slow to inflate the large tires of a 4WD vehicle; for instance, to reinflate from 15 to 35 pounds typically takes about 10 minutes for each tire. They are also unlikely to be rated for continuous use, which means that they will overheat and cut off before completing the job. If you're lucky, they will start up again when they have cooled down, but this means that you are unlikely to reinflate your tires in less than an hour.

The easiest way to identify a useful air compressor is by the price—good ones cost $200 or more. Many of the quality units feature a Thomas-brand pump and are built to last. Another good unit is sold by ARB. All these pumps draw between 15 and 20 amps and thus should not be plugged into the cigarette lighter socket but attached to the vehicle's battery with clips. The ARB unit can be permanently mounted under the hood. Quick-Air makes a range of units including a 10-amp compressor that can be plugged into the cigarette lighter socket and performs well.

Auxiliary Driving Lights

There is a vast array of auxiliary lights on the market today and selecting the best lights for your purpose can be a confusing process.

Auxiliary lights greatly improve visibility in adverse weather conditions. Driving lights provide a strong, moderately wide beam to supplement headlamp high beams, giving improved lighting in the distance and to the sides of the main beam. Fog lamps throw a wide-dispersion, flat beam; and spots provide a high-power, narrow beam to improve lighting range directly in front of the vehicle. Rear-mounted auxiliary lights provide greatly improved visibility for backing up.

For off-highway use, you will need quality lights with strong mounting brackets. Some high-powered off-highway lights are not approved by the Department of Transportation for use on public roads.

Roof Racks

Roof racks can be excellent for storing gear, as well as providing easy access for certain weatherproof items. However, they raise the center of gravity on the vehicle, which can substantially alter the rollover angle. A roof rack is best used for lightweight objects that are well-strapped down. Heavy recovery gear and other bulky items should be packed low in the vehicle's interior to lower the center of gravity and stabilize the vehicle.

A roof rack should allow for safe and secure packing of items and be sturdy enough to withstand knocks.

Packing Checklist

Before embarking on any 4WD adventure, whether a lazy Sunday drive on an easy trail or a challenging climb over rugged terrain, be prepared. The following checklist will help you gather the items you need.

Essential

- ❑ Rain gear
- ❑ Small shovel or multipurpose ax, pick, shovel, and sledgehammer
- ❑ Heavy-duty yank strap
- ❑ Spare tire that matches the other tires on the vehicle
- ❑ Working jack and base plate for soft ground
- ❑ Maps
- ❑ Emergency medical kit, including sun protection and insect repellent
- ❑ Bottled water
- ❑ Blankets or space blankets
- ❑ Parka, gloves, and boots
- ❑ Spare vehicle key
- ❑ Jumper leads
- ❑ Heavy-duty flashlight
- ❑ Multipurpose tool, such as a Leatherman
- ❑ Emergency food—high-energy bars or similar

Worth Considering

- ❑ Global Positioning System (GPS) receiver
- ❑ Cell phone
- ❑ A set of light-truck, off-highway tires and matching spare
- ❑ High-lift jack
- ❑ Additional tool kit
- ❑ CB radio
- ❑ Portable air compressor
- ❑ Tire gauge
- ❑ Tire-sealing kit
- ❑ Tire chains
- ❑ Handsaw
- ❑ Binoculars
- ❑ Firearms
- ❑ Whistle
- ❑ Flares
- ❑ Vehicle fire extinguisher
- ❑ Gasoline, engine oil, and other vehicle fluids
- ❑ Portable hand winch
- ❑ Electric cooler

If Your Credit Cards Aren' t Maxed Out

- ❑ Electric, vehicle-mounted winch and associated recovery straps, shackles, and snatch blocks
- ❑ Auxiliary lights
- ❑ Locking differential(s)

Engineer Pass Trail

STARTING POINT Ouray
FINISHING POINT Lake City—Intersection with
   Southwest #3: Cinnamon Pass Trail
TOTAL MILEAGE 31.0 miles
UNPAVED MILEAGE 27.2 miles
DRIVING TIME 3 hours
ROUTE ELEVATION 8,932 to 12,800 feet
USUALLY OPEN Mid-June to early October
DIFFICULTY RATING 4
SCENIC RATING 10

Special Attractions

- Part of the historic Alpine Loop, the
  location of many famous mining sites.
- Driving through the twenty-foot deep
  channel in the snow early in the season.
- Spectacular Rocky Mountain scenery.
- Whitmore Falls.

History

Six years before building the Million Dollar
Highway between Ouray and Silverton,
Otto Mears extended his toll road from
Saguache to Lake City and through to
Animas Forks, via Engineer Pass. Mears network
of toll roads continued south to Eureka
and Silverton and north to Mineral Point,
Poughkeepsie, and Ouray.

From its completion in August 1877, this
road was an important stagecoach route and
the principal freight route for the wagons
and mule trains that hauled supplies and ore
between all the main mining camps in the
area and Saguache, which was the closest
major supply center. Within three years, the
route had daily stages run by the Rocky
Mountain Stage and Express Company.

The Engineer Pass 4WD trail passes the
sites of some of the major mining camps that
were established in the area. The turnoff to
the first, Poughkeepsie, is located two and
one-half miles from the start of the trail. This
town was perched at an elevation of 11,650

Engineer Pass

feet and about seven miles south of Ouray; its remote location and the poor quality of access roads hindered its development. The winters were so long and harsh that miners could work only two or three months of the year. Despite the hardships Poughkeepsie residents had to endure, the town was surprisingly well-planned. It had a post office established in 1880, a newspaper called the *Poughkeepsie Telegraph*, stores, restaurants, saloons, and other businesses. Miners usually sent ore to Lake City or Silverton by burro via rough roads. Transporting the ore in this manner was so difficult and expensive that eventually mine owners decided the expense wasn't worth it and ceased operations. No buildings from the town remain.

Mineral Point mining camp was located about one and three-quarters of a mile southwest of Engineer Pass, at an elevation of 11,500 feet. Prospectors Abe Burrows and Charles McIntyre founded the camp in 1873. To generate interest in the camp and to raise capital, promoters of Mineral Point circulated far-fetched advertisements with unrealistic pictures and claims. One advertisement depicted a steamship running up the Animas River and streetcars running from Mineral Point to Animas Forks!

In truth, only very mediocre transportation was available, and miners had to use cumbersome wagons or burros to transport their ore. Most was sent either to Silverton via Animas Forks or to Lake City. Because of the inhospitable winters, the lack of transportation, and the silver crash of 1893, by the mid-1890s Mineral Point was on its way to becoming a ghost camp.

Just beyond Engineer Pass is the site of Engineer City, established around 1874 when H. A. Woods staked the first claim in the area and named it the Annie Woods Lode. By 1875, the population of prospectors grew to about four hundred. For a short time, Engineer City prided itself on being the largest city in the state without a saloon. The prospectors were simply too busy looking for silver to spend time in a bar. In 1882, the Frank Hough Mine was discovered. A camp of about fifty men operated the mine, located in American Flats on the eastern side of Engineer Mountain. Operations ceased in 1900, and the ruins of the mine remain.

Rose's Cabin was once a lively inn offering food, lodging, and entertainment to miners and travelers. Corydon Rose was one of the first pioneers to explore the San Juans after a treaty was signed with the Utes in 1873. Rose decided to build an inn to serve

Henson Creek runs alongside the trail

Palmetto Gulch cabin

the area, locating it about halfway between Ouray and Lake City to provide a convenient stopover for travelers along the route.

The area around the cabin began to grow in population as miners settled there. They built cabins nearby and worked mines in the surrounding hills. It is estimated that about fifty people settled in the vicinity. Rose's Cabin served the community as its local bar, restaurant, hotel, general store, and post office. Rose kept sixty burros in a stable to ship supplies to the miners and carry their ore down to his cabin. The cabin was the hive of activity in the region. Only a few traces of the cabin remain. The structure still standing is the old stable; the cabin was situated to the left.

Capitol City was established about ten miles west of Lake City after rich silver discoveries in 1877 brought prospectors to the area. The town of Galena City began as a tent city, but the tents were soon replaced by more permanent structures. George S. Lee, a miner with grand plans, had the town's name changed to Capitol City because he was certain that Colorado would move its capital to the San Juan Mountains, and he would live in the governor's mansion. To aid in the construction of Capitol City, Lee built a sawmill and planing

mill. He also erected the Henson Creek Smelter, one mile below the town, to process ore from the many mines nearby.

A town site of two hundred acres was laid out; a schoolhouse was built, although the population never exceeded four hundred and there were only a handful of students. Lee built himself a large and elegant house at the edge of town to be the governor's mansion, where he and his wife entertained lavishly. Their home even had a ballroom and orchestra pit. Bricks imported from Pueblo were estimated to have cost a dollar apiece! However, Lee's efforts did not bear fruit: Capitol City never even became the county seat.

About four miles before reaching Lake City the road passes through the town of Henson, a mining camp that grew up around the Ute-Ulay Mine. In 1871, Harry Henson discovered the mine, but the land belonged to the Indians, who did not take kindly to white trespassers. Henson was unable to develop the property until well after the Brunot Treaty of 1873, because violence with the Indians continued for several years. White settlers clashed with the native Indians near Lake City as late as 1879.

There was also a long, bitter, and violent miners' strike in Henson. Reportedly, the

Empire Chief Mill

The Empire Chief Mine adit

The building designed to become the governor's mansion at Capitol City in 1949

Whitmore Falls

strike started because the mine owners insisted that all single men board at the company boardinghouse. To protest, miners went on strike. When the owners hired non-union labor to replace the striking miners, fights erupted and some scabs were run out of town. The volatility of the situation prompted the governor of Colorado to send four companies of cavalry and two companies of infantry to settle the dispute. The dispute eventually went to trial, and all the miners were forced to leave camp.

Henson's post office, established in May 1883, was closed in November 1913. The buildings still standing in Henson are privately owned, and many are still in use.

Description

This route commences south of Ouray on the Million Dollar Highway, US 550.

If you wish to avoid the hardest section of the Engineer Pass Trail, the route can be commenced at Silverton by taking Southwest #6: Silverton to Animas Forks Ghost Town and then Southwest #5: North Fork Cutoff to connect with Engineer Pass Trail.

The turnoff from US 550 onto Engineer Pass Trail is well marked with a national forest access sign. This 4WD track gets straight down to business. In fact, the next five miles are the hardest of the entire trip. Sections of the road are steep and rough. It is also narrow with sheer drop-offs. Although it may appear threatening at first, it is readily passable for 4WD vehicles if taken slowly and carefully.

A tip for those who are nervous about driving shelf roads and encountering oncoming vehicles: Leave early. This road is popular, and oncoming 4WD vehicles will be encountered frequently later in the day, as those traveling from Lake City are descending. Pull-offs are reasonably frequent.

At the 1.6-mile point, you pass the Mickey Breene Mine, which was discovered in 1890. The mine yielded high-grade ore and produced copper and silver.

About two and one-half miles from US 550, the road intersects with the Poughkeepsie 4WD road. This road is difficult and should be taken

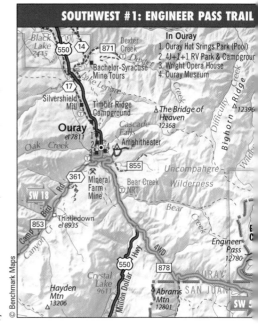

only by those willing to risk vehicle damage.

From the Mineral Point turnoff, the terrain starts to clear, with numerous open, although boggy meadows. The climb continues to Engineer Pass at 12,800 feet.

From the summit, the road descends through the southern edge of American Flats and past the site of Engineer City.

From this point, the road follows the path of Henson Creek all the way to Lake City.

About two miles after the summit, there is a scenic old cabin beside the creek at Palmetto Gulch; shortly after that, a bridge crosses the creek at what was the site of the Palmetto Gulch Mill. From this point, the road is passable by passenger vehicles.

The road passes close by Rose's Cabin, which was an important way station on the stage route. The remains of the buildings can still be seen. Less than a mile farther is the Empire Chief Mill that was worked from January to March 1929, when an avalanche killed four men and destroyed most of the buildings.

A few miles on, a sign marks a short walking trail down to beautiful Whitmore Falls. Though short, the hike back up is strenuous.

The original Capitol City, with its grand aspirations to be the state capital, is now

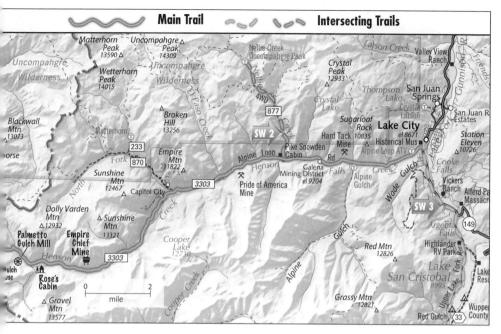

Main Trail	Intersecting Trails

reduced to the remains of the post office. However, the town site is on private land, and new homes continue to be built there.

The route continues to Henson and then through Henson Creek Canyon to Lake City.

Bulldozers plow portions of Engineer Pass, which is usually opened around mid-June. When the road crews get through, they leave in their wake a narrow channel through the snow, with walls of snow up to twenty feet high on either side.

Current Road Information

San Juan National Forest
Silverton Ranger District
PO Box 709
1246 Blair Street
Silverton, CO 81433
(970) 387-5530

Lake City Chamber of Commerce
800 Gunnison Avenue
Lake City, CO 81235
(970) 944-2527

Silverton Chamber of Commerce
414 Greene Street
Silverton, CO 81433
(970) 387-5654

Map References

Benchmark's *Colorado Road & Recreation Atlas,* pp. 110, 111

USFS   Uncompahgre National Forest and Gunnison National Forest

USGS   1:24,000   Ouray, Uncompahgre Peak, Lake City, Handies Peak, Ironton, Red Cloud Peak
1:100,000 Montrose, Silverton

Maptech CD-ROM:
Southwest/Durango/Telluride

Colorado Atlas & Gazetteer, pp. 66, 67, 76, 77

The Roads of Colorado, pp. 123, 124

Trails Illustrated, #141

Route Directions

▼ 0.0   In front of Beaumont Hotel at 5th and Main in Ouray, zero trip meter and proceed south out of town, remaining on US 550.

3.7 ▲   End in front of Beaumont Hotel at 5th and Main in Ouray.

           GPS: N 38°01.30′ W 107°40.29′

▼ 3.7   TL   National Forest access sign on right. Engineer Mountain and Alpine Loop signs are at the dirt track entrance. Zero trip meter.

0.0 ▲   Proceed on US 550 toward Ouray. Paved road.

Wildflowers blooming in early summer near the turnoff to Mineral Point

GPS: N 37°59.26' W 107°39.01'

▼ 0.0   Proceed along jeep trail.
7.0 ▲ TR Intersection with US 550. Zero trip meter.

▼ 1.6 SO Mickey Breene Mine ruins on left.
5.4 ▲ SO Mickey Breene Mine ruins on right.

▼ 1.7 SO Private road on left.
5.3 ▲ SO Private road on right.

▼ 2.0 SO Diamond Creek crossing. Track on right to backcountry campsites.
5.0 ▲ SO Track on left to backcountry campsites. Diamond Creek crossing.

▼ 2.4 TL Poughkeepsie Gulch 4WD trail to the right.
4.6 ▲ BR Intersection with Poughkeepsie Gulch 4WD trail on the left.
        GPS: N 37°58.01' W 107°37.60'

▼ 3.4 SO Track on left.
3.6 ▲ SO Track on right.

▼ 3.7 SO Track on right to backcountry campsites.
3.3 ▲ SO Track on left to backcountry campsites.

▼ 4.2 SO Miner's cabin on left. Tracks on left to Des Ouray Mine.

2.8 ▲ SO Tracks on right to Des Ouray Mine. Cabin on right.

▼ 4.4 SO Track on right. Stay on main road.
2.6 ▲ SO Track on left. Stay on main road.

▼ 4.6 SO Track on right to backcountry campsites.
2.4 ▲ SO Track on left to backcountry campsites.

▼ 5.0 SO Track on right to backcountry campsites.
2.0 ▲ SO Track on left to backcountry campsites.

▼ 5.1 TL Intersection: Signpost to Mineral Point. Follow sign to Engineer Mountain.
1.9 ▲ BR Intersection.
        GPS: N 37°57.72' W 107°35.71'

▼ 5.2 SO View across the valley to San Juan Chief Mill.
1.8 ▲ SO View across the valley to San Juan Chief Mill.

▼ 5.8 SO Public restrooms on right.
1.2 ▲ SO Public restrooms on left.

▼ 6.1 SO Tracks on right lead to series of open mine portals.
0.9 ▲ SO Tracks on left lead to series of open mine portals.

▼ 7.0   TL   Intersection with Southwest #5: North Fork Cutoff. Signs indicate Silverton and Animas Forks to the right; Lake City via Engineer Pass to the left. Zero trip meter.

0.0 ▲   Continue toward Ouray.
GPS: N 37°57.42′ W 107°34.47′

▼ 0.0   Continue on main road toward Engineer Pass.

6.1 ▲   TR   Three-way intersection. Straight ahead is Southwest #5: North Fork Cutoff, which leads to Animas Forks and Silverton. Zero trip meter.

▼ 0.8   UT   Follow sign to Engineer Pass. An unmarked track is straight ahead.

5.3 ▲   UT   Unmarked track is straight ahead.

▼ 1.9   SO   Road on left to Oh! Point.

4.2 ▲   SO   Road on right to Oh! Point.

▼ 2.3   BR   Summit of Engineer Pass. Two walking track trailheads are at summit: Bear Creek and Ridge Stock Driveway. Follow sign to Lake City.

3.8 ▲   BL   Summit of Engineer Pass. Two walking track trailheads are at summit: Bear Creek and Ridge Stock Driveway.
GPS: N 37°58.46′ W 107°35.08′

▼ 2.5   SO   Frank Hough Mine remains and American Flats.

3.6 ▲   SO   Frank Hough Mine remains and American Flats.

▼ 2.8   SO   Site of Engineer City.

3.3 ▲   SO   Site of Engineer City.

▼ 3.2   SO   Horsethief Trail walking track on left.

2.9 ▲   SO   Horsethief Trail walking track on right.

▼ 3.4   SO   Palmetto Gulch powderhouse and mine remains on right. Track on right to open mine shaft.

2.7 ▲   SO   Track on left to open mine portal. Palmetto Gulch powderhouse and mine remains on left.

▼ 4.4   SO   Palmetto Gulch cabin.

1.7 ▲   SO   Palmetto Gulch cabin.

▼ 4.6   SO   Thoreau's Cabin on left.

1.5 ▲   SO   Thoreau's Cabin on right.

▼ 4.8   SO   Bridge and Palmetto Gulch mill remains. 2WD vehicles sufficient beyond this point.

The trail being bulldozed in early summer

THE UTE AND CHIEF OURAY

Chief Ouray with Otto Mears in 1880

The vast area west of the Front Range was almost entirely controlled by various bands of Ute, who had lived there for approximately ten thousand years, longer than any other tribe lived within the future boundaries of Colorado. Ute domination of this entire area did not alter in the period leading up to the establishment of the Colorado Territory in 1861. In 1859, the Pikes Peak gold rush had erupted, and thousands of white prospectors and settlers poured across the eastern plains of Colorado, which were controlled by the Cheyenne and Arapaho. From his appointment in 1862, Governor Evans sought to open up eastern Colorado to these white settlers, but the two tribes refused to sell their lands and move to reservations. Evans decided to force the issue through what became known as the Cheyenne-Arapaho War, or the Colorado War, of 1864–1865.

During this period, the Ute maintained an uneasy peace with the whites, who were slowly encroaching on their lands. The initial fur trapping and prospecting had not greatly affected the Ute way of life, but numerous gold discoveries in central Colorado, from 1858 to 1860, led to greater incursions of white settlers into Ute territory.

In 1868, in response to the influx of miners and continued pressure for land to settle, a treaty known as the Kit Carson Treaty was negotiated by Chief Ouray, whereby the Ute gave up their land in the central Rockies and San Luis Valley and agreed to be settled on 16 million acres of land in western Colorado. The Colorado territory that the Ute retained was a rectangle that sat against the western and southern borders of the state, with its eastern border reaching almost to where Gunnison and Steamboat Springs are presently located, and its northern border located just south of the Yampa River. Two agencies, the White River Agency and the Los Pinos Agency, were established in 1869 to maintain the reservation and to distribute the promised $50,000 worth of supplies to the Ute every year.

Early prospecting efforts into the San Juan Mountains, the heartland of the Uncompahgre Ute, were slowed not so much by the Kit Carson Treaty or the fearsome reputation of the Ute, but by the lack of early success in finding gold and the intrusion of the Civil War. However, in the early 1870s, pressure from mining increased dramatically. Discoveries at Henson and in the Animas River Valley and prospecting in many other areas led to yet another treaty and further loss of land by the Ute. The Brunot Treaty, signed by

Chief Ouray and other Ute chiefs in Washington in 1873, ceded the San Juan region from their reservation. When Colorado achieved statehood in 1876, the miners and settlers again sought to have the treaties renegotiated. The political slogan became "The Utes Must Go."

Chief Ouray recognized the futility of resisting white expansion but was unable to control all the bands of Ute. The White River Ute especially resented the Brunot Treaty, which Ouray had been instrumental in negotiating. Nathan C. Meeker was appointed the Indian agent of the White River Ute in 1878. He was convinced that for their own good the Ute should give up hunting in exchange for agriculture and the Christian religion. When Meeker plowed the grazing land used by the Ute horses, a medicine man, Chief Johnson, attacked him. In response to this attack, in September 1879, federal officials

Chief Ouray

sent in 150 troops under the command of Major Thomas Thornburgh.

Chief Douglas and Chief Jack considered the calling of troops an act of war. Ute scouts warned the army not to enter reservation lands, which was prohibited by treaty agreement. The soldiers continued and were attacked. Major Thornburgh was killed and his troops besieged until Captain Francis S. Dodge and his cavalry of "Buffalo Soldiers" rescued them.

At the agency, the Ute burned the agency buildings, killed Meeker and the other white men, and took Meeker's daughter, his wife, and another woman into the mountains and held them captive for twenty-three days. Ouray acted swiftly to negotiate the release of the white women, but the political storm that ensued could not save the Ute from losing their reservation lands. After weeks of testimony before congressional committees in Washington, the Washington Treaty was signed in 1880 by Chiefs Ouray, Shavano, Antero, and others. It was necessary for three-quarters of the Ute males to sign this new treaty for it to come into effect. Otto Mears was appointed commissioner to secure the signatures. In August 1880, before all the signatures were obtained, Ouray died at the age of forty-six. Within a year, all the Ute were removed to reservations in Utah and southwestern Colorado.

Land developers and settlers gathered in Gunnison in the summer of 1881, waiting for the last of the Ute to vacate the old reservation, which they did on September 7, 1881. In 1882, Congress declared the Ute lands public and open for filing, but many settlers had already moved in and laid out towns.

1.3 ▲   SO Palmetto Gulch mill remains and bridge. 4WD vehicles recommended beyond this point.

▼ 5.1   SO Track on right to backcountry campsites along Henson Creek. Track networks with next two entries.

1.0 ▲   SO Track on left to backcountry campsites along Henson Creek.

▼ 5.4   SO Track on right goes to same vicinity as previous. Also goes across creek to Hurricane Basin and past a mine.

0.7 ▲   SO Track on left to backcountry campsites along Henson Creek.

▼ 6.1   BL Road to Rose's Cabin site on right. Zero trip meter.

0.0 ▲   Continue along main road toward Engineer Pass.
    GPS: N 37°58.58' W 107°32.20'

▼ 0.0   SO Continue along main road toward Lake City.

9.0 ▲   BR Road to Rose's Cabin site on left. Zero trip meter.

▼ 0.1   SO Public restrooms on right.
8.9 ▲   SO Public restrooms on left.

▼ 0.8   SO Empire Chief Mine and Mill on left.
8.2 ▲   SO Empire Chief Mine and Mill on right.

▼ 1.2   SO Waterfall on right.
7.8 ▲   SO Waterfall on left.

▼ 2.4   SO Smelter chimney on right from the Lee Mining and Smelter Company.

6.6 ▲   SO Smelter chimney on left from the Lee Mining and Smelter Company.

▼ 3.4   SO Whitmore Falls walking track on right.
5.6 ▲   SO Whitmore Falls walking track on left.

▼ 4.5   SO Corral on right.
4.5 ▲   SO Corral on left.

▼ 5.0   SO Capitol City town site. Private land and new homes.
4.0 ▲   SO Capitol City town site.

    GPS: N 38°00.35' W 107°28.05'

▼ 5.1   BR Bridge, then signpost on left indicating road to N. Henson Road via Matterhorn Creek and Uncompahgre Peak.

3.9 ▲   BL Walking trails on right, then bridge.

▼ 7.1   SO Bridge and track on right.
1.9 ▲   SO Bridge and track on left.

▼ 8.6   SO Open mine portal on left along road.
5.5 ▲   SO Open mine portal on right along road.

▼ 8.9   SO Public restrooms on left.
0.4 ▲   SO Public restrooms on right.

▼ 9.0   SO Track on left is Southwest #2: Nellie Creek Trail. Zero trip meter.

0.1 ▲   SO Continue on main road toward Engineer Pass.
    GPS: N 38°01.22' W 107°23.97'

▼ 0.0   Continue on main road toward Lake City.

5.1 ▲   SO Track on right is Southwest #2: Nellie Creek Trail. Zero trip meter.

▼ 1.3   SO Town of Henson.
3.7 ▲   SO Town of Henson.

▼ 1.7   SO Open mine portal on left along road.
3.4 ▲   SO Open mine portal on right along road.

▼ 2.5   SO Alpine Gulch Trailhead on right.
2.6 ▲   SO Alpine Gulch Trailhead on left.

▼ 4.0   SO Ruins of old mill on left.
1.2 ▲   SO Ruins of old mill on right.

▼ 5.1   TR Stop sign in Lake City. SO at next intersection, Silver Street.
0.1 ▲   BL And proceed along County 20.

▼ 5.2   Trail ends at the intersection of 1st Street and Gunnison Avenue (Colorado 149).

0.0 ▲   At the intersection of 1st Street and Gunnison Avenue (Colorado 149), zero trip meter and proceed northwest along 1st Street. SO across Silver Street.
    GPS: N 38°01.58' W 107°19.03'

Nellie Creek Trail

STARTING POINT Intersection of Southwest #1:
  Engineer Pass Trail and FR 877
FINISHING POINT Uncompahgre Peak Trailhead
TOTAL MILEAGE 4 miles (one-way)
UNPAVED MILEAGE 4 miles
DRIVING TIME 45 minutes
ROUTE ELEVATION 9,400 to 11,500 feet
USUALLY OPEN Mid-June to early October
DIFFICULTY RATING 4
SCENIC RATING 8

Special Attractions

- Interesting side road from Engineer Pass Trail.
- Scenery ranging from waterfalls to spectacular Uncompahgre Peak.
- Access to Uncompahgre Trailhead and the numerous hiking trails of the Uncompahgre Wilderness.

History

From much of the higher section of this trail you view the towering Uncompahgre Peak. At 14,309 feet, it is the highest mountain in the San Juans and the sixth highest in Colorado. The Hayden Survey Party made the first recorded ascent in 1874 and Lt. William Marshall of the later Wheeler Survey also climbed it. Prior to these times, the Ute used the peak as a lookout.

Hikers find the north face treacherous to climb, but access from the southwest and southeast is relatively easy. The mountain became notorious for its large population of grizzly bears, which was mentioned by both of the survey parties. However, evidently not everyone was deterred by their presence because in the late 1800s, the peak became a popular excursion for parties of hikers from the nearby mining towns of Capitol City and Lake City.

No major mines were ever found on the mountain itself.

Description

The initial section of this road is a gentle climb through the forest, following the course of Nellie Creek. This lower section of the creek and the nearby forest show the signs of many industrious beavers' labor. The trail is rough with occasional loose boulders, but generally they are embedded and it is not difficult to drive in a high-clearance vehicle. The biggest problem you are likely to have is passing vehi-

An early section of the trail that travels beside Nellie Creek

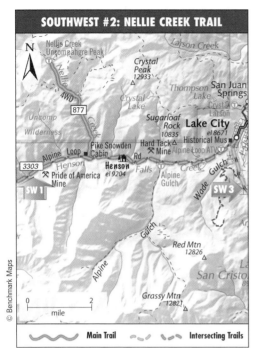

SOUTHWEST #2: NELLIE CREEK TRAIL

© Benchmark Maps

~~~~~ Main Trail   ~~~~ ~~~~ Intersecting Trails

Current Road Information
Gunnison National Forest
Gunnison Ranger District
216 N. Colorado
Gunnison, CO 81230
(970) 641-0471

Lake City Chamber of Commerce
800 Gunnison Avenue
Lake City, CO 81235
(970) 944-2527

Map References
Benchmark's *Colorado Road & Recreation Atlas,* p. 111
USFS   Gunnison NF or Uncompahgre NF
USGS   1:24,000   Uncompahgre Peak
           1:100,000 Montrose
Maptech CD-ROM:
           Southwest/Durango/Telluride
Colorado Atlas & Gazetteer, p. 67
The Roads of Colorado, p. 123
Trails Illustrated, #141

cles you encounter traveling the other way, as some sections are too narrow to pass without one driver reversing to a suitable spot.

There are numerous aspen trees at the lower reaches that add color in the fall to the already very attractive scenery provided by Nellie Creek, which flows beside the trail for much of the route, and a waterfall located at the 0.7-mile point.

After about three-quarters of a mile, there is a section of shelf road upon which you continue the climb. The road levels off after a little more than a mile and a half and you get a good view of Uncompahgre Peak. After you cross a shallow creek, the climb through the forest continues. The trail switchbacks up to another relatively level segment that can become quite boggy in wet weather conditions. The trail becomes rougher at this time and there are a number of shallow creek crossings. This section is the most difficult part of the trail but under dry conditions it only just warrants a rating of 4.

After about three miles, the trail levels off and enters an alpine meadow. A mile farther, the trail ends at the parking area for the Uncompahgre Peak Trailhead.

Route Directions

▼ 0.0   From Southwest #1: Engineer Pass Trail (5.1 miles from Lake City), zero trip meter and proceed along the 4WD track with sign to Nellie Creek Trailhead and Uncompahgre Peak Trail (FR 877).
           GPS: N 38°01.22' W 107°23.97'

▼ 0.7   SO   Waterfall in trees on left.
▼ 1.6   SO   Beaver lodge on right.
▼ 1.7   SO   Great view of rugged Uncompahgre Peak.
▼ 1.8   SO   Cross through Nellie Creek.
           GPS: N 38°02.58' W 107°24.23'

▼ 2.2   SO   Ruins of two log buildings across creek.
▼ 2.3   UT   Short track on right.
▼ 2.6   SO   Cross through creek.
▼ 3.4   SO   Cross through creek.
▼ 4.0   Public restrooms. Then end of track at trailhead and parking area.
           GPS: N 38°03.74' W 107°25.32'

Cinnamon Pass Trail

STARTING POINT Lake City at intersection with Southwest #1: Engineer Pass Trail
FINISHING POINT Animas Forks
TOTAL MILEAGE 26.8 miles
UNPAVED MILEAGE 20.4 miles
DRIVING TIME 2 hours
ROUTE ELEVATION 8,932 to 12,620 feet
USUALLY OPEN Late May to late October
DIFFICULTY RATING 3
SCENIC RATING 9

Special Attractions

- Animas Forks ghost town.
- Part of the Alpine Loop, the location of many historic mining towns.
- Moderately easy 4WD trail opened by snowplow early in the season.
- Wonderful, varied scenery.

History

The Ute used this pass road before white exploration of the area. Then, in the early 1860s, Charles Baker used the pass on his journey into the San Juan Mountains when he reported finding gold, triggering a minor gold rush. In 1873, Albert Burrows further explored the area, and in the following year, the Hayden Survey Party crossed the pass.

In the mid-1870s, Washington bureaucrats came to the conclusion that because the pass was not on the Continental Divide, the mail service should be able to cross it all year long; they awarded a contract on just that basis, despite the impossibility of the task.

In 1877, Enos Hotchkiss constructed the first wagon road over the pass. It was an important freight road for a period but was not maintained after the ore in the area declined.

The route starts at the still active town of Lake City. It was established following the discovery of the Golden Fleece Mine in 1874, originally named the Hotchkiss Mine, which

American Basin

Burrows Park

became the best ore producer in the area, although many other strikes followed.

In 1875, Lake City, named for nearby Lake San Cristobal, was registered and stagecoaches began making three trips a week to Saguache. That same year, Harry M. Woods published Lake City's first newspaper, *The Silver World.* The post office opened when the stagecoach service was extended to include a mail stage to Del Norte.

Lake City was one of the first towns in Colorado to have telephone service. In 1876, Western Union initiated telephone service, and by 1881, service had been extended to Silverton, Ouray, Capitol City, Rose's Cabin, Mineral Point, and Animas Forks. Musicians utilized the telephone service to perform popular telephone concerts for listeners along the various lines!

At its high point, Lake City had around 2,500 residents. Since the town was platted at the junction of two toll roads—Saguache to Silverton and Antelope Springs to Lake City—hundreds of people passed through the community each week. Stagecoaches continued

to stop in the city daily. The Denver & Rio Grande Railroad arrived in 1889. There were two trains daily in the 1890s, and ore shipments left aboard these trains regularly.

The wild red-light district on the west of town was known as Hell's Acres. Gambling dens and dance halls were interspersed among the many brothels. Lake City had its rough side: many of its residents were killed in mine accidents, snowslides, and shoot-outs.

Lake City experienced a series of economic fluctuations. It suffered greatly after the silver crash of 1893 and went into a long decline, relieved only by subsequent gold and lead production.

After the turn of the century, Lake City was on the decline; but camping, fishing, and hunting helped revive it as a summer community. In 1933, the railroad tracks were sold for scrap. Lake City never became a ghost town, although its population dwindled and it is currently a sleepy little community. Many original buildings were made of stone and still survive. The large stone schoolhouse was built in 1882. The courthouse where Alferd Packer was tried was built in 1877 and is still used.

From Lake City, the paved road extends past Lake San Cristobal, which was initially formed in about A.D. 1270 by the Slumgullion Slide, a huge mud and rockslide. A second major slide about 350 years ago completed the formation of Lake San Cristobal, the second largest natural lake in Colorado.

The route passes the turnoff to Sherman town site that was originally founded in 1877 and named for an early pioneer. The town grew slowly at first and then expanded quickly in the 1880s. Although several mines in the area yielded large amounts of gold, silver, copper, and lead, the principal mine was the Black Wonder. Located on the north side of town, the Black Wonder produced primarily silver and most of the mine's ore was transported to the smelters in Lake City. Sherman's population and prosperity fluctuated with the fortunes of the Black Wonder Mine, which continued to produce ore into the early 1900s. The town of Sherman peaked in the mid-1880s, when one summer the population reached about three hundred.

Sherman was a convenient stagecoach stop since it was located halfway between Animas Forks and Lake City. To travel on the toll road between Sherman and Lake City cost $2.50 and the cost to travel between Sherman and Animas Forks was $2.00 in either direction.

Around 1900, a 150-foot dam was constructed upstream of Sherman, but only a few days after the dam's completion, runoff from torrential rains flooded the mountainside, ripped the dam to pieces, and swept away much of the town of Sherman. The silver crash three years later ended Sherman's hopes for recovery, although the town was not completely deserted until the 1920s.

A cluster of mining camps sprouted up in the alpine meadow of Burrows Park between 1877 and 1880. The park was five miles long and a half-mile wide. The exact locations of the camps are disputed, but the general area is about ten miles southwest of Lake City, at the western end of the valley.

Burrows Park was the name of one of the camps, which was founded in 1877. About a mile south of Burrows Park, there was a community named Tellurium. This tiny camp had only about a dozen people, who hoped to find tellurium there. The highly optimistic group built an expensive mill. Unfortunately, Tellurium never became prosperous, and it was soon deserted. Another camp named Sterling was located a short distance beyond Tellurium, toward Animas Forks. Nearer the Continental Divide toward Cinnamon Pass, Whitecross was the largest of the settlements and served as the center of activity for the other camps. Whitecross's post office, established in 1880, was first called Burrows Park, after the region. Two years later it was renamed Whitecross.

Many men who lived in this area worked at the Tabasco Mine and Mill, which operated from 1901 to 1904 and was one of the first mines to use electric alternating current. Tabasco, the Louisiana hot sauce manufacturing company, owned both the mine and the mill. Ruins of the mine are scattered around the summit of Cinnamon Pass.

Description

Today Cinnamon Pass Trail is a seasonal, moderately easy 4WD road. It is part of the historic and majestic Alpine Loop. The other half of the loop is Southwest #1: Engineer Pass Trail. These two roads form the backbone of a network of roads throughout the region. Cinnamon Pass Trail is the easier of the two, but in the peak summer months both are extremely popular 4WD routes.

The scenery varies from the rugged alpine environment of year-round snow and barren talus slopes near the summit to the wildflower-covered valleys and rushing streams draining the melting snow. At either end of the route are wonderful, historic towns, one a ghost town, the other a hive of activity.

Initially, the gravel road is an easy, maintained road. After entering the Gunnison National Forest, the road intersects Southwest #4: Carson Ghost Town Trail on the left. The trail crosses Wager Gulch and passes the historic ghost town of Carson and continues over the Continental Divide.

Three miles farther along County 30 is the intersection with County 35—a short side

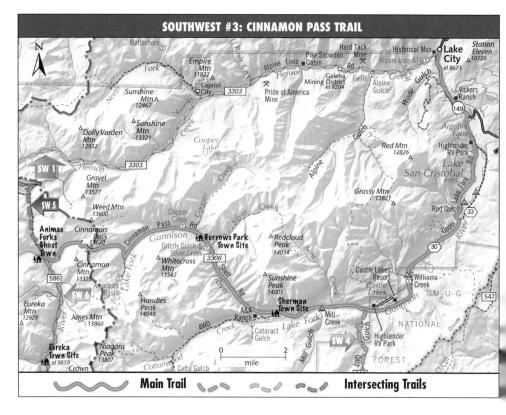

~~~~~ **Main Trail** 〜〜〜〜 〜〜〜 〜〜〜 **Intersecting Trails**

road leading to the site of Sherman. While the remains of the town are clearly visible, the forest has reclaimed the entire area.

After the Sherman turnoff, the road narrows into a shelf road overlooking the canyon. However, it remains comfortably wide even for full-sized 4WD vehicles, with a sufficient number of pull-offs available to facilitate passing.

A short distance farther, the road enters Burrows Park Basin—the region of Whitecross, Burrows Park, Tellurium, and Sterling townships. The road passes the two remaining buildings of Burrows Park and a public restroom.

About three and one-half miles farther, after passing the turnoff to the American Basin, which is renowned for its spring wildflowers, the road becomes more difficult as it ascends above timberline into alpine tundra. At this point, the views become expansive. From the summit of Cinnamon Pass, the road descends into the picturesque ghost town of Animas Forks, an amazingly well preserved ghost town where numerous buildings remain.

Bulldozers clear the snow on Cinnamon Pass, usually opening it by Memorial Day.

Current Road Information

San Juan National Forest
Silverton Ranger District
PO Box 709
1246 Blair Street
Silverton, CO 81433
(970) 387-5530

Lake City Chamber of Commerce
800 Gunnison Avenue
Lake City, CO 81235
(970) 944-2527

Silverton Chamber of Commerce
414 Greene Street
Silverton, CO 81433
(970) 387-5654

THE CANNIBALISM OF ALFERD PACKER

Alferd Packer was born in Pennsylvania. He served for a short time in the Union army during the Civil War and was discharged due to "disability." Packer, like many other men of his era, migrated westward with hopes of finding fabulous riches at the end of his arduous journey. He never made a fortune; he simply bummed around the mining camps, prospecting on occasion.

Alferd Packer

In November 1873, Packer led a party of twenty-one men from Provo, Utah to prospect in the San Juan Mountains of Colorado. Two months later, the group reached Ute Chief Ouray's winter camp at the junction of the Uncompahgre and Gunnison Rivers, near Montrose. Chief Ouray was friendly to the men and tried to warn them of the severe blizzards that regularly bombarded the mountains in the winter-time. Ouray tried to persuade the party to stay with him and his people to wait out the season. After a few days, Packer and five men decided they would continue their journey in search of gold, departing on February 9. The other sixteen men remained with Chief Ouray.

According to Packer, for some unknown reason, his group left camp with rations of only seven days' food for one man. It did not take the six men long to go through such a small supply, so after nearly a week, Packer separated from the group and ventured off in search of food.

In April, Packer arrived alone at Los Piños Indian Agency on Cochetopa Creek, carrying with him money and possessions from the other men in his party. The authorities' suspicions were aroused, and they questioned Packer about the fate of his five companions.

Packer claimed his companions had deserted him. He told the authorities that when he returned to camp after his fruitless search for food, he found one man sitting near the fire roasting a piece of meat cut from the leg of another man. Another three corpses lay near the fire; the head of each one had been bashed by a hatchet. Packer claimed that when the man saw him, he stood with his hatchet in hand, and Packer shot him through the belly.

In time, Packer finally admitted to killing the men and eating their bodies. He escorted a search party to recover the remains, but they quit the search before locating the bodies.

Packer was arrested and jailed in Saguache but escaped before he could be tried. Nine years later, he was arrested in Wyoming, where he had been living under another name.

In April 1883, he stood trial in Lake City and was found guilty and sentenced to hang the following month. An angry mob wanted to lynch him immediately, so he was moved to Gunnison for safekeeping.

Packer won a retrial, and his sentence was reduced to forty years at the State Prison in Cañon City for manslaughter. He had served almost fifteen years when Governor Thomas pardoned him in 1901. As part of the pardon agreement, Packer moved to Denver, where for a while he worked as a doorman at the *Denver Post's* offices.

In April 1907, Packer died and was buried in Littleton Cemetery. A memorial plaque marking the site of the murders overlooks Lake San Cristobal on Cannibal Plateau.

Map References

Benchmark's *Colorado Road & Recreation Atlas,* pp. 110, 111
USFS   Uncompahgre NF or Gunnison NF
USGS   1:24,000   Lake City, Lake San Cristobal, Redcloud Peak, Handies Peak
           1:100,000 Montrose
Maptech CD-ROM:
           Southwest/Durango/Telluride
Colorado Atlas & Gazetteer, pp. 67, 77
The Roads of Colorado, pp. 123, 124
Trails Illustrated, #141

Route Directions

▼0.0   At the intersection of Gunnison Avenue (Colorado 149) and 1st Street, zero trip meter and proceed south on Colorado 149.
14.0 ▲   End at intersection of Gunnison Avenue (Colorado 149) and 1st Street.
           GPS: N 38°01.58' W 107°19.03'

▼ 2.2   TR Follow Alpine Loop Drive sign.
11.8 ▲   TL Onto Colorado 149.

▼ 6.2   BR Before bridge. Follow Alpine Loop sign onto unpaved road.
7.8 ▲   BL Bridge on right. Turn onto paved road.

▼ 8.9   SO USFS Williams Creek Campground on right.
5.1 ▲   SO USFS Williams Creek Campground on left.

▼ 11.1   SO Southwest #4: Carson Ghost Town Trail on left.
2.9 ▲   SO Southwest #4: Carson Ghost Town Trail on right.
           GPS: N 37°54.39' W 107°21.60'

▼ 11.3   SO Cross over bridge.
2.7 ▲   SO Cross over bridge.

▼ 12.3   SO Public toilets on left.
1.7 ▲   SO Public toilets on right.

▼ 12.9   SO Mill Creek BLM campground on left.

1.1 ▲   SO Mill Creek BLM campground on right.

▼ 14.0   BR Intersection with County 35 on left to Sherman town site. Follow sign to Cinnamon Pass and Silverton. Zero trip meter.
0.0 ▲   Continue on main road toward Lake City.
           GPS: N 37°54.21' W 107°24.68'

▼ 0.0   Continue on main road toward Cinnamon Pass.
7.5 ▲   SO Intersection with County 35 to Sherman town site on right. Zero trip meter.

▼ 0.5   SO Cross bridge.
7.0 ▲   SO Cross bridge.

▼ 3.9   SO Cross over Silver Creek.
3.7 ▲   SO Cross over Silver Creek.

▼ 4.0   SO Burrows Park town site. Grizzly Gulch (left) and Silver Creek (right) trailheads. Public toilets.
3.5 ▲   SO Burrows Park town site. Grizzly Gulch (right) and Silver Creek (left) trailheads. Public toilets.
           GPS: N 37°56.24' W 107°27.63'

▼ 5.5   SO Mine on right.
2.0 ▲   SO Mine on left.

▼ 6.3   SO Cattle guard.
1.3 ▲   SO Cattle guard.

▼ 6.4   SO Creek crossing.
1.1 ▲   SO Creek crossing.

▼ 7.1   SO Track on left leads to mines.
0.4 ▲   SO Track on right leads to mines.

▼ 7.4   SO Creek cascade on right flows underneath road.
0.2 ▲   SO Creek cascade on left flows underneath road.

▼ 7.6   BR Intersection. Posted sign reads "4WD recommended past this point." American Basin on left. Zero trip meter.
0.0 ▲   Continue on main road toward Lake City.
           GPS: N 37°55.87' W 107°30.80'

▼ 0.0		Continue on main road toward Cinnamon Pass.
2.2 ▲	BL	Intersection. American Basin on right. Zero trip meter.

▼ 0.4	SO	Cross over creek.
1.8 ▲	SO	Cross over creek.

▼ 0.5	SO	Deserted cabin on right and then Tabasco Mill ruins.
1.6 ▲	SO	Tabasco Mill ruins and then deserted cabin on left.

▼ 2.2	SO	Summit of Cinnamon Pass. Zero trip meter.
0.0 ▲		Continue on main road toward Lake City.
		GPS: N 37°56.03′ W 107°32.25′

▼ 0.0		Continue on main road toward Animas Forks.
2.8 ▲	SO	Summit of Cinnamon Pass. Zero trip meter.

▼ 0.1	BL	Track on right.
2.7 ▲	BR	Track on left.

▼ 0.7	SO	Cross over Cinnamon Creek.
2.1 ▲	SO	Cross over Cinnamon Creek.

▼ 2.1	UT	Track straight ahead is Southwest #5: North Fork Cutoff. Continue on main road.
0.7 ▲	UT	Follow switchback toward Cinnamon Pass. Straight ahead is Southwest #5: North Fork Cutoff.

▼ 2.5	UT	Intersection. Go toward Animas Forks. Silverton is straight ahead.
0.3 ▲	UT	Intersection. Follow switchback toward Cinnamon Pass. Silverton is straight ahead.
		GPS: N 37°55.78′ W 107°33.90′

▼ 2.8		Cross bridge into Animas Forks and end at intersection. Southwest #6 to Silverton is to the left; Southwest #12: California Gulch Trail is to the right.
0.0 ▲		At three-way intersection in Animas Forks, zero trip meter and proceed across bridge toward Cinnamon Pass.
		GPS: N 37°55.89′ W 107°34.22′

Carson Ghost Town Trail

STARTING POINT Intersection of Southwest #3: Cinnamon Pass Trail and FR 568
FINISHING POINT Carson Ghost Town
TOTAL MILEAGE 3.7 miles (one-way)
UNPAVED MILEAGE 3.7 miles
DRIVING TIME 30 minutes
ROUTE ELEVATION 9,400 to 12,350 feet
USUALLY OPEN Mid-June to late September
DIFFICULTY RATING 4
SCENIC RATING 9

Special Attractions
■ Well-preserved ghost town of Carson.
■ Views from the Continental Divide.

History
Following the discovery of silver at Carson in 1881, a wagon road was built to service the mines, leading from the Gunnison River to Lake City. Carson was very close to the Continental Divide and was one of the most remote mining camps in Colorado. The silver crash of 1893 led to its demise, and no buildings remain standing.

In 1896, prospectors discovered gold in the area, and a new town was built at a lower elevation than the original. It is this second town of Carson that remains today as a ghost town. It was abandoned in 1903; the road that serviced it also fell into disuse.

Description
This short side trip from Cinnamon Pass Trail is well worth the time and effort of crossing a section of very slippery mud that exists on the trail most years. The rewards are exploring the well-preserved ghost town and spectacular panoramic views from the crest of the Continental Divide.

The route commences from Southwest #3: Cinnamon Pass Trail, 15.4 miles from Animas Forks and 11.3 miles from Lake City. A sign that reads "Wager Gulch/Carson" marks the turnoff.

The road is initially fairly steep but

reasonably wide and has an adequate number of pull-offs. Occasional rocks in the road and eroded surfaces can require care in selecting the right line, but the road should not be too rough for a normal 4WD vehicle.

The most difficult problem can be mud. The first two miles of this trail are usually spotted with muddy sections. The surface is firm, but it can be very slippery and wheel-rutted and because the forest shelters the road, the mud is slow to dry.

Getting adequate traction depends on the weight of your vehicle, the state of the road on the day you attempt it, and, most importantly, the tires you are using. Exercise care in order to avoid oncoming vehicles that can have difficulty steering or stopping on the downhill slope.

Once you pass the mud, this road is straightforward. Exploring Carson and witnessing the views from the Continental Divide are well worthwhile.

The Continental Divide is just over a mile past the creek crossing at Carson. From the Continental Divide, the route deteriorates into walking trails so you'll need to retrace your tracks and return to Cinnamon Pass Trail.

Current Road Information

Gunnison National Forest
Gunnison Ranger District
216 N. Colorado
Gunnison, CO 81230
(970) 641-0471

Stalls in the Carson ghost town stables

Carson ghost town, nestled in Wager Gulch

A view of Carson ghost town today

Map References

Benchmark's *Colorado Road & Recreation Atlas,* p. 111
USFS   Uncompahgre NF or Gunnison NF
USGS   1:24,000   Lake San Cristobal, Finger Mesa
1:100,000 Silverton
Maptech CD-ROM:
    Southwest/Durango/Telluride
Colorado Atlas & Gazetteer, p. 77
The Roads of Colorado, pp. 123, 139
Trails Illustrated, #141

A group of trail riders visiting Carson ghost town

SOUTHWEST #4: CARSON GHOST TOWN TRAIL

[Map]

N

Williams Creek

SW 3

Castle Lakes

River

Castle Lakes Resort

Fork

Rd

Mill Creek

Gunnison

Highlander RV Park

Lake Fork

NA

Gulch

FOREST

4WD

Gulch

568

Cabin Ruins

Continental

Wager

Carson Peak 13657

Carson Ghost Town

Heart Lake Road

0   mile   1

~~~ **Main Trail**   ~·~ **Intersecting Trail**

Route Directions

▼ 0.0   From intersection of Southwest #3: Cinnamon Pass Trail and FR 568, zero trip meter and proceed toward Carson on FR 568. This intersection is 11.3 miles from Lake City.
GPS: N 37°54.39′ W 107°21.60′

▼ 0.1   BL   Series of private driveways.
▼ 0.7   SO   Creek crossing.
▼ 1.7   BR   Fork in road. Continue uphill.
▼ 2.2   SO   Creek crossing.
▼ 2.8   SO   Cabin ruins on left.
▼ 3.5   BL   Fork in road. Turn toward Carson ghost town. Straight ahead will lead across the Continental Divide and to the site of Old Carson.
▼ 3.6   SO   Cross through creek.
▼ 3.7   BL   Carson town site with many well-preserved structures.
GPS: N 37°52.13′ W 107°21.72′

One of the larger buildings still standing in Carson ghost town

North Fork Cutoff

STARTING POINT Intersection with Southwest #3: Cinnamon Pass Trail
FINISHING POINT Intersection with Southwest #1: Engineer Pass Trail
TOTAL MILEAGE 2 miles
UNPAVED MILEAGE 2 miles
DRIVING TIME 20 minutes
ROUTE ELEVATION 11,489 to 12,169 feet
USUALLY OPEN Late May to late October
DIFFICULTY RATING 4
SCENIC RATING 9

Description

This route is straightforward and is included in this book to allow more flexibility in traveling the Alpine Loop, which primarily consists of Southwest #1: Engineer Pass Trail and Southwest #3: Cinnamon Pass Trail. By linking these two roads, the Alpine Loop can be started or finished from any of three towns: Lake City, Ouray, or Silverton.

The North Fork Cutoff usually opens before the summit of Engineer Pass is cleared, allowing access to the western end of Engineer Pass Trail, which can be used as a route between Ouray and Animas Forks.

Although the route includes sections of shelf road, it is not very narrow and has a reasonable number of pull-offs. However, it is sufficiently rough to require a high-clearance vehicle.

Current Road Information

San Juan National Forest
Silverton Ranger District
PO Box 709
1246 Blair Street
Silverton, CO 81433
(970) 387-5530

Map References

Benchmark's *Colorado Road & Recreation Atlas*, p. 110
USFS   Uncompahgre NF or Gunnison NF
USGS   1:24,000   Handies Peak

Denver Lake and open mine portals along the North Fork Cutoff

1:100,000 Silverton
Maptech CD-ROM:
    Southwest/Durango/Telluride
Colorado Atlas & Gazetteer, p. 77
The Roads of Colorado, p. 123
Trails Illustrated, #141

Route Directions

▼ 0.0   At the intersection of Southwest #3:
         Cinnamon Pass Trail and Southwest
         #5: North Fork Cutoff, 0.7 miles from
         Animas Forks, zero trip meter and
         proceed north.

2.0 ▲   End at intersection with Cinnamon
         Pass Trail. Bear left to Lake City.
         Bear right to Animas Forks.
         GPS: N 37°56.02' W 107°34.10'

▼ 0.3   SO Mine on left.
1.7 ▲   SO Mine on right.

▼ 0.4   SO Tram cables overhead.
1.6 ▲   SO Tram cables overhead.

▼ 0.6   SO Track on right.
1.4 ▲   SO Track on left.

▼ 0.9   SO Open mine portal in mountainside
         on the left.
1.1 ▲   SO Open mine portal in mountainside
         on the right.

▼ 1.0   SO Cross over creek.
1.0 ▲   SO Cross over creek.

▼ 1.2   SO Cross over creek.
0.8 ▲   SO Cross over creek.

▼ 1.4   BR Open mine portal on left. Track on left
         leads to mines along Burrows Creek
         and dead-ends in approximately 2
         miles. Follow sign to Engineer Pass
         and Alpine Loop.
0.6 ▲   BL Track on right leads to mines along
         Burrows Creek and dead-ends. Open
         mine portal on right.
         GPS: N 37°56.91' W 107°34.53'

▼ 1.6   SO Track on left to Denver Lake, cabin, and

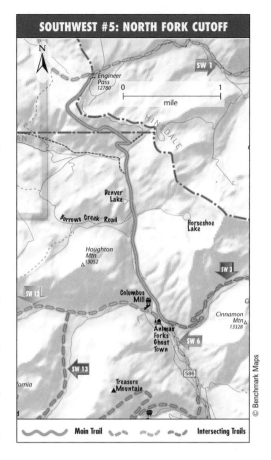

SOUTHWEST #5: NORTH FORK CUTOFF

© Benchmark Maps

〜〜〜 Main Trail 〜〜 ⌐〜⌐ 〜⌐〜 Intersecting Trails

         mine. Cross over creek. Track on right.
0.4 ▲   SO Track on left. Cross over creek. Track on
         right to Denver Lake, cabin, and mine.

▼ 1.7   SO Mine ruins on right.
0.3 ▲   SO Mine ruins on left.

▼ 2.0   End at intersection with Southwest
         #1: Engineer Pass Trail. Left goes to
         Ouray. Right goes to Engineer Pass
         and Lake City.
0.0 ▲   At the intersection of Southwest #1:
         Engineer Pass Trail and North Fork
         Cutoff, zero trip meter and proceed
         south along North Fork Cutoff toward
         Animas Forks.
         GPS: N 37°57.41' W 107°34.48'

Silverton to Animas Forks Ghost Town

STARTING POINT Silverton
FINISHING POINT Animas Forks
TOTAL MILEAGE 12.1 miles
UNPAVED MILEAGE 10.0 miles
DRIVING TIME 45 minutes
ROUTE ELEVATION 9,400 to 11,370 feet
USUALLY OPEN Mid-May to late October
DIFFICULTY RATING 1
SCENIC RATING 8

Special Attractions

- Animas Forks, one of Colorado's best ghost towns.
- The extremely historic road following part of the old railway grade, with innumerable points of historic interest.

History

This route commences in Silverton, a well-preserved, historic mining town that was founded in 1873. It is the terminus for the famed Durango and Silverton Narrow Gauge Railroad, which is a popular tourist destination in the summer months.

From Silverton, the route follows the Animas River as it passes numerous mines that dot the area known as Bakers Park, which extends all the way to Eureka. The park was named after Charles Baker, one of the first explorers in the area, who triggered a minor gold rush into territory still occupied by the Ute in the early 1860s.

At the six-mile point is the town site of Middleton, a small mining camp in the late 1800s, of which nothing remains. At the 7.7-mile point is the town site of Eureka. At the southern end of the town site is a turnoff on the right, which in days gone by was Saguache Street and led into the center of

The Casey Jones

The Columbus Mill in Animas Forks

SILVERTON

In July 1860, before the Brunot Treaty, Charles Baker (a native Virginian) and a party of six men explored Ute Indian territory in search of gold. They crossed the peaks of the San Juan Mountain ranges and set up camp in an area they called Baker City or Baker's Park. The miners lived in almost constant dread of the Utes, who were fierce fighters and the original occupants of the land.

When the Brunot Treaty was signed in 1873, the land was opened up for settlement to white men. At this time, twelve houses were recorded in Baker City, and the settlement's name was changed to Silverton. It is rumored that the town earned its name when a prospector exclaimed there was not much gold in the area, but there was "silver by the ton."

Prospectors discovered an enormous number of rich silver properties in the surrounding area, and miners began flooding in from all over.

A packtrain of burros and donkeys preparing to depart from Silverton, circa 1890

La Plata Miner, Silverton's first newspaper, was published in 1875. Some of the other early businesses established at the same time were the Greene & Company general store, a general merchandise store, a meat market, a drugstore, an attorney's office, an assay office, a doctor's office, and a post office. There was no jail at this time, and it has been reported that the first lawbreaker was actually chained to the floor of a cabin.

While Greene Street was considered the main commercial district, Blair Street was alive with numerous saloons and the red lights of prostitutes' bordellos. Blair Street became one of the West's most notorious hell-raising areas, 24 hours a day, seven days a week. Silverton's 37 saloons and numerous whorehouses lined the several block stretch. It is also reported that the underworld settled in on Blair Street and began to control Silverton. Wyatt Earp ran the gambling rooms for a while at the Arlington, a fancy saloon and gaming hall. Crime was so rampant that local vigilantes could not settle the town, so they hired Bat Masterson from Dodge City to take charge of the Silverton police department. He was able to calm things down a bit but did not close down Blair Street completely because he enjoyed what it had to offer a bit too much.

Up until 1880, Silverton's buildings consisted mainly of all-wood frames. From that time onwards, brick and stone construction became commonplace, and many of the buildings from that era remain. One of Silverton's most elegant establishments, the Grand Hotel at the corner of 12th and Green Streets, opened in 1882. The name of the hotel later changed to the Grand Imperial Hotel. It was a lavish, grandly decorated, three-story showplace.

Because Silverton was situated in a mountain valley, like Ouray it had a problem with transportation over the San Juan ranges. Only the richest gold and silver ores were worth shipping out by pack trains of burros, which brought supplies on the return trip. Because the mountain passes were navigable only in summer, residents had to haul in enough supplies to last the snowy winter months.

Mid-1882 saw the arrival of the Denver & Rio Grande Railroad from Durango. Otto Mears established three other narrow-gauge lines from Silverton, making a total of four railway lines serving Silverton. This solved Silverton's transportation problems and opened it up economically and geographically to the rest of the world. To this day, the Denver & Rio Grande narrow-gauge railway still makes trips between Durango and Silverton during warm months.

The railroad did not guarantee comfortable living in the San Juan Mountains. During the winter of 1884, avalanches blocked the railroad for 73 continuous days, leaving Silverton desperate for supplies. Crews of men eventually dug from both directions to clear an 84-foot snowslide. When the train finally reached Silverton, it was met by a cheering crowd of townspeople, many of whom were down to their last morsels of food.

View of Silverton in 1909 looking down 12th Street

Several wealthy characters lived in Silverton. Thomas Walsh of the Camp Bird Mine had interests there. The Guggenheims accumulated a sizable portion of their fortune from the Silverton area. Lena Stoiber, married to the owner of the Silver Lake Mine, was a rich woman who shared her wealth by piling gifts into her sleigh at Christmastime and delivering toys to the town's children.

Silverton never did become a ghost town. It survived the silver crash of 1893, primarily because gold was discovered in the region. Also, copper and lead were mined locally. The Durango-Silverton narrow-gauge railway attracts tourists to the area and accounts for a major part of Silverton's economy today. Hollywood also discovered Silverton—with its authentic Victorian storefronts still intact and its nineteenth-century train—an ideal site for filming. Such films as *Ticket to Tomahawk*, *Around the World in Eighty Days*, and *The Naked Spur* were filmed in Silverton.

The much-photographed Walsh House in Animas Forks

Another well-preserved cabin in Animas Forks

town. The square building is the restored water tank; the room below was used as the town jail. The foundations of several other buildings are evident.

The massive foundations that rise up the mountainside on the other side of the Animas River are the remains of the Sunnyside Mill. The Sunnyside Mine, located in Eureka Gulch behind the mill, was discovered in 1873. By 1910, it consisted of 10 miles of tunnel and employed 300 miners. The first wooden mill opened in 1899 and is located to the left of the existing foundations, which belong to the second Sunnyside Mill (which started production in 1918). The second mill incorporated much of the dismantled Gold Prince Mill, relocated from Animas Forks.

About half a mile from Eureka, the ruins of a boardinghouse and a bridge across the Animas River can be seen on the right. The boardinghouse was built in 1907 to house the workers from the Tom Moore Mine.

The road at this point follows the old Silverton Northern Railroad line, built by Otto Mears in 1903–1904. Four hundred men worked on this section of the railroad line; it had an average grade of seven percent, which resulted in the train having an average speed of only four miles per hour. Going up, the train could only pull a coal car and one empty car, and on the downhill, it was limited to a maximum of three ore cars.

The other natural obstacle that challenged the railroad was snow. On the left of the road can be seen the remnants of one of the snowsheds built by Otto Mears to protect the railroad from the snowslides, which are prevalent in the area. Despite Mears' best endeavors, nature proved too strong an adversary, and the snowsheds were destroyed in the first winter. High operating costs and declining mineral production led to the closure of the railroad in 1916.

Across the river from the snowshed can be seen the remnants of the last toll road built

A view of Animas Forks today

by Otto Mears in the mid-1880s—the only one he lost money on.

As you cross the Animas River on the entry into Animas Forks ghost town, the foundations on the right are the remains of the Gold Prince Mill, the largest concentrating mill in Colorado when it was built in 1904. On the left is the location of the railroad turntable used to turn around the steam engine of the Silverton Northern Railroad for the return to Silverton.

Farther into Animas Forks, a number of buildings remain to the left of the road. The most famous of these is the two-story Walsh House with the front bay window. This was the home of William Duncan, and was constructed in 1879. It has been speculated that Thomas Walsh's daughter stayed there when writing her father's biography and also that Walsh rented a room there in his younger (and poorer) days. It is extremely unlikely that either story is true. The build-ings across the Animas River as you leave town are the Columbus Mine and Mill, built in about 1880. This mill ceased operations in 1948.

Description
The entire route is an easy, well-maintained, gravel road suitable for passenger vehicles under good weather conditions.

Current Road Information
San Juan National Forest
Silverton Ranger District
PO Box 709
1246 Blair Street
Silverton, CO 81433
(970) 387-5530

Silverton Chamber of Commerce
414 Greene Street
Silverton, CO 81433
(970) 387-5654

A snow bridge across the Animas River in late spring

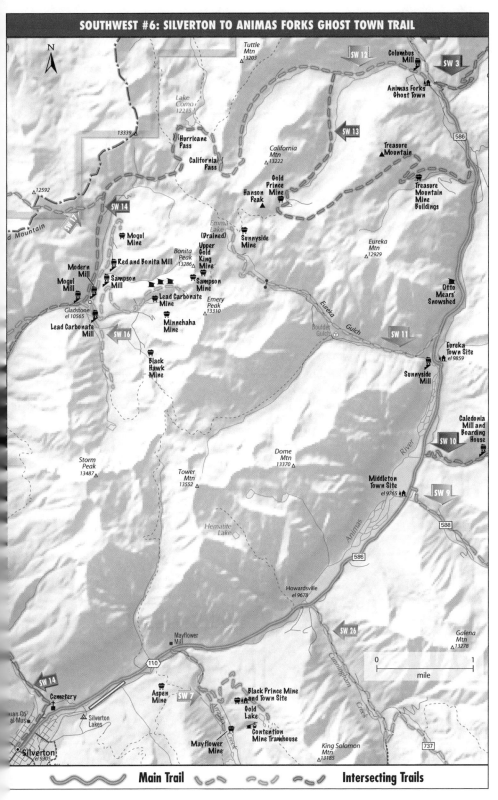

N

Tuttle Mtn 13203

SW 12

Columbus Mill

SW 3

Animas Forks Ghost Town

Lake Como 12215

SW 13

13339

Hurricane Pass

California Pass

California Mtn 13222

Treasure Mountain

586

12592

SW 14

SW 17

ed Mountain

Gold Prince Mine

Hanson Peak

Treasure Mountain Mine Buildings

Mogul Mine

Emma Lake (Drained)

Sunnyside Mine

Eureka Mtn 12929

Bonita Peak 13286

Upper Gold King Mine

Red and Bonita Mill

Modern Mill

Sampson Mill

Mogul Mill

Sampson Mine

Otto Mears' Snowshed

Lead Carbonate Mine

Emery Peak 13310

Eureka Gulch

Gladstone el 10565

Minnehaha Mine

Boulder Gulch

SW 11

Eureka Town Site el 9859

Lead Carbonate Mill

SW 16

Sunnyside Mill

Black Hawk Mine

Caledonia Mill and Boarding House

SW 10

Storm Peak 13487

Dome Mtn 13370

River

Tower Mtn 13552

Middleton Town Site el 9765

SW 9

588

Hematite Lake

586

Animas

Howardsville el 9678

SW 26

Galena Mtn 13278

Mayflower Mill

0   1
mile

110

Cunningham Creek

SW 14

Cemetery

Aspen Mine

SW 7

Black Prince Mine and Town Site

uan Co- al Mus

Silverton Lakes

Gold Lake

Mayflower Mine

Contention Mine Tramhouse

King Solomon Mtn 13185

737

Silverton el 9305

~~~ **Main Trail** ~~~   ~~~ **Intersecting Trails**

ANIMAS FORKS

Animas Forks, originally called La Plata City, experienced its first silver strike in 1875. As an enticement to live near timberline and brave the harsh winters, the government offered settlers free lots and aid for building homes.

Within a year, settlers had erected 30 cabins, a post office, a saloon, a general store, a hotel, and two mills; the town soon boasted a population of 200 residents. All the buildings were well-constructed, with finished lumber and shingled roofs. The jail-house, a rough, box-like structure made of two-by-six lumber and consisting of two cells and a jailer's office in front, was a rare exception to the general building standards.

In 1877, Otto Mears constructed a wagon road to Eureka and through to Silverton. This resulted in his

Animas Forks with the bay-windowed Walsh House

network of toll roads connecting Lake City, Ouray, and Silverton. Animas Forks became the central junction for these and other roads that connected the area's many mining camps. The other main contributor to the town's economy was its mill, which treated ore from Red Cloud Mine in Mineral Point.

Snow presented a huge problem for Animas Forks. Although the town was considered a year-round mining community, the population dropped in the wintertime. In 1884, the population reached 400 in the summer but dropped to a dozen men, three women, and

A view of Animas Forks in 1875

20 dogs in the winter. A winter storm that same year lasted for 23 days.

During the 1880s, telephone lines were installed, running from Lake City and passing over the 12,500-foot Continental Divide near Engineer Pass. Stagecoaches ran daily from Lake City to Silverton via Engineer Pass.

Mrs. Eckard, the first woman in Animas Forks, ran an extremely popular boarding-house. Eckard won the favor of the local miners by extending them credit. When one freeloader slipped out of town without settling his account for three months of lodging, a vigilante committee set out after him. They caught him in Silverton and threatened to lynch him. He paid up, and no further bad debts were reported!

A photograph of Animas Forks in the 1880s taken by William Henry Jackson

At its peak, Animas Forks was home to about 1,500 residents. Located at an elevation of 11,584 feet, it once boasted that it was the largest city in the world at this elevation.

Although its prosperity began to wane by the 1890s and the town was nearly deserted by 1901, Animas Forks experienced a resurgence of activity between 1904 and 1916. Otto Mears extended the railroad in 1904 and planned an elaborate system of seven snowsheds to permit the line to operate from Lake City to Silverton. Snowdrifts in the area were sometimes over 25 feet high. When the first big snowslide of the season destroyed the first of Mears' sheds, his idea was abandoned. The remains of this shed are clearly visible along Southwest #6: Silverton to Animas Forks Ghost Town.

The Gold Prince Mill, constructed in 1904, operated until 1910 and was moved to Eureka in 1917. Animas Forks rapidly declined once more.

In 1942, the railroad tracks were removed and scrapped. The railroad bed became a road again after the tracks were removed.

Today, Animas Forks is a fascinating ghost town, consisting of about a dozen houses. The Columbus Mill still stands, as

The famous Walsh House in Animas Forks

do several other structures, including the elaborate Walsh house with its prominent bay window. The foundations of the Gold Prince Mill remain at the southern end of town.

A view of Animas Forks nestled in the valley with the road continuing beyond toward California Gulch

Map References

Benchmark's *Colorado Road & Recreation Atlas*, p. 110
USFS Uncompahgre NF or San Juan NF
USGS 1:24,000   Howardsville, Silverton, Handies Peak
      1:100,000 Silverton
Maptech CD-ROM:
      Southwest/Durango/Telluride
Colorado Atlas & Gazetteer, p. 77
The Roads of Colorado, p. 123
Trails Illustrated, #141

Route Directions

▼ 0.0   From the Silverton City Hall at Greene (main) Street and 14th Street, zero trip

meter and proceed northeast out of town.
7.8 ▲   End in front of the Silverton City Hall at Greene and 14th Streets.
         GPS: N 37°48.79′ W 107°39.72′

▼ 0.2   BR Road forks. Bear right onto Colorado 110. Remain on paved road.
7.6 ▲   BL Road forks. Bear left and remain on paved road.

▼ 0.4   SO Campground on the right.
7.4 ▲   SO Campground on the left.

▼ 0.5   SO Lackawanna Mill on right across the river. Hillside Cemetery on left.
7.3 ▲   SO Hillside Cemetery on right. Lackawanna Mill on left across the river.

▼ 0.7   BR   Road fork entering on left.
7.0 ▲   BL   Road fork entering on right.

▼ 1.6   SO   Aspen Mine ruins on right across the river.
6.2 ▲   SO   Aspen Mine ruins on left across the river.

▼ 1.7   SO   On the right side of the road, in the distance about 3 miles east, the tram house and boardinghouse of the Old Hundred Mine are evident about three-quarters of the way up Galena Mountain.
6.1 ▲   SO   The tramhouse and boardinghouse of the Old Hundred Mine are evident on the left, in the distance about 3 miles southeast, three-quarters of the way up Galena Mountain.

▼ 2.0   SO   Silver Lake Mill on right.
5.8 ▲   SO   Silver Lake Mill on left.

▼ 2.1   SO   Southwest #7: Arrastra Gulch Trail and Southwest #8: Silverton Northern Railroad Grade on right.
5.7 ▲   SO   Southwest #7: Arrastra Gulch Trail and Southwest #8: Silverton Northern Railroad Grade on left.

▼ 2.2   SO   Mayflower Mill and tram on left.
5.6 ▲   SO   Mayflower Mill and tram on right.

▼ 3.8   SO   Little Nation Mine on right, halfway up the mountainside.
4.0 ▲   SO   Little Nation Mine on left, halfway up the mountainside.

▼ 4.0   SO   Bridge across the Animas River.
3.8 ▲   SO   Bridge across the Animas River.

▼ 4.2   SO   Bridge across Cunningham Creek, then turnoff for Southwest #26: Cunningham Gulch and Stony Pass Trail on the right. Town site of Howardsville. Little Nations Mill.
3.6 ▲   SO   Little Nations Mill. Town site of Howardsville. Turnoff for Southwest #26: Cunningham Gulch and Stony Pass Trail on the left. Bridge across Cunningham Creek.
GPS: N 37°50.06′ W 107°35.68′

▼ 6.0   SO   Southwest #9: Maggie Gulch Trail on right. Town site of Middleton.
1.8 ▲   SO   Town site of Middleton. Southwest #9: Maggie Gulch Trail on left.

▼ 6.6   SO   Cross over creek. Southwest #10: Minnie Gulch Trail on right.
1.2 ▲   SO   Southwest #10: Minnie Gulch Trail on left. Cross over creek.

▼ 6.7   SO   Track to campsites on right.
1.1 ▲   SO   Track to campsites on left.

▼ 7.7   BL   Entry to Eureka town site on right. Campsites.
0.1 ▲   BR   Entry to Eureka town site on left. Campsites.

▼ 7.8   SO   Bridge over Animas River. Zero trip meter.
0.0 ▲   Continue along main road.
GPS: N 37°52.76′ W 107°33.92′

▼ 0.0   Continue along main road.
4.3 ▲   SO   Bridge over Animas River. Zero trip meter.

▼ 0.1   BR   Sunnyside Mill on left.
4.2 ▲   BL   Sunnyside Mill on right.

▼ 0.3   SO   Southwest #11: Eureka Gulch Trail on left.
4.0 ▲   SO   Southwest #11: Eureka Gulch Trail on right.

▼ 0.5   SO   Historic boardinghouse for mine workers on right.
3.7 ▲   SO   Historic boardinghouse for mine workers on left.

▼ 1.0   SO   Log remains of a snowshed built by Otto Mears on left.
3.3 ▲   SO   Log remains of a snowshed built by Otto Mears on right.

▼ 1.8   SO   Silver Wing Mine on right.
2.5 ▲   SO   Silver Wing Mine on left.

▼ 2.7   SO   Remains of dam used to feed the Silver Wing Mine.

1.6 ▲	SO	Remains of dam used to feed the Silver Wing Mine.
▼ 2.8	SO	Southwest #13: Picayne Gulch and Placer Gulch Trail on left. Track on right crosses Animas River and joins the road to Burns Gulch.
1.5 ▲	SO	Southwest #13: Picayne Gulch and Placer Gulch Trail on right. Track on left crosses Animas River and joins the road to Burns Gulch.
▼ 2.9	SO	Track on left. Cross over Animas River. Turnoff to Burns Gulch on right.
1.4 ▲	SO	Turnoff to Burns Gulch on left. Cross over Animas River. Track on right.
▼ 3.5	SO	Cross over Cinnamon Creek.
0.8 ▲	SO	Cross over Cinnamon Creek.
▼ 3.6	BL	Proceed toward Animas Forks. Cutoff to Cinnamon Pass Trail on right. Public restrooms on left.
0.7 ▲	BR	Public restrooms on right. Cutoff to Cinnamon Pass Trail on left. Proceed on main road toward Silverton.
▼ 3.9	SO	Cross over Animas River. Gold Prince Mill ruins on right.
0.4 ▲	SO	Gold Prince Mill ruins on left. Cross over Animas River.
▼ 4.1	SO	Public restrooms on right. Animas Forks jailhouse site behind the restrooms.
0.2 ▲	SO	Animas Forks jailhouse site behind the public restrooms on left.
▼ 4.3		Animas Forks ghost town. Bridge across Animas River is on the right, leading to Southwest #3: Cinnamon Pass and Southwest #1: Engineer Pass. The Columbus Mill is straight ahead.
0.0 ▲		At the bridge over the Animas Forks River at the north end of Animas Forks, zero trip meter and proceed south toward Silverton.
		GPS: N 37°55.89′ W 107°34.22′

Arrastra Gulch Trail

STARTING POINT Intersection with Southwest #6: Silverton to Animas Forks Ghost Town road

FINISHING POINT Gold Lake in Little Giant Basin

TOTAL MILEAGE 5.3 miles

UNPAVED MILEAGE 5.3 miles

DRIVING TIME 1 hour (one-way)

ROUTE ELEVATION 9,850 to 12,200 feet

USUALLY OPEN Mid-June to early October

DIFFICULTY RATING 5

SCENIC RATING 10

Special Attractions

- Picturesque Gold Lake.
- Black Prince mining camp.
- Numerous other old mining remains.

History

The historic interest of this 4WD trail centers on the numerous mines that were located in the area. Many of the mining operations built mills to process their ore and tramways to transport the ore from the mines to the mills.

The first historic site along the route is the Whale Mill, which was an early, water-powered mill erected in about 1888 and eventually incorporated into the Silver Lake Mill operation.

The Mayflower Mine was discovered in the late 1880s. Following the construction of Mayflower Mill in 1929, ore from the mine was carried nearly two miles by a steel tramway down to the mill for processing.

The Contention tramway carried ore one and one-quarter miles from the Big Giant and Black Prince mines to Contention Mill, located on the north side of the Animas River, beside the railroad. Near the Black Prince Mine is a mining camp that still contains a number of long-deserted buildings. The mining company constructed them in 1915 to house its workers.

Near the end of the route is the Big Giant Mine, which was discovered in the 1870s

The shelf road cut into the talus rock above Arastra Creek

A view of the Black Prince mining camp

Contention Mine tramhouse

Gold Lake

but was only a marginal operation. After being bought by the Contention Mining Company, its tramway was used to carry ore to the Contention Mill for processing.

Description

This route is another side road of Colorado 110, Southwest #6: Silverton to Animas Forks Ghost Town. It starts at the unmarked turnoff to Arrastra Gulch. Shortly after the start, the trail crosses a bridge over the Animas River, and then a shelf road that climbs toward Arrastra Gulch commences. Progressing along this road, there is a good view of the creek and valley below. The road is sound and reasonably wide.

At the 0.8-mile point the road forks. The route directions follow the right-hand fork first and then return to explore the other fork. The right-hand section follows the gulch to end just below the Mayflower Mine at which point the road gets much narrower and is washed out a short distance ahead.

The left-hand fork is the harder of the two roads. It leads to the Black Prince Mine and the buildings that have survived from the mining camp. From there, the road climbs to the majestic surrounds of Gold

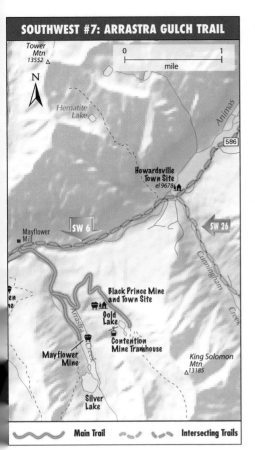

Tower Mtn 13552 △

N

Hematite Lake

Animas

586

Howardsville Town Site el 9678

SW 6

SW 26

Mayflower Mill

Cunningham Creek

Black Prince Mine and Town Site

en ne

Arrastra Creek

Gold Lake

Contention Mine Tramhouse

Mayflower Mine

King Solomon Mtn △13185

Silver Lake

〜〜〜 **Main Trail**   ⌒⌒ ⌒⌒ **Intersecting Trails**

Lake, nestled in Little Giant Basin. This fork of the route starts by ascending a narrow shelf that has limited opportunity for passing. It is rough and rocky but not extremely difficult because the surface is fairly sound. The rocks on the trail are not large enough to pose clearance problems for a 4WD vehicle, but some are sharp. From the Black Prince mining camp the road gets narrower with a very steep drop-off. The scenic location of Gold Lake makes the journey well worthwhile.

Most of this trail rates a 3 for difficulty. The latter section, exploring the left-hand fork, rates a 4 until the Black Prince mining camp and then the trail becomes rated 5 for the last short section to Gold Lake. The trail is particularly scenic, especially along the upper reaches and in the vicinity of Gold Lake. There are numerous aspens to provide autumn color in the lower section of the trail.

Current Road Information

Silverton Chamber of Commerce
414 Greene Street
Silverton, CO 81433
(970) 387-5654

Map References

Benchmark's *Colorado Road & Recreation Atlas,* p. 110
USFS   Uncompahgre NF or San Juan NF
USGS   1:24,000   Howardsville, Silverton
          1:100,000 Silverton
Maptech CD-ROM:
          Southwest/Durango/Telluride
Colorado Atlas & Gazetteer, p. 77
The Roads of Colorado, p. 139
Trails Illustrated, #141

Route Directions

▼ 0.0   From Southwest #6: Silverton to Animas Forks Ghost Town (County 110) opposite the Mayflower Mill, zero trip meter and proceed downhill on the Arrastra Gulch road towards the river. This intersection is 2.1 miles from Silverton City Hall.
          GPS: N 37°49.62′ W 107°37.77′

▼ 0.2   SO Track on the left and right is Southwest #8: Silverton Northern Railroad Grade. Then cross Arrastra Creek.

▼ 0.3   SO Cross under Mayflower Mill tram. Track on right goes to up Arrastra Gulch to the Silver Lake Mine.

▼ 0.5   SO Ruins of dam in creek on right.

▼ 0.7   SO Whale Mill ruins down at the creek on the other side. Level with the road, across the steam are the ruins of a wooden support for the Silver Lake Tram.

▼ 0.8   BL Track straight ahead into meadow.
          BR At the fork in the road. Zero trip meter. (You will return to this point to explore the left-hand fork.)
          GPS: N 37.49.21′ W 107.37.23′

▼ 0.0   Cross under tram line.

▼ 0.2   SO Wooden tram structure on right.

▼ 0.3   SO Track on left.

▼ 0.6   SO Track on left to Mayflower Mine and

EUREKA

Eureka was founded in the early 1870s. Although not a boom town, it grew slowly and steadily.

The Sunnyside Mine was located in 1873 and became one of the best producers in the area. Sunnyside Mill was built in 1899, with a three-mile cable tramway connecting the mine to the new mill. The Sunnyside Mill was easily the leading producer of income for the town.

Eureka flourished and boasted a population of 2,000 and many stores, meat markets, saloons, and a restaurant. It was incorporated in 1883, making it one of only two incorporated towns in San Juan County (Silverton was the other). Eureka had its own post office, and the monthly newspaper, the *San Juan Expositor*, was published there. Otto Mears routed the

The Sunnyside Mill, circa 1920

Silverton Northern Railroad through the town in 1896, further strengthening Eureka's economy.

The Gold Prince Mill was moved to Eureka from Animas Forks in 1917 but did not begin operation until 1918, because it was damaged by fire and had to be rebuilt. Eureka also served the Toltec, the Golden Fleece, the Tom Moore, the Silver Wing, and the Sound Democrat mines. The Sunnyside Mine operated continuously until 1931, when it shut down for a few years and then reopened in 1937. Two years later the miners went on strike, and since an agreement could not be reached, the mine was shut down again.

Toward the end of its operation, the Silverton Northern Railroad's steam engines were replaced by a combination of auto and locomotive parts called the Casey Jones, which could speed down the tracks between Silverton and Eureka in just 20 minutes. To clear snow off the tracks, the Casey Jones carried brooms strapped behind its cowcatcher. Service between Silverton and Eureka ended in 1939 and the railroad was sold and junked in 1942.

In 1976, the state of Colorado decided that the town had had no municipal government for the past five years and declared Eureka formally abandoned. Today, only a reconstructed two-story building stands on what was Eureka's flat town site. You also can still see the enormous skeleton of the Sunnyside Mill.

The foundations of the Sunnyside Mill in Eureka today

A view of Eureka and the Sunnyside Mill in 1929

tram station.

▼ 0.7 SO Cross under tram line. Tram towers on the right.

▼ 1.0 SO Road deteriorates.

▼ 1.2 UT Trail is washed out at head of gulch. Mayflower Mine on hill to the left. Turn around and return to the fork where you last reset the trip meter.
GPS: N 37°48.33′ W 107°36.69′

▼ 2.4 TR At intersection. Zero trip meter.
GPS: N 37°49.21′ W 107°37.23′

▼ 0.1 SO Pass under tram cable.

▼ 0.3 SO Both wooden and steel tram supports on right.

▼ 0.4 TL Turn sharply onto the road to Little

Giant Basin.
GPS: N 37°49.06′ W 107°36.99′

▼ 0.9 SO Pass under tram cables for the Contention tram.

▼ 1.0 SO Pass under tram cables.

▼ 1.3 SO Pass under tram cables.

▼ 1.5 SO Pass under tram cables.

▼ 2.1 BL Black Prince mining camp.
GPS: N 37°48.35′ W 107°36.29′

▼ 2.4 SO King Solomon Mine portal on left.

▼ 2.7 SO Big Giant/Contention Mine and Mill on right.

▼ 2.9 End at beautiful Gold Lake.
GPS: N 37°48.39′ W 107°35.96′

A pond with the Black Prince mining camp in the background

Silverton Northern Railroad Grade

STARTING POINT Intersection with Southwest #7: Arrastra Gulch Trail

FINISHING POINT Intersection with Southwest #6: Silverton to Animas Forks Ghost Town road, near Howardsville

TOTAL MILEAGE 2.6 miles

UNPAVED MILEAGE 2.6 miles

DRIVING TIME 30 minutes

ROUTE ELEVATION 9,550 to 10,250 feet

USUALLY OPEN Mid-May to October

DIFFICULTY RATING 2

SCENIC RATING 8

Special Attractions

■ Historic Silverton Northern Railroad grade.
■ Remains of the Silver Lake Mill.
■ Numerous additional mining sites.

History

Otto Mears incorporated the Silverton Northern Railroad in November 1895 to connect Silverton to Animas Forks, located 14 miles apart. His original plan was to continue the tracks beyond Animas Forks all the way to Lake City. The first section of railway to Howardsville and Eureka opened in June 1896. The second section to Animas Forks opened in 1903, with an average grade of seven percent. The line above Eureka was removed in 1920, and the lower section ceased operations in 1939; the tracks were removed in 1942. This route follows the old

Howardsville

railroad grade from just below Arrastra Gulch to Howardsville.

The foundations of the Silver Lake Mill are a prominent feature along this route. Ore had been discovered at the Silver Lake Mine in about 1890 and was greatly developed by the incorporation of further claims. The original claim was located at an elevation of 12,275 feet beside Silver Lake at the top of Arrastra Gulch. Two mills were built to process ore from this mine. The first was located at the mine. The second, more substantial mill was built in the late 1890s. This mill is still evident beside the Animas River and the Silverton Northern Railroad grade.

A tramway was constructed to carry ore over two and one-half miles from the mine to the new mill. The Silver Lake operation processed more than $7 million worth of ore before being bought by the Guggenheim empire in 1901 for $1.25 million. In 1906, the mill burned down. It was rebuilt but ceased operations in 1914. It burned down again in 1949 and what remained was sold for scrap.

The route also passes the site of the Wifley Mill. From 1913 to 1919, Otto Mears and Arthur Wifley leased the Silver Lake Mine and chose to process the ore, which they mainly recovered from the tailing dumps at the Wifley Mill, which was located on the north side of the Animas River at the bottom of Arrastra Gulch.

The site of the Silver Lake Mill today

The Silver Lake Mill, circa 1890

Description

The route starts a short distance along Southwest #7: Arrastra Gulch Trail. Initially, it heads southwest to the location of the Silver Lake Mill. This section dead-ends after a short distance, at which point the route returns to the Arrastra Gulch road, crosses it and continues along the old railway grade all the way to Howardsville.

This trail, which is easy the entire length, is a very interesting short side route because of its mining and railroad history. It travels closely beside the scenic Animas River.

Current Road Information

Silverton Chamber of Commerce
414 Greene Street
Silverton, CO 81433
(970) 387-5654

Map References

Benchmark's *Colorado Road & Recreation Atlas*, p. 110
USGS 1:24,000 Silverton, Howardsville
    1:100,000 Silverton (incomplete)
Maptech CD-ROM:
    Southwest/Durango/Telluride
Trails Illustrated, #141 (incomplete)

Route Directions

▼ 0.0   From the 0.1 mile point along Southwest #7: Arrastra Gulch Trail, zero trip meter and turn right onto track that was once the Silverton Northern Railroad grade. This intersection is before Southwest #7 crosses the river.

1.0 ▲   End at intersection with Southwest #7: Arrastra Gulch Trail.

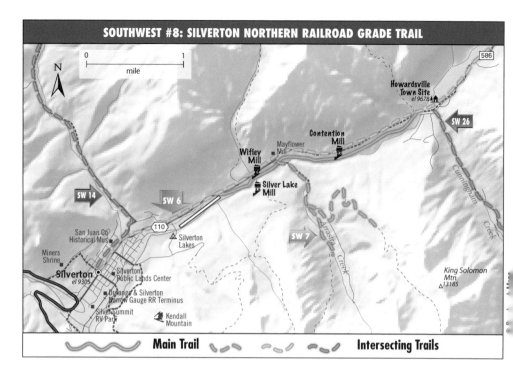

Main Trail   **Intersecting Trails**

GPS: N 37°49.66' W 107°37.63'

▼ 0.1 SO Site of the Wifley Mill on hillside to the right.

0.5 ▲ UT Fork in the road. Left crosses through creek. Right is closed. Turn around and retrace tracks.

▼ 0.2 SO Silver Lake Mill ruins across the Animas River on left.

0.2 ▲ SO Silver Lake Mill ruins across the Animas River on left.

▼ 0.5 UT Fork in the road. Left crosses through creek. Right closed. Turn around and retrace tracks.

Howardsville, circa 1875

0.1 ▲	SO	Site of the Wifley Mill site on hillside to the right.

▼ 1.0	SO	Cross Southwest #7: Arrastra Gulch Trail. Pass under the Mayflower tram lines. Zero trip meter.
0.0 ▲		Proceed along the river road on the south side of Arrastra Gulch Trail.
		GPS: N 37°49.65' W 107°37.55'

▼ 0.0		Continue along the river road on the north side of Arrastra Gulch Trail.
1.6 ▲	SO	Pass under the Mayflower tram lines. Then cross Southwest #7: Arrastra Gulch Trail. Zero trip meter.

▼ 0.4		Ruins of tram stands are visible on the mountainside across the river. Foundation and timbers on the left are from the Contention Mill.
1.2 ▲	SO	Foundation and timbers from the Contention Mill on right. Then tram stand ruins are on mountainside across the river.

▼ 0.5	SO	Remains of a swing bridge (cables and occasional timbers) cross overhead. Then timbers and a decaying structure are evident high on the valley wall, which were part of a wooden flume.
1.1 ▲	SO	Timbers and a decaying structure are part of a wooden flume across the river, high on the valley wall. Then remains of a swing bridge (cables and occasional timbers) cross overhead.

▼ 1.6		End at intersection with Southwest #6: Silverton to Animas Forks Ghost Town road (County 110), just south of Howardsville.
0.0 ▲		From Southwest #6: Silverton to Animas Forks Ghost Town road at the southern side of Howardsville, zero trip meter at the bridge over the Animas River and turn onto a small trail marked "Private Property-stay on road" and proceed south.
		GPS: N 37°50.08' W 107°35.95'

Maggie Gulch Trail

STARTING POINT Intersection of Southwest #6: Silverton to Animas Forks Ghost Town road and FR 588 at the town site of Middleton

FINISHING POINT Intersection Mill

TOTAL MILEAGE 4.1 miles (one-way)

UNPAVED MILEAGE 4.1 miles

DRIVING TIME 1 hour

ROUTE ELEVATION 9,800 to 11,900 feet

USUALLY OPEN June to October

DIFFICULTY RATING 3

SCENIC RATING 8

Special Attractions

■ Varied, easy and scenic side road.

■ Numerous mining remains.

History

At the beginning of this trail is the town site of Middleton. The town was named for Middle Mountain, which in turn got its name because it was located midway between Howardsville and Eureka. There were as many as a hundred claims being worked in the area in the 1890s. The town was formed in 1894, the year after the first mine was discovered. The town never amounted to much and many of the residents relocated to Howardsville or Eureka.

Maggie Gulch still contains plenty of evidence of early mining activity. The structures from the Ridgway tramway were used to transport ore from the Ridgway Mine located some 2,000 feet higher. It carried the ore nearly a mile to the floor of the gulch for carting to the railroad.

Farther along, above and to the left of the road, is the Little Maud Mine, which was worked from the 1890s with intermittent success. The washed out road that crosses Maggie Creek leads to the Empire Mine, a product of mining activity in recent times.

The Intersection Mine and Mill date back to around 1900. Much of the mill machinery is still located at the site. The

The trail crosses a talus slope

mines above this site, along the hiking trail, were also part of this operation.

Description

This trail starts at the town site of Middleton. Nothing remains today, but a public toilet is located at the site. The road forks almost immediately, and you bear left up a straightforward shelf road that switch-

The remains of the Intersection Mill

backs up the mountain. The right-hand fork is a short road that leads to several back-country camping spots.

As the road climbs, it affords a good view through the gulch. The track travels along a fairly wide shelf that is lined with pine and aspen. At this point, the route is easy, with a smooth, sound surface and adequate places to pass any oncoming vehicles.

In less than a mile, the trail climbs almost 1,000 feet and the scenery changes dramatically as it emerges above the timberline and crosses an expansive talus slope. The aspens in the gulch below provide a particularly scenic view in the fall. The Ridgway Mine tram is also evident in the valley below.

The route then crosses a short, narrow section of shelf road as it passes a scenic waterfall at the top of the gulch. Entering a broad alpine basin, the scenery changes again as the trail proceeds along the last section of the journey, which ends at the Intersection Mill. There are extensive ruins of the mill and its machinery that operated in the early 1900s. At this point, the road

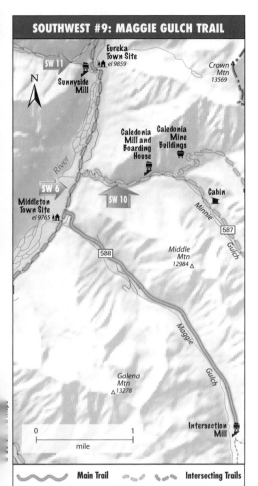

Southwest/Durango/Telluride
Colorado Atlas & Gazetteer, p. 77
The Roads of Colorado, p. 139
Trails Illustrated, #141

Route Directions

▼ 0.0   From Southwest #6: Silverton to Animas Forks Ghost Town road in Middleton, zero trip meter and proceed east on FR 588 toward Maggie Gulch. The road immediately forks, so bear left and proceed up hill.
         GPS: N 37°51.30′ W 107°34.30′

▼ 0.9   SO Track on left.
▼ 1.1   SO Attractive view of waterfall at head of gulch.
▼ 1.2   BL Track on the right goes across the gulch to the Ruby Mine.
▼ 1.6   SO Track enters on left.
▼ 3.0   SO Track on left to the Little Maud Mine.
▼ 3.7   BL Road forks. To the right it crosses Maggie Creek and leads to the Empire Mine, but the bridge has been washed out.
         GPS: N 37°49.14′ W 107°32.12′

▼ 3.9   SO Cross through creek.
▼ 4.1   SO Cross through creek.
▼ 4.1   End at Intersection Mill with plenty of room to turn around.
         GPS: N 37°48.85′ W 107°32.14′

contracts into a hiking trail, which continues to the Continental Divide, crossing it about three-quarters of a mile northeast of Stony Pass.

Current Road Information

Silverton Chamber of Commerce
414 Greene Street
Silverton, CO 81433
(970) 387-5654

Map References

Benchmark's *Colorado Road & Recreation Atlas*, p. 110
USFS   Uncompahgre NF or San Juan NF
USGS 1:24,000   Howardsville
         1:100,000   Silverton
Maptech CD-ROM:

The trail above Maggie Creek

Minnie Gulch Trail

STARTING POINT Intersection with Southwest #6: Silverton to Animas Forks Ghost Town road and FR 587
FINISHING POINT Kittimac Mine
TOTAL MILEAGE 3.9 miles (one-way)
UNPAVED MILEAGE 3.9 miles
DRIVING TIME 1 hour
ROUTE ELEVATION 9,800 to 11,800 feet
USUALLY OPEN June to October
DIFFICULTY RATING 4
SCENIC RATING 8

Special Attractions

- Historic mining district with many, well-preserved buildings.
- Moderately difficult trail with good scenery.

History

Caledonia Mine was established in 1872 and the Caledonia Mill was built in the early 1900s to treat ore extracted from the Caledonia Mine. The mill is located half a mile northeast and 1,200 feet above the mill. Stone foundations of the mill are clearly visible stretching up the hillside. Remains of the tram that transported ore down from the mine are also visible above the mill. Shortly past the mill are remains of three buildings. On the right-hand side of the road is the mill superintendent's house, and on the left, the larger building is the boardinghouse for mill workers. Both these buildings are well-preserved.

Near the end of this trail is the Kittimac Mine, which may have been part of the same discovery as the Caledonia Mine in 1872. A tramway was constructed around 1900 to carry ore from the mine to the new Kittimac Mill, which was built beside the Silverton

The Caledonia Mill boardinghouse

Remains of the Caledonia Mill

Northern Railroad tracks next to the Animas River. The tramway was nearly two miles long and descended nearly 2,000 feet.

The Esmerelda Mine operated at its peak in the early 1900s and continued to operate for many years. Its longevity was due to high assays of both the mine's silver and gold ore.

Description

This route heads east from Southwest #6: Silverton to Animas Forks Ghost Town road, initially traveling through the forest beside Minnie Creek. A little over a mile from the start is the site of the Caledonia Mill on the left, across Minnie Creek.

Continuing along the route you come to a fork in the road; both legs of this fork are included in this route. The left-hand fork is described first. This road switchbacks up the mountain and although it is narrow, the surface is sound. The trail passes a tram support for the Kittimac Mine that transported ore to the Kittimac Mill located on the Animas River, just south of the start of this 4WD trail.

Farther along is the Caledonia Mine boardinghouse and stables. The boardinghouse is leaning at a precarious angle, only saved from collapse by the supports that have been put in place. The road continues to the Caledonia and Kittimac mines. As it does, it gets narrower and steeper. Turn around at an appropriate place and head back down to the fork in the road to explore the other leg of the fork, which leads to the Esmerelda Mine.

Once on the right-hand fork, the road heads farther up Minnie Gulch traveling above the creek. It passes two cabins, a waterfall from a side creek, and another cabin with a stone foundation—all on the left side of the road. The road gets more difficult as you travel along this last section, so turn around whenever you think conditions warrant and return to the beginning of the trail.

The difficulty rating for this trail reflects conditions at the upper reaches of both forks. The earlier stages are quite easy. The varied scenery and the numerous mining remains make this short trail well worth doing.

Current Road Information

Silverton Chamber of Commerce
414 Greene Street
Silverton, CO 81433
(970) 387-5654

Map References

Benchmark's *Colorado Road & Recreation
    Atlas*, p. 110
USFS Uncompahgre NF or San Juan NF
USGS 1:24,000 Howardsville
      1:100,000 Silverton
Maptech CD-ROM:
      Southwest/Durango/Telluride
Colorado Atlas & Gazetteer, p. 77
The Roads of Colorado, pp. 123, 139
Trails Illustrated, #141

Route Directions

▼ 0.0   From Southwest #6: Silverton to

The Caledonia Mine boardinghouse and stables

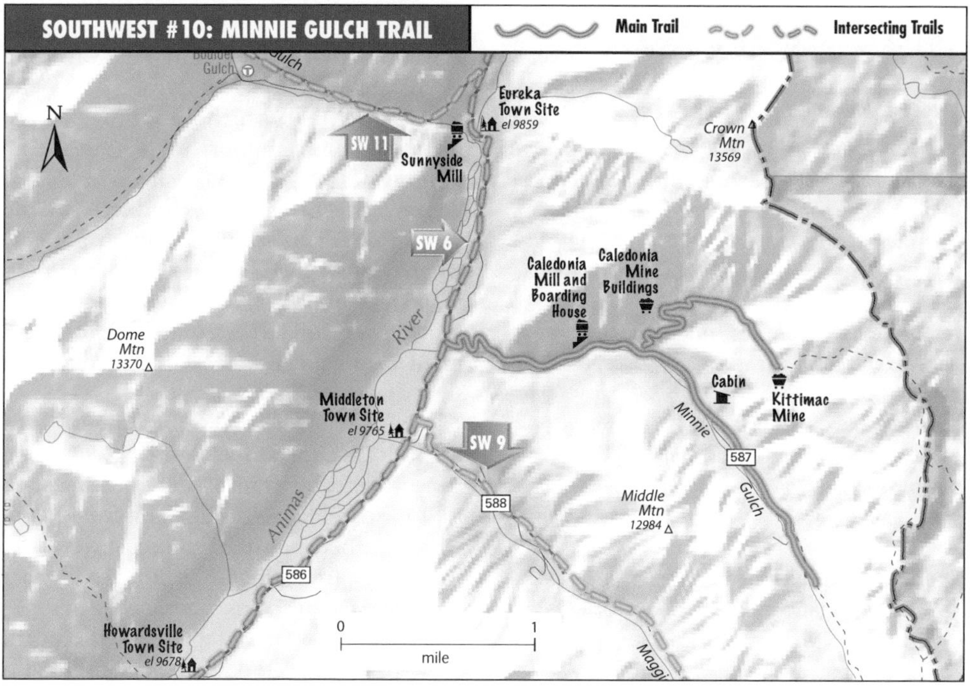

Main Trail   **Intersecting Trails**

N

SW 11
Sunnyside Mill

Bouldr Gulch

Eureka Town Site
el 9859

Crown Mtn
13569

SW 6

Caledonia Mill and Boarding House

Caledonia Mine Buildings

Dome Mtn
13370 △

River

Cabin

Kittimac Mine

Middleton Town Site
el 9765

SW 9

587

588

Middle Mtn
12984 △

Minnie Gulch

586

Animas

Howardsville Town Site
el 9678

0   mile   1

Maggi

Animas Forks Ghost Town road (County 110), zero trip meter and proceed east along FR 587 toward Minnie Gulch. This intersection is about 6.6 miles from Silverton City Hall.
GPS: N 37°51.77′ W 107°34.07′

▼ 1.0 SO Cross over Minnie Creek.
▼ 1.1 SO Stone foundation from the Caledonia Mill on left across the creek.
▼ 1.2 SO Building on the right; then two on the left. The large, well-preserved structure on the left was the Caledonia Mill boardinghouse.
GPS: N 37°51.48′ W 107°33.06′

▼ 1.4 BL Cross over creek; then zero trip meter and bear left at the intersection. This route will later return to explore the track on the right, which goes to the Esmerelda Mine.
GPS: N 37°51.27′ W 107°32.27′

▼ 0.0   Proceed uphill.
▼ 0.2 SO Kittimac Mine tram structure on left.
▼ 0.7 SO At switchback, proceed toward the well-preserved Caledonia Mine board-

inghouse and ruins of a stable. From these buildings, turn around and continue up the mountain.
▼ 0.9 SO Caledonia Mine on left.
▼ 1.0 BR Track on left; then end at the Kittimac Mine a short distance farther. From here, the route directions will return to complete the fork that was passed earlier.
GPS: N 37°51.93′ W 107°32.22′

Continuation from the fork in the road

▼ 0.0   Zero trip meter at fork in the road. Turn left to continue along the other leg towards the Esmerelda Mine.
GPS: N 37°51.27′ W 107°32.27′

▼ 1.6 SO Two cabins on left.
▼ 2.2 SO Cross through creek with waterfall on left.
GPS: N 37°51.26′ W 107°32.26′

▼ 2.6 SO Cabin ruins with stone foundation on left.
▼ 2.7 SO Esmerelda Mine tramway ruins on right. End of trail.
GPS: N 37°50.90′ W 107°31.94′

Eureka Gulch Trail

STARTING POINT Intersection with Southwest #6: Silverton to Animas Forks Ghost Town road

FINISHING POINT Sunnyside Mine at Lake Emma (drained)

TOTAL MILEAGE 3.6 miles (one-way)

UNPAVED MILEAGE 3.6 miles

DRIVING TIME 30 minutes

ROUTE ELEVATION 10,000 to 12,100 feet

USUALLY OPEN June to October

DIFFICULTY RATING 3

SCENIC RATING 7

Special Attractions

■ Visiting the location of the historic Sunnyside Mine.

■ Lake Emma, accidentally drained in 1978.

History

This trail starts at the Sunnyside Mill at the town site of Eureka and finishes at the Sunnyside Mine, which once provided the main economic support for the area. The Sunnyside Mine, established in 1873, became one of the best producers in the area. It operated continuously until 1931, when it shut down for a few years and then reopened in 1937. Two years later the miners went on strike, and since an agreement could not be reached, the mine was shut down again.

The first of the two Sunnyside Mills to be built in Eureka opened in 1899, with a three-mile cable tramway connecting it to the mine. The second Sunnyside Mill, which incorporated much of the machinery from the Gold Prince Mill that had operated at Animas Forks, began operations in 1918. It was built on the north side of the old mill. Eureka's mills also

A tram angle station for the cable tramway that ran from the Sunnyside Mine to the Midway and Sunnyside mills

served the Toltec, the Golden Fleece, the Tom Moore, the Silver Wing, and the Sound Democrat mines. Finally, the mill was dismantled and sold for salvage in 1948.

For further historical information and photographs of the town of Eureka turn to pages 72 and 73.

As you drive up Eureka Gulch, there is much evidence of the mining activity that once existed. The Midway Mill, named for its location between the Sunnyside Mine and Eureka township, was constructed in 1890 and was connected to the Sunnyside Mine by a tramway. At the turn of the century, this tramway was extended to Eureka when the first Sunnyside Mill opened. A second tramway was constructed in 1917 to service the new mill. The new tram incorporated some of the upper section of the old tramway, which brought its total length to three miles.

Continuing up Eureka Gulch, you pass a closed track on the left, which leads to the mile-long Terry Tunnel. Constructed in 1906, the tunnel was bored into the mountainside to connect with the Sunnyside vein.

One-half mile farther up the gulch is a large portal from the Ben Franklin Mine, which dates from the early 1870s.

Many remnants of the Sunnyside tramway can be seen in the vicinity of the Sunnyside Mine. In 1888, a mill was built at the site of the mine but proved too expensive to operate. In the early 1900s, as many as 200 men were employed at the mine. The Sunnyside Mine continued to operate on and off until 1991. In the 1960s, it was still producing 600 tons of ore per day. The foundations of many of the buildings remain. Extensive reclamation work was undertaken in the area in the 1990s.

The Sunnyside Mine buildings were clustered along the shore of Lake Emma. On Sunday, June 4, 1978, a tunnel that was being excavated about 70 feet under Lake Emma collapsed and completely drained the lake. Thousands of gallons of water and millions of tons of mud and rocks drained into the American Tunnel before exiting at Gladstone, some two miles away and 1,500 feet lower. The Terry Tunnel was also filled. The cleanup took more than two years to complete. Because the disaster occurred on a Sunday, the miners were not working, and fortunately, no one was killed.

Description

The route starts with a climb along a shelf road that is well-maintained and reasonably wide with plenty of opportunities for passing. After about half a mile, the road levels off and continues along the wall of the gulch.

The route is simple to navigate and easy to drive. The scenery is attractive, but the real attraction of the trail is its historical significance, evidence of which is abundant.

Current Road Information

Silverton Chamber of Commerce
414 Greene Street
Silverton, CO 81433
(970) 387-5654

A close-up of the tramway angle station

The Sunnyside mine buildings beside Lake Emma in 1929

Map References

Benchmark's *Colorado Road & Recreation Atlas*, p. 110
USFS Uncompahgre National Forest or San Juan National Forest
USGS 1:24,000 Handies Peak
      1:100,000 Silverton
Maptech CD-ROM:
      Southwest/Durango/Telluride

Colorado Atlas & Gazetteer, p. 77
The Roads of Colorado, p. 123
Trails Illustrated, #141

Route Directions

▼ 0.0   From Southwest #6: Silverton to Animas Forks Ghost Town road (about 0.3 miles north of Eureka), zero trip

Eureka townsite viewed from near the start of the trail

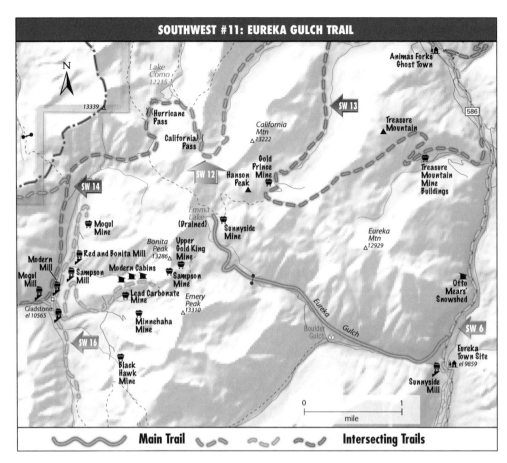

Main Trail ∿∿ ⌒⌐ ⌐⌐⌐ **Intersecting Trails**

meter and turn onto Eureka Gulch Trail. Proceed up the hill.

GPS: N 37°53.09' W 107°33.82'

▼ 0.4 SO Ruins of the second Sunnyside Mill are on left directly below road. On right is a tram structure that carried ore from the mine to the mill, almost three miles.

▼ 0.7 BR Fork in road.

▼ 0.9 SO Snowslide defense structure beside the road on left and a private cabin on left across Eureka Creek.

▼ 1.0 SO Track on left to Midway Mill in the South Fork of Eureka Gulch.

▼ 1.8 SO Johnson Tower on left across the valley, halfway up mountain.

▼ 2.1 SO Cross over Parson's Creek with waterfall on right.

▼ 2.3 SO Tram tension station on left across valley on the mountain slope.

▼ 2.4 SO Track on left is gated and goes to the next entry.

▼ 2.5 SO Reclamation ponds on left for the Terry Tunnel.

▼ 2.7 SO Cross over Eureka Creek.

▼ 2.8 SO Large portal beside the road is from the Ben Franklin Mine.

▼ 2.9 BR Fork in the road.

▼ 3.0 BR Road joins on left.

▼ 3.3 SO Sunnyside Mine tram station on right.

▼ 3.4-3.6 SO Remains of mine buildings.

▼ 3.6 SO End at site of drained Lake Emma.

GPS: N 37°54.17' W 107°36.86'

California Gulch Trail

STARTING POINT Animas Forks

FINISHING POINT Intersection with Southwest #14: Silverton to Lake Como Trail

TOTAL MILEAGE 4.2 miles

UNPAVED MILEAGE 4.2 miles

DRIVING TIME 1 hour

ROUTE ELEVATION 11,400 to 12,930 feet

USUALLY OPEN June to late October

DIFFICULTY RATING 4

SCENIC RATING 9

Special Attractions

- Spectacular scenery, especially the view from California Pass.
- Many historic mining sites and structures.
- A short, moderately easy 4WD trail.
- Part of a large network of 4WD trails.

History

Numerous mines and mills operated in California Gulch and plenty of evidence of this activity remains today.

The Columbus Mine, located at the northern edge of Animas Forks, was discovered in the early 1880s. The mine yielded a large tonnage of ore, but it was low-grade,

The Columbus Mine and Mill

The Columbus Mill standing beside the West Fork of the Animas River

and high transportation costs meant that the mine was barely economical. As a producer of zinc, it had some of its best years during World War II. The mill, located at the mine, was built in 1927. The whole operation closed in 1948.

The Bagley Mill, built in 1912 to treat ore from Frisco Tunnel, was regarded as one of the best mills in the area; it had a capacity of 150 tons of ore a day. Construction on Frisco Tunnel, which burrows over a mile into Houghton Mountain, began in 1904 and took four years to complete. The mining operations ceased in about 1915.

ake Como

About a mile farther is Vermilion Mine, which started operations in the early 1900s, with the mill being constructed in 1909.

Close to the pass as you climb out of the gulch is the Mountain Queen Mine, which was discovered in 1877 and operated until the 1940s. Rasmus Hanson owned the mine, and it has been speculated that Thomas Walsh managed it before he made his fortune from Camp Bird Mine.

Description

This route departs to the northwest of Animas Forks and is clearly marked to California Gulch. Traveling along California Gulch entirely above timber line, the trail is relatively easy, with numerous mine remains and open mine portals in evidence.

The road ascends to California Pass from which there is a spectacular 180° view. From the pass, you look down onto Lake Como and Poughkeepsie Gulch, the road back to Animas Forks, and across to Hurricane Pass and Hurricane Peak.

The section of the road descending from California Pass is the harder part of this route and traverses quite different terrain. There is a series of tight switchbacks along a narrow shelf road. At times, the road is steep, and passing other vehicles can be difficult.

The road is usually open from mid-June to late October, but snow often remains

The Bagley Mill

along the side of the road throughout the summer. This trail is likely to be muddy early in the season.

Current Road Information

San Juan National Forest
Silverton Ranger District
PO Box 709
1246 Blair Street
Silverton, CO 81433
(970) 387-5530

Silverton Chamber of Commerce
414 Greene Street
Silverton, CO 81433
(970) 387-5654

Map References

Benchmark's *Colorado Road & Recreation Atlas*, p. 110
USFS Uncompahgre National Forest or Gunnison National Forest
USGS 1:24,000 Handies Peak
1:100,00 Silverton
Maptech CD-ROM:
Southwest/Durango/Telluride
Colorado Atlas & Gazetteer, p. 77
The Roads of Colorado, p. 123
Trails Illustrated, #141

Route Directions

▼ 0.0   At the north end of Animas Forks, zero

The road climbing out of the west end of California Gulch

Main Trail   **Intersecting Trails**

trip meter beside the bridge over the Animas River and proceed northwest (do not cross bridge), following signs to California Gulch. Cross over the West Fork of Animas River; pass the Columbus Mine and Mill on the right.

4.2 ▲ End at bridge in Animas Forks.

GPS: N 37°55.89' W 107°34.22'

▼ 0.5 SO Bagley Mill and Frisco Tunnel on right.
3.6 ▲ SO Bagley Mill and Frisco Tunnel on left.

▼ 0.7 BL Track to Bagley Mill on right.
3.5 ▲ BR Track to Bagley Mill on left.

▼ 1.0 BR Southwest #13: Picayne Gulch and Placer Gulch Trail on left.
3.1 ▲ BL Southwest #13: Picayne Gulch and Placer Gulch Trail on right.

▼ 1.1 BR Track on left to cabin.
3.1 ▲ BL Track on right to cabin.

▼ 1.5 SO Vermilion Mine and Mill ruins on right.
2.7 ▲ SO Vermilion Mine and Mill ruins on left.

▼ 1.7 SO Burrows Mine ruins on right.
2.4 ▲ SO Burrows Mine ruins on left.

▼ 2.9 SO Cross over creek.
1.3 ▲ SO Cross over creek.

▼ 3.0 SO Open mine portal on right side of road.
1.2 ▲ SO Open mine portal on left side of road.

▼ 3.4 UT Intersection.
0.8 ▲ UT Intersection.

▼ 3.5 SO Road on left.
0.7 ▲ BL Fork in the road.

▼ 3.6 SO Mountain Queen Mine on right.
0.6 ▲ SO Mountain Queen Mine on left.

▼ 3.8 UT Summit of California Pass. The lake you look down upon is Lake Como.
0.4 ▲ UT Summit of California Pass.

GPS: N 37°55.02' W 107°36.91'

▼ 4.2 End at intersection with Southwest #14: Silverton to Lake Como Trail to the left. Corkscrew Gulch, Poughkeepsie Gulch, and Lake Como are 0.3 miles ahead.

GPS: N 37°55.26' W 107°37.26'

Picayne Gulch and Placer Gulch Trail

STARTING POINT Intersection with Southwest #12: California Gulch Trail

FINISHING POINT Intersection with Southwest #6: Silverton to Animas Forks Ghost Town road

TOTAL MILEAGE 6.2 miles

UNPAVED MILEAGE 6.2 miles

DRIVING TIME 1 hour

ROUTE ELEVATION 10,500 to 13,000 feet

USUALLY OPEN June to October

DIFFICULTY RATING 4

SCENIC RATING 8

Special Attractions

- Varied, scenic trail.
- Many interesting mining buildings and other mining structures.
- Abundant wildflowers in early summer.

History

At the start of the trail, remains of the Gold Prince Tramway are visible on the face of Treasure Mountain to the left. Built in 1905, the tramway ran a mile and a half from the mine at the top of the gulch down to the angle station at Treasure Mountain and then another three-quarters of a mile to the Gold Prince Mill in Animas Forks. The tram transported 50 tons of ore each hour.

About a mile farther are the concrete foundations of the Mastodon Mill, which was constructed in the mid-1880s and

A view of the road behind the buildings remaining from Treasure Mountain Gold Mining Company

treated ore from both the Mastodon and the Silver Queen Mines.

The Sound Democrat Mine was established in 1899. Initially ore had to be transported to the mill constructed at the Sunnyside Mine. In 1906, the Sound Democrat Mill began operations and continued until 1914.

At the top of the gulch is the Gold Prince Mine, which had been known previously as the Sunnyside Extension and the Mountain Pride. Nearby is the concrete foundation of the boardinghouse that once housed 150 miners. Beside it is the tram tower used to unload supplies for the boardinghouse. The Gold Prince began ore production in 1874 and worked the same veins as the Sunnyside Mine, located less than a mile to the south-

west on the other side of Hanson Peak. Rasmus Hanson built the Hanson Mill in 1889 to process the ore. The mine was still being worked in the 1950s.

In the early 1900s, Treasure Mountain Gold Mining Company built the cluster of buildings that the trail passes in Picayne Gulch, which include a substantial boardinghouse. This mining company consolidated and worked some thirty claims in the area including the Golden Fleece, the Scotia and the San Juan Queen. The tunnel near the buildings is the Santiago Tunnel, built in 1937.

Description

At the start of this route, the road immediately crosses the West Fork of the Animas

The Treasure Mountain boardinghouse

The Treasure Mountain mill and other buildings

River. The road continues into the gulch and travels above Placer Creek. The scenery in the gulch is treeless alpine tundra. The beauty of the open countryside is enhanced in the early summer by massive displays of wildflowers. Placer Gulch still holds much evidence of the mines, mills, and tramways that turned it into a hive of activity long ago.

The road to the Gold Prince Mine located at the top of the gulch is the easier part of the trail and only rates a 3 for difficulty. From the Gold Prince, the road switchbacks up to the ridge and crosses into Picayne Gulch. This segment is fairly steep but is quite wide; there are plenty of opportunities to pass oncoming vehicles. Once into Picayne Gulch, the route travels through broad, open meadows where flocks of sheep are left to graze in the summer. This section of road is cleared by snowplow at the start of the season and can be quite muddy when wet.

The road reenters the forest and passes the cluster of buildings constructed by the Treasure Mountain Gold Mining Company. Among these is a substantial boardinghouse that had an adjoining bathroom with bath, toilet, and hot and cold running water. The bathroom was connected to the boarding-house by an enclosed corridor.

The last section of the trail is a narrow shelf road that descends to intersect with Southwest #6: Silverton to Animas Forks Ghost Town road. Passing opportunities are limited on this short section, but the surface is sound and it is not very difficult.

Current Road Information

Silverton Chamber of Commerce
414 Greene Street
Silverton, CO 81433
(970) 387-5654

Map References

Benchmark's *Colorado Road & Recreation Atlas*, p. 110
USFS Uncompahgre NF or San Juan NF
USGS 1:24,000 Handies Peak
1:100,000 Silverton
Maptech CD-ROM:
Southwest/Durango/Telluride
Colorado Atlas & Gazetteer, p. 77
The Roads of Colorado, p. 123
Trails Illustrated, #141

Route Directions

▼ 0.0   From Southwest #12: California Gulch Trail (approximately 1 mile northwest of Animas Forks), zero trip meter at sign to Placer Gulch and proceed south toward Placer Gulch. Cross over the West Fork of the Animas River.

6.2 ▲   Cross over the West Fork of the Animas River and end at intersection with Southwest #12: California Gulch Trail. Animas Forks is approximately 1 mile to the right.

GPS: N 37°48.79′ W 107°39.72′

▼ 0.1   SO   Mine ruins on left directly below road.
6.1 ▲   SO   Mine ruins on right directly below road.

▼ 1.1   SO   Concrete foundations of Mastodon Mill on left.
5.1 ▲   SO   Concrete foundations of Mastodon Mill on right.

▼ 1.3   SO   Red-roofed mill on left across river is the Sound Democrat Mill.
4.9 ▲   SO   Red-roofed mill on right across river is the Sound Democrat Mill.

▼ 1.5   SO   Two standing tram supports on left.
4.7 ▲   SO   Two standing tram supports on right.

▼ 1.6   SO   Concrete foundation for Gold Prince boardinghouse on left with tram tower beside it. Mine building on right.
4.6 ▲   SO   Concrete foundation for Gold Prince boardinghouse on right with tram tower beside it. Mine building on left.

SOUTHWEST #13: PICAYNE GULCH & PLACER GULCH TRAIL

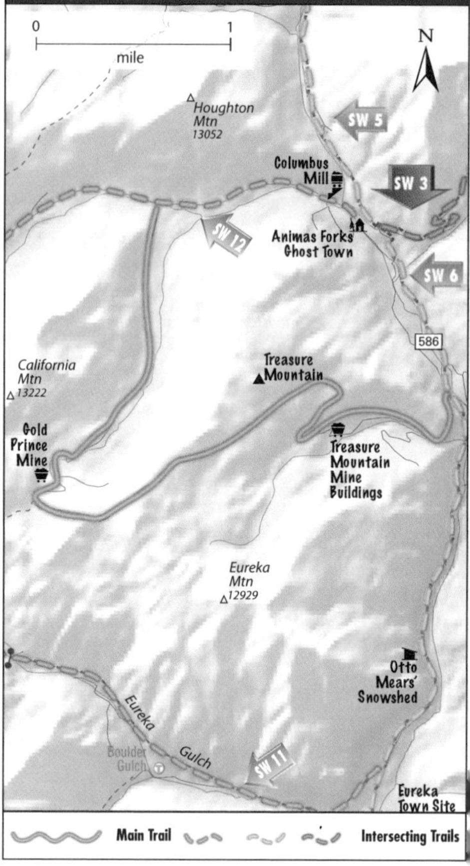

▼ 1.7   SO   Track on left; then cross creek. Shortly after, ruins of the Sunnyside Mine Extension/Gold Prince Mine structure on right.
4.5 ▲   SO   Mine ruins of the Sunnyside Mine Extension/Gold Prince Mine structure on left. Cross creek; then track on right.

▼ 1.8   UT   Track on left to Hidden Treasure, Silver Queen and Sound Democrat Mines.
4.4 ▲   UT   Track on right to Hidden Treasure, Silver Queen and Sound Democrat Mines.

▼ 2.7   BL   Tracks on right to scenic overlook.
3.5 ▲   SO   Tracks on left to scenic overlook.

▼ 2.9   SO   View to the Sound Democrat Mill in the gulch below on left.
3.3 ▲   SO   View to the Sound Democrat Mill in

A view across Picayne Gulch

the gulch below on right.

▼ 3.8	SO	Faint track on right.
2.4 ▲	SO	Faint track on left.

▼ 4.1	SO	Short access track on left to ruins from Golden Fleece and Scotia Mines.
2.1 ▲	SO	Short access track on right to ruins from Golden Fleece and Scotia Mines.

▼ 4.3	SO	Open mine portal on left.
1.9 ▲	SO	Open mine portal on right.

▼ 4.5	SO	View across the valley to the southeast is Burns Gulch Trail.
1.7 ▲	SO	View across the valley behind you to the southeast is Burns Gulch Trail.

▼ 4.9	SO	Treasure Mountain Gold Mining Company buildings and mine on right; then track on right goes into Upper Picayne Basin.
1.3 ▲	SO	Track on left goes into Upper Picayne Basin; then Treasure Mountain Gold Mining Company buildings and mine

on left.

▼ 5.0	SO	Open mine portals on right.
1.2 ▲	SO	Open mine portals on left.

▼ 5.2	SO	Treasure Mountain Gold Mining Company buildings on right.
1.0 ▲	BR	Treasure Mountain Gold Mining Company buildings on left.

▼ 5.8	SO	Track on right to the Toltec Mine.
0.4 ▲	BR	Track on left to the Toltec Mine.

▼ 6.0	SO	Open mine portal on left.
0.2 ▲	SO	Open mine portal on right.

▼ 6.2		End at intersection with Southwest #6: Silverton to Animas Forks Ghost Town road.
0.0 ▲		From Southwest #6: Silverton to Animas Forks Ghost Town road (approximately 1.5 miles south of Animas Forks and 2.8 miles north of Eureka), zero trip meter and turn onto track to Picayune Gulch.
		GPS: N 37°54.99′ W 107°33.45′

The deep snow that must be bulldozed in the spring

Silverton to Lake Como Trail

STARTING POINT Silverton
FINISHING POINT Intersection with Southwest #12: California Gulch Trail near Lake Como
TOTAL MILEAGE 10.3 miles
UNPAVED MILEAGE 10.3 miles
DRIVING TIME 1 hour
ROUTE ELEVATION 9,200 to 12,407 feet
USUALLY OPEN Silverton to Gladstone: year-round; Gladstone to Lake Como: June to October
DIFFICULTY RATING 4
SCENIC RATING 10

Special Attractions

- Spectacular, rugged scenery.
- Beautiful Lake Como encircled by mountains.
- Numerous mining sites.
- Access to a network of other 4WD trails.

Assorted mining remains before the ascent to Hurricane Pass

An old boiler located below Hurricane Pass

History

From Silverton to Gladstone, this route closely parallels the tracks laid by the Silverton, Gladstone & Northerly Railroad. In April 1899, the Gold King Mining Company established the railroad to reduce its freight costs to the new mill it was constructing in Gladstone. The train commenced operations on August 4th of that year. Then in 1910, Otto Mears leased the Gold King Mine and Mill operations and with it the Silverton, Gladstone & Northerly Railroad. In 1915, he purchased the railroad from the mine owners. The railway continued to operate until 1924 and was officially abandoned in 1937. The last of the tracks were torn up and sold for scrap during World War II.

About halfway along Cement Creek Valley (on the other side of the creek) is the site of the Boston and Silverton Mill, which had an output of 100 tons per day when it was built in the 1890s, making it one of the larger mining operations in the valley. A newer mill is on the site of first mill. The Gold Hub Mining Company acquired the

Lake Como

whole operation in the late 1930s. The Yukon Tunnel located just behind the mill continued to operate until the 1980s.

The Gold King Mining Company bought the Anglo-Saxon Mine, which had been discovered in the late 1890s; it produced tungsten used in the manufacture of bulletproof steel during World War II.

On the left shortly after the road crosses to the east side of the creek is the Elk Mountain Mine, which operated for about 20 years before closing in the 1920s.

On the western edge of the town of Gladstone stand the foundations of the Mogul Mill, which was constructed in 1906 to treat ore from the Mogul Mine. It was connected to the Mogul Mine by a two-mile-long tramway.

Description

Navigating the route from Silverton to Gladstone, a well-maintained gravel road, is straightforward.

From the turnoff to Lake Como, just past the Mogul Mill foundations in Gladstone, the road becomes much narrower and travels

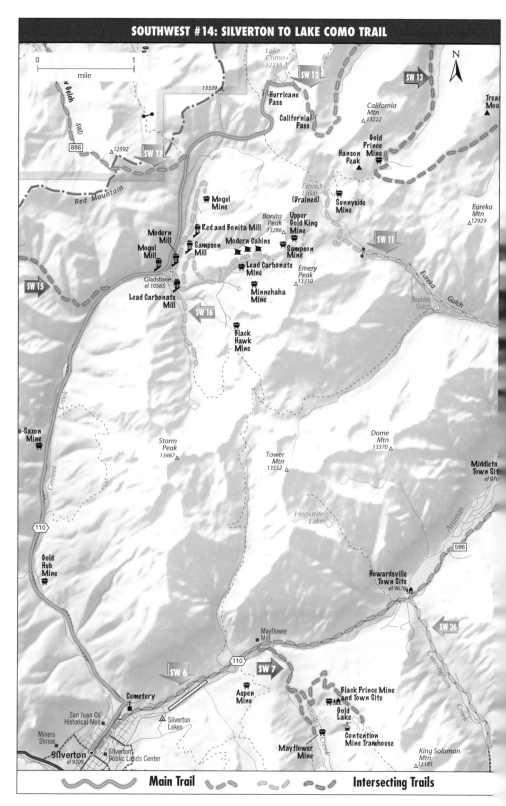

0
mile
1

N Gulch

4WD

13339

886

△*12592*

SW 17

Red Mountain

Lake
Como
12215

SW 12

Hurricane
Pass

California
Pass

California
Mtn
△*13222*

SW 13

Treas
Mou

Gold
Prince
Mine

Hanson
Peak

Emma
Lake
(Drained)

Sunnyside
Mine

Eureka
Mtn
△*12929*

Mogul
Mine

Bonita
Peak
13286△

Upper
Gold King
Mine

SW 11

Modern
Mill

Mogul
Mill

Red and Bonita Mill

Sampson
Mill

Modern Cabins

Sampson
Mine

Lead Carbonate
Mine

Emery
Peak
△*13310*

Eureka

Gladstone
el 10565

Minnehaha
Mine

SW 15

Lead Carbonate
Mill

SW 16

Black
Hawk
Mine

Boulder
Gulch

Gulch

o-Saxon
Mine

Storm
Peak
13487△

Tower
Mtn
13552△

Dome
Mtn
13370△

Middleto
Town Sit
el 976

Cement

Creek

Hematite
Lake

Animas

586

Gold
Hub
Mine

110

Howardsville
Town Site
el 9678

SW 26

Mayflower
Mill

Cunningham
Creek

SW 6

110

SW 7

Cemetery

San Juan Co
Historical Mus

Silverton Lakes

Aspen
Mine

Mirasol
Creek

Black Prince Mine
and Town Site

Gold
Lake

Contention
Mine Tramhouse

King Solomon
Mtn
△*13185*

Miners
Shrine

Silverton
el 9305

Silverton
Public Lands Center

Mayflower
Mine

~~~~~ **Main Trail** ~~~~~ ~ ~ ~ ~ ~ **Intersecting Trails**

along a shelf above the North Fork of Cement Creek for about two and one-half miles. Although this section is much more difficult than the road between Silverton and Gladstone, the surface is quite sound, albeit bumpy, and the only real difficulty is negotiating your way past oncoming vehicles.

As you travel along this shelf section, the 4WD trail to Mogul Mine can be seen to the east across the creek.

As you continue, you quickly climb above timberline; the scenery becomes much more rugged and offers some spectacular mountain views. There is a wonderful view of Lake Como and Poughkeepsie Gulch from near Hurricane Pass. Signs of mining activity abound along this route.

Current Road Information

Silverton Chamber of Commerce
414 Greene Street
Silverton, CO 81433
(970) 387-5654

Map References

Benchmark's *Colorado Road & Recreation Atlas,* p. 110
USFS   Uncompahgre NF
USGS   1:24,000   Ironton, Silverton
        1:100,000 Silverton
Maptech CD-ROM:
        Southwest/Durango/Telluride
Colorado Atlas & Gazetteer, pp. 76, 77
The Roads of Colorado, pp. 123, 139
Trails Illustrated, #141

Route Directions

▼ 0.0   From the Silverton City Hall at Greene (main) Street and 14th Street, zero trip meter and proceed northeast out of town.
▲ 6.5   End in front of the Silverton City Hall at Greene Street and 14th Street.
         GPS: N 37°48.79′ W 107°39.72′

▼ 0.2   SO Follow County 110 straight ahead. County 110 also turns to the right.
▲ 6.3   BR Proceed toward Silverton.

▼ 0.4   BL Hillside Cemetery is straight ahead.

▲ 6.1   BR Hillside Cemetery is to the left.

▼ 0.7   BR Track on left. Then cross over creek.
▲ 5.8   BL Cross over creek. Then track on right.

▼ 1.0   SO Unpaved.
▲ 5.5   SO Paved.

▼ 2.5   SO Bridge over Cement Creek and track on left.
▲ 4.0   SO Track on right and bridge over Cement Creek.

▼ 3.1   SO Boston and Silverton Mill site on the right. Newer buildings are part of the Gold Hub Mining Company.
▲ 3.4   SO Boston and Silverton Mill site on the left. Newer buildings are part of the Gold Hub Mining Company.

▼ 3.5   SO Track on left.
▲ 3.0   SO Track on right.

▼ 3.8   SO Logs and building behind it on left are remnants of the Anglo-Saxon Mine.
▲ 2.7   SO Logs and building behind it on right are remnants of the Anglo-Saxon Mine.

▼ 4.1   SO Bridge over Cement Creek.
▲ 2.3   SO Bridge over Cement Creek.

▼ 4.6   SO Cabin on left is part of the Elk Mountain Mine.
▲ 1.9   SO Cabin on right is part of the Elk Mountain Mine.

▼ 5.0   SO Cross over creek and railroad bed. Track on left goes through Georgia Gulch to the Kansas City Mine.
▲ 1.5   BL Track on right goes through Georgia Gulch to the Kansas City Mine. Cross over creek.

▼ 6.0   SO Southwest #15: Prospect Gulch Trail (County 35) on left.
▲ 0.5   SO Road on right is Southwest #15: Prospect Gulch Trail (County 35).
         GPS: N 37°53.31′ W 107°39.66′

▼ 6.5   SO Site of the Mogul Mill on left. Town

site of Gladstone existed in the flat area to the right. Zero trip meter at the mill.

0.0 ▲   Continue along track toward Silverton.

GPS: N 37°53.44' W 107°39.10'

▼ 0.0   Continue along main road.

1.5 ▲   SO   Site of the Mogul Mill on right. Town site of Gladstone existed in the flat area to the left. Zero trip meter at the mill.

▼ 0.1   BL   Turn onto County 10 towards Hurricane Pass, California Pass, and Corkscrew Gulch on left.

1.4 ▲   BR   Onto Cement Creek Road.

GPS: N 37°53.46' W 107°38.99'

▼ 0.7   SO   Track from the road to Mogul Mine joins in on right.

0.8 ▲   BR   Road forks.

▼ 0.9   SO   Track on right is private property to a modern cabin.

0.6 ▲   SO   Track on left is private property to a modern cabin.

▼ 1.5   SO   Southwest #17: Corkscrew Gulch Trail (County 11) on left goes to US 550.

The road you can see in valley on right is Mogul Mine Road. Zero trip meter.

0.0 ▲   BL   Proceed along County 10 toward Gladstone.

GPS: N 37°54.61' W 107°38.68'

▼ 0.0   Proceed toward Hurricane Pass

2.3 ▲   BL   Southwest #17: Corkscrew Gulch Trail on right. Zero trip meter.

▼ 1.1   SO   Lower Queen Anne Mine ruins on left.

1.2 ▲   SO   Lower Queen Anne Mine ruins on right.

▼ 1.2   SO   Track on right.

1.1 ▲   SO   Track on left.

▼ 1.4   SO   Mine on right is the Upper Queen Anne Mine.

0.9 ▲   SO   Mine on left is the Upper Queen Anne Mine.

▼ 1.6   SO   Open mine portal on left.

0.7 ▲   SO   Open mine portal on right.

▼ 1.8   SO   Hurricane Pass summit with a viewpoint on left down to Lake Como.

0.5 ▲   SO   Summit of Hurricane Pass.

GPS: N 37°55.19' W 107°37.56'

▼ 2.3   End at intersection with Southwest #12: California Gulch Trail. Lake Como and Poughkeepsie Gulch are 0.3 miles to the left at GPS: N 37°55.41' W 107°37.38'.

0.0 ▲   From Southwest #12: California Gulch Trail near Lake Como, zero trip meter at sign to Silverton and Corkscrew Gulch and proceed in that direction toward Hurricane Pass.

GPS: N 37°55.26' W 107°37.26'

The Hurricane Pass summit

Prospect Gulch Trail

STARTING POINT Intersection of Southwest #14: Silverton to Lake Como Trail and CR 35

FINISHING POINT Galena Queen Mine

TOTAL MILEAGE 1.9 miles

UNPAVED MILEAGE 1.9 miles

DRIVING TIME 30 minutes

ROUTE ELEVATION 10,600 to 11,900 feet

USUALLY OPEN June to October

DIFFICULTY RATING 3

SCENIC RATING 8

Special Attractions

■ Numerous old mines.

■ The remaining buildings and equipment at the Galena Queen Mine.

A boiler from the Galena Queen Mine

History

Prospect Gulch contains many mines dating back to early 1880s. The first major operation that you will see evidence of is the Henrietta Mine, where deposits were discovered in the 1890s. Initially, ore produced at the mine was treated at the Fisher Mill in Gladstone. In the early 1900s, a mile-long tramway was built to transport the ore to the

Machinery once used by the Galena Queen Mine

Silverton, Gladstone & Northerly Railway, which passed the entrance to this route as it headed up Cement Creek Valley. The railroad took the ore back down to Silverton for treatment.

At the top of the gulch is the Galena Queen Mine, established around 1890. It was only a small mining operation but continued production into the early 1900s; much of the old machinery is still located at the site. Reclamation works are being undertaken in the vicinity.

Description

This route commences at the intersection of Southwest #14: Silverton to Lake Como Trail and CR 35, about half a mile east of Gladstone. The entrance to this road is at the bottom of Dry Gulch. The road wraps around the southwest of the mountain before entering Prospect Gulch; from there, it parallels the creek to the head of the gulch.

From the start of this route, the road ascends through the forest. The graded gravel surface is wide. The route is fairly easy to drive and very easy to navigate for the 1.9-mile route we have described. From there the road becomes much more difficult as it continues

© Benchmark Maps

Route Directions

▼ 0.0   From Southwest #14: Silverton to Lake Como Trail (Cement Creek Road), zero trip meter at sign for County 35 and proceed up hill toward Prospect Gulch. This turnoff is about 6 miles north of Silverton and 0.5 miles south of Gladstone.
         GPS: N 37°53.31′ W 107°39.66′

▼ 0.7   SO   Old tram tower that serviced the Henrietta Mine on left.

▼ 1.0   SO   Track on left to the Henrietta Mine.

▼ 1.1   SO   Cabin on right.

▼ 1.2   SO   Modern mine building on right.

▼ 1.3   BR   Road forks. Left goes to the Crown Prince Mine.

▼ 1.4   SO   John and Joe Mine and mine buildings on right.

▼ 1.7   BR   Fork in the road. Left goes to the Henrietta Mine. Track on right goes up Red Mountain.
         GPS: N 37°53.46′ W 107°41.13′

▼ 1.9   End at the Galena Queen Mine.
         GPS: N 37°53.52′ W 107°41.35′

to climb Red Mountain; it is steep and narrow, and the surface is loose. Although we have not driven to the end of the road, we believe that the road does not go through.

Current Road Information

Silverton Chamber of Commerce
414 Greene Street
Silverton, CO 81433
(970) 387-5654

Map References

Benchmark's *Colorado Road & Recreation Atlas,* p. 110
USFS   Uncompahgre NF or San Juan NF
USGS   1:24,000   Ironton
          1:100,000 Silverton
Maptech CD-ROM:
          Southwest/Durango/Telluride
Colorado Atlas & Gazetteer, p. 77
The Roads of Colorado, p. 123
Trails Illustrated, #141

Gladstone Network

STARTING POINT Mogul Mill site in Gladstone
FINISHING POINT Mogul Mill site in Gladstone
TOTAL MILEAGE 11.8 miles (round trip)
UNPAVED MILEAGE 11.8 miles
DRIVING TIME 2 hours
ROUTE ELEVATION 10,800 to 11,800 feet
USUALLY OPEN Mid-June to early October
DIFFICULTY RATING 5
SCENIC RATING 9

Special Attractions

■ Network of short trails out of Gladstone.
■ Many old mines and mine buildings.
■ Wildflowers in spring and early summer.

A view of Gladstone thought to be in the 1930s or 1940s

History

This network of three trails commences from the mining town of Gladstone and explores the area in which the scores of mining claims that once sustained the town's economy were located. Gladstone, founded in 1878, was named for the prime minister of Great Britain from 1880 to 1885. The town got a post office that same year, which would close three times in subsequent years as the town went through cycles of boom and bust. In its first year, the town consisted of a general store, a meat market, a two-story hotel, a boardinghouse, and a small schoolhouse. There was also a newspaper: The Gladstone Kibosh.

Following ore discovery at the Sampson Mine in 1882, development in the area started to accelerate. In 1887, the town was given its largest boost by Olaf Nelson's venture, the Gold King Mine. With little capital, he worked the Gold King for three years until his death, and in 1894, Nelson's widow sold the mine for $15,000. Under new ownership the mine produced $1 million in gold, silver, and copper during the next three years. In the late 1890s, the Gold King Mill was constructed. The mill was expanded several times and at its peak produced 300 tons of treated ore per day. The site of the Gold King Mill at the east end of

The Lead Carbonate Mill today

The Mogul Mill ruins, located at the western edge of Gladstone

yields of both silver and gold after the discovery of its deposits in the 1880s. Its period of greatest activity was after World War II. A mill at the site was destroyed by a snow slide shortly after it was constructed in the 1930s. During its period of greatest production, the ore was treated at the mill in Gladstone.

The Sampson Mine expanded its production following the completion of its mill near the North Fork of Cement Creek in about 1890. A tramway was constructed to haul the ore about two-thirds of a mile to the mill. In later years, the Sampson operation was amalgamated into the Gold King.

Along the third trail of this group are a number of old mill ruins as well as the substantial Mogul Mine site. Ore was discovered at the Mogul Mine in the 1870s, and a small mining camp was established at the mine. The mine tunneled nearly four miles into the mountain to connect with the Sunnyside Mine located at Lake Emma. By 1906, ore from the Mogul Mine was transported by a two-mile-long tramway to a new mill in Gladstone.

Most recently, Gladstone was also the location of the outflow of mud and water from the collapse of Lake Emma in 1978 (see Southwest #11: Eureka Gulch Trail, page 86).

Description

This route consists of three connecting trails extending from Gladstone: Colorado (Velocity) Basin, Minnehaha Basin, and Mogul Mine. The three trails split off from each other as the road winds around behind the metal building at the site of the Gold King Mill.

The Velocity Basin trail splits off first and follows the South Fork of Cement Creek. The first mile of the trail is through the forest traveling above the creek. Once above timberline, the scenery is majestic as you approach the end of the barren, gray, steeply sided basin. The road is moderately easy for

Gladstone is now occupied by the steel mining buildings.

The Lead Carbonate Mill, located just behind the site of the Gold King Mill, was built in 1947 to process ore from the Lead Carbonate Mine in Minnehaha Basin about a mile away.

The first trail of this network goes to Colorado Basin, which was renamed Velocity Basin in the early 1990s when the world speed-skiing championships were held there. About a mile past the Lead Carbonate Mill are ruins from the Big Colorado Mine, which operated for about a decade from the mid-1890s. Storm Peak, recognizable by the microwave tower at its summit, towers about 1,400 feet above the mine.

The second trail heads towards Minnehaha Basin, an area dotted by many signs of the once-abundant mining activity. The Minnehaha Mine began ore production in the 1880s and operated into the 1930s. The Black Hawk Mine dates back to the late 1890s.

The Lead Carbonate Mine produced good

The Mogul Mill and the town of Gladstone, circa 1940

The Gold King Mill, circa 1900

its entire length.

Returning to where the road to Velocity Basin split from the rest of the route, turn right and proceed north a short way to the turnoff, also to the right, that leads into Minnehaha Basin.

Minnehaha Basin is the location of the Minnehaha Mine, the Black Hawk Mine, and the Lead Carbonate Mine. This road affords some particularly good views, including across the South Fork of the Cement Creek Valley, Velocity Basin, and Minnehaha Basin. This trail has a length of shelf road with a steep drop-off. However, the road is reasonably wide and there are adequate passing opportunities. The route ends shortly after the three deserted modern cabins, where there is plenty of room to turn around. The road continues beyond this point but is narrow and has been washed out before reaching the Sampson and Gold King

Mines. Looking across to the mines, the Sampson is to the left and the upper Gold King is located to the right.

Returning to where the road to Minnehaha Basin split off, turn right and proceed toward Mogul Mine. This road is rough and rocky. Some of the rocks are quite sharp, so care is needed to minimize the risk of a punctured tire. From Mogul Mine, where we end the route, the trail gets very narrow as it ascends into the upper Ross Basin. Even without proceeding into the upper part of the basin, this trail is the hardest of the three and is the basis for the difficulty rating.

This network of trails offers an engaging mix of scenery: from spectacular, rugged mountains, protected valleys with swiftly flowing streams at their bases, steep-sided canyons, and many interesting remains from the bustling mine workings that once spread

The Gold King tramway in 1906

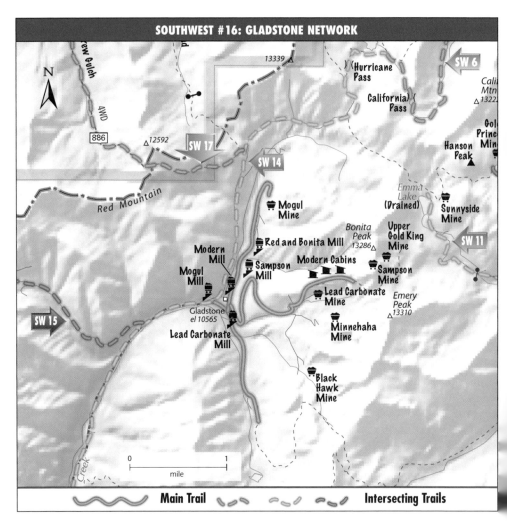

throughout the entire district. The numerous snow slide splitters are testament to the difficult winters endured by these miners.

Current Road Information
Silverton Chamber of Commerce
414 Greene Street
Silverton, CO 81433
(970) 387-5654

Map References
Benchmark's *Colorado Road & Recreation Atlas*, p. 110
USFS Uncompahgre National Forest
USGS 1:24,000 Ironton
1:100,000 Silverton
Maptech CD-ROM:

Southwest/Durango/Telluride
Colorado Atlas & Gazetteer, p. 77
The Roads of Colorado, p. 123
Trails Illustrated, #141

Route Directions

Section one: Colorado (Velocity) Basin

▼ 0.0   On Southwest #14: Silverton to Lake Como Trail at the Mogul Mill ruins along in Gladstone, zero trip meter and proceed toward the modern mining buildings.
      GPS: N 37°53.44' W 107°39.10'

▼ 0.1   BR Southwest #14: Silverton to Lake Como Trail (County 10) forks off to the left.

▼ 0.2 TL/TR   As you approach the Lead Carbonate Mill ruins, turn left and then immediately turn right. Note: You will return to this intersection to continue along the road to the left after completing the segment of the route into Colorado (Velocity) Basin.
▼ 0.4   SO   Cabin on left.
▼ 0.5   SO   Cross over creek.
▼ 0.6   SO   Private track on left.
▼ 1.1   SO   Big Colorado Mine on right.
▼ 1.2   SO   Open mine portal on left. Then cross over creek.
▼ 1.5   SO   Cross through creek.
▼ 1.7   End in steep-sided basin. Return to the intersection at the 0.2-mile point above.
             GPS: N 37°52.14′ W 107°38.65′

Section Two: Minnehaha Basin
▼ 0.0   BR   When you return to the intersection where you split off to go to Colorado (Velocity) Basin, bear to the right of the modern mine entrance and go past the Lead Carbonate Mill on the right. Zero trip meter.
▼ 0.1   TR   At the next intersection turn right to head toward Minnehaha Basin. Note: You will return to this intersection to continue along the road to Mogul Mine to complete this network of trails.
▼ 1.4   TR   Track straight ahead leads to the Gold King Mine. Follow switchback to the right.
▼ 2.0   TL   Straight ahead about a hundred yards is a fork in the road. The left fork goes to Minnehaha Mine. The right fork goes to Black Hawk Mine and some private lots—it dead-ends in approximately one mile.
▼ 2.2   SO   Eastern Star Road on left is gated. Track on right goes to two modern cabins.
▼ 2.4   BL   Lead Carbonate Mine on right.
             GPS: N 37°53.51′ W 107°37.98′

▼ 2.6   SO   Three deserted modern cabins on left.
▼ 2.7   End of track—it is washed out ahead. You can see an outcropping of quartz approximately 50 feet onward along the road. Return to the intersection where you started this section of the route.

GPS: N 37°53.56′ W 107°37.98′

Section Three: Mogul Mine
▼ 0.0   TR   Zero your trip meter when you return to the intersection where you split off to go to Minnehaha Basin. Continue towards Mogul Mine.
▼ 0.2   SO   Faint track on right.
▼ 0.4   BR   Fork in road. Left fork crosses through creek and joins County 10 toward Hurricane Pass.
▼ 0.5   SO   Site of the Sampson Mill and faint track to it on right.
▼ 0.6   SO   Red and Bonita Mill site.
▼ 0.8   SO   Track on right.
▼ 0.9   SO   Snowslide defense structure on left.
▼ 1.0   SO   Track rejoins on right.
▼ 1.5   SO   Mogul Mine and dump on right.
▼ 1.6   End at entrance to Mogul Mine on right. Beyond this point, the road is too narrow for full-sized vehicles, so turning around here is advised. Return to Mogul Mill in Gladstone.
             GPS: N 37°54.60′ W 107°38.27′

Corkscrew Gulch Trail

STARTING POINT Intersection of US 550 and FR 886
FINISHING POINT Intersection with Southwest #14: Silverton to Lake Como Trail
TOTAL MILEAGE 4.8 miles
UNPAVED MILEAGE 4.8 miles
DRIVING TIME 30 minutes
ROUTE ELEVATION 9,800 to 12,600 feet
USUALLY OPEN Mid-June to late October
DIFFICULTY RATING 4
SCENIC RATING 9

Special Attractions
■ Exceptional scenery, with panoramic views of the Red Mountain Peaks and the more distant mountains both west and east of the trail.
■ Provides access to a large network of 4WD trails.

The unmarked entrance to Corkscrew Gulch Trail along US 550

History

This route commences near the town site of Ironton, which was located at the southern end of the old tailings pond. The town was formed in 1883 as a tent colony following the mining craze around Red Mountain four years earlier. Ironton developed into a somewhat refined town. Some merchants of the better stores in Ouray and Silverton opened branches in Ironton. Ironton served as the residential center for workers in the nearby mines, such as the Yankee Girl and the Guston.

The town also served as an important stage and supply center for the region. Wagons arrived at regular intervals, and ore wagons left from the city continuously. When Otto Mears opened the Rainbow Route, extending his railroad from Silverton, over Red Mountain Pass, through to Ironton in 1889, the town had a grand welcoming celebration.

Prospectors found gold in nearby mountains, which helped create another rush. New mine shafts were drilled deeper into the mountains. The digging of deep mine shafts resulted

in the discovery of underground water; unfortunately, the water was found to contain deadly sulfuric acid, which often ate through machinery, making equipment maintenance a constant and expensive endeavor.

The modest success of the gold mines was not sufficient for the town to survive the impact of the silver crash of 1893, and most of Ironton's residents moved on to other areas. A few hardy residents remained until the early 1930s. Some old buildings are left in the area.

Description

This route is moderately difficult to drive because some sections of the road are rough, steep, and narrow, and there are several sharp switchbacks to negotiate. However, other than locating the start of the trail, which is unmarked, navigation is straightforward.

The route commences at the Idarado Mine tailing pond on US 550. Initially the road, which is unmarked but designated FR 886, travels through the forest as it starts the ascent into Corkscrew Gulch. Sections of the road surface are clay and become very boggy in wet conditions. After crossing a couple of shallow creeks, you encounter several switchbacks as the road climbs out of the gulch.

Once above timberline, you have a panoramic view of adjoining mountains and valleys, including the three Red Mountains. As the road starts to descend, it reenters the forest. From the turnoff to Gray Copper Gulch, the road is quite steep immediately prior to coming to an end at the intersection with Southwest #14: Silverton to Lake Como Trail.

Current Road Information

Grand Mesa, Uncompahgre and Gunnison
National Forests
Ouray Ranger District
2505 South Townsend Avenue
Montrose, CO 81401
(970) 240-5300

Map References

Benchmark's *Colorado Road & Recreation Atlas,* p. 110
USFS Uncompahgre NF
USGS 1:24,000 Ironton
1:100,000 Silverton
Maptech CD-ROM:
Southwest/Durango/Telluride
Colorado Atlas & Gazetteer, pp. 76, 77
The Roads of Colorado, p. 123
Trails Illustrated, #141

Route Directions

▼ 0.0   Begin at the sign for the Idarado Mine and its tailings on US 550. Zero trip meter and proceed east onto FR 886, crossing over plank bridge. This intersection is about 15 miles from Silverton and 7.7 miles from Ouray.

Ironton, circa 1908

View of abandoned mine buildings and tailings piles in Ironton, circa 1941

4.8 ▲   Cross plank bridge and end at US 550. Ouray is to the right and Silverton is to the left.

GPS: N 37°56.33′ W 107°40.27′

▼ 0.2 BR Sign indicates Brown Mountain left; Corkscrew Gulch right.

4.6 ▲ BL Continue on trail.

▼ 0.3 SO Sign reads "Corkscrew Gulch 4x4 only."

4.5 ▲ SO Continue on trail.

▼ 0.6 SO Track on right is the North Pipeline Trailhead.

4.2 ▲ SO Track on left is the North Pipeline Trailhead.

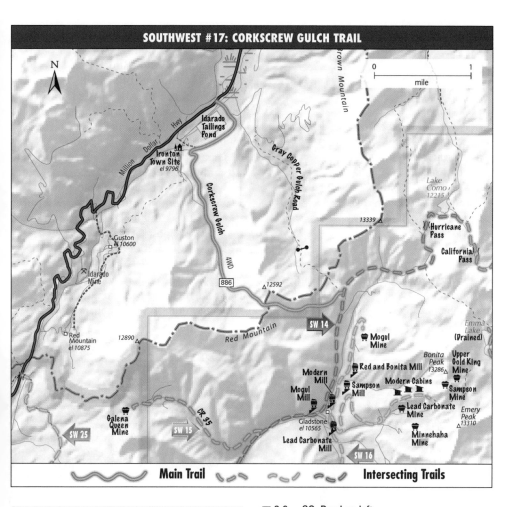

~~~~~ **Main Trail** ~~~ ~~~ **Intersecting Trails**

▼ 1.1 SO Track on left.
3.7 ▲ SO Track on right.

▼ 1.5 SO Track on left.
3.3 ▲ SO Track on right.

▼ 1.6 SO Cross through creek.
3.2 ▲ SO Cross through creek.

▼ 2.0 SO Cross through creek.
2.8 ▲ SO Cross through creek.

▼ 2.7 BL Cabin on right.
2.1 ▲ BR Cabin on left.

▼ 2.8 SO Sign to Gladstone and Silverton.
2.0 ▲ SO Sign to US 550.

▼ 3.6 SO Pond on left.
1.2 ▲ SO Pond on right.

▼ 3.7 SO Intersection.
1.1 ▲ SO Intersection.

▼ 4.7 SO Track on left to Gray Copper Gulch.
0.1 ▲ SO Track on right to Gray Copper Gulch.

▼ 4.8 End at intersection with Southwest #14: Silverton to Lake Como Trail.

0.0 ▲ From Southwest #14: Silverton to Lake Como Trail (1.5 miles from Gladstone), zero trip meter and turn onto County 11 toward Corkscrew Gulch.

GPS: N 37°54.61' W 107°38.68'

Yankee Boy Basin Trail

STARTING POINT Ouray
FINISHING POINT Yankee Boy Basin
TOTAL MILEAGE 9.1 miles (one-way)
UNPAVED MILEAGE 8.6 miles
DRIVING TIME 1 hour
ROUTE ELEVATION 7,800 to 11,850 feet
USUALLY OPEN Mid-June to early October
DIFFICULTY RATING 3
SCENIC RATING 8

Special Attractions
- Historic mines and old mining camps.
- Canyon Creek shelf road.
- Abundant wildflowers in Yankee Boy Basin.

History
On the way to Yankee Boy Basin you pass the famous Camp Bird Mine. In 1896, Thomas Walsh, an Irishman, discovered very rich gold in Imogene Basin. He immediately purchased more than one hundred claims in the area and consolidated them under the name Camp Bird.

Camp Bird, a company town that grew up around the Camp Bird Mine, soon became the second largest gold producer in Colorado, turning out ore that was worth more than $1 million per year. The camp had its own post office, which was established in 1898 and discontinued in 1918.

Walsh furnished a boardinghouse for his employees with marble-topped lavatories, electric lights, steam heat, and even a piano. Meals were deliciously prepared and served on china plates.

A cutting along the Camp Bird shelf road

Yankee Boy Basin

OURAY

Ouray is located in a beautiful box canyon at the base of steep and colorful mountains. When miners first came to the area in the early 1870s, the land belonged to the Ute Indians. The first mining camp was called Uncompahgre City.

Ute leader Chief Ouray functioned as a peace ambassador between the Indians and the white prospectors. Realizing that the influx of white men was inevitable, Ouray continued his peaceful arbitration between the whites and Utes, saving countless lives. Chief Ouray signed the Brunot Treaty of 1873, giving the San Juan Mountains to the United States. The town's name was changed to honor Chief Ouray in 1876.

In its early days, the town was quite isolated. Roads were so poor that there was little

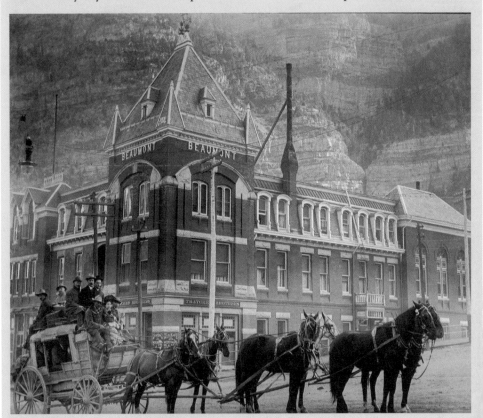

A stagecoach in front of the famous Beaumont Hotel in Ouray, circa 1888

transportation into or out of Ouray. Food was scarce, particularly in winter months. Supplies were hard to get and expensive. The postal service had such difficulties negotiating the roads that mail carriers often arrived behind a team of sled dogs. Since local mines could not afford to ship out all of their ore, they transported only their high-grade ore and had to scrap the lower-grade commodity. Mining implements freighted in were outrageously priced.

By 1877, the town reached a population of 800. Two newspapers were published in Ouray. The printing presses had to be carried over the mountains by wagon train. The people of Ouray used their saloons in more ways than one. Early in the town's history, residents held church services in saloons and used kegs of beer for seating. When Ouray became the county seat a few years later, the Star Saloon was renovated as the first courthouse. The bar was removed, the first floor functioned as city hall, and the second-floor rooms were changed into county offices.

Otto Mears earned his nickname, "Pathfinder of the San Juans," by constructing a toll road in 1881. His ambitious 12-mile road from Ouray to Red Mountain cost $10,000 per mile to construct. Some sections cost $1,000 per foot! However, improved accessibility boosted Ouray and its economy. The toll road enabled the mining companies to ship their lower-grade ore at reasonable expense instead of throwing it away. This road was the beginning of Mears' Million Dollar Highway from Silverton to Ouray. He later followed the route with his railroad but could go only as far north as Ironton. Supplies from Ouray reached the northern end of the railroad by wagon. Because Mears still wanted to reach Ouray by train, he began building the Rio Grande Southern from Durango, through Ophir and Ridgway, and into Ouray. This line was completed in 1887.

Ouray today

By the 1890s, much of Ouray's downtown area had been replaced with brick and stone buildings. Ouray became one of the most elegant mining towns in the San Juans. The remarkable Beaumont Hotel at Main and 5th Streets, with its three-story rotunda and divided stairway, displayed French architectural influences. The furnishings came from Marshall Fields in Chicago, and the dining room staff was trained at the Brown Palace Hotel in Denver. Its interior was lush and luxurious. Many prominent people stayed there, including Herbert Hoover. The Beaumont was closed in 1965 as a result of a dispute between the owner and the city. It sat empty until 1998 when it was bought at auction and after a 5-year, multi-million dollar renovation was reopened in December, 2003.

Thomas Walsh, owner of the Camp Bird Mine, was a miner who struck it rich and became famous. Walsh gave Ouray a 7,500-volume library, although it has been said he was illiterate. The Walsh family became so rich from the Camp Bird Mine that Walsh's daughter, Evalyn, purchased the Hope Diamond. Later, Harry Winston bought the diamond from her and donated it to the Smithsonian Institution.

Today, Ouray is an attractive Victorian town prospering by tourism, particularly during summer months. Its population peaked at around 6,500 in 1890; for the past 50 years it has stabilized at around 2,500. As virtually all of Ouray's major public buildings and commercial structures were constructed over one hundred years ago, the town's appearance is largely unchanged. Some popular vacation activities in the area include hiking, bathing in the Ouray Hot Springs Pool, and exploring countless 4WD routes.

Camp Bird shelf road with Canyon Creek below

Winter and snow were always problems for the community. The men often had to tunnel out of their quarters to reach the mine. Avalanches killed several men over the years. It was necessary to construct a two-mile aerial tramway from the mines to the mill. Underground tunnels linked the Camp Bird and the Tomboy Mines.

Six years after establishing the prosperous mine, millionaire Walsh sold the properties to an English company for $3.5 million cash, a half million in shares of stock, and royalties on future profits. Upon selling the mine, Walsh showed his appreciation to his employees by issuing bonus checks of up to $5,000.

With profits from Camp Bird, Walsh bought a mansion in Washington, D.C., and his wife and daughter hobnobbed with international society. They became the "jet-setters" of their era. Walsh's daughter, Evalyn, married Edward B. McLean, whose family owned the Washington Post. As wedding gifts, each family gave the couple $100,000, which they supposedly spent before the honeymoon was over. Evalyn Walsh McLean later purchased the famed Hope Diamond, which is now on display at the Smithsonian Institution.

The first cabin in Yankee Boy Basin was built during the winter of 1874–1875 when several prospectors endured the harsh, snowy

Waterfalls along Sneffels Creek In Yankee Boy Basin

Camp Bird Mine in 1911

winter. As the snow thawed, it was clear they had chosen a very successful locale for mining; they discovered both gold and silver and founded a mining camp called Porters. This was before Ouray was established and several years prior to the first strikes at Camp Bird.

During the peak production years of this mining district as many as 3,000 men worked the silver and gold mines in Yankee Boy Basin. Sneffels served as the headquarters for local mines, although some smaller camps were situated around the more distant mines. Some of the profitable mines included the Yankee Boy, the Ruby Trust, the Wheel of Fortune, and the best producer of all, the Virginius Mine. In 1884, the Revenue Tunnel was constructed to intercept the Virginius at a cost of $600,000. The Virginius-Revenue project was so successful it paid for itself almost immediately and then many times over.

A shelf road was cut into the mountain to Ouray, passing the future site of Camp Bird. The narrow ledges and steep grades were dangerous; rockslides and snowslides were frequent.

Although the silver crash of 1893 saw the closure of some local mines, rich ore and good management kept the Virginius open. Prospectors discovered additional gold veins. Operations were suspended in 1905 for some improvements to the mining works, but in 1906, a fire badly damaged the mine.

In 1909, operations resumed as normal but the activity was short lived. When miners began sending their ores to the more economical Tomboy Mill on Imogene Pass, the Revenue Mill ceased operations. Ten years later, the mill was destroyed by fire.

The Sneffels post office closed down in 1930. The town experienced a brief revival during the late 1940s when some enterprising folks rehabilitated several of the town's buildings and attempted to get the Revenue Tunnel operating again, but the town was never the same. The Revenue-Virginius properties later became the property of Camp Bird.

Description

Yankee Boy Basin is a very popular location during the peak summer months for both sightseers and hikers. To help alleviate traffic jams, accidents that can be fatal, and ultimately trail closures, please refer back to the Before You Go chapter at the beginning of the book and follow our 4WD Road Rules (page 12). Being courteous and following proper trail etiquette makes the journey more enjoyable for everyone.

The trail is short, varied, and is a good introduction to four-wheel driving. Attractions include historic mines, deserted town sites, rugged mountain scenery, and wonderful natural beauty, including alpine meadows that are covered with wildflowers in the late spring. About five miles from

Ouray, the route traverses a spectacular shelf road perched above Canyon Creek. The road is well-maintained and relatively wide.

From Camp Bird, the route takes you through a fairly wide, flat valley to the Revenue Mine and Mill and the old mining town of Sneffels, which can be viewed from the road but is on private property.

About half a mile farther, the road forks, with the road to Governor Basin to the left and the road to Yankee Boy Basin to the right. Until this point, the road is negotiable by passenger vehicles; farther on, high clearance 4WD vehicles have an advantage.

The Governor Basin 4WD trail is a narrow shelf road that is much more difficult than the Yankee Boy road. Passing is difficult in many sections, and snow can block the road late into summer, necessitating the sometimes-difficult job of turning around. Nonetheless, for those with the experience and nerve, the Governor Basin road offers some majestic scenery and historic mines (difficulty rating: 5).

The road into Yankee Boy Basin passes Twin Falls and numerous mines as it follows

The miners' dining room at Camp Bird Mine, circa 1900

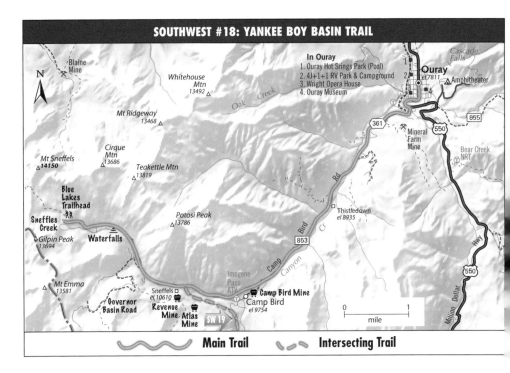

N

Blaine Mine

Whitehouse Mtn 13492 △

Mt Ridgeway 13468 △

Oak Creek

In Ouray
1. Ouray Hot Srings Park (Pool)
2. 4J+1+1 RV Park & Campground
3. Wright Opera House
4. Ouray Museum

Cascade Falls

Ouray
el 7811

Amphitheater

361

855

Cirque Mtn 13686

Mt Sneffels 14150 △

Teakettle Mtn 13819 △

Mineral Farm Mine

550

Bear Creek NRT

Blue Lakes Trailhead

Sneffels Creek

Gilpin Peak 13694

Waterfalls

Potosi Peak 13786 △

Thistledown el 8935

Rd

853

Bird Cr

Hwy

550

Mt Emma 13581 △

Sneffels el 10610

Imogene Pass ATV

Camp Canyon

Camp Bird Mine

Camp Bird el 9754

Million Dollar

Governor Basin Road

Revenue Mine

Atlas Mine

SW 19

0   1
|—————————————|
mile

~~~~~~ **Main Trail**   ~~~ **Intersecting Trail**

alongside Sneffels Creek to the end of the trail, some two miles farther. Towering peaks including Stony Mountain (12,698 feet) and Mount Sneffels (14,150 feet) surround the basin. The abundant, spring wildflowers include columbine, bluebells, and Indian paintbrush.

Numerous backcountry camping sites are located near the trail, but camping is not permitted within a quarter mile of Sneffels Creek in Yankee Boy Basin or the tributary creek from Governor Basin. Also, camping is not allowed on private lands without written permission. Firewood is scarce in the basin, so if you are planning to camp, we recommend that you either bring wood with you or use a gas stove according to local fire regulations.

Current Road Information

Grand Mesa, Uncompahgre and Gunnison National Forests
Ouray Ranger District
2505 South Townsend Avenue
Montrose, CO 81401
(970) 240-5300

Map References

Benchmark's *Colorado Road & Recreation Atlas,* p. 110
USFS   Uncompahgre National Forest
USGS   1:24,000   Ouray, Ironton, Telluride
             1:100,000 Montrose, Silverton
Maptech CD-ROM:
             Southwest/Durango/Telluride
Colorado Atlas & Gazetteer, pp. 66, 76
The Roads of Colorado, pp. 122, 123
Trails Illustrated, #141

Route Directions

▼ 0.0   In front of Beaumont Hotel at 5th
                 Avenue and Main Street in Ouray, zero
                 trip meter and proceed south out of
                 town, remaining on US 550.
6.4 ▲   End at Beaumont Hotel in Ouray at 5th
                 Avenue and Main Street.
                 GPS: N 38°01.30' W 107°40.29'

▼ 0.5   TR Toward Box Canyon Falls on Camp
                 Bird Road, County 361.
5.9 ▲   TL On US 550 toward Ouray.

▼ 0.6   BL Box Canyon Falls on right. Bear left.

Camp Bird Mine

Sneffels town site

5.8 ▲	BR	Box Canyon Falls on left. Bear right.
▼ 2.4	SO	Bridge over Canyon Creek. Campsites.
4.0 ▲	SO	Campsites. Bridge over Canyon Creek.
▼ 3.1	SO	Camping on the left and right.
3.3 ▲	SO	Camping on the left and right.
		GPS: N 38°59.61′ W 107°42.02′
▼ 3.3	SO	Bridge over Weehawken Creek.
3.1 ▲	SO	Bridge over Weehawken Creek.
▼ 5.0	SO	Camping on the left and right.
1.4 ▲	SO	Camping on the left and right.
▼ 5.1	SO	Camp Bird Mine turnoff to the left.

1.3 ▲	SO	Camp Bird Mine turnoff to the right.
▼ 5.7	SO	Canyon wall dramatically overhangs the road.
0.7 ▲	SO	Canyon wall dramatically overhangs the road.
▼ 6.2	SO	Track on right.
0.2 ▲	SO	Track on left.
▼ 6.4	SO	Intersection. Southwest #19: Imogene Pass Trail on left. Track on right. Zero trip meter.
0.0 ▲		At intersection of Southwest #19: Imogene Pass Trail and Yankee Boy Basin Trail, zero trip meter and proceed northeast toward Ouray and US 550. **GPS: N 37°58.53′ W 107°44.70′**
▼ 0.0		Continue along road toward Yankee Boy Basin.
▼ 0.1	SO	Road on right.
▼ 0.3	SO	Revenue Mine and Sneffels site on left. Track on right.
▼ 0.5	SO	Road on right.
▼ 0.7	BR	Numerous campsites on left and right. Atlas Mine ruins on left across the river. Go past the information board. **GPS: N 37°58.67′ W 107°45.36′**
▼ 0.9	BR	Road forks. Governor Basin road is to the left. **GPS: N 37°58.73′ W 107°45.52′**
▼ 1.2	SO	Closed track on left.
▼ 1.3	SO	Dual waterfall view on left.
▼ 1.5	SO	Private road on left. Walker Ruby Mining.
▼ 1.6	SO	Public restrooms on left.
▼ 1.7	SO	Short road on left goes to a mine portal and then rejoins the main track.
▼ 1.9	SO	Cross through creek. Yankee Boy Mine and tailing dump on right. Track on left rejoins from previous entry.
▼ 2.1	SO	Tracks on left and right.
▼ 2.7		End of track. **GPS: N 37°59.45′ W 107°46.76′**

Imogene Pass Trail

STARTING POINT Intersection with Southwest #18: Yankee Boy Basin Trail
FINISHING POINT Telluride
TOTAL MILEAGE 12.8 miles
UNPAVED MILEAGE 12.2 miles
DRIVING TIME 2.5 hours
ROUTE ELEVATION 9,000 to 13,114 feet
USUALLY OPEN Late June to late September
DIFFICULTY RATING 4
SCENIC RATING 10

Special Attractions

■ The highest pass road in the San Juan Mountains, with spectacular scenery and a wealth of historical interest.
■ The ghost town of Tomboy.
■ Views of Bridal Veil Falls and the switchbacks of Southwest #22: Black Bear Pass Trail.

History

The Imogene Pass road was built in 1880 for access to Ouray from the Tomboy Mine. It was named for Imogene Richardson, the wife of one of Thomas Walsh's partners in the Camp Bird Mine. Wires carrying the first commercial transmission of alternating current electricity were strung across this pass in the 1890s. The power was generated in Ames and transmitted to Ouray.

The Tomboy Mine, located in 1880 by Otis C. Thomas, was situated high above Telluride. Tomboy was Thomas' nickname. For several years there was little activity at Tomboy because it was so difficult to reach. However, after the silver crash in 1893, prospectors struck gold at the Tomboy, and the mine began to produce handsomely. At its peak, the mining camp supported about 900 people.

In 1901, the Western Federation of Miners called their first strike in the Telluride area. This strike was successful, and non-union laborers were chased out of

Crossing through Imogene Creek during the spring runoff

A view of the trail on the east side of Imogene Pass

Social Tunnel

An information board at Tomboy

Mill foundations at Tomboy

Tomboy over Imogene Pass. In 1903, the Tomboy Mill again began to use non-union labor, and a second strike was called. The mine owners asked Governor James Peabody to call up the state militia, and the governor, in turn, called on President Theodore Roosevelt to send federal troops. The U.S. army stayed away, but when 500 state troopers arrived, the violence escalated.

The union even brought in a hired gun, Harry Orchard, whom they had previously commissioned to assassinate the governor of Idaho. On union orders, he attempted to murder Governor Peabody, but the plot failed. With the area under military rule, the union and the strike were broken. The union labor was run out of town but set up camp at Red Mountain and plotted to recapture Tomboy and Telluride. Fort Peabody was constructed at the top of the pass in 1903 to protect against such an attack. The attack never occurred.

Although Tomboy's residents relied on Telluride for supplies, they did not necessarily turn to Telluride for entertainment. About halfway between the Tomboy and the Smuggler Mine was a renegade district called The Jungle, offering a mix of brothels, poker dens, and saloons.

The Tomboy Mine was sold for $2 million to the Rothschilds of London in 1897 and continued to operate until 1927.

This route was reopened as a 4WD road in 1966, following the efforts of various 4WD clubs.

Description

Imogene Pass is a very popular 4WD trail during the peak summer months. To help alleviate traffic jams, accidents that can be fatal, and ultimately trail closures, please refer back to the Before You Go chapter at the beginning of the book and follow our 4WD Road Rules (page 12). Being courteous and following proper trail etiquette makes the journey more enjoyable for everyone.

Imogene Pass is the second highest pass road in the United States and provides a wonderfully scenic route through the San Juan Mountains. The route passes two major mining camps: Camp Bird and Tomboy.

From the Yankee Boy Basin turnoff, the standard of the road deteriorates and high

Tomboy Mine, circa 1900

ridal Veil Falls and powerplant

clearance and 4WD become necessary. The track travels through the forest and Imogene Creek Valley. There are a number of creek crossings as the track proceeds toward the pass, although none should prove to be any problem for a high clearance 4WD vehicle. The road narrows for the final ascent to the pass, but there are adequate pull-offs available for passing.

About two miles from the pass, the track enters the ghost town of Tomboy, 2,880 feet above Telluride and three miles distant. The town site has numerous historic remains. Although the buildings of Tomboy continue to deteriorate from the onslaught of harsh weather, Tomboy remains one of the better ghost towns to explore; many of the foundations and some of the structures are clearly evident.

Some two miles past Tomboy, the road passes through Social Tunnel, a short passage through a rock outcrop that provides a popular photo opportunity. This location on the trail is also a spectacular overlook with views of the switchbacks of Southwest #22: Black Bear Pass Trail as well as both Ingram Falls and Bridal Veil Falls.

Current Road Information

Grand Mesa, Uncompahgre and Gunnison National Forests
Norwood Ranger District
PO Box 388
1150 Forest Street
Norwood, CO 81423
970-327-4261

Mining debris at Tomboy

Tomboy Mill ruins

The trail heading to Telluride with Tomboy in the foreground

Map References

Benchmark's *Colorado Road & Recreation Atlas,* p. 110
USFS   Uncompahgre National Forest
USGS   1:24,000   Ironton, Telluride
       1:100,000 Silverton
Maptech CD-ROM:
       Southwest/Durango/Telluride
Colorado Atlas & Gazetteer, p. 76
The Roads of Colorado, pp. 122, 123
Trails Illustrated, #141

Route Directions

▼ 0.0   At intersection of Southwest #18:
           Yankee Boy Basin Trail and Imogene
           Pass Trail (FR 869), zero trip meter and
           proceed across bridge over Sneffels
           Creek. Track on right, bear left.
5.3 ▲   Track on left. Cross bridge over Sneffels

Creek. End at intersection with Southwest #18: Yankee Boy Basin Trail.
GPS: N 37°58.53′ W 107°44.70′

▼ 0.2   SO Track on right—no access.
5.1 ▲   SO Track on left—no access.

▼ 0.4   SO Creek crossing.
4.9 ▲   SO Creek crossing.

▼ 0.8   SO Old cabin on left.
4.5 ▲   SO Old cabin on right.

▼ 1.2   BR Private road to Camp Bird Mine on left.
4.1 ▲   BL Private road to Camp Bird Mine on right.

▼ 1.5   SO Imogene Creek cascading down
            through valley on left.
3.8 ▲   SO Imogene Creek cascading down
            through valley on right.

〰〰〰 Main Trail   ⌒⌒ ⌒⌒ Intersecting Trails

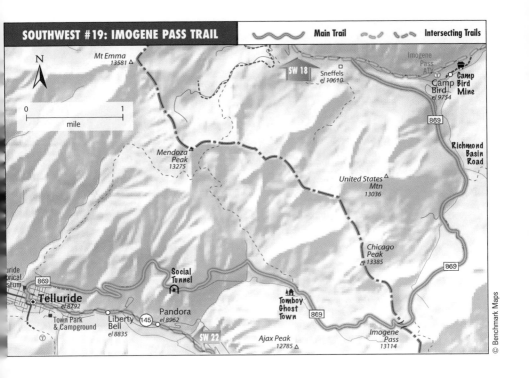

© Benchmark Maps

▼ 1.9   SO   Track on right. Old sign to Imogene Pass.
             Cross through Imogene Creek with
             cascade on left. Another track on right
             goes to an old log building and mine.
3.4 ▲   SO   Track on left goes to an old log building
             and mine. Cross through Imogene Creek.
             Track on left.

▼ 2.0   SO   Spectacular view of Imogene Creek
             cascading into valley.
3.3 ▲   SO   Spectacular view of Imogene Creek
             cascading into valley.

▼ 2.3   SO   Cross bridge over Imogene Creek.
             Track on left to Richmond Basin.
3.0 ▲   SO   Track on right to Richmond Basin.
             Cross bridge over Imogene Creek.
             GPS: N 37°57.22′ W 107°43.45′

▼ 2.7   SO   Track on right to buildings and mine.
             Cross through creek.
2.6 ▲   SO   Cross through creek. Track on left to
             buildings and mine.

▼ 2.9   SO   Track on right. Follow Imogene Pass sign.
2.4 ▲   SO   Track on left.

▼ 3.0   BR   Series of tracks; continue to the right.
2.3 ▲   SO   Roads rejoin on the right.

▼ 3.1   SO   Roads rejoin on the left.
2.2 ▲   BL   Roads on the right.

▼ 4.1   SO   Cross through creek.
1.2 ▲   SO   Cross through creek.

▼ 4.4   SO   Cross through creek.
0.9 ▲   SO   Cross through creek.

▼ 5.2   BR   Track on left to Ptarmigan Lake.
0.1 ▲   BL   Track on right to Ptarmigan Lake.

▼ 5.3   SO   Summit of Imogene Pass. Zero trip meter.
0.0 ▲   Continue along main road.
             GPS: N 37°55.88′ W 107°44.07′

▼ 0.0   Stay on main road and proceed downhill.
7.5 ▲   SO   Summit of Imogene Pass. Zero trip meter.

▼ 1.2   SO   Track on left. Stay on main road.
6.3 ▲   SO   Track on right. Stay on main road.

▼ 1.4   SO   Cross over drainage.

Imogene Pass summit

6.1 ▲	SO	Cross over drainage.	

▼ 1.5	SO	Tracks on right.
6.0 ▲	SO	Tracks on left.

▼ 1.7	SO	Stone building remains on left.
5.8 ▲	SO	Stone building remains on right.

▼ 1.8	UT	Overlook of Tomboy mining township.
5.7 ▲	UT	Overlook of Tomboy mining township.

▼ 2.1	SO	Tomboy site.
5.4 ▲	SO	Tomboy site.

GPS: N 37°56.18′ W 107°45.23′

▼ 2.4	SO	Mill; then bridge over creek.
5.1 ▲	SO	Bridge over creek; then mill.

▼ 2.5	SO	Track on right.
5.0 ▲	SO	Track on left.

▼ 3.0	BR	Track on left.
4.5 ▲	BL	Track on right.

▼ 3.1	SO	Bridges over two creeks.
4.4 ▲	SO	Bridges over two creeks.

▼ 3.3	SO	Tomboy Mine remains.

4.2 ▲	SO	Tomboy Mine remains.

▼ 3.8	SO	Colorful mine buildings.
3.7 ▲	SO	Colorful mine buildings.

▼ 4.3	SO	Social Tunnel.
3.2 ▲	SO	Social Tunnel.

▼ 6.6	SO	Seasonal closure gate.
0.9 ▲	SO	Seasonal closure gate.

▼ 6.9	UT	Onto Gregory Avenue at intersection with North Oak. Then turn right onto North Fir.
0.5 ▲	TL	Onto Gregory Avenue. Then U-turn to the right at North Oak.

▼ 7.1	TR	Intersection of N. Fir and W. Colorado.
0.4 ▲	TL	Intersection of N. Fir and W. Colorado.

▼ 7.5		End at Visitor Information Center on W. Colorado in Telluride.
0.0 ▲		From Visitor Information Center on W. Colorado in Telluride, zero trip meter and proceed east on W. Colorado (main street).

GPS: N 37°56.37′ W 107°49.15′

THE SILVER CRASH OF 1893

In the eighteenth century, currencies were typically backed by one or more precious metals. All major countries chose either gold or silver, or a combination of the two, as the basis of their currency. At the time, choice of currency was a major political issue both in Europe and in the United States; most countries changed their policy more than once during the course of the 1700s and 1800s.

Adherents of the system believed that it stabilized not only the prices of gold and silver but also the value of all commodities, thereby simplifying foreign exchange. Most economists came to oppose the practice.

In 1792, Secretary of the Treasury Alexander Hamilton led the U.S. Congress to adopt a bimetallic monetary standard, meaning that both gold and silver were used to back the currency. Silver dollars contained 371.25 grains, and gold dollars 24.75 grains—a 15:1 ratio.

One of the difficulties of this system is that as the relative market value of gold or silver changes, one coin becomes more valuable than the other; the more-valuable coin's circulation decreases as people melt it down and sell the metal and use the less-valuable coin for commerce. A metal's market value can change because of major discoveries of one of the metals or because one nation has changed its policy about the value of a metal backing its currency. In 1834, the United States was forced to change the gold content of its coins because France changed its policy. The U.S. ratio of silver to gold was increased to 16:1.

The Californian and Australian gold rushes in 1849 and 1850 resulted in a decline in the relative price of gold. The value of the silver in silver dollars became greater than the face value of the coins, resulting in widespread melting down of silver dollars. During the course of the Civil War, silver dollars disappeared from circulation; and in 1873, the United States moved to a gold standard, eliminating the free coinage of silver.

Subsequently, the large discoveries of silver in Colorado led to the price of silver falling below the old mint price, which created a political clamor for the government to revert to the old policy that supported the silver price. In 1878, Congress responded by reintroducing the minting of silver dollars but restricted silver purchases to between $2 million and $4 million per month. This was insufficient to quiet the clamor, and in 1890 Congress passed the Sherman Silver Purchase Act to provide for the purchase of $4.5 million per month. The result was an immediate increase in the price of silver from 84¢ to $1.50 per ounce, which had a dramatic effect on the silver miners in Colorado; times were booming.

However, the act caused the U.S. Treasury to start stocking silver bullion, since the value of silver decreased as increasing amounts were discovered. The government's stockpiling led to a lack of confidence in the currency and caused speculators to hoard gold, thus depleting U.S. reserves.

On August 7, 1893, President Cleveland called an emergency session of Congress and repealed the Sherman Act. The demand for silver was reduced by $4.5 million per month, and the price of silver crashed. Overnight, many Colorado mines became unprofitable and ceased operations. Populations moved, and many silver mining towns were doomed to become ghost towns.

In 1896, the presidential election was fought on the issue of gold versus silver. William Jennings Bryan supported silver, but William McKinley won. In 1900, McKinley succeeded in passing the Gold Standard Act, which led to further decline in the depressed silver price, more mine closures, and more ghost towns in the West.

In 1967, the United States eliminated the gold backing from the currency; by 1970, all silver content had been eliminated from U.S. coins, and the government sold the remaining silver reserves.

Ophir Pass Trail

STARTING POINT Intersection of Colorado 145 and FR 630 south of Telluride

FINISHING POINT Intersection of FR 679 and US 550 between Ouray and Silverton

TOTAL MILEAGE 9.8 miles

UNPAVED MILEAGE 9.8 miles

DRIVING TIME 1.75 hours

ROUTE ELEVATION 9,500 to 11,789 feet

USUALLY OPEN Mid-June to October

DIFFICULTY RATING 3

SCENIC RATING 9

Special Attractions

- Driving through the 20-foot-high channel in the snow early in the season.
- The long, narrow shelf road set into the talus slope on the west side of the pass.
- Varied scenery, with exceptional views from near the summit.

History

This route was originally called the Navajo Trail and was a well-used Indian hunting trail. The remains of an Indian camp were still visible near the pass in the 1880s.

Trappers were the first white men to use the pass. Explorers and prospectors followed in the 1860s, and the road across the pass became a recognized pass route. In the mid-

The channel cut through the snow near Ophir Pass in late spring each year

The railroad track on the Ophir Pass route in 1951

View of Ophir Loop, west of Ophir in 1947

OTTO MEARS, THE PATHFINDER OF THE SAN JUANS

Otto Mears, born in Russia in 1840, was orphaned at the age of four. Various relatives took care of him, first in Russia, then in England, then in New York, and finally in San Francisco. At the age of twelve, he arrived in San Francisco to live with an uncle, but he found that the uncle had left for the gold rush in Australia; Mears was on his own.

He drifted through the mining camps of Nevada before serving in the First California

Otto Mears

A stagecoach on Mears' narrow toll road that became the Million Dollar Highway, circa 1905

Volunteers in the Civil War. From 1863–1864, he served under Kit Carson in the Indian Campaign against the Navajos. After the war, Mears first went to Santa Fe before moving to Colorado, where he opened a store in Saguache. He prospered and expanded his business interests. He farmed in the San Luis Valley and operated a sawmill and a grain mill.

Mears standing in front of a steam locomotive operated by his Silverton Northern Railroad, circa 1900

To expand market access for his wheat, Mears constructed a road over Poncha Pass. The government gave permission for this road to become a toll road. Thus, Mears acquired the sobriquet Pathfinder of the San Juans. By the mid-1880s, Mears had built 450 miles of roads in the region. His most famous road is what has become known as the Million Dollar Highway, U.S. Highway 550 between Silverton and Ouray.

As the railroads expanded in Colorado, Mears naturally expanded his interests into railroad construction. In partnership with the Denver & Rio Grande Railroad, he built a network of four narrow-gauge rail lines. In 1887, he built the main line from Durango to Rico, over Lizard

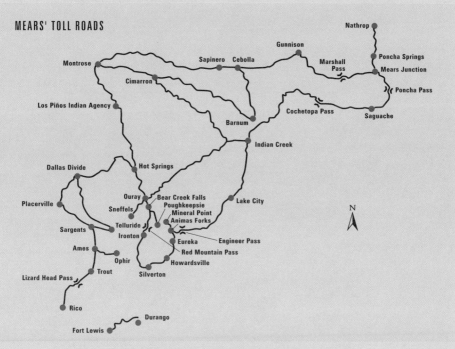

MEARS' TOLL ROADS

Nathrop

Gunnison

Poncha Springs

Montrose

Sapinero   Cebolla

Marshall
Pass

Mears Junction

Cimarron

Poncha Pass

Los Piños Indian Agency

Cochetopa Pass

Saguache

Barnum

Indian Creek

Dallas Divide   Hot Springs

Ouray   Bear Creek Falls   Lake City

Placerville   Poughkeepsie

Sneffels   Mineral Point

Animas Forks

N

Sargents   Telluride

Ironton

Ames   Eureka   Engineer Pass

Ophir   Red Mountain Pass

Trout   Howardsville

Lizard Head Pass   Silverton

Rico

Durango

Fort Lewis

Head Pass on what is now Colorado Highway 145, descending with the aid of the Ophir Loop and proceeding to Placerville, Ridgway, and south to Ouray.

Mears learned the Ute language and was friendly with Chief Ouray. He served as an interpreter in the Brunot Treaty negotiations. Following the Meeker Massacre, he assisted Chief Ouray in freeing the women captives. As a result, Mears worked with Ouray to negotiate the resulting Washington Treaty, which was signed in March 1880. In June, Mears was chosen by President Rutherford Hayes as one of five commissioners to implement the treaty. In 1884, he was elected to the Colorado legislature and became influential in the Republican Party.

Mears suffered heavily in the silver crash of 1893, with many of his enterprises being jeopardized or bankrupted. In

Mears' Million Dollar Highway in 1909

1907, Mears returned to Silverton and remained there until his retirement to Pasadena, California, in 1917. He died on June 24, 1931, at the age of 91.

Ophir Loop, circa 1940

Ophir Loop, circa 1890

1870s after the Brunot Treaty opened the region, a wagon road was built across the pass. The wagon road was converted into a toll road in 1880. When Otto Mears built his railroad through the area in 1891, the need for the pass road declined.

Throughout the mining period, the name Ophir referred to two towns: Old Ophir and Ophir Loop. Located at the foot of Ophir Pass, Old Ophir, or just Ophir, was established in 1870, shortly before Ophir Loop. Early settlers named the towns after an Old Testament reference to a region rich in gold in hopes that the nearby mines would bring similar fortunes. The first claims were staked in 1875, after which time prospectors worked the area sporadically.

By 1885, the population of Ophir grew

A packtrain of mules on the old Ophir Pass toll road, circa 1920

to 200. In three years, it blossomed to 500. Ophir had five saloons, several churches, a school, and its own electricity and water works.

The town was often snowbound because of avalanches. In December 1883, a mail carrier named Swen Nilson left Silverton to deliver 60 pounds of Christmas packages and letters to Ophir and was never seen or heard from again. Although some people believed he had stolen the mail and fled the country, Swen's brother set out to search for him. After two years, he finally discovered Swen's skeleton with the mail sack still around his neck.

New Ophir, or Ophir Loop, was founded in the mid-1870s, just two miles from Ophir. Although a railway in this area

Ophir Pass

seemed inconceivable, Otto Mears did not know the word impossible. Getting trains started up the steep grade to Lizard Head Pass was a true feat of railroad engineering. Mears oversaw the construction of three tiers of tracks with loops crossing above and below each other and trestles as high as 100. Over this incredible structure, the railroad ran from Telluride to Durango. Two cars of ore were shipped from Ophir Loop each day, and the town accumulated a small population as a few of Ophir's residents moved closer to the railroad.

The population of Ophir dwindled after the turn of the twentieth century, and the area was close to being a ghost town by 1929. In 1960, it was listed as one of four incorporated towns in the United States with no residents. However, the town is now home to a number of summer residents.

The current 4WD road was opened in 1953.

Description
The trail commences at the turnoff from Colorado 145 at the site of the Ophir Loop; but it is not well marked, so we recommend that you measure the distance from Telluride on your odometer. Those with GPS receivers will be glad to have the benefit of modern technology to easily locate the trail.

Across the highway from the start of this trail is a short road to the township of Ames, the site of the first commercial, alternating current electricity generating plant in the United States.

As you leave the old township of Ophir, the road starts to ascend immediately through a scenic wooded area and aspen stands. As the ascent continues, the road rises above the timberline and becomes a narrow shelf road cut into the talus slope with some tight switchbacks and high, sheer drop-offs. This section is the most difficult part of the route. For a short stretch, passing requires careful negotiation. Traveling slowly and carefully, moderately experienced drivers should not have any difficulty. The road is certainly easier than Southwest #22: Black Bear Pass Trail, but those who are tempted to

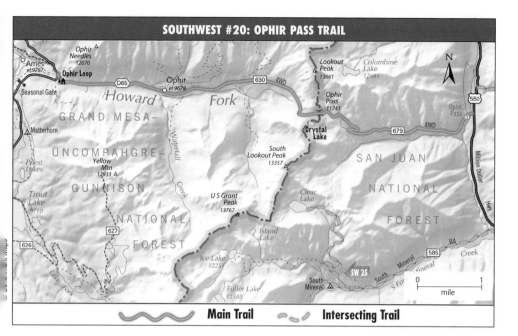

Main Trail   **Intersecting Trail**

take the route too lightly should heed the lesson offered by the remains of a wrecked vehicle that rolled off the road near this location.

From the summit of the pass to US 550, the route is much easier. Although the road is wider and the surface more sound, it remains a shelf road for much of the balance of the journey.

The varied scenery offers particularly panoramic views on the west side of the pass. The east side is more heavily wooded than the west side, and the wildflowers in the valley add vivid color in season.

The trail intersects with FR 820 and the forest road is an alternative route to US 550. The road, about 1.5 miles long, provides a challenging crossing through Mineral Creek when water levels are high. FR 820 joins US 550, 0.7 mile north of where the main route intersects. Ouray is about 18 miles north and Silverton is five miles south of the intersection with US 550.

The road opens in early to mid-June each year. The snowplow only clears the east side of the pass to the summit. When the road first opens, the plow leaves a narrow channel through the snow—the sides can be up to 20 feet high.

Current Road Information

San Juan National Forest
Columbine Ranger District (East)
PO Box 439
367 South Pearl Street
Bayfield, CO 81122
(970) 884-2512

Map References

Benchmark's *Colorado Road & Recreation Atlas,* p. 110
USFS   Uncompahgre NF or San Juan NF
USGS   1:24,000   Silverton, Ophir
            1:100,000   Silverton
Maptech CD-ROM:
            Southwest/Durango/Telluride
Colorado Atlas & Gazetteer, p. 76
The Roads of Colorado, pp. 122, 138, 139
Trails Illustrated, #141

Route Directions

▼ 0.0   At intersection of Colorado 145 and FR 630 at Ophir Loop (no signpost, but opposite the Ames turnoff), zero trip meter and turn onto FR 630 heading east toward Ophir. This is 10 miles from the Telluride Visitor Center.

5.7 ▲   End at intersection of Colorado 145

TELLURIDE

Telluride began as a small mining camp along the San Miguel River in 1878. The first residents called it Columbia. Because the post office sometimes confused Columbia with other towns of the same name, the town was renamed in 1881. Telluride, derived from tellurium (a metallic substance that is often attached to silver and gold in their natural states), was an apt name, since tellurium was widespread in the region.

Colorado Avenue in Telluride after a flood, circa 1914

In 1881, business sites in Telluride were being sold for 25 dollars, and residential lots went for 75 cents. At this time, Telluride had a population of around a thousand people to patronize two grocery stores, and a whopping 13 saloons! Two newspapers were established, and a school district was organized, with classes held in private homes. The following year, the townspeople raised funds to erect the first schoolhouse. The building still stands, but now it serves as Telluride's city hall. The first church, built in 1889, was followed by a number of others. One unconventional pastor even held services in a local saloon.

Butch Cassidy

Telluride's mountains held fortunes in silver and gold. Zinc, copper, and lead were also mined in the area, but transporting the ores presented a major difficulty. At the Liberty Bell, miners tried to send ore from the mine to the mill downhill on sleds. This failed, because the ore kept falling off the sleds. The miners tried to steady the toboggans by constructing and adding wings, but too many sleds practically flew off the mountainside!

Telluride was isolated, so the townspeople often had trouble obtaining supplies and food. Lack of transportation also made shipping ore to Ouray on burros an arduous task. From Ouray, teams of oxen towed the ore to Alamosa. Finally, the ore traveled on to Denver by rail to reach the smelter.

When Otto Mears brought the Rio Grande Southern Railroad to Telluride in 1890, population growth was colossal, but little did people know what lay ahead of them. "To hell you ride!" the conductor would shout to passengers headed for Telluride.

Telluride was a wild place, where guns and tempers often got out of hand. The town's three dozen saloons and gambling halls never shut their doors. Telluride's saloon patrons seemed prone to drunken brawls and fights, and gun battles and murders were common. "The law" itself committed much of the lawlessness. Prostitutes were plentiful, especially along Pacific Avenue. The residents of town tolerated the prostitutes because the bordello madams paid all the town's taxes in regular installments on their behalf.

Butch Cassidy robbed his first bank in Telluride in 1889. Cassidy and two other men held up a bank at the corner of First and Colorado in broad daylight. Although they had three fresh horses waiting for them outside of town, they had no time to make the exchange as they rode for their lives toward Rico with the posse on their tails. Cassidy and his cohorts never were caught for the robbery, but several weeks later three dead horses were found still tied to the tree.

The Wild Bunch pose for a photo in Fort Worth, Texas in 1900

Set magnificently in a box canyon surrounded by snowy mountains and breathtaking waterfalls, Telluride has suffered problems from the elements. Historically, snow piling up in the mountain bowls has presented the greatest threat. In 1902, several men were swept away in an avalanche that also took out the Liberty Bell's tramway. More were killed when a slide buried the rescue party recovering the first bodies. The following day a third slide hit, bringing the death toll to 19. It took months to locate all the bodies. Two years later, nearly 100 people lost their lives in snowslides. Floodwaters once washed out a dam on the San Miguel River, depositing up to eight feet of mud on the streets and isolating the town for weeks. To counteract this problem, residents constructed a flume leading from the town to the creek so that mud would wash into the creek, sometimes assisted by fire hoses.

Largely because of numerous complicated disputes between labor unions and mining companies, Telluride's economy declined dramatically in the early part of last century. One by one, the mines ceased operation. The most recent to close its doors was the Smuggler Union, renamed the Idarado in the 1970s.

The destroyed car from the real Wild Bunch train robbery that was depicted in the 1969 movie

Today, Telluride's gold is the ski industry, which started in the 1970s and has boomed ever since. Thanks to successful efforts at architectural preservation of Victorian houses and other buildings, the town looks much as it did a century ago. Telluride's community is currently prosperous and thriving with year-round resort activities.

and FR 630 at Ophir Loop.
GPS: N 37°51.74' W 107°52.11'

▼ 0.6 SO Seasonal gate.
5.1 ▲ SO Seasonal gate.

▼ 2.0 SO Seasonal gate. Enter town of Ophir.
              Follow sign to Ophir Pass.
3.7 ▲ SO Leave Ophir. Seasonal gate.

▼ 2.1 BR Road forks. Then Ophir Pass sign.
3.6 ▲ BL Road forks.

▼ 2.6 BL/TR Stay on main road.
3.1 ▲ TL/BR Stay on main road.

▼ 2.7 SO Leaving town on Ophir Pass Trail.
3.0 ▲ SO Enter Ophir town limits.

▼ 3.2 SO Track on right.
2.4 ▲ SO Track on left.

▼ 3.7 SO Two tracks on left.
2.0 ▲ SO Two tracks on right.

▼ 3.8 SO Track on left.
1.9 ▲ SO Track on right.

▼ 4.1 SO Track on left.
1.6 ▲ SO Track on right.

▼ 4.2 SO Tracks on left and right. Track on right
              goes to the lake and campsites.

1.5 ▲ SO Track on left goes to the lake and
              campsites. Tracks on right.

▼ 5.7 SO Summit of Ophir Pass. Zero trip meter.
0.0 ▲   Continue along main track toward Ophir.
              GPS: N 37°51.00' W 107°46.72'

▼ 0.0   Continue along main track.
4.1 ▲ SO Summit of Ophir Pass. Zero trip meter.

▼ 0.5 SO Tracks on left.
3.6 ▲ SO Tracks on right.

▼ 1.0 UT Track on left.
3.1 ▲ BL Track on right.

▼ 3.2 SO Track on right.
0.9 ▲ SO Track on left.

▼ 3.7 SO Columbine Lake Trail on left (FR 820).
0.4 ▲ SO Columbine Lake Trail on right (FR 820).

▼ 3.9 SO Cross bridge.
0.2 ▲ SO Cross bridge.

▼ 4.1   End at intersection with US 550.
0.0 ▲   From intersection of US 550 and San
              Juan County 8 (FR 679), zero trip
              meter and proceed along County 8
              toward Ophir.
              GPS: N 37°50.84' W 107°43.44'

Talus mounds beside the road at the Ophir Pass summit

Alta Ghost Town Trail

STARTING POINT Telluride
FINISHING POINT Alta Lakes
TOTAL MILEAGE 12.4 miles (one-way)
UNPAVED MILEAGE 4.2 miles
DRIVING TIME 1 hour
ROUTE ELEVATION 9,700 to 11,100 feet
USUALLY OPEN Mid-June to October
DIFFICULTY RATING 2
SCENIC RATING 8

Special Attractions

■ Alta, a well-preserved ghost town.
■ The picturesque Alta Lakes.

History

Alta was the company town for the Gold
King Mine, where ore deposits were discovered in 1878. The mine operated as recently
as the 1940s. Gold, silver, copper, and lead
were mined and transported in aerial tram-
cars from the Gold King and other mines to
Ophir Loop, two miles farther down the
mountain.

Alta's Gold King was a very rich mine, but
it was expensive to operate because of its
high elevation. Fortunately, L. L. Nunn
found a way to reduce expenses by running
electrical power to the mine. In 1881, he
organized a contract with the Westinghouse
company to construct an electrical plant in
Ames, less than three miles away. George
Westinghouse was a supporter of alternating
current electricity against the strong opposi-
tion of Thomas Edison.

The plant harnessed the power of the San
Miguel River, transmitting 3,000 volts of
alternating current back up to the Gold King
Mine. Encouraged by the success of this first
alternating current power transmission plant
in America, Nunn expanded his venture to
supply the city of Telluride, as well as many
nearby mines, and installed transmission
lines across Imogene Pass. Subsequently,
alternating current electricity became widely
used in Colorado and the world.

A makeshift sign along the trail

There were three mills at Alta, all of which have burned down. The last one burned in 1945 while seven men were underground. The superintendent ordered the portal to be dynamited in order to cut off the draft that was feeding the fire even though his son was one of the men inside.

Due to the longevity of the Gold King Mine, Alta thrived longer than most high-country mining towns. Visitors can still see quite a few well-preserved historic buildings, including a boardinghouse, cabins, and some more substantial homes. Alta never had a church or a post office.

Description

FR 632 is a well-maintained, unpaved road that leaves Colorado 145 and proceeds east to the township of Alta. In good weather conditions, passenger vehicles can easily traverse the road.

FR 632 leaves Colorado 145, 1.7 miles north of the intersection with the start of Southwest #20: Ophir Pass Trail. On the west side of Colorado 145 at the Ophir Pass turnoff is the road to the township of Ames, where the electricity for Alta was generated from the power station built in 1881.

The very scenic Alta Lakes are located at timberline, a short distance above Alta ghost

The boardinghouse at the Gold King Mine

town. The lakes have good picnic facilities and public toilets.

The road to the lakes is also easy, but the road that encircles the lakes can be extremely rutted and muddy. This section of road would have a difficulty rating of 5.

A number of maps suggest that there is a road from the Alta Lakes to the Telluride ski area. However, when we were last there, this road had been blocked off. We were not able to confirm that this road would be reopened.

Current Road Information

Grand Mesa, Uncompahgre and Gunnison National Forests
Norwood Ranger District

PO Box 388
Norwood, CO 81423
970-327-4261

Map References

Benchmark's *Colorado Road & Recreation Atlas,* p. 110
USFS   Uncompahgre National Forest
USGS   1:24,000   Telluride, Gray Head, Ophir
1:100,000 Silverton
Maptech CD-ROM:
Southwest/Durango/Telluride
Colorado Atlas & Gazetteer, p. 76
The Roads of Colorado, p. 122
Trails Illustrated, #141

Built in 1881, Ames power station serviced the Alta Mine (circa 1933)

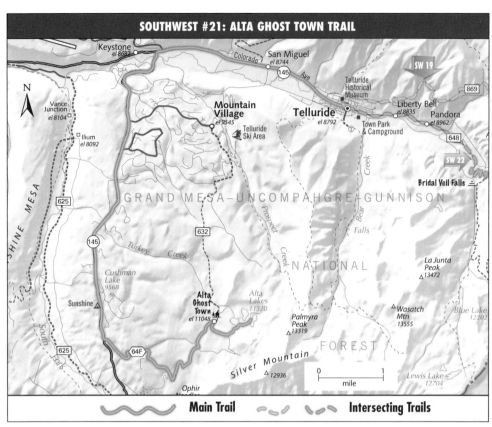

N

Keystone *el 8682*
San Miguel *el 8744*
Colorado
Colorado Ave
145
SW 19
869

Vance Junction *el 8104*
Mountain Village *el 9545*
Telluride Ski Area
Telluride *el 8792*
Telluride Historical Museum
Town Park & Campground
Liberty Bell *el 8835*
Pandora *el 8962*

Ilium *el 8092*

648

SW 22

Bridal Veil Falls

625

GRAND MESA–UNCOMPAHGRE–GUNNISON

SHINE MESA

632

Prospect Creek

Bear Creek

Falls

NATIONAL

La Junta Peak △13472

145

Turkey Creek

Cushman Lake 9568

Sunshine △

Alta Ghost Town *el 11048*

Alta Lakes 11320

Palmyra Peak △13319

Wasatch Mtn 13555

Blue Lake 12202

FOREST

South Park

625

64F

Silver Mountain △12936

0   1
mile

Lewis Lake 12704

Ophir Needles

~~~ **Main Trail**   ~~ ~~ **Intersecting Trails**

Alta Lakes

Route Directions

▼ 0.0   In front of the Telluride Visitor Information Center on W. Colorado in Telluride, zero trip meter and proceed west out of town.
GPS: N 37°56.37' W 107°49.15'

▼ 3.1   TL   Follow Colorado 145 south toward Ophir.
▼ 7.8   SO   Sunshine Campground on right.
▼ 8.2   TL   National Forest access sign on right (FR 632) toward Alta and Alta Lakes. Unpaved. Zero trip meter.
GPS: N 37°53.02' W 107°53.25'

▼ 0.0   Proceed toward Alta on FR 632.
▼ 2.9   SO   Track on right.

▼ 3.0   SO   Track on left with private property sign. Gate. Sign to stay on designated roads.
▼ 3.0   SO   Track on right.
▼ 3.4   SO   Private track on left. Private track on right.
▼ 3.7   BR   Ghost town of Alta. Zero trip meter at small sign for Alta Lakes.
GPS: N 37°53.13' W 107°51.28'

▼ 0.0   Follow track on right toward Alta Lakes.
▼ 0.3   BL   Road forks.
▼ 0.5   Road forks. End at Alta Lakes. There are numerous spots for picnics and tracks winding around the lakes.
GPS: N 37°52.83' W 107°50.87'

view of Alta in about 1895

MINING OPERATIONS

Gold and silver deposits are frequently found together. Both are formed when molten minerals are forced up from deep within the earth into the bedrock. Usually gold and silver also exist with other minerals such as pyrite (fool's gold) and galena (which has a silvery appearance). Commonly, the host rock is quartz.

Over time, erosion breaks down the rock deposits and the gold is freed and left in pure form. Water then disperses the free gold along streambeds. In its free form, gold exists in a variety of shapes: nuggets, scale, shot, grains, and dust. These free deposits are known as "placers" when the gold is found in streambeds or along stream banks. A deposit of gold that is contained in a rock formation is called a "lode."

Placer Mining. Because placers are relatively easy to find, they are normally the first gold deposits discovered in any area. Miners typically follow the placers upstream to the mother lode.

Placer mining is the simplest form of mining operations, because it merely involves separating the free gold from the dirt, mud, or gravel with which it is mixed. The process takes a number of forms:

- simple panning
- sluicing, the method for processing larger volumes, using the same principle as panning
- dredging, the method for processing even larger volumes of rock (Dredge mining utilizes a power-driven chain of small buckets mounted on a barge, leaving in its wake squalid piles of washed rock, marking its course for decades to come. Processing tons of rock and soil quickly, dredges overcame the problem of large quantities of low-grade gravel. Dredges could move up to three-quarters of a million yards of earth per annum.)
- hydraulic mining is used where the ancient riverbeds had long since disappeared, leaving the gold on dry land and some distance from any existing stream. Hydraulic mining uses hoses to bring water from up to three miles distant and wash away the extraneous material to recover the gold.

Placer mining was known as "poor man's mining" because panning a creek could be done with very little capital. Colorado's placer production has been nearly all gold.

Hard-Rock Mining. Hard-rock mining involves digging ore out of the ground and recovering it from the quartz (or other minerals) surrounding it. Hard-rock mining in its simplest form involves tunneling horizontally under the vein (either directly or from an initial vertical shaft), then digging out the ore into mine cars placed beneath it. In the 1800s, mining cars were pulled by mules along tracks laid in the mines. If the mine incorporated a vertical shaft, then a hoist would lift the ore to the surface. Digging the shafts was made much easier during the 1870s, when hand drilling techniques were made obsolete by machine drills and dynamite.

Once extracted from the mine, the gold had to be separated from the host rock. To do this economically in the latter half of the nineteenth century, mining companies made use of stamp mills. Large structures that processed the ore in stages, stamp mills required water and a downhill slope. Milling involved progressively crushing the ore, then processing it chemically to extract the precious metal. Mine workers brought the ore into the mill and fed it into a stamper, which weighed up to a ton. The stamper crushed the host rock; then a slurry of the crushed ore and water was fed over a series of mercury-coated amalgamation plates, which captured the precious metal.

Because hard-rock mining required substantial capital, only large mining corporations normally undertook hard-rock mining operations. The men who worked the mines were employees of the larger corporations.

Typical Amalgamation/Concentration Mill

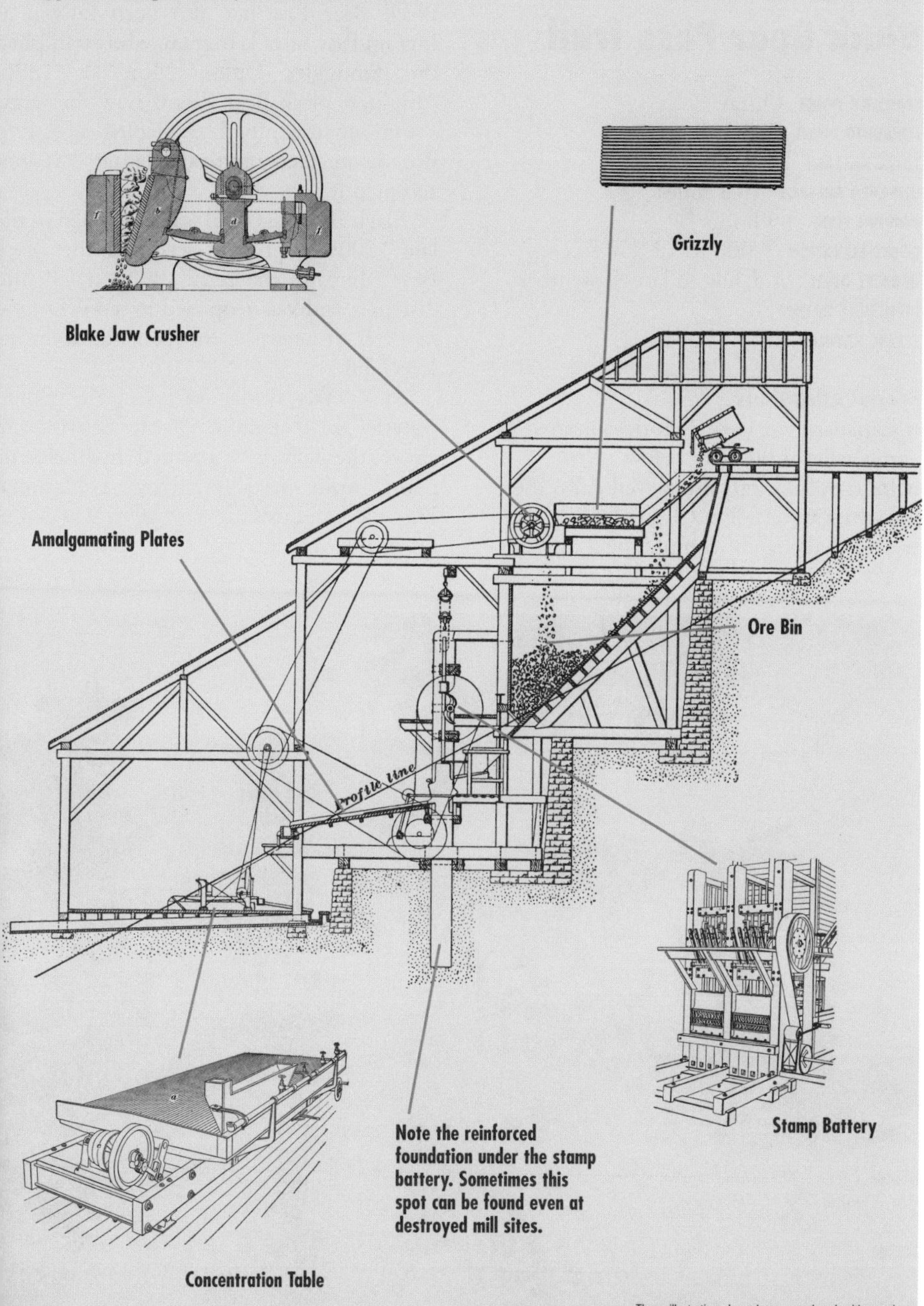

Blake Jaw Crusher

Grizzly

Amalgamating Plates

Ore Bin

Profile line

Stamp Battery

Note the reinforced foundation under the stamp battery. Sometimes this spot can be found even at destroyed mill sites.

Concentration Table

These illustrations have been reproduced with permission of BenchMark Publishing of Colorado. These pictures and many others can be found in *The Mining Camps Speak*, an invaluable reference to a better understanding of mining camps, ghost towns, and mining techniques of the American West, by Beth and Bill Sagstetter.

Black Bear Pass Trail

STARTING POINT Ouray
FINISHING POINT Telluride
TOTAL MILEAGE 25.2 miles
UNPAVED MILEAGE 10.1 miles
DRIVING TIME 2.5 hours
ROUTE ELEVATION 9,000 to 12,840 feet
USUALLY OPEN Mid-July to late September
DIFFICULTY RATING 6
SCENIC RATING 10

Special Attractions

- Expansive views of Telluride, nestled in the valley 4,000 feet below.
- Ingram Falls and Bridal Veil Falls, the highest waterfall in Colorado.
- The challenge of completing a difficult 4WD trail.

History

Black Bear Pass has also been known as Ingram Pass, after J. Ingram, who established the Smuggler Union Mine in 1876. Although Black Bear Pass is now the name commonly used, the U.S. Geological Survey Board on Geographical Names has not accepted it.

Black Bear Pass Trail was developed in the late 1800s to provide access to the Black Bear Mine. In the early 1900s, it fell into disrepair and was reopened as a 4WD road in 1959 through the efforts of the Telluride Jeep Club.

At 365 feet, Bridal Veil Falls is the highest waterfall in Colorado. On the canyon rim above the falls is a restored hydroelectric plant, built in 1904. Now a National Historic Landmark, it once generated power for nearby mines.

Pack train on Black Bear Pass trail, circa 1908

A view descending from Black Bear pass toward Telluride

Description

The one-way Black Bear Pass Trail is one of the more difficult 4WD trails included in this book. It can be dangerous and has claimed many lives during the past 30 years. Just how difficult you will find it depends on your vehicle, your 4WD experience, and current road conditions. We have included it here for drivers who wish to try a more demanding road and because it is justly famous for its scenery.

The trail is not suitable for a full-sized vehicle due to the very tight switchbacks on the steep, western side of the pass. It is the only trail in this book that we have never traveled in our Suburban. Taken slowly and carefully in a small vehicle, this pass should not be beyond the abilities of any driver who has comfortably undertaken a broad selection of the easier trails included in this book.

The portion of the trail that earns its difficulty rating stretches from the summit of the pass to the U-turn at the entrance to the power station at Bridal Veil Falls, about four miles below. This section is one way and can only be traveled from east to west.

From the Million Dollar Highway, US 550, the road starts its climb toward the pass.

About a mile before the summit of the pass, the road flattens out, leading through lovely meadows with alpine lakes and waterfalls in beautiful tundra countryside.

At the summit, a network of tracks provides a multitude of wide, panoramic views. The abundance of tracks makes it difficult to identify the main track down to the west side; but by looking down into the valley (to the northwest of the summit), you can easily see the road you need to take.

Dropping down from the pass, the road heads into a treeless alpine valley but remains quite easy. The water crossings may be of concern to some drivers, but the base of the road is sound and should pose little problem when taken carefully. Some slipping on the talus surface must be anticipated. Up to this point, the degree of difficulty would be rated only 3. As you will have noticed, though, the spectacular views are already evident.

The road continues to get rougher and more difficult as you descend. Obstacles that may prove too challenging for inexperienced four-wheelers include tight, off-camber switchbacks, loose talus, and narrow shelf roads with thousand-foot-plus drop-offs. Because of the difficulty of this section of road, local 4WD rental businesses do not permit their vehicles to cross this pass.

The very tight switchbacks commence about two miles below the summit. The road has a formidable reputation, and when you arrive at this series of switchbacks, it is easy to see why. One switchback is particularly notorious and is justly considered impassable for full-sized vehicles. A short distance farther, the road crosses the creek directly above Ingram Falls.

The route provides many scenic views of Bridal Veil Falls and the historic hydroelectric power station. Numerous mines and tramways are evident during the journey down into Telluride.

We think this is one of the great 4WD roads of Colorado. Although experienced

Near Black Bear Pass

Telluride viewed from the trail

four-wheelers may not find it as difficult as it is reputed to be, we are sure they will consider it a great drive.

Current Road Information

Grand Mesa, Uncompahgre and Gunnison
National Forests
Norwood Ranger District
PO Box 388
1150 Forest Street
Norwood, CO 81423
970-327-4261

Map References

Benchmark's *Colorado Road & Recreation Atlas,* p. 110
USFS   Uncompahgre NF or San Juan NF
USGS   1:24,000   Telluride, Ironton
1:100,000   Silverton
Maptech CD-ROM:
Southwest/Durango/Telluride
Colorado Atlas & Gazetteer, p. 76
The Roads of Colorado, pp. 122, 123
Trails Illustrated, #141

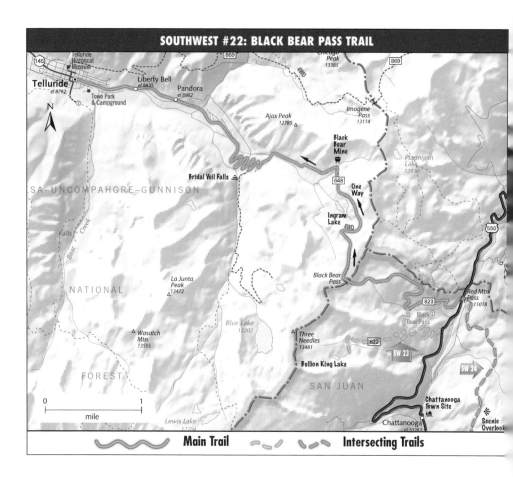

SOUTHWEST #22: BLACK BEAR PASS TRAIL

Main Trail **Intersecting Trails**

Route Directions

▼ 0.0   In front of Beaumont Hotel at 5th and Main in Ouray, zero trip meter and proceed south out of town, remaining on US 550.
GPS: N 38°01.30' W 107°40.29'

▼ 12.9   TR   Onto Black Bear Pass Trail (FR 823), just beyond the summit marker of Red Mountain. Only a small, brown 4WD signpost marks the track. Zero trip meter.
GPS: N 37°53.81' W 107°42.78'

▼ 0.1   SO   Mine remains.
▼ 1.0   BR   Road forks. To the left is Southwest #23: Bullion King Lake Trail.
▼ 1.2   BR   Track on left. Waterfall on right.
▼ 1.3   SO   Track on right.
▼ 2.9   BL   Road forks.
▼ 3.2   Summit of Black Bear Pass. Zero trip meter.
GPS: N 37°53.99' W 107°44.52'

▼ 0.0   Proceed from the summit on main track, heading northwest down the hill.
▼ 1.6   SO   Track on left to Ingram Lake.
▼ 1.8   SO   Spectacular view of Telluride on left.
▼ 2.1   BL   Track on right goes to Black Bear Mine. Cross through creek.
▼ 2.6   SO   Very tight downhill switchback.
▼ 2.8   SO   Mine portal on the right side of road.
▼ 3.2   SO   Mine on left.
▼ 3.3   SO   Cross through Ingram Creek at Ingram Falls. Mine ruins.
GPS: N 37°55.34' W 107°45.60'

▼ 4.1   UT   One-way sign. End of difficult section. Closed driveway to old power station on left.
▼ 4.7   SO   Mine entrance (closed) on right.
▼ 5.0   SO   Parking at Bridal Veil Falls.

▼ 5.5   SO   Cross Ingram Falls runoff.
▼ 5.8   SO   Cross over creek.
▼ 6.4   SO   Tracks on left and right.
▼ 6.5   BL   Entrance to Pandora Mill on right
             (no access).
▼ 6.6   SO   Tailing ponds on left and Pandora Mill
             on right.
             GPS: N 37°55.84′ W 107°46.70′

▼ 6.9   SO   Road changes from dirt to paved surface.
▼ 8.0   SO   Telluride Cemetery on right.
▼ 8.4   SO   Enter Telluride's main street (W. Colorado).
▼ 9.1   End at Visitor Information Center on W.
             Colorado (main street) in Telluride.
             GPS: N 37°56.37′ W 107°49.15′

Bridal Veil Falls and the power station built to generate power for the Smuggler-Union Mine

Bullion King Lake Trail

STARTING POINT Southwest #22: Black Bear
Pass Trail
FINISHING POINT US 550
TOTAL MILEAGE 2.8 miles (one-way)
UNPAVED MILEAGE 2.8 miles
DRIVING TIME 30 minutes
ROUTE ELEVATION 11,000 to 12,400 feet
USUALLY OPEN Mid-July to late September
DIFFICULTY RATING 3
SCENIC RATING 7

Special Attractions
■ Panoramic scenery.
■ Small alpine lakes.

Description

Most maps do not show this road, and those that do are not accurate.

This road can be used as a side route of Southwest #22: Black Bear Pass Trail or as an alternative for those not wishing to tangle with Black Bear—one of the most notorious 4WD roads in the San Juan Mountains. This trail provides some wonderfully panoramic scenery and an opportunity for a short hike to a few small, tranquil alpine lakes at the end of the trail.

The route commences one mile from the beginning of Southwest #22: Black Bear Pass Trail. It includes a section of narrow shelf road, a hundred feet or more above Porphyry Gulch Creek, which is sound but provides little opportunity for passing oncoming vehicles. It pays to look ahead and let any oncoming vehicles come through before proceeding.

Taking a side road toward Silverton rather than returning all the way to Black Bear Pass Trail can vary the return trip.

Current Road Information
Grand Mesa, Uncompahgre and Gunnison
National Forests
Ouray Ranger District
2505 South Townsend Avenue
Montrose, CO 81401
(970) 240-5300

Map References
Benchmark's *Colorado Road & Recreation
Atlas,* p. 110
USFS San Juan National Forest
USGS 1:24,000 Ironton
1:100,00 Silverton
Maptech CD-ROM:
Southwest/Durango/Telluride
Colorado Atlas & Gazetteer, p. 76
The Roads of Colorado, p. 123
Trails Illustrated, #141

Route Directions

▼ 0.0   Begin at the intersection of US 550 and
Southwest #22: Black Bear Pass Trail
(FR 823), just south of the summit
marker of Red Mountain. Only a small,
brown 4WD signpost marks the track.
Zero trip meter and proceed along FR 823.
2.8 ▲   End at intersection with US 550.
     GPS: N 37°53.81′ W 107°42.78′

▼ 0.1   SO   Mine remains.
2.7 ▲   SO   Mine remains.

▼ 1.0   BL   Road forks. Black Bear Pass Trail
continues on the right fork.
1.8 ▲   BR   Intersection with Southwest #22: Black
Bear Pass Trail. Left goes to Black Bear
Pass and right goes to US 550.
     GPS: N 37°53.70′ W 107°43.51′

▼ 1.1   SO   Cross through creek.
1.7 ▲   SO   Cross through creek.

▼ 1.3   SO   Track on left to campsite. Then cross
through creek.
1.5 ▲   SO   Cross through creek. Track on right to
campsite.

▼ 1.4   SO   Track on left to campsite on cliff.
1.4 ▲   SO   Track on right to campsite on cliff.

▼ 1.5   BR   Track on left to campsite. Then alternate
route from US 550 enters on left.
1.3 ▲   BL   Alternate route from US 550 enters
on right.

▼ 2.3   SO   Mine remains on the left. Cross through
creek. Mine remains on the right.

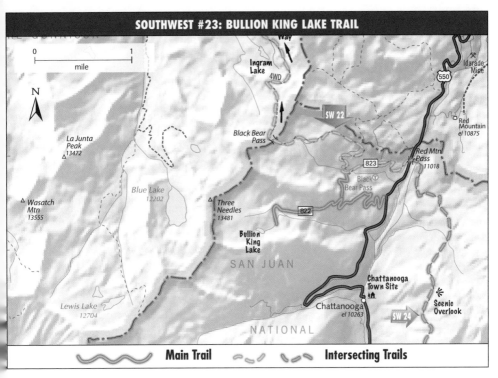

0		1
	mile	

N

Ingram Lake 4WD

Way

SW 22

Idarado Mine

550

Black Bear Pass

Red Mountain el 10875

La Junta Peak 13472

823

Red Mtn Pass 11018

Blue Lake 12202

Black Bear Pass

Wasatch Mtn 13555

Three Needles 13481

822

Bullion King Lake

SAN JUAN

Chattanooga Town Site

Lewis Lake 12704

Chattanooga el 10263

Scenic Overlook

SW 24

NATIONAL

Main Trail   **Intersecting Trails**

0.5 ▲ SO Mine remains on the left. Cross through creek. Mine remains on the right.

▼ 2.6 SO Cross through creek.
0.2 ▲ SO Cross through creek.

▼ 2.7 SO Waterfall on right.
0.1 ▲ SO Waterfall on left.

▼ 2.8 Road comes to an end. Follow walking path to Bullion King Lake. Zero trip meter.
0.0 ▲ UT Turn around and proceed back down the mountain away from Bullion King Lake.
       GPS: N 37°53.16′ W 107°44.42′

▼ 0.0 UT Turn around and proceed back down the mountain away from Bullion King Lake.
2.8 ▲ Road comes to an end. Follow walking path to Bullion King Lake. Zero trip meter.

▼ 0.1 SO Waterfall on left.
2.7 ▲ SO Waterfall on right.

▼ 0.2 SO Cross through creek.
2.6 ▲ SO Cross through creek.

▼ 0.5 SO Mine remains on the left. Cross through

creek. Mine remains on the right.

2.3 ▲ SO Mine remains on the left. Cross through creek. Mine remains on the right.

▼ 1.3 BR Fork in road. Left reconnects with Black Bear Pass Trail.
1.5 ▲ BL Fork in road.

▼ 1.6 BR Track on left.
1.2 ▲ BL Track on right.

▼ 2.2 SO Campsite on right.
0.6 ▲ SO Campsite on left.

▼ 2.7 SO Fork in road to private cabin.
0.1 ▲ BR Fork in road to private cabin.

▼ 2.8 End at US 550.
0.0 ▲ At the intersection of US 550 and FR 822, zero trip meter and proceed west on FR 822.
       GPS: N 37°53.33′ W 107°43.12′

Brown's Gulch Trail

STARTING POINT Intersection with US 550, 0.2 miles south of Red Mountain Pass

FINISHING POINT Intersection with US 550, 0.7 mile north of turnoff to Southwest #20: Ophir Pass Trail

TOTAL MILEAGE 5.8 miles

UNPAVED MILEAGE 5.8 miles

DRIVING TIME 1 hour

ROUTE ELEVATION 10,200 to 12,100 feet

USUALLY OPEN June to October

DIFFICULTY RATING 3

SCENIC RATING 8

Special Attractions

- Great views of the of U.S. Basin and the surrounding mountains.
- Historic mining area.
- Located near many other trails.

Description

The entrance to this trail is unmarked. It is located opposite the entrance to Southwest #22: Black Bear Pass Trail. There are some old buildings that were part of the Longfellow Mine on the left of the entrance to the trail. Although long since deserted, they are in good condition.

The trail climbs through the forest after leaving US 550. It is narrow, but passing oncoming vehicles is not a problem. After about two miles, the trail rises above timberline and views are expansive. Initially, there is a good view to the west of Red Mountain in the foreground and beyond it to the row of mountain peaks from Ophir Pass to Black Bear Pass. A short distance farther, as you travel just below the ridgeline, walk the short distance to a wonderful overlook into U.S. Basin and across to McMillan Peak to the east.

Continuing, the trail descends back into

Old buildings from the Longfellow Mine

A view of the trail near an overlook into U.S. Basin

the forest. The road travels through some recent mining operations before it proceeds to switchback down the mountain and then to rejoin US 550.

The road is reasonably steep in places and can become muddy. However, in good weather conditions the surface is sound and should not pose problems. Only a few short sections of shelf road, all of which are low on the "white knuckle" rating, are encountered along this route.

Current Road Information

San Juan National Forest
Columbine Ranger District (East)
PO Box 439
367 South Pearl Street
Bayfield, CO 81122
(970) 884-2512

Map References

Benchmark's *Colorado Road & Recreation Atlas,* p. 110
USFS San Juan National Forest or Uncompahgre National Forest
USGS 1:24,000 Ironton, Silverton
        1:100,00 Silverton
Maptech CD-ROM:
        Southwest/Durango/Telluride
Colorado Atlas & Gazetteer, p. 76
The Roads of Colorado, p. 123
Trails Illustrated, #141

Route Directions

▼ 0.0   From the top of Red Mountain Pass on US 550, proceed east onto the unmarked track beside old buildings from the Longfellow Mine and zero trip meter.

This turn is approximately opposite Southwest #22: Black Bear Pass Trail.

5.8 ▲ End at intersection with US 550 at Red Mountain Pass.
GPS: N 37°53.76′ W 107°42.79′

▼ 0.1 BR Track on left. Follow sign to US Basin (FR 825).
5.7 ▲ BL Track on right.

▼ 0.2 SO Track on right.
5.6 ▲ SO Track on left.

▼ 0.7 BR Track on left. Then cross over creek.
5.1 ▲ BL Cross over creek. Then track on right.

▼ 0.8 BL Fork in road. Track on right goes to private property.
5.0 ▲ SO Entrance to private property is on left.

▼ 0.9 SO Cross over creek.
4.9 ▲ SO Cross over creek.

▼ 1.0 BR Track on left.
4.8 ▲ BL Track on right.

▼ 1.3 SO Cross through creek.
4.5 ▲ SO Cross through creek.

▼ 2.8 SO Faint track on left to a scenic overlook of mountains and basin; a cabin is visible on mountain across the valley.
3.0 ▲ SO Faint track on right to an overlook; a cabin is visible on mountain across the valley.
GPS: N 37°52.98′ W 107°42.33′

▼ 3.6 SO Track on right.
2.2 ▲ SO Track on left.

▼ 3.7 BL Track on right. Then bear right at the fork in road.
2.1 ▲ BR Continue past track entering on right. Then bear right at the next fork.

▼ 3.8 SO Road enters on left. Pass through mining area.
1.9 ▲ BL Mining operations area. Fork in road.

▼ 3.9 SO Mine portal on left.

SOUTHWEST #24: BROWNS GULCH TRAIL

1.8 ▲ SO Mine portal on right.

▼ 4.1 SO Cross over creek.
1.7 ▲ SO Cross over creek.

▼ 5.8 End at intersection with US 550.
0.0 ▲ From US 550 (about 0.7 miles north of Southwest #20: Ophir Pass Trail), zero trip meter and proceed east along FR 825-an unmarked dirt track.
GPS: N 37°51.50′ W 107°43.40′

Bandora Mine and Clear Lake Trail

STARTING POINT Intersection of US 550 and CR 7/FR 585

FINISHING POINT Clear Lake

TOTAL MILEAGE 14.5 miles (to Clear Lake)

UNPAVED MILEAGE 14.5 miles

DRIVING TIME 1 hour

ROUTE ELEVATION 9,600 to 12,300 feet

USUALLY OPEN June to October

DIFFICULTY RATING 3

SCENIC RATING 9

Special Attractions

■ Scenic, particularly the picturesque setting of Clear Lake.

■ Good camping, both developed and backcountry.

History

Silver was first discovered near Mineral Creek in 1882 and several rich strikes followed. The Bandora Mine was acquired by the Blanco Mining Company in 1940 and worked into the 1950s. By that time there were no accommodations for the miners at the mine and most commuted from Silverton.

Description

To start this trail, turn off US 550 onto CR 7, a maintained gravel road, and proceed toward Mineral Creek Campground. The road travels beside South Mineral Creek, along which you can see numerous ponds and lodges created by ever-industrious beavers.

The route directions first guide you to Bandora Mine and then to Clear Lake. At the 3.7-mile point, you pass the turnoff for the lake on the right-hand side, which is worth noting as you pass. After traveling to

A section of the trail as it switchbacks up to Clear Lake

The abandoned Bandora Mine and Mill, 1950

the Bandora Mine and South Park, the route directions will direct you back to this point to visit Clear Lake.

Shortly after this intersection, you pass the USFS Mineral Creek Campground on the left. Many good backcountry camping opportunities are also located along this trail. After passing the campground, the road becomes rougher but it is not difficult. After traveling through a short section of dense forest, then through open scrub country, the trail passes below Bandora Mine and enters a large, level meadow known as South Park. This segment of the route ends at an old cabin on the far side of the park.

Returning to the turnoff to Clear Lake, zero your trip meter and turn left, proceeding toward Clear Lake. Immediately starting to ascend, you travel through pine and spruce forest. Although this part of the route is along a shelf, it is not difficult, and there are plenty of passing spots. The segment to Clear Lake is a little rough and rocky, but the surface is sound.

The road proceeds to switchback up the mountain, climbing above timberline and providing a couple of good observation points for the waterfalls created by Clear Creek. Finally, the road levels off as you enter the very picturesque basin that cradles Clear Lake.

Current Road Information
San Juan National Forest
Columbine Ranger District (East)
PO Box 439
367 South Pearl Street
Bayfield, CO 81122
(970) 884-2512

A camping site at the end of the trail

An old cabin at the end of the trail

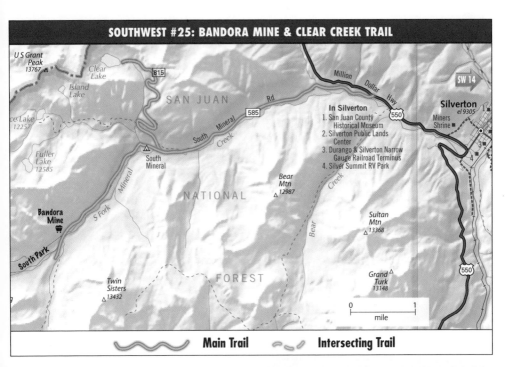

Main Trail   Intersecting Trail

Map References

Benchmark's *Colorado Road & Recreation
        Atlas,* p. 110
USFS   San Juan NF or Uncompahgre NF
USGS   1:24,000   Silverton, Ophir
        1:100,000 Silverton
Maptech CD-ROM:
        Southwest/Durango/Telluride
Colorado Atlas & Gazetteer, p. 76
The Roads of Colorado, pp. 138, 139
Trails Illustrated, #141

Route Directions

▼ 0.0   From US 550, zero trip meter and turn
           onto County 7/FR 585. A sign indicates
           this is a NF Access road to South
           Mineral Campground.
           GPS: N 37°49.11' W 107°42.10'

▼ 1.0   SO   Cross over bridge.
▼ 1.6   SO   Track on right.
▼ 2.3   SO   Cross over creek.
▼ 3.7   BL   Fork in road. Turning right goes to
             Clear Lake (you will return to this inter-
             section later). Continue toward USFS
             Mineral Campground, remaining on

A waterfall on the side road to Clear Lake

main road.
GPS: N 37°48.32' W 107°45.74'

▼ 4.3   SO USFS South Mineral Campground on left. Parking on right. Continue straight ahead.
GPS: N 37°48.29' W 107°46.31'

▼ 4.5   SO Cross over creek with Rico-Silverton Trailhead and waterfall on the right.

▼ 6.3   SO Cross through creek.

▼ 6.4   SO Bandora Mine and Mill ruins on the right.
GPS: N 37°47.20' W 107°47.99'

▼ 6.6   SO Track on left goes to a cabin.

▼ 6.7   SO Cross though creek.

▼ 6.9   End of track. A mining cabin is across the creek.
GPS: N 37°46.80' W 107°48.11'

Continuation from Clear Lake turnoff

▼ 0.0   From County 7 (South Mineral Creek Campground access road), zero trip meter and proceed up the hill.
GPS: N 37°48.32' W 107°45.74'

▼ 2.8   SO Closure gate.

▼ 3.3   SO Waterfall on left.
GPS: N 37°49.22' W 107°46.46'

▼ 3.5   SO Mine straight ahead at switchback. Proceed up hill.
GPS: N 37°49.17' W 107°46.33'

▼ 4.1   BR Track on left goes on up the mountain.

▼ 4.4   End of trail at beautiful Clear Lake.
GPS: N 37°49.58' W 107°46.90'

Clear Lake

Cunningham Gulch and Stony Pass Trail

STARTING POINT Howardsville from Southwest #6: Silverton to Animas Forks Ghost Town road

FINISHING POINT Intersection of FR 520 and Colorado 149, between Lake City and Creede

TOTAL MILEAGE 37.7 miles

UNPAVED MILEAGE 37.2 miles

DRIVING TIME 3.25 hours

ROUTE ELEVATION 9,200 to 12,588 feet

USUALLY OPEN Mid-June to late October

DIFFICULTY RATING 5

SCENIC RATING 9

Special Attractions

- A varied and scenic 4WD trail.
- A challenging stream crossing.
- Relative solitude; this trail has less traffic than many others in the peak summer months.

History

Cunningham Gulch is named for Major W. H. Cunningham, who brought a party of mining investors from Chicago through the area. Stony Pass got its name because of its rocky terrain. It was also known as Hamilton Pass, after the builder of the first wagon road over the pass, and as Rio Grande Pass.

The Stony Pass crossing holds a great deal of historic interest. The Ute used the trail for centuries, and Spanish artifacts have also been found in the area. It is believed that Charles Baker discovered the pass in 1860. Baker led a party of prospectors to the area

Cunningham Gulch

well before the Brunot Treaty officially opened the territory to white settlers in 1873.

Major E. M. Hamilton built a wagon road along the route in 1872, which was improved seven years later. During this period, the road was heavily used as a stage route and a major supply line for the 4,000 mines working claims in the area.

When the railroad reached Silverton in 1882, the pass was less frequently used. However, the route remained open and was classified as a state highway at one point in the early 1900s. Eventually, it was completely abandoned until the Forest Service reopened it in the 1950s as a 4WD recreational route.

This trail starts in the town of Howardsville, originally named Bullion City for the Bullion City Company, which laid out the town as a promotional settlement in late 1872. However, the following year the residents changed the name to Howardsville, for the individual who built the first cabin on the site.

Because Howardsville was growing at the same time as nearby Silverton, the two towns became rivals. Howardsville was named the first county seat in Colorado in 1874, but the following year voters moved the county seat to Silverton. Howardsville consisted of about 30 buildings and at its peak had about 150 residents. The post office that served Howardsville was claimed to have been the first in western Colorado; it operated from 1874 to 1939.

Two brothers who headed west from New York to seek their fortunes in silver, established Highland Mary, a town near the Highland Mary Mill and Highland Mary Mine at the top of Cunningham Gulch. The enterprising Ennis brothers took the rather eccentric step of consulting a fortune-teller to decide where they should begin prospecting. The fortune-teller reportedly pointed to an area on the map where the two would find treasure.

The brothers named the area Highland Mary and continued to visit the spiritualist for advice. Her instructions regarding where

and how to find ore led the brothers on a peculiar search through the mountains, during which they unknowingly crossed over some rich gold veins. Occasionally they made some lucky discoveries. By 1885, the Ennis brothers had invested about a million dollars in the mine and had paid the spiritualist another fifty thousand. The pair ended up bankrupt; they sold the mine and their nearby elaborate house and returned to New York.

The new owners of the mine prospected by more conventional methods, and Highland Mary immediately began to pay off. It became one of the best producing mines in Cunningham Gulch and operated sporadically through the years until 1952. All that remains today are the ruins of the mill.

On the eastern side of the pass, near where Pole Creek flows into the Rio Grande River, is the site that was proposed for Junction City. The town was platted after ore was found in 1894, but the ore soon ran out and most of the miners left before any construction occurred.

Description

The route is a long 4WD trail with varied scenery. It is lightly used compared to other, better-known routes in the San Juan Mountains during summer. It is usually open by the middle of June.

The trail begins in Howardsville, between Silverton and Animas Forks, as an attractive 2WD road, running alongside Cunningham Creek and up Cunningham Gulch. Within a couple of miles it becomes steeper, narrower, and rougher as it climbs up a ledge overlooking the gulch. It soon narrows to the width of one vehicle with occasional pull-offs for passing.

As the road approaches the summit of Stony Pass, it levels out into a beautiful alpine valley with typical vegetation and many wildflowers. Open portals of mines and decaying cabins remain.

From the pass, the road tracks along the edge of the Weminuche Wilderness Area and follows the headwaters of the Rio Grande

River. At around the ten-mile point, the road reveals great access to some quiet and scenic fishing spots.

The road from the summit has a relatively gentle grade. The biggest potential problems in the first ten miles of the descent are mud and occasional shallow creek crossings. The few rough stretches are relatively short.

At the 11.8-mile point is the Pole Creek crossing, which is the deepest of all of the stream crossings included in this book. If you are traveling early in the season, we advise you to start this trail in the morning because snowmelt causes the creek to rise significantly throughout the day. Later in the day, this crossing could be impassable or cause vehicle damage. Later in the season, the creek can still be two feet deep, but the creek bed is sound. With good tires and a slow, steady pace, high clearance 4WD vehicles should have no problem crossing.

The degree of difficulty of the next few miles is a matter of how long it has been since the last rain. When wet, the road can be very muddy. Assess the situation and proceed cautiously when crossing the creeks; sharp approach and departure angles at these crossings can hang up your vehicle. The trail winds through forest in this section, so once it gets muddy, it can stay that way for some time. Clearance between the trees is narrow at times, and the road has a couple of short, rocky sections.

Current Road Information

San Juan Public Lands Center
BLM & National Forest Combined Office
15 Burnett Court
Durango, CO 81301
(970) 247-4874

Rio Grande National Forest
Divide Ranger District (Creede)
Third and Creede Avenue
Creede, CO 81130
(719) 658-2556

Old, lonely miner's cabin and some of the many mines near the summit of Stony Pass

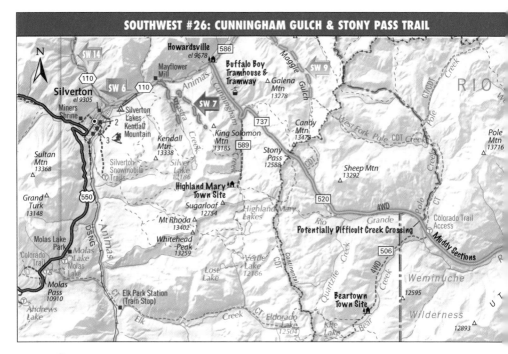

Map References

Benchmark's *Colorado Road & Recreation Atlas,* pp. 110, 111

USFS   Uncompahgre NF
        Rio Grande NF

USGS   1:24,000   Howardsville, Finger Mesa, Weminuche Pass, Pole Creek Mtn., Rio Grande Pyramid, Hermit Lakes, Little Squaw Creek
        1:100,00   Silverton

Maptech CD-ROM:
        Southwest/Durango/Telluride

Trails Illustrated, #140, #141

The Roads of Colorado, pp. 139, 140

Colorado Atlas & Gazetteer, pp. 77, 78

Route Directions

▼ 0.0   At intersection of Southwest #6 and the turnoff to Cunningham Gulch in Howardsville, zero trip meter and proceed toward Cunningham Gulch and Stony Pass.

5.8 ▲   End at intersection with Southwest #6: Silverton to Animas Forks Ghost Town.
         GPS: N 37°50.12' W 107°35.69'

▼ 0.2   BR Fork in road. Left goes to Old Hundred Mine.

5.6 ▲   SO Road on right to Old Hundred Mine.

▼ 1.0   SO Old Hundred Mine and Mill on left.
4.8 ▲   SO Old Hundred Mine and Mill on right.

▼ 1.3   SO Site of Green Mountain Mill on right.
4.5 ▲   SO Site of Green Mountain Mill on left.

▼ 1.5   SO Buffalo Boy Tramhouse and Tramway on left.
4.3 ▲   SO Buffalo Boy Tramhouse and Tramway on right.

▼ 1.7 BR/BL Follow sign to Creede via Stony Pass on County 3. Road enters on left and goes back to Old Hundred Mine. Then road forks and the track on right goes to the town site of Highland Mary in 3.4 miles.
4.1 ▲BL/BR Intersection. Roads enter on left and right. Continue on middle road.

▼ 2.5   SO Cross through creek.
3.3 ▲   SO Cross through creek.

▼ 3.2   BR Short track on left.
2.6 ▲   BL Short track on right.

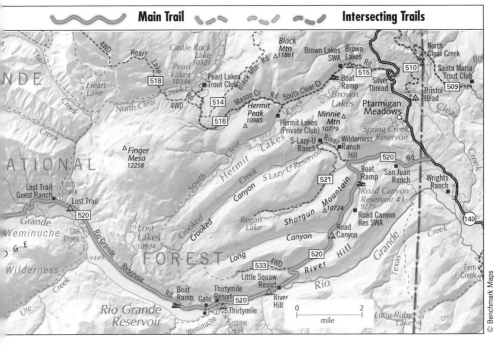

Main Trail   **Intersecting Trails**

▼ 3.3   BR   Track on left.
2.5 ▲   BL   Track on right.

▼ 3.5   BL   Cross under tramway. Track entering on right.
2.3 ▲   BR   Track entering on left. Cross under tramway.

▼ 3.7   SO   Small bridge over creek.
2.1 ▲   SO   Small bridge over creek.

▼ 4.0   SO   Cross over creek. Small track on right.
1.8 ▲   SO   Small track on left. Cross over creek.

▼ 4.7   SO   Small track on right.
1.1 ▲   SO   Small track on left.

▼ 5.8   SO   Summit of Stony Pass. Zero trip meter.
0.0 ▲   Continue along road.
      GPS: N 37°47.75′ W 107°32.93′

▼ 0.0   Continue along road.
6.2 ▲   SO   Summit of Stony Pass. Zero trip meter.

▼ 0.2   SO   Cabin and mine tracks on right.
6.0 ▲   SO   Cabin and mine tracks on left.

▼ 1.0   SO   West Ute Creek and Ute Creek trails.
5.2 ▲   SO   West Ute Creek and Ute Creek trails.

▼ 1.3   SO   Cross over creek.
4.9 ▲   SO   Cross over creek.

▼ 3.6   SO   Cross over creek.
2.6 ▲   SO   Cross over creek.

▼ 5.3   SO   Track to river on right.
0.9 ▲   SO   Track to river on left.

▼ 5.4   SO   Pass through fence line.
0.8 ▲   SO   Pass through fence line.

▼ 6.0   SO   Cross through Pole Creek. Beware that this crossing may be deep.
0.2 ▲   SO   Cross through Pole Creek. Beware that this crossing may be deep.
      GPS: N 37°45.86′ W 107°28.00′

▼ 6.2   BL   Intersection. FR 506 on right goes to Beartown site and Kite Lake. Town site of Junction City. Zero trip meter.
0.0 ▲   Continue toward Stony Pass and Silverton.
      GPS: N 37°45.72′ W 107°27.97′

▼ 0.0　　Continue toward Rio Grande Reservoir and Creede. Pole Creek Trail is on left.

16.2 ▲　SO　Pole Creek Trail on right. Intersection. FR 506 on left goes to Beartown site and Kite Lake. Town site of Junction City. Zero trip meter.

▼ 0.7　SO　Cross through creek.
15.5 ▲　SO　Cross through creek.

▼ 1.0　SO　Gate.
15.2 ▲　SO　Gate.

▼ 2.1　SO　Cross through Sweetwater Creek.
14.1 ▲　SO　Cross through Sweetwater Creek.

▼ 2.3-2.5 SO　Beaver ponds and dams on right.
13.7-13.9 ▲ SO　Beaver ponds and dams on left.

▼ 2.9　SO　Cross through creek.
13.3 ▲　SO　Cross through creek.

▼ 3.0　SO　Water crossing. This one can be deep.
13.2 ▲　SO　Water crossing. This one can be deep.

▼ 3.2　SO　Cross through creek.
13.0 ▲　SO　Cross through creek.

▼ 3.5　SO　Cross through creek.
12.7 ▲　SO　Cross through creek.

▼ 4.3　SO　Cross through creek.
11.9 ▲　SO　Cross through creek.

▼ 4.4-4.8 SO　Series of water crossings. None difficult.
11.4-11.8 ▲　SO　Series of water crossings. None difficult.

▼ 5.0　SO　Cattle guard. Cross through creek.
11.2 ▲　SO　Cross through creek. Cattle guard. Sign reads "Brewster Park."

▼ 5.7　SO　Track on right to river.
10.5 ▲　SO　Track on left to river.

▼ 6.5　BR　Track on left. Cross through creek.
9.7 ▲　SO　Cross through creek. Track on right.

▼ 6.7　SO　Track to campsites on right.

9.5 ▲　SO　Track to campsites on left.

▼ 7.1　SO　Track on right.
9.1 ▲　SO　Track on left.

▼ 7.9　SO　Lost Trail Creek Trailhead on left. Cattle guard.
8.3 ▲　SO　Cattle guard. Lost Trail Creek Trailhead on right.

▼ 8.3　SO　Bridge over creek. Lost Trail Campground on right.
7.9 ▲　SO　Lost Trail Campground on left. Bridge over creek.

▼ 9.1　SO　Ute Creek Trailhead on right. Public restrooms.
7.1 ▲　SO　Public restrooms. Ute Creek Trailhead on left.

▼ 10.1　SO　Cattle guard. Overlook to Rio Grande Reservoir.
6.1 ▲　SO　Overlook to Rio Grande Reservoir. Cattle guard.
GPS: N 37°44.99′ W 107°19.87′

▼ 13.2　SO　Track on right to reservoir. Public restrooms available.
3.0 ▲　SO　Track on left to reservoir. Public restrooms available.

▼ 14.2　SO　Seasonal closure gate. Track on right to Rio Grande Reservoir (no access).
2.0 ▲　SO　Track on left to Rio Grande Reservoir (no access). Seasonal closure gate.
GPS: N 37°43.35′ W 107°16.00′

▼ 14.8　SO　Turnoff on right to USFS Thirtymile Campground, Weminuche Trailhead, Thirtymile Resort, and Squaw Creek Trailhead.
1.4 ▲　SO　Turnoff on left to USFS Thirtymile Campground, Weminuche Trailhead, Thirtymile Resort, and Squaw Creek Trailhead.

▼ 16.2　SO　USFS River Hill Campground. Zero trip meter.
0.0 ▲　　Continue along main road toward Stony Pass.

The trail crossing Pole Creek

GPS: N 37°43.81' W 107°13.86'

▼ 0.0   Continue along main road.
9.5 ▲ SO USFS River Hill Campground. Zero trip meter.

▼ 1.2 SO Cattle guard. Road on left to Sawmill Canyon.
8.3 ▲ SO Road on right to Sawmill Canyon. Cattle guard.

▼ 2.8-4.8 SO Road Canyon Reservoirs #1 and #2 on right.
4.7- ▲ SO Road Canyon Reservoirs #1
6.7   and #2 on left.

▼ 3.3 SO USFS campground.
6.2 ▲ SO USFS campground.

▼ 3.6 SO Seasonal gate.
5.9 ▲ SO Seasonal gate.

▼ 4.4 SO Public toilets.
5.1 ▲ SO Public toilets.

▼ 5.1 SO Public toilets.
4.4 ▲ SO Public toilets.

▼ 6.2 BR Fork in the road.
3.3 ▲ BL Track on right.

▼ 6.8 SO Cattle guard.
2.7 ▲ SO Cattle guard.

▼ 9.0 SO Pavement begins.
0.5 ▲ SO Unpaved road.

▼ 9.5   Cattle guard. Stop sign. End at intersection with Colorado 149. Lake City is approximately 32 miles to the left; Creede is approximately 20 miles to the right.
0.0 ▲   At intersection of Colorado 149 with FR 520, zero trip meter and proceed onto FR 520. Creede is approximately 20 miles east.
          GPS: N 37°47.41' W 107°07.71'

Old Lime Creek Road

STARTING POINT Intersection of US 550 and south end of FR 591

FINISHING POINT Intersection of US 550 and north end of FR 591

TOTAL MILEAGE 11.2 miles

UNPAVED MILEAGE 11.2 miles

DRIVING TIME 1.5 hours

ELEVATION RANGE 8,757 to 9,810 feet

USUALLY OPEN Year-round

BEST TIME TO TRAVEL Mid-April through mid-October

DIFFICULTY RATING 2

SCENIC RATING 10

Special Attractions

- Amazing views of Lime Creek, Twilight Peak, and Weminuche Wilderness across Lime Creek Valley from an exciting shelf road.
- Shady backcountry or developed campsites and scenic picnic areas on Lime Creek.
- Scenic lake with beaver dams and lily pads.
- Aspen fall color viewing.
- Snowmobile trail in winter.
- Scenic, leisurely side trip off US 550.
- Interesting, historic original route of US 550.

History

The Ute Indians, who lived in this area as early as the fourteenth and fifteenth centuries, first used this track for hunting. Game, fowl, and wild vegetation were plentiful, allowing the Ute to live prosperously.

Things began changing when Spanish explorers, who ventured into the rugged San Juans searching for silver, first visited the area in 1765 and then again in 1776. Although the Spanish were unsuccessful extracting silver from the San Juans, in the mid-1800s white settlers from the east came to the San Juans to test their own silver and gold thumbs. Indian hunting trails helped prospectors penetrate the rugged wilderness.

At first ore-seekers attempted to extract silver, but a discovery of gold near Denver in 1858 caused gold miners to flock to this area as well. Supplies were brought in and ore was initially shipped out using burros over the primitive animal and Indian

Intricate stone workings added to Lime Creek Road by the Civilian Conservation Corps in the 1930s.

ording Lime Creek on the short spur at the end of the trail

hunting trails, but as the size and weight of the loads increased, wider roads were needed for freight wagons. Teams of oxen and horses were needed to power these loads over the steep terrain.

Sturdy roadbeds began being constructed for these freight wagons. Work to develop a viable freight route between Durango and Silverton began in earnest in the early 1900s after the federal government passed road legislation and the state of Colorado instituted a Highway Department. The intro-duction of the automobile, and along with it the tourism industry, necessitated even more road improvements, including the elimination of steep grades and sharp turns where possible.

Many of the original wagon roads were abandoned in favor of an easier route, which would become the highway we know today as US 550, the Million Dollar Highway. Construction was complete on the highway in July 1924, when the road was dedicated on Red Mountain Pass.

Lime Creek Valley

This road was originally part of the highway, when in 1918 construction began to upgrade the wagon roads. This section of road was constructed as part of the highway in order to avoid Coal Bank Hill and Potato Mountain. With advancements in road building technology and the debris clearing from the 26,000-acre Lime Creek wildfire (1879), the road took its current route along the shale slopes of Engineer Mountain and over Coal Bank Pass. The San Juan National Forest now maintains this beautiful and historic section of the original Million Dollar Highway.

Description

The trail, FR 591, begins off of US 550, approximately three miles north of Purgatory Ski Area and 20 miles south of Silverton. It starts out as a wide, maintained dirt road with plenty of room for two oncoming cars to pass. Beginning to gain elevation almost immediately, the trail alternately travels through large, open meadows

Lime Creek flows beside Lime Creek USFS Campground

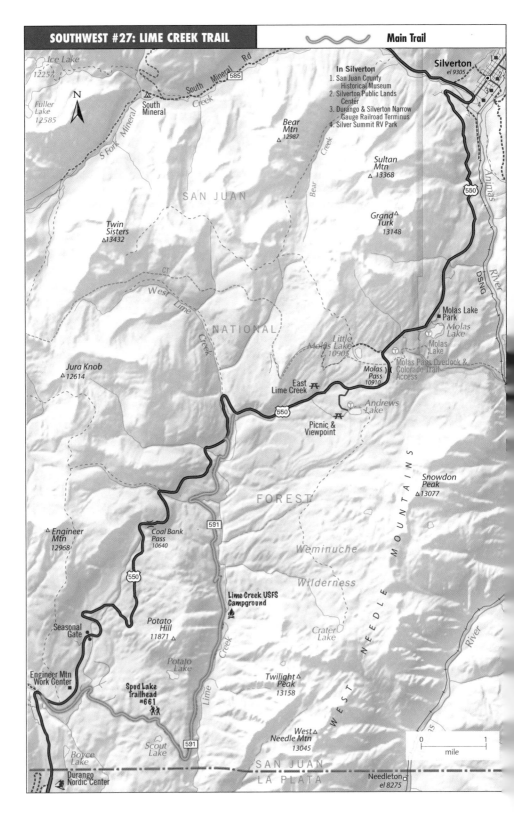

~~~~~~ **Main Trail**

In Silverton
1. San Juan County Historical Museum
2. Silverton Public Lands Center
3. Durango & Silverton Narrow Gauge Railroad Terminus
4. Silver Summit RV Park

Silverton el 9305

Ice Lake 12257

Fuller Lake 12585

South Mineral

S Fork Mineral

South Mineral Creek

585

Bear Mtn △ 12987

Bear Creek

Sultan Mtn △ 13368

Animas

550

SAN JUAN

Twin Sisters △13432

Grand Turk △ 13148

CT

West Lime Creek

NATIONAL

Molas Lake Park

Molas Lake

Little Molas Lake 10905

Molas Lake

Jura Knob △ 12614

Molas Pass 10910

Molas Pass Overlook & Colorado Trail Access

East Lime Creek

Andrews Lake

550

Picnic & Viewpoint

Snowdon Peak △ 13077

FOREST

591

Weminuche

Engineer Mtn △ 12968

Coal Bank Pass 10640

550

Wilderness

Lime Creek USFS Campground

River

Crater Lake

Potato Hill 11871 △

Seasonal Gate

WEST

Potato Lake

Lime Creek

Engineer Mtn Work Center

Spud Lake Trailhead #661

Twilight Peak △ 13158

NEEDLE

MOUNTAINS

Scout Lake

591

West Needle Mtn △ 13045

Boyce Lake

Durango Nordic Center

SAN JUAN
LA PLATA

Needleton el 8275

N

0 ——— 1
mile

and thick forest of aspens and conifer trees.

At mile 2.8, you arrive at Scout Lake. An attractive spot for landscape painters, in summer the lake is thick with blooming lily pads. The lake is also home to abundant wildlife, including geese, ducks, and beaver and their lodges. In fact, if you stay on the lookout for wildlife along the entire length of the trail, you will more than likely be rewarded. The area is home to an abundance of deer and other wildlife.

Past Scout Lake, the road becomes a wide shelf road with scenic views down into Lime Creek Valley below. Rocks embedded in the shelf section of this road give this trail its difficulty rating of 2, no obstacle for a high-clearance 4WD vehicle. The track continues to climb and is corrugated in sections. As the ascent levels off, the road becomes a narrow, very high shelf with sheer drop-offs. Although the trail is narrow, there are plenty of pullouts for passing oncoming vehicles. High above Lime Creek, views along this section of the trail are quite spectacular, especially in fall when brilliant yellow aspens blanket the valley. Also along this section of the trail, worthy of note are the intricate, stone "road guards" constructed by the Civilian Conservation Corps in the 1930s.

Gradually the trail descends into the valley and follows alongside Lime Creek, a wide meandering creek. As the trail follows the creek over a talus slide, the trail becomes quite rocky. On Lime Creek, a pleasant USFS campground (East Lime Creek USFS Campground) has well-shaded spots with picnic tables, fire grates, a pit toilet. The site is also a pristine fishing spot. If you plan to camp at this idyllic location in the summer months, remember to bring the bug spray for mosquitoes.

Beyond the campground, the trail begins to climb again away from creek. In general the trail evens out and becomes a smooth dirt road at its north end as it winds through stands of aspen. In some sections, the road is still a shelf, although it is wider and the drop-off less severe than along previous sections of the trail.

Just beyond the historical marker and before the trail ends, a track to the right follows the old route of US 550 just less than a mile to the north of the main trail. This dead-end sidetrack has a fun crossing through Lime Creek and is interesting to explore. The original route of US 550 is still quite evident and even some pavement from the original road remains. The track also passes a few old, wrecked cars that appear to have fallen from US 550 above. The track dead-ends after 0.7 mile. Both this sidetrack and the track off the main trail to the south (a left turn off the main trail) both have some nicely shaded backcountry campsites.

The trail ends at the intersection with US 550, 11 miles south of Silverton and 12 miles north of Purgatory Ski Area. This route is a scenic and exciting snowmobile trail in winter months.

Current Road Information

San Juan National Forest
Columbine Ranger District (East)
PO Box 439
367 South Pearl Street
Bayfield, CO 81122
(970) 884-2512

Map References

Benchmark's *Colorado Road & Recreation Atlas,* p. 110
USFS   San Juan National Forest
USGS   1:24,000   Snowdon Peak, Engineer Mtn.
　　　　1:100,000 Silverton
Maptech CD-ROM:
　　　　Southwest/Durango/Telluride
The Roads of Colorado, pp. 38, 39
Colorado Atlas & Gazetteer, p. 76
Trails Illustrated, #140
Other: *Jeep Trails of the San Juans*

Route Directions

▼ 0.0　　Trail begins at intersection of US 550 and FR 591, signed National Forest Access Old Lime Creek Road, approximately 3 miles north of Purgatory Ski Area and 20 miles south of Silverton. Turn onto unpaved road and head south.

2.8 ▲ SO Trail ends at intersection with US 550 at south end at FR 591, Old Lime Creek Road.
GPS: N37°39.51' W107°48.56'

▼ 0.11 SO Cattle guard.
2.69 ▲ SO Cattle guard.

▼ 0.40 SO Undeveloped camping area on right.
2.4 ▲ SO Undeveloped camping area on left.

▼ 0.82 SO Private road on left.
1.98 ▲ SO Private road on right.
GPS: N37°39.44' W107°47.88'

▼ 1.03 SO Private road on left.
1.77 ▲ SO Private road on right.
GPS: N37°39.59' W107°47.73'

▼ 1.2 SO Private driveway on left and track on right.
1.6 ▲ SO Private driveway on right and track on left.

▼ 1.31 SO Private driveway on left.
1.49 ▲ SO Private driveway on right.
GPS: N37°39.51' W107°47.66'

▼ 2.8 SO Pond on right. Zero trip meter.
0.0 ▲ Continue southwest on FR 591.
GPS: N37°39.12' W107°46.45'

▼ 0.0 Continue northeast on FR 591.
3.0 ▲ SO Pond on left. Zero trip meter.

▼ 0.1 SO Trailhead on left is #661 to Potato Lake.
2.9 ▲ SO Trailhead on right is #661 to Potato Lake.

▼ 0.53 SO Track on left.
2.47 ▲ SO Track on right.
GPS: N37°38.96' W107°46.12'

▼ 1.05 SO Trailhead on right.
1.95 ▲ SO Trailhead on left.

▼ 3.0 SO USFS East Lime Creek Campground on right. Zero trip meter.
0.0 ▲ Continue south on FR 591, Old Lime Creek Road.
GPS: N37°40.00' W107°45.26'

▼ 0.0 Continue north on FR 591, Old Lime Creek Road.
5.4 ▲ SO USFS East Lime Creek Campground

An old car that may have fallen from US 550 directly above now rests on the spur that runs north from Old Lime Creek Road on left. Zero trip meter.

▼ 0.42 SO Track on right to undeveloped campsites.
4.98 ▲ SO Track on left to undeveloped campsites.
GPS: N37°40.34' W107°45.12'

▼ 1.8 SO Track on right to overlook of creek.
3.6 ▲ SO Track on left to overlook of creek.

▼ 2.8 SO Campsite on right.
2.6 ▲ SO Campsite on left.

▼ 3.5 SO Cross over creek.
1.9 ▲ SO Cross over creek.
GPS: N37°42.37' W107°45.68'

▼ 3.7 SO Track on left.
1.7 ▲ SO Track on right.

▼ 4.1 SO Track on right.
1.3 ▲ SO Track on left.

▼ 4.8 SO Cross over creek.
0.6 ▲ SO Cross over creek.

▼ 5.2 SO Track on right and Historical Marker on left.
0.2 ▲ SO Track on left and Historical Marker on right.
GPS: N37°43.27' W107°44.94'

▼ 5.3 SO Track on left to undeveloped campsites and track on right follows old US 550 north 0.7 mile.
0.1 ▲ SO Track on right to undeveloped campsites and track on left follows old US 550 north 0.7 mile.

▼ 5.4 SO Trail ends at intersection with US 550, signed National Forest Access Old Lime Creek Road, approximately 11 miles south of Silverton and 12 miles north of Purgatory Ski Area.
0.0 ▲ Trail begins at intersection of US 550 and the north end of FR 591 signed National Forest Access Old Lime Creek Road.
GPS: N37°43.27' W107°45.01'

Bolam Pass Trail

STARTING POINT Silverton
FINISHING POINT Intersection of FR 578 and Colorado 145
TOTAL MILEAGE 45.7 miles
UNPAVED MILEAGE 24.3 miles
DRIVING TIME 2.5 hours
ROUTE ELEVATION 9,200 to 11,340 feet
USUALLY OPEN Early July to October
DIFFICULTY RATING 2
SCENIC RATING 7

Special Attractions
■ Attractive stream valley through the Purgatory ski area.
■ Historic mining area of special significance in the effort to develop the first atomic bomb during World War II.
■ Can connect with Southwest #29: Fall Creek Trail.

History
The Ute Indians used Bolam Pass long before miners entered the area in the early 1860s. In 1881, the pass was surveyed as a railroad route. The road was improved during World War II to provide access to the Graysill Mine.

This mine produced the vanadium and uranium used in the first atomic bombs. It continued to supply these substances for bomb construction until 1963. At its peak, there were 450 working claims in the area, but only about 20 men endured the harsh winters (not to mention the odorless, tasteless, radioactive radon gas), enabling the mine to remain in production year-round.

Description
The route commences in Silverton and follows US 550, the Million Dollar Highway, south for 21 miles to the Purgatory ski resort. The route passes through the resort and its network of paved roads without signs to guide you. An unpaved road exits the resort area and travels through the winter ski runs.

Numerous camping spots with good creek access are just off the road for about 10 miles from the Purgatory ski resort.

Until the creek crossing 9.9 miles from the resort, the road is a well-maintained, unpaved, passenger-vehicle road. From this point, it gets narrower and rougher but remains an easy road for 4WD vehicles.

At the 16.1-mile point from Purgatory ski resort, the road passes the only remaining building (and a Forest Service information board) for the Graysill Mine. A mile and one-half farther, past an attractive alpine lake, is Bolam Pass, at which point the road traverses a relatively level ridge through open meadows and patches of forest. Through the alpine meadows along this section of the trail, pleasant views of adjoining hillsides and many wildflowers are abundant.

After about two miles, the road starts its descent and becomes rougher, with considerable erosion evident. It is not difficult, but it does require caution.

Around 22 miles from the Purgatory ski resort, the road returns to easy passenger-vehicle conditions and follows Barlow Creek as it descends into the valley.

The trail ends when it intersects with Colorado 145, 5.3 miles south of Lizard Head Pass. On the opposite side of the highway is FR 535, which is Southwest #29: Fall Creek Trail.

Current Road Information

San Juan National Forest
Columbine Ranger District (East)
PO Box 439
367 South Pearl Street
Bayfield, CO 81122
(970) 884-2512

San Juan National Forest
Dolores Ranger District
100 North Sixth
PO Box 210
Dolores, CO 81323
(970) 882-7296

Map References

Benchmark's *Colorado Road & Recreation Atlas,* p. 110
USFS   San Juan NF
Maptech CD-ROM:
    Southwest/Durango/Telluride
USGS 1:24,000   Engineer Mtn.,
    Hermosa Peak, Mt. Wilson
    1:100,000 Silverton
The Roads of Colorado, p. 138
Colorado Atlas & Gazetteer, p. 76
Trails Illustrated, #141

Route Directions

▼ 0.0   In front of the Silverton Visitor Center (at the intersection of Greene Street and US 550), zero trip meter and proceed south on US 550.
21.0 ▲   End at the Silverton Visitor Center.
    GPS: N 37°48.29' W 107°40.18'

▼ 21.0   TR Into Purgatory ski resort and zero trip meter.
0.0 ▲   Continue along US 550 toward Silverton.
    GPS: N 37°37.71' W 107°48.59'

▼ 0.0   Keep to the right.
8.4 ▲   TL Onto US 550. Zero trip meter.

▼ 0.3   SO Intersection. Dirt road enters from the right.
8.1 ▲   SO Intersection. Remain on paved road.

▼ 0.4   TR Paved road continues to the left. Follow unpaved road.
8.0 ▲   TL Onto paved road.

▼ 1.0   SO Hermosa Travel board to the right has a map posted. Sign to Bolam Pass.
7.4 ▲   BR Continue toward Purgatory Ski Resort.

▼ 2.1   BR Track on left.
6.3 ▲   BL Track on right.

▼ 3.1   BR Elbert Creek Road on left to Cafe de Los Piños. Follow Hermosa Creek Trail.
5.3 ▲   BL Elbert Creek Road on right to Cafe de Los Piños. Stay on main road.

~~~~ Main Trail   **~~/ ~~~ Intersecting Trails**

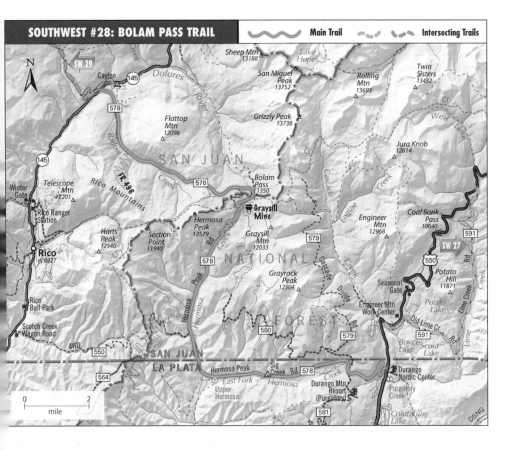

▼ 3.5   BL   Intersection. Remain on FR 578.
4.9 ▲   BR   Intersection. Remain on FR 578.

▼ 4.4   SO   Intersection.
4.0 ▲   SO   Intersection.

▼ 4.8   SO   Access to trout streams.
3.6 ▲   SO   Access to trout streams.

▼ 6.6   SO   USFS Sig Creek Campground.
1.8 ▲   SO   USFS Sig Creek Campground.

▼ 6.7   SO   Track on left.
1.7 ▲   SO   Track on right.

▼ 7.5   SO   Track on left to campsites.
0.9 ▲   SO   Track on right to campsites.

▼ 7.6   SO   Cross over creek.
0.8 ▲   SO   Cross over creek.

▼ 8.4   SO   Road on left crosses through East Fork

of Hermosa Creek to Hermosa Creek
Trailhead FR 577. Follow sign toward
Bolam Pass. Zero trip meter.

0.0 ▲   Continue along route.
GPS: N 37°37.92′ W 107°54.95′

▼ 0.0   Continue along main road.
7.9 ▲   Road on right. Zero trip meter.

▼ 0.4   SO   Cattle guard.
7.5 ▲   SO   Cattle guard.

▼ 0.7-1.6   SO   Numerous campsites.
6.4-7.2 ▲   SO   Numerous campsites.

▼ 1.5   SO   Cross through creek.
6.4 ▲   SO   Cross through creek.
GPS: N 37°38.80′ W 107°55.65′

▼ 2.2   SO   Intersection. FR 550 on left has signs
to Rico and Hotel Draw via Scotch
Creek. Follow FR 578 toward Bolam

The last cabin remaining at the Graysill Mine site

and Rico via Barlow Creek.

5.7 ▲   SO Intersection on right to Rico and Hotel Draw. Remain on FR 578.

▼ 2.9   SO Cattle guard.
3.4 ▲   SO Cattle guard.

▼ 3.5   SO Cross through creek.
4.4 ▲   SO Cross through creek.

▼ 5.7   SO Cross over creek.
2.2 ▲   SO Cross over creek.

▼ 5.8   SO Cross through creek.
2.1 ▲   SO Cross through creek.

▼ 6.2   SO Cross over creek.
1.7 ▲   SO Cross over creek.

▼ 7.6   SO Cross over creek.
0.3 ▲   SO Cross over creek.

▼ 7.7   SO Graysill Mine ruins on right.
0.2 ▲   SO Graysill Mine ruins on left.

▼ 7.9   SO Cabin and historic marker. Zero trip meter.
0.0 ▲   Continue along main road.
        GPS: N 37°42.82′ W 107°53.93′

▼ 0.0   Continue along main road.
8.4 ▲   SO Cabin and historic marker. Zero trip meter.

▼ 0.3   SO Lake on left.
8.1 ▲   SO Lake on right.

▼ 0.4   SO Track on right is FR 578B.
8.0 ▲   SO FR 578B on left.

▼ 1.4   SO Bolam Pass summit (unmarked).
7.0 ▲   SO Bolam Pass summit (unmarked).
        GPS: N 37°43.15′ W 107°53.89′

▼ 2.3   TR Cross over creek. Intersection.
6.1 ▲   TL Intersection. Cross over creek.

▼ 4.6   SO Cross through creek.
3.8 ▲   SO Cross through creek.

| ▼ 4.8 | SO | Track on left to creek. |
| 3.6 ▲ | SO | Track on right to creek. |

| ▼ 5.0 | SO | Cabin. |
| 3.4 ▲ | SO | Cabin. |

| ▼ 5.8 | SO | Cross over creek. |
| 2.6 ▲ | SO | Cross over creek. |

| ▼ 5.9 | SO | Intersection with FR 496 on left. |
| 2.5 ▲ | SO | Intersection with FR 496 on right. |

| ▼ 6.9 | SO | Barlow Lake on right. |
| 1.5 ▲ | SO | Barlow Lake on left. |

▼ 8.1	BL	FR 476 Intersection on right. USFS Cayton Campground.
0.3 ▲	BR	USFS Cayton Campground. FR 476 on left.
		GPS: N 37°46.15′ W 107°58.91′

▼ 8.4		Bridge over Dolores River. End at intersection with Colorado 145. Southwest #29: Fall Creek Trail is across Colorado 145.
0.0 ▲		At intersection of Colorado 145 and FR 578, zero trip meter and proceed along FR 578. Cross bridge over Dolores River.
		GPS: N 37°46.14′ W 107°59.25′

SOUTHWEST REGION TRAIL #29

Fall Creek Trail

STARTING POINT Intersection of Colorado 145 and County 57P

FINISHING POINT Intersection of FR 535 and Colorado 145

TOTAL MILEAGE 48.6 miles

UNPAVED MILEAGE 47.7 miles

DRIVING TIME 3 hours

ROUTE ELEVATION 7,600 to 10,800 feet

USUALLY OPEN Early July to October

DIFFICULTY RATING 2

SCENIC RATING 7

Special Attractions

■ Long, but fairly easy, trail through Uncompahgre and San Juan National Forests.

■ Relatively remote country with good backcountry campsites.

■ Numerous side roads, including many that are challenging 4WD trails.

■ Provides access for other activities, including good hiking, hunting, and fishing.

■ Can connect with Southwest #28: Bolam Pass Trail.

Description

This route starts on paved road for the first mile and then becomes a maintained, gravel road until Woods Lake. The lake is a scenic fishing and picnic spot, but overnight camping is not allowed. However, there are plenty of backcountry camping sites outside the immediate vicinity of the lake. From Woods Lake, the road narrows slightly but remains easy and continues to travel through the forest of cottonwood, pine, spruce, and aspen trees. Along the road, after passing the lake, there are some large stands of aspen that make for a particularly scenic drive in the fall.

As you continue towards Beaver Park, the forest opens up to a number of large meadows. When dry, the road remains easy, but there are sections that become quite boggy when wet. Most of the way navigation is easy. On occasion multiple forest side roads intersect within a short distance.

Other than in hunting season, when the area becomes a hive of activity, this route offers the opportunity for a solitary, tranquil journey through two of Colorado's magnificent national forests.

The trail ends at the intersection with Colorado 145. On the opposite side of the highway is FR 578, which is Southwest #28: Bolam Pass Trail.

Current Road Information

San Juan National Forest
Dolores Ranger District
100 North Sixth

PO Box 210
Dolores, CO 81323
(970) 882-7296

Grand Mesa, Uncompahgre and Gunnison
National Forests
Ouray Ranger District
2505 South Townsend Avenue
Montrose, CO 81401
(970) 240-5300

Map References

Benchmark's *Colorado Road & Recreation
Atlas,* p. 109
USFS   San Juan NF or Uncompahgre NF
USGS 1:24,000   Little Cone, Beaver
Park, Groundhog Mtn., Dolores
Peak, Mt. Wilson
1:100,000 Dove Creek
Maptech CD-ROM:
Southwest/Durango/Telluride
Colorado Atlas & Gazetteer, p. 76
The Roads of Colorado, pp. 122, 137, 138
Trails Illustrated, #141 (incomplete)

Route Directions

▼ 0.0   From Colorado 145 (northwest of
Telluride), zero trip meter and proceed
along County 57 P. This road is marked
with a National Forest access sign to
Fall Creek Road. Then cross bridge
over the San Miguel River.
3.7 ▲   End at intersection with Colorado 145.
Telluride is to the right.
GPS: N 37°59.60' W 108°01.28'

▼ 0.9   SO Cross over creek.
2.8 ▲   SO Cross over creek.

▼ 1.1   SO Picnic spot with grill on right.
2.6 ▲   SO Picnic spot with grill on left.

▼ 3.7   BR Road forks. Proceed toward Woods
Lake on 57 P (also FR 618). County
Road 56 L goes to the left. Zero
trip meter.
0.0 ▲   Continue along road.
GPS: N 37°56.76' W 108°02.16'

▼ 0.0   Continue toward the lake.
3.6 ▲   BR Onto County Road 57 P. Zero trip
meter.

▼ 1.3   SO Enter Uncompahgre National Forest.
2.2 ▲   SO Leave Uncompahgre National Forest.

▼ 2.5   SO Track on right.
1.1 ▲   SO Track on left.

▼ 2.7   SO Cross bridge over creek.
0.9 ▲   SO Cross bridge over creek.

▼ 3.1   SO Small track on left.
0.5 ▲   SO Small track on right.

▼ 3.6   TR Intersection. Woods Lake is straight
ahead. Zero trip meter and cross over
creek.
0.0 ▲   Continue along main road toward
Colorado 145.
GPS: N 37°53.16' W 108°03.23'

▼ 0.0   Continue along FR 618 toward Beaver
Park.
11.3 ▲ TL Cross over creek, then T-intersection.
Woods Lake is to the right. Zero
trip meter.

▼ 0.6   SO Small track on right.
10.7 ▲ SO Small track on left.

▼ 1.7   SO Small track crosses the road.
9.5 ▲   SO Small track crosses the road.

▼ 3.6   BR Track on left.
7.7 ▲   BL Track on right.

▼ 4.8   SO Track on left.
6.5 ▲   SO Track on right.

▼ 6.3   SO Cross over McCulloch Creek.
5.0 ▲   SO Cross over McCulloch Creek.

▼ 7.2   SO Track on left.
4.1 ▲   SO Track on right.

▼ 8.0   SO Small track on right.
3.3 ▲   SO Small track on left.

Main Trail   **Intersecting Trail**

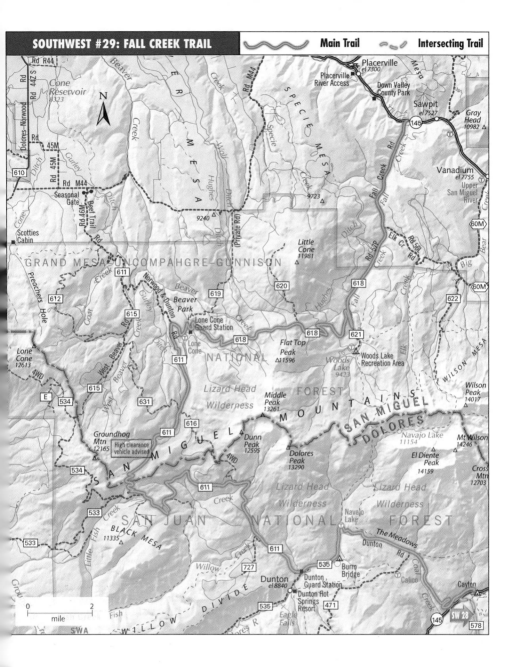

▼ 8.4   SO   Cattle guard.
 .9 ▲   SO   Cattle guard.

▼ 8.8   BL   Track on left.
 .5 ▲   BR   Track on right.

▼ 9.1   SO   Track on left.
 .2 ▲   SO   Track on right.

▼ 10.1   TL   FR 619 intersects on right. Then cross Main Beaver Creek.
1.2 ▲   TR   Cross Main Beaver Creek; FR 619 is straight ahead.
       GPS: N 37°53.41' W 108°07.96'

▼ 10.6   TR   Intersection. Proceed toward Noorwood and Dunton. Lone Cone

Station is to the left.

0.7 ▲ TL Lone Cone Station is straight ahead.
GPS: N 37°53.37′ W 108°10.29′

▼ 10.9 SO Cattle guard.
0.4 ▲ SO Cattle guard.

▼ 11.3 TL Intersection. Noorwood is to the right. Turn toward Dunton onto FR 611 and zero trip meter.
0.0 ▲ Continue along FR 618.
GPS: N 37°53.95′ W 108°10.17′

▼ 0.0 Continue along FR 611.
9.3 ▲ TR Turn onto FR 618.

▼ 0.6 SO Cross bridge over Beaver Creek.
8.6 ▲ SO Cross bridge over Beaver Creek.

▼ 0.8 SO Cattle guard.
8.5 ▲ SO Cattle guard.

▼ 3.3 SO Track on left, then track on right.
6.0 ▲ SO Track on left then track on right.

▼ 4.8 SO Cross over creek.
4.5 ▲ SO Cross over creek.

▼ 4.9 SO Track on right is FR 611.2.
4.3 ▲ Track on left is FR 611.2.

▼ 5.6 SO Cross over creek. Track on left.
3.7 ▲ Track on right. Cross over creek.
GPS: N 37°52.06′ W 108°09.48′

▼ 5.7 SO Track on right.
3.6 ▲ SO Track on left.

▼ 7.1 SO Track on right.
2.2 ▲ SO Track on left.

▼ 9.3 SO Fork in road.
0.1 ▲ SO Track enters on left.
GPS: N 37°49.05′ W 108°11.31′

▼ 9.4 BL Intersection. Zero trip meter and follow FR 611.
0.0 ▲ Continue along FR 611.
GPS: N 37°48.98′ W 108°11.15′

▼ 0.0 Continue along FR 611 and pass track on right.
10.9 ▲ BR Track on left. Then road forks; stay to the right. Zero trip meter.

▼ 2.8 SO Cross over creek.
8.1 ▲ SO Cross over creek.

▼ 4.7 SO Track on left.
6.2 ▲ SO Track on right.

▼ 6.3 SO Track on left. Cross creek.
4.6 ▲ BL Cross creek. Then track on right.

▼ 7.1 SO FR 305 on right.
3.8 ▲ SO FR 305 on left.

▼ 7.8 SO Track on left.
3.1 ▲ SO Track on right.

▼ 8.7 SO Cattle guard; then FR 727 on right.
2.2 ▲ SO FR 727 on left; then cattle guard.

▼ 10.8 SO Cattle guard. Then track to cabin on right.
0.1 ▲ SO Track to cabin on left. Cattle guard.

▼ 10.95 TL Intersection with FR 535. Zero trip meter at intersection and cross over creek.
0.0 ▲ Continue on FR 611.
GPS: N 37°46.83′ W 108°05.32′

▼ 0.0 Proceed along FR 535.
9.7 ▲ TR Cross over creek. Zero trip meter at intersection and turn onto FR 611 (Black Mesa Road).

▼ 1.25 SO USFS Burro Bridge Campground on right.
8.4 ▲ SO USFS Burro Bridge Campground on left.

▼ 1.9 SO Cross Burro Bridge over Dolores River
7.7 ▲ SO Cross Burro Bridge over Dolores River

▼ 2.3 SO Cross over Meadow Creek.
7.4 ▲ SO Cross over Meadow Creek.

▼ 2.6	SO	Short track on left to Navajo Trailhead.
7.1 ▲	SO	Short track on right to Navajo Trailhead.

▼ 4.7	SO	Track on left to Kilpacker Trailhead.
5.0 ▲	SO	Track on right to Kilpacker Trailhead.

▼ 4.8	SO	Private cabin on left.
4.8 ▲	SO	Private cabin on right.

▼ 5.5	SO	FR 471 on right passes Calico Trailhead.
4.1 ▲	SO	FR 471 on left passes Calico Trailhead.

▼ 5.7	SO	Cross over Coal Creek.
3.9 ▲	SO	Cross over Coal Creek.

▼ 8.1	SO	Track on left at switchback.
1.6 ▲	SO	Track on right at switchback.

▼ 9.7		End at intersection with Colorado 145.
0.0 ▲		From Colorado 145 (5.3 miles south of Lizard Head Pass), zero trip meter and turn onto FR 535 toward Dunton.
		N 37°46.34' W 107°58.84'

SOUTHWEST REGION TRAIL #30

Jersey Jim Lookout Loop

STARTING POINT Highway 160 and CO 184 in Mancos

FINISHING POINT 3.6 miles southeast of Dolores on CO 184

TOTAL MILEAGE 41.4 miles

UNPAVED MILEAGE 39.9 miles

DRIVING TIME 2 hours

ELEVATION RANGE 7,031 to 10,103 feet

USUALLY OPEN Mid-April to mid-October

BEST TIME TO TRAVEL June to September

DIFFICULTY RATING 1

SCENIC RATING 9

Special Attractions

■ Multitude of aspen with amazing fall color.

■ Historic Jersey Jim Fire Lookout that can be rented for overnight stays.
■ Large network of 4WD trails.
■ Shady backcountry campsites as well as developed Transfer USFS campground.
■ Access to numerous hiking, mountain biking, ATV, motorbike, and equestrian trails.

History

Among the first humans to populate the area include the Anasazi, or Ancestral Puebloans, the constructors of Mesa Verde National Park's amazing cliff dwellings. While the civilization's disappearance is a mystery, some believe these people migrated to Arizona and New Mexico where they still reside.

Sometime in the fourteenth or fifteenth century, Navajo and Ute Indians settled in the area. They farmed and hunted and continue to live in the area today. In the late 1700s, Spanish explorers blazed the Spanish Trail through the area.

In more recent years, farmers worked the fertile lands to grow important resources for the mines in the San Juan Mountains. Timber was harvested from the Dolores area, cattle ranchers in the Mancos Valley supplied meat, while produce and other agricultural products were grown in the fertile, lower elevation fields around Cortez. Then the products were sent into the mines.

As the ore disappeared near the turn of the twentieth century, agriculture and tourism took over as the main industry driving the local economy, as it does today. The mining and agricultural history is evident in the San Juan National Forest, a haven for outdoor recreation. Miners accessing mining claims in the La Platas and loggers supplying the mines with timber created many of the current forest roads.

The Jersey Jim Fire Lookout, which towers 55 feet above the surrounding terrain, was used by the forest service from the 1940s to the 1970s to spot forest fires. The tower was named after an early-day rancher who grazed Jersey cattle in the area. Under permit, cattle still graze the forestlands today.

Jersey Jim Lookout is available for overnight rentals from late May through mid-October

The tower would have been demolished in 1991 except for the efforts of the Jersey Jim Foundation, a volunteer organization that renovated the cabin and now operates it under permit from the Forest Service. The cabin is available for one- or two-night stays from late May to mid-October. Rental fees go toward the maintenance of the landmark. The one-room cab is furnished with its original fixtures and propane heating and lighting. No water is available in the tower. Starting in March, call 970-533-7060 for more information.

The Aspen Guard Station is another structure of historical interest on the trail. The Civilian Conservation Corps built the structure, which was originally used as the District Office for forest rangers in the 1930s. Later fire crews and seasonal forest employees lived in the cottage.

The cabin fell into disuse for decades until 1994 when the Artist-in-Residence Program began. Writers, painters, sculptors, musicians, photographers, dancers, performers, poets, and other artists have been selected to stay at the cabin for one or two weeks where they can practice their art in a beautiful, secluded setting. Oftentimes, participants donate a piece of artwork that represents their experience at the cabin. They also take part in open houses for the public and attend an annual art show each fall after their residency.

View from West Mancos Overlook at Transfer USFS Campground

In fall aspens turn brilliant yellow before dropping their leaves

Description

This trail begins as a paved road in the city of Mancos, just less than 30 miles west of Durango on US 160. Begin by traveling north from Mancos on CO 184 then turn east on FR 561 (W. Mancos Road) after about 0.25 mile, following signs to Jackson Lake and Mancos State Park. After about a mile and a half, the pavement ends and the road becomes a wide, well-maintained dirt road through private land. Vegetation around the trail mostly consists of low oak scrub and pinyon and juniper pines over which there are good views to the east of the La Plata Mountains.

The road gains elevation and narrows slightly after entering San Juan National Forest, but passing is not an issue. Heavy corrugations can develop along this section depending on how recently repairs to the road have been made. Within the boundaries of San Jan National Forest abundant, shady backcountry campsites are available. At the 10-mile point, Transfer USFS campground has facilities that include grills, picnic tables, and restrooms. The campground also has 5 sites adjacent to corrals for equestrian recreation.

West Mancos Overlook is also located at the campground, with views over Crystal Creek Ditch, the Mancos River, and Hesperus Mountain, as well as number of other 13,000-foot plus peaks in the La Plata Mountains. The West Fork of the Mancos River is also visible from the overlook. Aspens dominate the vegetation in this area and are brilliant yellow in fall, creating an impressive scene. The dense aspen growth along the entire length of the trail makes for some of the best fall aspen viewing in Colorado.

Continue north on FR 561 past the intersections and forks, following the signs to Jersey Jim Lookout. Beyond the fork with FR 560 on the left, the trail narrows, but the

The trail winds through dense aspen forest

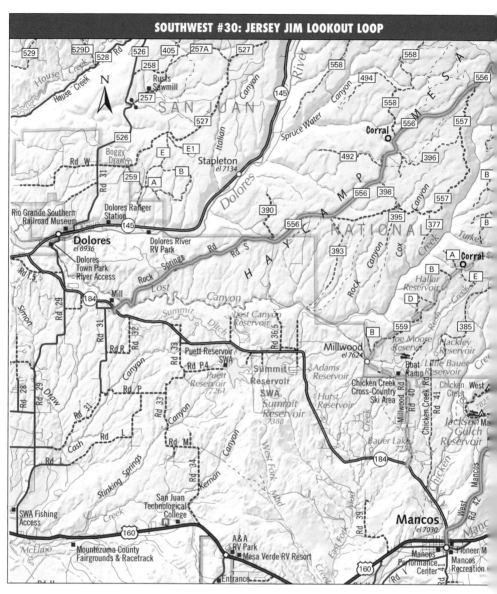

drive is still easy with ample room for passing. Avoid using this trail in wet conditions when travel through mud could damage the road or strand vehicles. Along this section, many hiking trails crisscross the trail making their way into the wilderness in all directions. Also along this section, the shady backcountry campsites are popular with hunters in fall.

At mile 11.6, the trail passes the Aspen Guard Station, which is used by the Artist-

in-Residence Program between June and September each year. Just beyond the guard station, continue on FR 561 past the intersection with the end of Southwest #32: Gold Run Loop (FR 350). Just beyond past the intersection with Southwest #31: Turkey Creek Trail (FR 352) is the historic Jersey Jim Fire Lookout at the 13.6-mile point. A local volunteer organization, the Jersey Jim Foundation, restored the tower and saved it from demolition in 1991. Under permit from the San Juan National Forest, the foun-

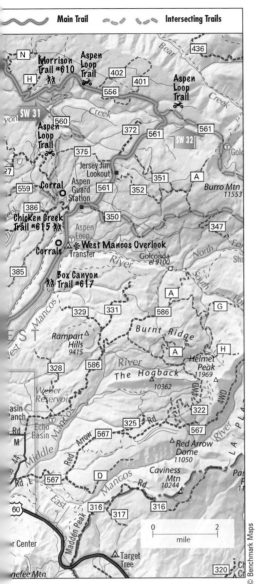

Main Trail ~~ ~~ **Intersecting Trails**

guards, the cattle grazed under permit in this area are trucked in and out from the substantial stock facilities here. The trail begins descending in this section and is a wide, maintained gravel road.

Toward the end of the trail around the 34-mile point, the trail leaves the boundaries of the San Juan National Forest and travels through private land. Stay on the road and respect private property owners. The road continues to descend to lower elevations and aspens give way to ponderosa pine trees and oak scrub.

The forest roads that make up the first section of this trail are good snowmobiling, snowshoeing, and cross-country skiing trails in the winter months. The trail ends at the intersection with CO 184, 3.6 miles east of Dolores.

Current Road Information

San Juan National Forest
Dolores Ranger District
100 North Sixth
PO Box 210
Dolores, CO 81323
(970) 882-7296

Map References

Benchmark's *Colorado Road & Recreation
    Atlas,* p. 121
USFS   San Juan National Forest
USGS 1:24,000   Mancos, Millwood,
    Rampart Hills, Wallace Ranch,
    Stoner, Dolores East
    1:100,000 Cortez, Dove Creek
Maptech CD-ROM:
    Southwest/Durango/Telluride
Colorado Atlas & Gazetteer, pp. 75, 85
The Roads of Colorado, pp. 137, 138

Route Directions

▼ 0.0   Trail begins at the intersection of
    US 160 and CO 184 in the town of
    Mancos. Proceed north on US 184.
10.0 ▲   Trail ends at US 160 in the town of
    Mancos. Turn left for Durango. Turn
    right for Cortez.
    GPS: N37°20.84' W108°17.34'

dation rents the tower for overnight stays, and rental fees are put toward maintaining the landmark.

Beyond the tower at mile 16.5 is the intersection with the beginning of Southwest #32: Gold Run Loop on the right. Continuing on FR 556 or Rock Springs Road, the trail is a similarly wide and well-maintained, dirt and gravel road. Other than corrugated sections, the drive is easy and is passable by passenger vehicle in good conditions.

As is evident from the corrals and cattle

▼ 0.35 TR Road 42 on right sign posted to Jackson Lake, Mancos State Park, and FR 561.

9.65 ▲ TL T-intersection with CO 184.

GPS: N37°21.15' W108°17.34'

▼ 1.50 SO Pavement ends.

8.5 ▲ SO Pavement begins.

GPS: N37°21.83' W108°16.56'

▼ 4.4 SO Road to Mancos State Park on left.

5.6 ▲ SO Road to Mancos State Park on right.

▼5.6 SO Cattle guard; then road becomes West Mancos Road, FR 561 entering San Juan National Forest.

4.4 ▲ SO Leave San Juan National Forest.

GPS: N37°24.85' W108°15.29'

▼ 5.9 SO Seasonal closure gate.

4.1 ▲ SO Seasonal closure gate.

▼6.2 SO Cattle guard.

3.8 ▲ SO Cattle guard.

GPS: N37°25.33' W108°15.05'

▼ 7.6 SO Track on right.

2.4 ▲ SO Track on left.

GPS: N37°26.32' W108°14.23'

▼ 7.85 SO Cattle guard; then track on right.

2.15 ▲ SO Track on left; then cattle guard.

GPS: N37°26.41' W108°14.03'

▼ 7.92 SO Corral then track on left.

2.08 ▲ SO Track on right then corral.

GPS: N37°26.44' W108°13.96'

▼ 8.9 SO Cattle guard; then Rim Trail Road on right.

1.1 ▲ SO Rim Trail Road on left; then cattle guard.

GPS: N37°27.10' W108°13.36'

▼ 9.28 SO Trail on right to Box Canyon.

0.72 ▲ SO Trail on left to Box Canyon.

GPS: N37°27.38' W108°13.14'

▼ 10.0 SO Intersection with FR 358 on right. Transfer Campground, West Mancos Overlook, and corral also on right.

0.0 ▲ Proceed south on FR 561.

▼ 0.0 SO Proceed north on FR 561. Sign posted to Gold Run Trailhead and Sharkstooth Trail.

2.09 ▲ SO Intersection with FR 358 on left. Transfer Campground, West Mancos Overlook, and corral also on left. Zero trip meter.

GPS: N37°27.97' W108°12.66'

▼ 0.23 SO TR 615, Chicken Creek Trail on left.

1.86 ▲ SO TR 615, Chicken Creek Trail on right.

GPS: N37°28.18' W108°12.61'

▼ 0.86 BR Road forks with FR 560 on left. Continue on FR 561 following signs to Jersey Jim Lookout.

1.23 ▲ SO FR 560 U-turn to the right.

GPS: N37°28.70' W108°12.65'

▼ 1.2 SO Cross over Chicken Creek.

0.89 ▲ SO Cross over Chicken Creek.

▼1.42 SO Cattle guard.

0.67 ▲ SO Cattle guard.

GPS: N37°28.97' W108°12.30'

▼ 1.5 SO Cross over Rush Reservoir Ditch.

0.59 ▲ SO Cross over Rush Reservoir Ditch.

▼1.6 SO Aspen Guard Station on right.

0.49 ▲ SO Aspen Guard Station on left.

GPS: N37°29.00' W108°12.12'

▼ 2.00 SO Cattle guard.

0.9 ▲ SO Cattle guard.

▼ 2.09 BL Trail forks; the end of Southwest #32: Gold Run Loop (FR 350) to the right. Zero trip meter.

0.0 ▲ Continue southwest on FR 561.

▼ 0.0 Continue northeast on FR 561.

4.46 ▲ BR Intersection with Southwest #32: Gold Run Loop to the left. Zero trip meter.

GPS: N37°28.94' W108°11.71'

▼ 0.8 SO Track on right.

3.66 ▲ SO Track on left.

GPS: N37°29.35' W108°11.28'

▼ 1.35 SO Southwest #31: Turkey Creek
Trail (FR 352) on right.
3.11 ▲ SO Southwest #31: Turkey Creek
Trail (FR 352) on left.
GPS: N37°29.73' W108°11.02'

▼ 1.49 SO Jersey Jim Lookout on right.
2.97 ▲ SO Jersey Jim Lookout on left.
GPS: N37°29.84' W108°11.06'

▼ 1.59 SO Cattle guard.
2.87 ▲ SO Cattle guard.

▼2.12 SO FR 372 on left.
2.34 ▲ SO FR 372 on right.
GPS: N37°30.29' W108°10.82'

▼ 2.72 SO Road on right.
1.74 ▲ SO Road on left.
GPS: N37°30.39' W108°10.40'

▼ 4.07 SO Cross over Turkey Creek Ditch.
0.39 ▲ SO Cross over Turkey Creek Ditch.

▼ 4.15 SO Cross over Lost Canyon Creek.
0.31 ▲ SO Cross over Lost Canyon Creek.
GPS: N37°31.03' W108°09.26'

▼ 4.46 BL Intersection with Southwest #32:
Gold Run Loop (FR 561) on right and
FR 556 on left. Zero trip meter.
0.0 ▲ Continue northeast on FR 556.

▼ 0.0 Continue northwest on FR 556,
signposted Rock Springs Road.
5.6 ▲ BR Intersection with Southwest #32:
Gold Run Loop on left (FR 561) and FR
556 on right. Zero trip meter.
GPS: N37°31.26' W108°09.41'

▼ 1.57 SO FR 556R on left.
4.03 ▲ SO FR 556R on right.
GPS: N37°31.64' W108°10.50'

▼ 1.65 SO FR 401 on right.
3.95 ▲ SO FR 401 on left.
GPS: N37°31.65' W108°10.59'

▼ 2.03 SO Cattle guard.

3.57 ▲ SO Cattle guard.

▼ 2.79 SO FR 402 on right.
2.81 ▲ SO FR 402 on left.
GPS: N37°31.89' W108°11.62'

▼ 3.47 SO Aspen Loop Trail on right.
2.13 ▲ SO Aspen Loop Trail on left.
GPS: N37°32.12' W108°12.18'

▼ 3.57 SO Pond on left.
2.03 ▲ SO Pond on right.

▼ 3.69 SO Aspen Loop Trail on left.
1.91 ▲ SO Aspen Loop Trail on right.
GPS: N37°32.24' W108°12.22'

▼ 4.0 SO Aspen Loop Trail on right.
1.6 ▲ SO Aspen Loop Trail on left.
GPS: N37°32.26' W108°12.44'

▼ 4.63 SO Cattle guard.
0.97 ▲ SO Cattle guard.

▼ 4.75 SO Morris Trail on right and left.
0.85 ▲ SO Morris Trail on left and right.
GPS: N37°32.01' W108°12.97'

▼ 5.6 SO Intersection with Southwest #31:
Turkey Creek Trail on left and Aspen
Loop Trail on left and right. Zero trip
meter.
0.0 ▲ Continue northeast on FR 556.

▼ 0.0 Continue southwest on FR 556.
7.78 ▲ SO Intersection with Southwest #31:
Turkey Creek Trail on right and Aspen
Loop Trail on right and left. Zero trip
meter.
GPS: N37°31.77' W108°13.69'

▼ 0.32 SO FR 556K on left.
7.46 ▲ SO FR 556K on right.
GPS: N37°31.67' W108°14.00'

▼ 0.63 BL FR 556H on right; then cross over
Morgan Gulch.
7.15 ▲ BR Cross over Morgan Gulch; then FR
556H on right.
GPS: N37°32.30' W108°14.48'

▼ 1.61 SO FR 556N on right.
6.17 ▲ SO FR 556N on left.
           GPS: N37°32.30' W108°14.48'

▼ 1.85 SO Cattle guard.
5.93 ▲ SO Cattle guard.

▼ 2.49 SO Track on right.
5.29 ▲ SO Track on left.
           GPS: N37°32.50' W108°14.86'

▼ 2.63 SO FR 556M on left.
5.15 ▲ SO FR 556M on right.
           GPS: N37°32.39' W108°14.93'

▼ 4.20 SO Road on right.
3.58 ▲ SO Road on left.
           GPS: N37°32.50' W108°16.14'

▼ 4.78 SO Cattle guard and corral on right.
3.0 ▲   SO Corral on left and cattle guard.

▼ 4.95 SO Track on right.
2.83 ▲ SO Track on left.
           GPS: N37°32.06' W108°16.67'

▼ 7.07 SO Cattle guard.
0.71 ▲ SO Cattle guard.

▼ 7.78 SO FR 558 on right to Haycamp Point.
           Zero trip meter.
0.0 ▲   Continue northeast on FR 556.

▼ 0.0   Continue southwest on FR 556.
11.5 ▲ SO FR 558 on left to Haycamp Point.
           Zero trip meter.
           GPS: N37°30.85' W108°19.12'

▼ 0.34 SO Cattle guard and private corral on right
           and left.
11.16 ▲ SO Private corral on right and left and
           cattle guard.
           GPS: N37°30.58' W108°19.08'

▼ 1.39 SO Cattle guard.
10.11 ▲ SO Cattle guard.
           GPS: N37°29.96' W108°19.57'

▼ 3.56 SO FR 557 and FR 393 on left.

7.94 ▲ SO FR 557 and FR 393 on right.
           GPS: N37°28.88' W108°21.32'

▼ 5.21 SO Cattle guard then private property of
           Lost Canyon Ranch on left.
6.29 ▲ SO Private property signed Lost Canyon
           Ranch on right then cattle guard.
           GPS: N37°28.37' W108°22.82'

▼ 7.25 SO Cattle guard.
4.25 ▲ SO Cattle guard.
           GPS: N37°27.99' W108°24.84'

▼ 8.19 SO Cattle guard.
3.31 ▲ SO Cattle guard.
           GPS: N37°27.82' W108°25.66'

▼ 8.75 SO Cattle guard.
2.75 ▲ SO Cattle guard.
           GPS: N37°27.67' W108°26.22'

▼ 9.57 SO Stop sign at unmarked intersection.
1.93 ▲ BR Unmarked intersection.
           GPS: N37°27.30' W108°26.92'

▼ 9.99 SO Cattle guard.
1.51 ▲ SO Cattle guard.
           GPS: N37°27.15' W108°27.57'

▼ 10.4 SO Cattle guard.
1.1 ▲   SO Cattle guard.
           GPS: N37°27.01' W108°27.70'

▼ 11.1 SO Cross bridge over Lost Canyon Creek.
0.4 ▲   SO Cross bridge over Lost Canyon Creek.

▼ 11.5 SO Cattle guard; then trail ends at inter-
           section with CO 184. Turn left for
           Durango and right for Dolores.
0.0 ▲   Trail begins 3.6 miles east of Dolores
           on CO 184.
           GPS: N37°26.60' W108°28.45'

Turkey Creek Trail

STARTING POINT Intersection of Southwest #30: Jersey Jim Lookout Loop and FR 560

FINISHING POINT Intersection of CO 184 and CR 40, north of Mancos

TOTAL MILEAGE 21.3 miles

UNPAVED MILEAGE 21.3 miles

DRIVING TIME 1.25 hours

ELEVATION RANGE 7,256 to 9,358 feet

USUALLY OPEN Year-round

BEST TIME TO TRAVEL Mid-April to mid-October

DIFFICULTY RATING 1 with rough spots that can be as hard as 3

SCENIC RATING 8

Special Attractions

- Thousands of aspens with brilliant yellow foliage in fall.
- Lightly used trail within a network of 4WD trails.
- Access to the Aspen Loop Trail for ATVs and motorbikes.
- Numerous backcountry campsites.

Description

This lightly used trail begins at the intersection with Southwest #30: Jersey Jim Lookout Trail and the intersection of FR 560. Although the ride is bumpy from embedded rocks, it is still an easy trail for a high clearance 4WD vehicle.

Winding through an aspen tunnel, the views of the brilliant yellow foliage in fall are stunning. The view of the rugged Sharkstooth Mountain cloaked in aspens near the beginning of the trail is particularly beautiful.

The trail narrows as it descends from Southwest #30: Jersey Jim Lookout Loop and it can be quite boggy in wet conditions. Embedded rocks in the trail can be quite large. Sections of the trail are shelf road along Fish Creek, and although the road is relatively narrow, the shelf is not high above the creek. The rugged, surrounding terrain is sloping and thickly vegetated. Just beyond a sharp turn crossing over the creek at approximately 3.5 miles, the standard of the trail improves to a smooth dirt road through a dense aspen forest.

Between the 4- and 5-mile points, the road intersects with the Aspen Loop Trail, designed by the forest service for motorbikes and ATVs. The 39-mile OHV loop consists of easy to moderately difficult tracks and is estimated by the forest service to be a 3 to 5 hour trip.

The trail continues on FR 561 until mile 6.7, where, taking a right turn, it picks up FR 559 (Millwood Road). This one-lane road has isolated sections that can be very rutted and embedded with large rocks that can be as challenging as a 3 difficulty rating. However, the majority of the trail is not difficult. Also along this section of trail are places for shady backcountry camping or pleasant picnic spots.

As the trail continues to descend to the south, it exits USFS land briefly and runs alongside private property where the road can be very muddy in wet conditions. Mud tires are an asset if you must travel in wet weather.

After crossing over a creek near mile 10.5, the standard of the road begins to improve with fewer sections of rocks and ruts, but the road remains narrow. Near the end of the trail, the road widens and becomes a smooth, maintained gravel road (CR 40) through private ranch land on either side. The trail ends at the intersection of CR 40 and CO 40, north of Mancos.

Current Road Information

San Juan National Forest
Dolores Ranger District
100 North Sixth
PO Box 210
Dolores, CO 81323
(970) 882-7296

Map References

Benchmark's *Colorado Road and Recreation Atlas,* p. 121

A good fall color aspen viewing trail

~~~~~ **Main Trail**   ~~~ ~~~ **Intersecting Trails**

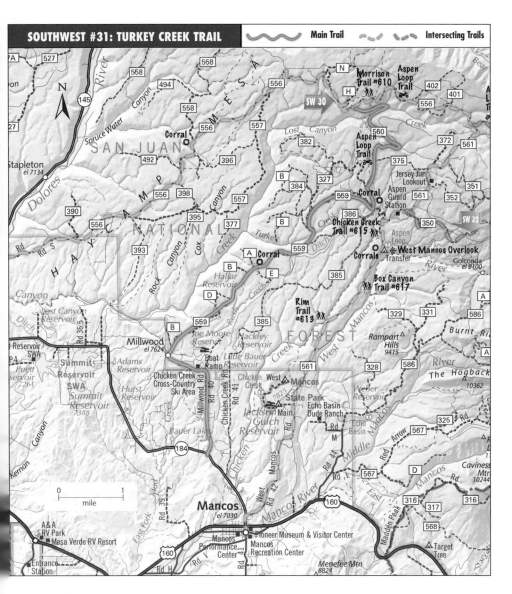

Atlas, p. 121
USFS San Juan National Forest
USGS 1:24,000 Wallace Ranch, Rampart
      Hills, Millwood
      1:100,000 Cortez, Dove Creek
Maptech CD-ROM:
      Southwest/Durango/Telluride
Colorado Atlas & Gazetteer, pp. 75, 85
The Roads of Colorado, pp. 137, 138

Route Directions

▼ 0.0   Trail begins at intersection with FR 560
          on Southwest #30: Jersey Jim
          Lookout Loop.

5.76 ▲   Trail ends at intersection with
          Southwest #30: Jersey Jim Lookout
          Loop.
          GPS: N37°31.76' W108°13.69'

▼ 0.8 SO Trail 610 on right then left.
4.96 ▲ SO Trail 610 on left then right.

▼ 1.3 SO Cattle guard; then cross over Fish
           Creek.
4.46 ▲ SO Cross over Fish Creek; then Cattle

▼ 3.37 SO Gated track on left.
2.39 ▲ BL Gated track on right.
GPS: N37°30.74' W108°12.03'

▼ 3.45 SO Cross over creek; then cattle guard.
2.31 ▲ SO Cattle guard; then cross over creek.

▼ 4.32 SO Aspen Loop Trail on right, gated.
1.44 ▲ SO Aspen Loop Trail on left, gated.

▼ 4.54 SO Track on left.
1.22 ▲ SO Track on right.

▼ 4.9 SO Aspen Loop Trail on left.
0.86 ▲ SO Aspen Loop Trail on right.
GPS: N37°30.31' W108°12.89'

▼ 5.76 TL Intersection with FR 327 on right and FR 560 continues on left. Zero trip meter.
0.0 ▲ Continue north on FR 560.
GPS: N37°29.65' W108°13.18'

▼ 0.0 Continue south on FR 560.
0.97 ▲ TR Intersection with FR 327 on left and FR 560 continues on right. Zero trip meter.

▼ 0.12 SO Cattle guard.
0.85 ▲ SO Cattle guard.

▼ 0.33 SO Cross over Turkey Creek.
0.64 ▲ SO Cross over Turkey Creek.
GPS: N37°29.59' W108°12.98'

▼ 0.85 SO Cabin and corral on left.
0.12 ▲ SO Cabin and corral on right.

▼ 0.97 TR Intersection with FR 559 on right signed Millwood Road. Zero trip meter.
0.0 ▲ Proceed east on FR 560.
GPS: N37°29.22' W108°13.00'

▼ 0.0 Proceed west on FR 559.
2.57 ▲ TL Intersection with FR 560 on left signed Millwood Road. Zero trip meter.

▼ 0.12 SO Cross through creek.
2.45 ▲ SO Cross through creek.

▼ 1.31 SO Cattle guard.
1.26 ▲ SO Cattle guard.

▼ 1.40 SO Track on left.
1.17 ▲ SO Track on right.

▼ 1.59 SO Dead end track on right.
0.98 ▲ SO Dead end track on left.

▼ 2.57 SO FR 327 on right. Zero trip meter.
0.0 ▲ Proceed northeast on FR 559.
GPS: N37°29.08' W108°15.12'

▼ 0.0 Continue southwest on FR 559.
1.52 ▲ BR FR 327 on left. Zero trip meter.

▼ 0.57 SO Intersection with FR 303 on right.
0.95 ▲ BR Intersection with FR 303 on left.
GPS: N37°28.63' W108°15.24'

▼ 0.63 SO Track on left.
0.89 ▲ SO Track on right.

▼ 1.13 SO Cross over Turkey Creek.
0.39 ▲ SO Cross over Turkey Creek.
GPS: N37°28.48' W108°14.90'

▼ 1.52 BR Intersection with FR 386 on left; then cattle guard. Zero trip meter.
0.0 ▲ Proceed northeast on FR 559.
GPS: N37°28.23' W108°15.18'

▼ 0.0 Proceed southwest on FR 559.
7.37 ▲ BL Cattle guard; then intersection with FR 386 on right. Zero trip meter.

▼ 0.01 SO Cross under power lines.
SO Cross under power lines.

▼ 0.75 SO Cattle guard.
6.62 ▲ SO Cattle guard.

▼ 1.73 SO Track on left.
5.64 ▲ SO Track on right.

▼ 2.17 SO Large corral on right; then cattle guard. FR 519 E on left then FR 559A on right.
5.2 ▲ SO FR 559 A on left; then FR 519 E on

right. Cattle guard then large corral on left.

GPS: N37°27.55' W108°17.09'

▼ 2.5   SO Seasonal closure gate.
4.87 ▲ SO Seasonal closure gate.

▼ 2.55 SO FR 559K on right.
4.82 ▲ SO FR 559K on left.

▼ 3.06 SO FR 559D on right.
4.31 ▲ SO FR 559D on left.

▼ 4.14 SO Seasonal closure gate.
3.23 ▲ SO Seasonal closure gate.

▼ 4.77 SO Cattle guard.
2.6 ▲   SO Cattle guard.

▼ 5.38 SO Drill hole on left.
1.99 ▲ SO Drill hole on right.

▼ 7.37 TL T-intersection with Road P. Zero trip meter.
0.0 ▲   Proceed west on FR 556 following signs for Millwood and FR 560.
            GPS: N37°24.95' W108°19.28'

▼ 0.0   Proceed east on Road P.
3.10 ▲ TR FR 556 on right.

▼ 0.22 SO Road 40.2 on left.
2.88 ▲ SO Road 40.2 on right.

▼ 0.52 BR Track on left to Joe Moore Reservoir and Chicken Creek Cross Country Ski Area; then cattle guard.
2.58 ▲ BL Cattle guard; then track to Joe Moore Reservoir and Chicken Creek Cross Country Ski Area on right.

▼ 2.77 SO Bauer Lake on left.
0.33 ▲ SO Bauer Lake on right.

▼ 3.10   Trail ends at intersection of CO 184 and CR 40.
0.0 ▲   Trail begins at intersection of CO 184 and CR 40. Proceed north on CR 40.
            GPS: N37°22.76' W108°18.67'

Gold Run Loop

STARTING POINT Intersection with Southwest #30: Jersey Jim Lookout Loop and FR 561

FINISHING POINT Intersection with Southwest #30: Jersey Jim Lookout Loop and FR 350

TOTAL MILEAGE 15.8 miles, including spur one-way

UNPAVED MILEAGE 15.8 miles

DRIVING TIME 1.50 hours, including spur

ELEVATION RANGE 8,972 to 10,994 feet

USUALLY OPEN Year-round

BEST TIME TO TRAVEL Mid-April through mid-October

DIFFICULTY RATING 2

SCENIC RATING 8

Special Attractions

■ Numerous hiking, mountain biking, horseback riding, ATV, and motorbike trailheads.

■ Scenic, shady backcountry campsites.

■ Views of Sharkstooth Mountain.

Description

At the intersection of Southwest #30: Jersey Jim Lookout Loop (FR 556) and FR 561, travel east on the wide one-lane, dirt road. Avoid this road in wet conditions and use caution if it has recently rained or snowed. As is evident from the deep ruts in this road, vehicles will easily become bogged.

Engleman Spruce trees mixed with a few aspens shade the trail in summer. In spring, abundant wildflowers blanket the surrounding terrain. In the warmer months, hike, mountain bike, or ride your horse, ATV, or motorbike from any of the numerous trailheads. The trail is also excellent for snowmobiling, cross country-skiing, or snowshoeing in winter, and in the fall the area is a popular base for hunters.

The trail becomes a wide shelf road descending into Bear Creek Canyon. Although the trail is a shelf road, the drop-

Although the trail is a shelf road, the drop-offs are not sheer and the main obstacle drivers must contend with are the ruts, some of which are quite deep. Picking a good line will get you through them easily. Along the shelf section, there are beautiful overlooks of the valley below.

At the 2.3-mile point, the trail passes the Gold Run Trailhead, which has a corral, restrooms, and a parking lot. Beyond the trailhead, the trail is lightly used and backcountry campsites are abundant. These scenic, quiet spots are also great for picnicking or wildlife viewing.

The trail crosses short sections of steep, talus slopes, what appears to be the remains of significant rockslides. The road across the slides is wide and sound, and they are not an obstacle, but are scenic. Travelers crossing the slides will hear the warning cries of the rock-dwelling pikas.

At 5.5-mile point, the trail intersects with FR 346, a 3-rated spur to Sharkstooth Trailhead. An unmaintained 4WD road, the spur is narrow, very rocky, and deeply rutted, but not overly challenging for a high clearance 4WD vehicle. Depending on the time of year and recent precipitation, you may also encounter pools of standing water on the trail. Avoid the spur in wet conditions as vehicles could easily get bogged.

The spur climbs steadily over flat terrain and yields fabulous views of Sharkstooth Mountain. Gradually the 1.5-mile trail winds its way in and out of forests and through meadows, ending at Sharkstooth Trailhead at the foot of Hesperus Mountain. The non-motorized Sharkstooth Trail accesses the Colorado Trail, Centennial Peak (13,062 feet), La Plata Canyon, and Windy Gap.

Beyond Sharkstooth spur, the main trail widens and becomes smooth and maintained with good views of Sharkstooth Mountain to the south. The end of the trail

Twin Lakes and Sharkstooth Mountain

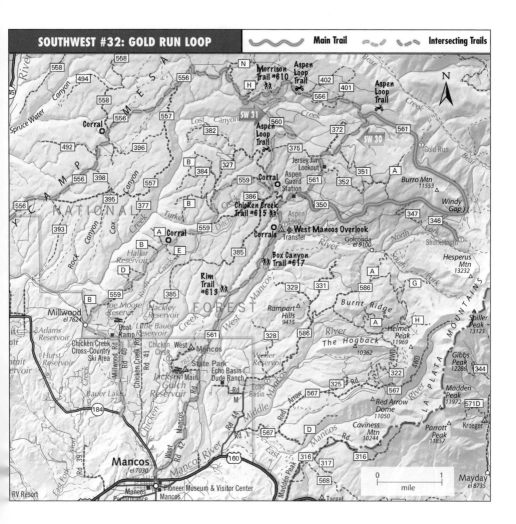

canopy of yellow in the fall, and ends at the intersection with Southwest #30: Jersey Jim Lookout Loop (FR 561).

Current Road Information
San Juan National Forest
Dolores Ranger District
100 North Sixth
PO Box 210
Dolores, CO 81323
(970) 882-7296

Map References
Benchmark's *Colorado Road and Recreation Atlas,* p. 121
USFS San Juan National Forest
USGS 1:24,000 Rampart Hills, La Plata, Wallace Ranch, Orphan Butte

1:100,000 Cortez, Dove Creek
Maptech CD-ROM:
Southwest/Durango/Telluride
Colorado Atlas & Gazetteer, pp. 85, 86
The Roads of Colorado, p. 138

Route Directions

▼ 0.0   Trail begins at intersection of Trail #30: Jersey Jim Lookout Loop (FR 556) and FR 561. Proceed east on FR 561.

2.34 ▲   Trail ends at intersection with Trail #30: Jersey Jim Lookout Loop (FR 556).
         GPS: N37º31.26' W108º09.40'

▼ 0.37 SO Aspen Loop Trailhead on left.

1.97 ▲ SO Aspen Loop Trailhead on right.
         GPS: N37º31.35' W108º09.04'

The pleasant, lightly-used Gold Run Loop

GPS: N37°28.54' W108°06.37'

▼ 2.34 SO Gold Run Trailhead with
            corral on left. Zero trip meter.
0.0 ▲   Proceed northwest on FR 561.
            GPS: N37°30.53' W108°07.43'

▼ 0.0   Proceed southeast on FR 561.
5.57 ▲ SO Gold Run Trailhead with corral on right.
            Zero trip meter.

▼ 0.56 SO Track on right.
5.01 ▲ SO Track on left.

▼ 4.73 BR Tracks on left and FR 358 gated closed.
0.84 ▲ BL Tracks FR 358 gated closed and tracks
            on right.

▼ 5.57 SO Intersection with FR 350 straight on
            and FR 346 to Sharkstooth Trailhead
            on left. Zero trip meter.
0.0 ▲   Proceed east on FR 561.

Spur to Sharkstooth Trailhead

▼ 0.0   Proceed southwest on FR 346.
            GPS: N37°28.54' W108°06.37'

▼ 0.8   SO Twin Lakes on left.
            GPS: N37°28.11' W108°06.14'

▼ 0.92 SO Aspen Loop Trail on left for ATVs, hik-
            ers, bikers, and horses.
            GPS: N37°28.07' W108°06.04'

▼ 1.5   Trail ends at trailheads for Sharkstooth
            Trail and Highline Loop National
            Recreation Trail.
            GPS: N37°27.72' W108°05.70'

Continuation of main trail

▼ 0.0   Continue northwest on FR 350.

6.36 ▲	BL	Intersection with spur trail to Sharkstooth Trailhead, FR 346, on right and FR 561 straight on. Zero trip meter. **GPS: N37°28.54' W108°06.37'**
▼ 2.09	SO	Cattle guard on one side of road.
4.27 ▲	SO	Cattle guard on one side of road.
▼ 2.47	SO	Intersection with FR 351 on right and track on right to Jersey Jim Lookout.
3.89 ▲	SO	Intersection with FR 351 on left and track on left to Jersey Jim Lookout. **GPS: N37°28.88' W108°08.60'**
▼ 3.45	BL	Track on right; then cattle guard.
2.91 ▲	BR	Cattle guard; then track on left. **GPS: N37°28.72' W108°09.36'**
▼ 3.7	SO	Pond on left and undeveloped campsites on right and left.
2.66 ▲	SO	Undeveloped campsites on left and right and pond on right.
▼ 4.28	SO	Track on left.
2.08 ▲	SO	Track on right.
▼ 4.58	SO	Cross over Crystal Creek.
1.78 ▲	SO	Cross over Crystal Creek. **GPS: N37°28.51' W108°10.20'**
▼ 4.73	SO	Cattle guard.
1.63 ▲	SO	Cattle guard.
▼ 5.25	SO	Tracks on right.
1.11 ▲	SO	Tracks on left.
▼ 6.32	SO	Cross over Chicken Creek.
0.04 ▲	SO	Cross over Chicken Creek.
▼ 6.36		Trail ends at intersection with Southwest #30: Jersey Jim Lookout Loop.
0.0 ▲		Trail begins at the intersection of Southwest #30: Jersey Jim Lookout Loop and FR 350. Proceed southeast on FR 350. **GPS: N37°28.94' W108°11.71'**

Columbus Mine Trail

STARTING POINT Intersection of CR 124 off US 160 in Hesperus

FINISHING POINT Closure gate a short hike from mine adit

TOTAL MILEAGE 11.8 miles (one-way)

UNPAVED MILEAGE 7.2 miles

DRIVING TIME 1 hour

ELEVATION RANGE 8,166 to 11,647 miles

USUALLY OPEN May through mid-October

BEST TIME TO TRAVEL May through September

DIFFICULTY RATING 4

SCENIC RATING 10

Special Attractions

- Much remaining evidence of historic mining activity.
- Exciting shelf road.
- Terrific photo opportunities.
- Remote-feeling, high elevation trail close to Durango.
- Developed and dispersed USFS campgrounds.

History

Named after the Spanish word for silver, the La Plata Mountains have drawn silver and gold seekers since the 1700s, and were one of the first places to be prospected in southwestern Colorado. The search for precious metals created a thriving mining industry, and settlements within the La Platas developed, supported by some of the richest mines in the state.

Juan Maria de Rivera, the leader of a Spanish expedition through the area, is believed to have made the first gold discovery in these hills in 1765. It wasn't until roughly a century later that the first town site, Parrott City, was located in La Plata County. Nothing remains of the site, which is now located on private property.

A successful prospector, John Moss, planned the settlement after leading a small expedition into the La Plata Valley in 1873. Upon discovering veins of gold and quartz,

La Plata City, circa 1894

Moss established with Chief Ignacio, the leader of the southern Ute, a private treaty for mining and farming rights on 36 square miles of land. Moss then returned to his hometown in California to secure financial backing.

In his absence, the Brunot Treaty of 1873, in which the Ute relinquished 4 million acres of mineral rights within the San Juan Mountains, was signed. Word spread east about gold strikes in the vicinity and people flocked to the La Plata area, as well as Silverton, among other locations in the mineral-rich San Juans. Tensions between the Ute and white settlers were still high after the treaty was signed, but Moss maintained diplomatic relations while building Parrott City, named for his investor, Tiburcia Parrott of San Francisco.

Eventually Parrott City included a court-house, a jail, a two-story hotel, two stores, several cabins, and even a weekly newspaper

(1876-1877) called *The Gazette.* In 1876, Parrott City became the official seat of La Plata County, and the population grew, some speculate, to as many as 1,000 residents. During the town's heyday, residents apparently had a habit of carrying whiskey around town in a communal water bucket, and a visitor remarked that the atmosphere was of a continual celebration. The ringleader, John Moss, kept a tapped barrel of whiskey in his office that visitors were welcome to sample any time, as many times as they wished.

Parrott City's prospects soon began to wane, first when Tiburcia Parrott withdrew funding, and then again when the builders of the Denver & Rio Grande Railroad laid tracks south of Parrott City to the new town of Durango. The railroad gave Durango a strategic advantage over the less accessible mountain towns, and by 1881 the county seat relocated there. The founding of La Plata City three miles to the north and nearer to the main mining activity further diminished Parrott City. The town was mostly abandoned by 1883.

Farther to the north, the town of La Plata City was established on the site of early Spanish explorer's first gold discoveries. By 1882, when the town gained a post office, La Plata City's population was roughly 200. In 1889, records approximate La Plata City residents to number nearly 500, becoming crowded with rowdy, gold seeking miners migrating from Parrott City and other dying towns in the area.

During La Plata City's prime, one of the town's brothels became known as "The Convent" or "Jesse's Convent," and subsequent histories recount that the town was so pious it was even home to a convent of nuns. Also officially named "La Plata" and "LaPlata," the locality maintained a post office until 1934, even though miners largely deserted the short-lived settlement around the turn of the twentieth century.

The fortunes of the area's mining communities rose and fell with the mines. Despite the initial promise of mines in the area, the ore was often scattered in small amounts rather than concentrated in large veins. Between John Moss' discovery in 1873 and the turn of the twentieth century, many mines opened in the area, but overall production did not meet expectations. The Comstock Mine near La Plata City, for example, yielded only somewhere between $15,000 and $75,000 in total.

While many of the mines yielded little, there were some notable exceptions. The two mines just north of Parrott City, the May Day, and the Idaho, produced more than half of the $6 million, which totaled the district's mining productivity from the years 1873-1943.

The May Day Mine proved so successful that in 1905 the May Day Gold Mining and Milling Company paid the construction costs to run a short branch from the Rio Grande Railroad to the mine. The spur operated until 1926. One gold nugget discovered there was valued at roughly $4,000. During

La Plata River and Campground at La Plata City town site

its 40 years of operation, the May Day Mine yielded a total of 75,000 ounces of gold and 759,000 ounces of silver and supported the nearby town of Mayday.

The town of Hesperus, where the trail begins, sprung up after investor, John Porter, opened the Hesperus Coal Mine in 1882. The town's post office was established in 1891. The Porter Fuel Company eventually produced 150,000 tons of coal annually and employed 175 men. Also serving as a supply point and railroad stop for the gold mining activities in the La Plata Mountains, the Rio Grande Southern Railroad chose the name Hesperus for the tallest nearby mountain, Hesperus Peak (13,225 feet).

Although the town grew quiet along with the La Plata mines, it is still an active coal mining location. Today investors also hope to revive gold and silver mining in La Plata Canyon. The May Day Mine along with the Idaho Mine and Idaho Mill (located just north of the May Day Mine) are part of a 141-acre parcel that the Wildcat Mining Corporation of San Diego is leasing to restore mining operations.

New activity, possibly prompted by the 30-year high prices of precious metals, is unusual, with only a few other active mines on record in the area, including the Mason Mine, the Incas Mine, and the Neglected Mine. Not without controversy, local residents are resisting the establishment of corporate mining operations in tranquil La Plata Canyon. Wildcat has been tied up for years in the process of permit approvals from numerous state, local, and regional governing agencies.

Description
This scenic and historic trail begins at the intersection of US 160 and CR 124 in the town of Hesperus, 11 miles west of Durango. Enjoy the impressive scenery of rugged peaks jutting above timberline and cloaked with aspen while traveling north on paved CR 124 for approximately 4.6 miles. Along this section, the trail runs through private land, so please respect private property owners and stay on the road.

At first the trail runs through flat, open land. Where the pavement ends the road enters the San Juan National Forests, and nearby is the historic town site of Mayday.

Remains of the Columbus Mine near the end of Columbus Mine Trail

The spectacular shelf road switchbacks up Lewis Mountain

Old mine adit from the Bessie G Mine

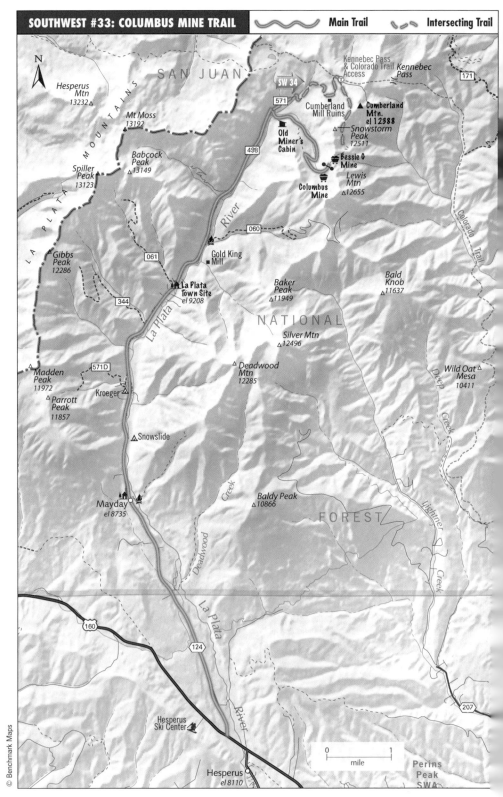

Main Trail · Intersecting Trail

N

Hesperus Mtn 13232△

SAN JUAN

Kennebec Pass & Colorado Trail Access · Kennebec Pass

171

SW 34

571

Cumberland Mill Ruins

▲ Cumberland Mtn. el 12388

△ Snowstorm Peak 12511

Mt Moss 13192

498

Old Miner's Cabin

MOUNTAINS

Babcock Peak △ 13149

Bessie G Mine

Spiller Peak 13123

Columbus Mine

Lewis Mtn △12655

River

060

LA PLATA

Gibbs Peak 12286

061

Gold King Mill

Baker Peak △11949

Bald Knob △11637

Colorado Trail

344

△ La Plata Town Site el 9208

NATIONAL

Silver Mtn △12496

La Plata

571D

Madden Peak 11972

△ Deadwood Mtn 12285

Wild Oat △ Mesa 10411

Parrott Peak 11857

Kroeger △

Deep Creek

Snowslide

Creek

Baldy Peak △10866

Lightner Creek

Mayday el 8735

FOREST

Deadwood

160

La Plata

124

207

Hesperus Ski Center

River

0   1
mile

Perins Peak SWA

Hesperus el 8110

About a mile beyond that is the Snowslide USFS Campground.

The two Forest Service campgrounds along this trail have fire rings, picnic tables, and pit toilets. Water is available at Kroeger USFS Campground, located about a half a mile north of Snowslide. These campgrounds are fee areas. The campgrounds are generally open for use from Memorial Day through Labor Day, and a host is on site. The sites at these campgrounds are first come, first served.

Two other camping options are available at Miners Cabin and Madden Dispersed USFS Camping Areas. Camping is not allowed near this trail other than in these designated areas. There is no fee to camp in the dispersed sites.

After the pavement ends, the ride becomes bumpy due to the trail's embedded and loose rock surface, but the road is not difficult for high clearance 4WD vehicles. The scenery is magnificent as the trail travels alongside the La Plata River through mixed forest of aspens, cottonwoods, engleman spruce, and other conifers. The trail is spectacular for wildlife viewing, and elk, deer, and blue birds among other animals are commonly sited.

At the 7.7-mile point is the La Plata City town site. Very little remains in the clearing where the town was once located, but information boards commemorate the short-lived settlement.

Gradually the road becomes a wide shelf road with sheer, high drop-offs to the La Plata River below. The road begins to climb and is quite steep in sections. Several waterfalls are visible along this section of trail. The scenery is quite dramatic, with amazing views of the surrounding peaks jutting above timberline.

The trail's difficulty increases as the trail climbs. Embedded rocks can be very large and erosion to the road adds to the obstacles over which the driver must navigate. These sections and the shelf sections give the trail its difficulty rating of 4. This trail and its side tracks are also popular for ATV and motorbike riders. High clearance 4WD is recommended for vehicles traveling this trail.

Near the intersection with Southwest #34: Kennebec Pass Trail (FR 571) at approximately the 12-mile point, the road starts to climb more aggressively and begins to switchback.

As the trail makes its way above timberline and enters Columbus Basin, the scenery changes dramatically. The floor of the basin is a beautiful alpine meadow with a creek flowing through it. Wildflowers abound in spring. The shelf road narrows and switchbacks up the steep talus slopes of Lewis Mountain, and there are substantially high drop-offs along this section of shelf.

After about 14 miles, the trail ends at a gate. Beyond the gate is an adit of the Bessie G Mine, a high-grade gold telluride deposit. More interesting old mine remains from the Columbus Mine are located just to the east beside the trail. Among the numerous remains are an old mine shaft, boiler, portable hoist, and a stove.

Current Road Information

San Juan National Forest
Columbine Ranger District (East)
PO Box 439
367 South Pearl Street
Bayfield, CO 81122
(970) 884-2512

Map References

Benchmark's *Colorado Road and Recreation Atlas,* p. 121
USFS   San Juan National Forest
USGS   1:24,000   Hesperus, La Plata
           1:100,000 Cortez
Maptech CD-ROM:
           Southwest/Durango/Telluride
Colorado Atlas & Gazetteer, p. 86
The Roads of Colorado, pp. 138, 154

Route Directions

▼ 0.0   Trail begins at the intersection of US 160 and CR 124 in Hesperus.
           GPS: N37°17.63' W108°02.08'

▼ 4.60 SO Pavement ends. Mayday town site on right.

ELK

Elk are large deer with brown bodies, tawny-colored rumps, thick necks, and sturdy legs. Cows range in weight from five hundred to six hundred pounds, and bulls range from six hundred to one thousand pounds. Only the males have antlers, which they shed each year.

From the eastern foothills to the western border of Colorado, elk are often found in the timberline or in grassy clearings just below the timberline. They remain in herds throughout the year and feed on grasses, shrubs, and trees.

In the late summer and early fall, bulls display behavior caused by their high levels of testosterone: They begin thrashing bushes and "bugling"—making a sound that begins as a bellow, changes to a shrill whistle or scream, and ends with a series of grunts. This vocalization broadcasts a bull's presence to other bulls and functions as a call of domination to the cows. Bulls

A bugling elk

become territorial and make great efforts to keep the cows together (a harem may consist of up to sixty cows), mating as they come into heat and keeping other bulls at distance. Bulls often clash antlers in mating jousts but are seldom hurt.

Calves are born in the late spring after a gestation period of about nine months.

Colorado has the largest elk population in the United States.

GPS: N37°21.24' W108°04.68'

▼ 5.76 SO Snowslide USFS Campground on right. Zero trip meter.
GPS: N37°22.20' W108°04.69'

▼ 0.0   Continue northeast on CR 124.
▼ 0.4   SO Kroeger Campground on left.
▼ 0.96 SO Track on left.
▼ 1.24 SO Maden Campground on right.
▼ 1.7   SO FR 344 on left.
GPS: N37°23.50' W108°04.29'

▼ 1.98 SO La Plata City site on right.
GPS: N37°23.70' W108°04.15'

▼ 2.46 SO Cross Boren Creek.
▼ 3.49 SO Private drive on right.
GPS: N37°24.68' W108°03.16'

▼ 3.85 SO Lewis Creek Campground. Zero trip meter.
GPS: N37°24.90' W108°03.08'

▼ 0.0   SO Continue north on CR 124.
▼ 0.55 SO Cross over Basin Creek.
▼ 0.88 SO Track on left to old foundations and undeveloped campsites.
GPS: N37°25.49' W108°02.61'

▼ 2.34 SO Intersection with FR 571 to Kennebec Pass on left and FR 498 to Columbus Basin on right. Zero trip meter.
GPS: N37°26.53' W108°01.90'

▼ 0.0   Continue northeast on FR 498.
▼ 0.1   SO Cross over Columbus Creek.
▼ 0.88 SO Old cabin on right.
GPS: N37°26.28' W108°01.84'

▼ 1.0   SO Track on left is steep 0.4-mile climb to old mine ruins.
GPS: N37°26.17' W108°01.22'

▼ 2.08 SO Short walk to the right to old mine remains.
▼ 2.16 SO Trail ends at gate.
GPS: N37°25.78' W108°00.99'

Kennebec Pass Trail

STARTING POINT Intersection Southwest #33: Columbus Mine Trail and FR 571
FINISHING POINT Kennebec Pass
TOTAL MILEAGE 2.9 miles (one-way)
UNPAVED MILEAGE 2.9 miles
DRIVING TIME 35 minutes
ELEVATION RANGE 10,477 to 11,999 feet
USUALLY OPEN May through mid-October
BEST TIME TO TRAVEL Mid-May through mid-October
DIFFICULTY RATING 5
SCENIC RATING 10

Special Attractions

- Mine and mill ruins.
- Spectacular, high-elevation shelf road.
- Interesting historic pass road.
- Access to the Colorado Trail.

History

High atop the La Plata Mountains near Kennebec Pass are a number of abandoned gold and silver mines, which first began operating in the 1870s. John Moss, on a prospecting mission in 1873, discovered gold and quartz roughly 5 miles south of Kennebec Pass. A year later he founded Parrot City and mining began in earnest.

The mines directly along the Pass trail did not prove particularly profitable. Well

Kennebec Pass Trail winds up to the shelf road that ends at the notch in the ridge between Cumberland Mountain and Snowstorm Peak

Sections of the trail are rocky and eroded

The last section of trail is a narrow shelf road that ends at the notch on the slopes of Cumberland Mountain

Cumberland Mill remains

Spectacular view from the end of Kennebec Pass Trail

Plata River

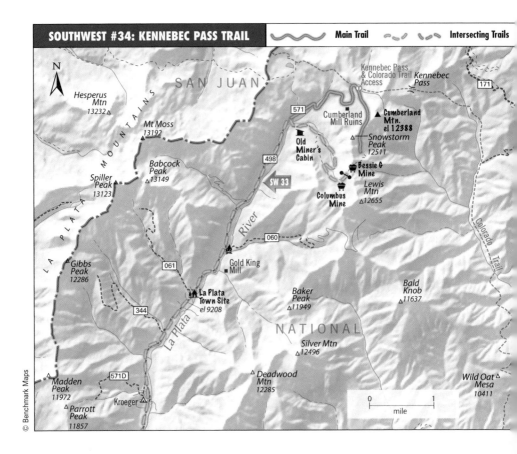

over half of all the money from mining in the area came from the May Day and Idaho mines. Four other mines—the Neglected, the Incas, the Gold King, and the Red Arrow—produced over $1 million in metals.

Just as the mines near Kennebec Pass failed to meet expectations during the height of the gold rush, much more recently, a number of investors found themselves deceived as to the wealth of mining claims in the vicinity. An unscrupulous California telemarketing company promised a 10 to 1 return from stock investments in a company opening a mine near Kennebec Pass called the Tippecanoe Mine. In 1997, the courts ruled the company pay $2.4 million in damages.

This trail also provides an access point to the Colorado Trail, a continuous 468-mile recreational trail from Denver to Durango.

Administered jointly by the US Fores Service and the Colorado Trail Foundation the Forest Service first proposed the idea i 1973. This hiking trail, which can also b used by mountain bikers and horsebac riders in sections, traverses seven nation: forests, six wilderness areas, five major rive complexes, and accesses eight of Colorado mountain ranges. Thousands of volunteer helped complete the trail in 1987.

The last leg of the 468-mile trail, th section follows Junction Creek Canyon int Durango and is also the most difficult. Th segment negotiates rugged terrain wit nearly 6,000 feet of elevation change.

Description

This short, exciting trail begins at the inte section of Southwest #33: Columbus Mir Trail and FR 571. It is also quite a scen trail through grassy meadows filled wi

© Benchmark Maps

wildflowers in spring; and surrounding the trail are engleman spruce, other conifers, and aspens, and historic mining remains.

From its beginning the trail has a higher difficulty rating due to the large loose and embedded rocks, and steep, narrow shelf road with high drop-offs. At the half-mile point, the trail crosses through the La Plata River and again at approximately mile 1.4. In general, the trail climbs steeply, gaining 1,523 feet in its short 2.9-mile length.

Above timberline, open views of the rugged, surrounding terrain are amazing, and you catch your first glimpse of the incredible man-made notch carved into the ridge between Snowstorm Peak and Cumberland Mountain on the horizon. The last section of shelf road leading to the "pass" clings dramatically to the rocky slope of Columbus Mountain.

The trail travels through a short section of flat alpine meadow with numerous old mine adits and other relics. Beyond the mine ruins, the trail leaves the basin and begins climbing again up toward Kennebec Pass. At the two mile point there is a parking lot at a scenic overlook and access to the Colorado Trail. Views of the Needles Range to the northeast are impressive. The true Kennebec Pass is accessed from this point by hiking southeast along the Colorado Trail about a half-mile.

Before attempting to drive the final stretch of shelf road, you should wait for any vehicles already on the road to return to the overlook area. This section is narrow and passing another vehicle on the shelf would be impossible. The surface of the spectacular shelf road is sound, but the track is narrow and the drop-off is sheer and high, more than 300 feet.

The trail ends at the 12,000-foot man-made pass, which was carved into the ridge in order to connect the area's mines. It is worth the extra effort to drive to the last section of trail for the fabulous views on both sides of the pass.

Current Road Information

San Juan National Forest
Columbine Ranger District (East)
PO Box 439
367 South Pearl Street
Bayfield, CO 81122
(970) 884-2512

Map References

Benchmark's *Colorado Road and Recreation Atlas,* p. 121
USFS   San Juan National Forest
USGS   1:24,000   La Plata
           1:100,000 Cortez
Maptech CD-ROM: Southwest Colorado/ Durango/Telluride
Colorado Atlas & Gazetteer, p. 86
The Roads of Colorado, p. 138

Route Directions

▼ 0.0   Trail begins off Southwest #33: Columbus Mine Trail at intersection of FR 498 and FR 571. Proceed northeast on FR 571.
           GPS: N37°26.54' W108°01.89'

▼ 0.27   SO   Hiking trail on left.
           GPS: N37°26.67' W108°01.67'

▼ 0.57   SO   Cross through the La Plata River.
           GPS: N37°26.80' W108°01.39'

▼ 1.39   SO   Cross through La Plata River.
▼ 1.64   BL   Track on right and old mine remains. Zero trip meter.
           GPS: N37°26.79' W108°00.77'

▼ 0.0   Continue northeast on FR 571 to Kennebec Pass.
▼ 0.19   SO   ATV track on right.
▼ 0.42   BR   Scenic Overlook and intersection with Colorado Trail on left.
           GPS: N37°27.10' W108°00.68'

▼ 1.26   Trail ends at a notch in the ridge between Cumberland Mountain (12,388 feet) and Snowstorm Peak (12,511 feet).
           GPS: N37°26.48' W108°00.48'

Junction Creek Trail

STARTING POINT Intersection of Main Avenue and Junction Road (25th Street) in Durango
FINISHING POINT Dead end
TOTAL MILEAGE 23.3 miles (one-way)
UNPAVED MILEAGE 19.8 miles
DRIVING TIME 1.25 hours
ELEVATION RANGE 6,567 to 10,669 feet
USUALLY OPEN Year-round
BEST TIME TO TRAVEL Mid-April through mid-October
DIFFICULTY RATING 1
SCENIC RATING 10

Special Attractions

- Numerous campsites, multi-use trail heads, and river access right in Durango.
- Easy, scenic drive starting in Durango.
- Animas Overlook.
- Colorado Trail access.

History

Junction Creek, located in the La Plata Mountains, was once an active part of the La Plata Mining District, one of the first areas to be prospected in southwest Colorado. The Neglected Mine, just off Junction Creek Trail, was established in 1895 and became among the highest producing mines in the region. From 1895 to 1901, small-scale operations worked the claim until the discovery of rich tellurides of gold and silver.

View over Animas Valley from Animas Overlook

After intensive development, the mine reached peak production between 1902 and 1904, yielding 7,000 ounces of silver and 13,000 ounces of gold with an estimated value of $270,000. With ore exhausted, the mine ceased operations in 1905. Optimistic investors, who hoped to discover new gold or silver tellurides, re-established operations in 1911 and 1912, but yields totaled a disappointing $10,000 in ore. In the 1930s, another outfit called the Colorado Juno Mining Company revisited the mine but abandoned it after tests revealed more lackluster results.

During peak production years in the La Plata District, Durango's famous female pioneer and cowgirl amazingly began running supplies by mule train for the Neglected Mine and most other mines in the La Platas. The story goes that in the early 1900s during an especially harsh winter, Frank Rivers, who operated the Rivers and the Gorman Ruby Mine, could not find anyone to pack supplies to his men at the mines. He asked one of Durango's best-known cowhands, the 26-year-old Olga Schaaf, to make a one-time run.

At a time when trails to the mines were narrow, underdeveloped foot-paths on the sheer slopes of the rugged La Plata Mountains and covered in feet of snow, she successfully led a train of burros loaded with supplies up to the remote mines. Subsequently she was contracted by the owner of the Neglected Mine to pack supplies to the mine for three years.

Famously, she packed supplies in the worst of conditions using trains of as many as 35 burros. She provided custom saddles for each pack animal and knew each by name. Her pack teams transported tons of equipment, including food, coal, rails, timber, 25-foot coils, and once the corpse of a miner. Incredibly, one story recounts how, becoming stranded by a severe snowstorm at the Neglected Mine, she led 18 miners and 25 burrows through snowdrifts as high as 10 feet in well-below freezing temperatures back to safety.

Other mines she serviced in the La Plata District included the May Day, the Durango Girl, the Bessie G, the Monarch, the Lucky Moon, and the Gold King. After she retired in the 1940s, she ranched cattle on her homestead near Mayday.

Miners and settlers both braved the rugged terrain and harsh elements to settle the Animas Valley, an incredible view of which can be seen from the Animas Overlook on Junction Creek Trail. In fact, settlers established two towns of the same name, Animas City, in the valley visible from the overlook.

Charles Baker helped established the first Animas City, which was located about 15 miles farther north, near Rockwood. The would-be gold baron convinced hundreds of men, women, and children from Denver that the Animas River at Baker Park flowed over nuggets of gold. The Baker Expedition embarked on their arduous journey west in December 1860. Arriving at the Animas River in March 1861, the party constructed a substantial bridge that became known as Baker's Bridge. After crossing the river and advancing to Baker's Park, the party discovered little if any gold, but stranded with winter setting in, they constructed cabins for shelter from the elements. The following spring, the "settlement" was abandoned and the party disbanded.

Although the settlement failed, Baker's Bridge became a toll station and the bridge was used for decades until a flood in 1911 washed it away. In more recent times the location made history again when Robert Redford and Paul Newman jumped from this spot into the Animas River while filming a scene of the movie *Butch Cassidy and the Sundance Kid* (1969).

The second and more successful Animas City, part of which is visible from Animas Overlook, was settled as a farming community sometime around 1874. The Animas City post office opened in 1877. Finding ample market in the mining camps for its agricultural products grown on the fertile banks of the Animas River, the town slowly grew, and the 1880 census reported a population of 286 residents.

Junction Creek Trail winds through the La Plata Mountains.

The town grew slowly in part because of its constant fear of attacks from the Ute, who relinquished their lands to the US government under conditions that were never met. So great was the town's fear of retribution from the tribe, on one occasion they sent a messenger north to bring back protection for the settlement.

The winded rider made a stop at a Howardsville bar where he announced that the Indians had burned Animas City and wiped out the town. Through the sympathies of the bar patrons, he was rewarded with free drinks, which encouraged him to spread the fictional story from town to town.

The tall tale spread by the thirsty messenger may have caused the abandon-ment of several of the smaller camps and settlements in the area—at least until the cavalry arrived in Animas City. Stationed at Fort Flagler, the troops remained until the scare passed.

By 1880, the town had as many as 50 structures, including residences, a school, and a small business district of several stores, and a newspaper, *The Southwest*. At the time, Animas City was the largest town in southwest Colorado and eagerly anticipated the arrival of the Denver & Rio Grande Railroad. When the railroad made demands on the city that it refused to meet, the D&RG ran its line right past Animas City, 2 miles south to Durango. Almost overnight Durango became the center of commerce in southwest Colorado. Eventually what remained of Animas City became a northern suburb of the railroad hub, Durango.

Description
Junction Creek Trail begins in the outskirts of Durango at the intersection of Main Avenue (US 550) and Junction Road (25th Street). Traveling west on paved Junction Road through a residential area, follow the signs to Junction Creek Campground in San Juan National Forest. After three and a half miles, the pavement ends after crossing a cattle guard. Here the trail enters the national forest and the road becomes FR 171.

Within the forest, the trail is a wide, maintained dirt road through ponderosa pine and scrub oak forest, and the trail becomes a wide shelf road. The easygoing road is passable by passenger vehicles in good conditions. Approximately 5 miles from the start of the trail, you will pass Junction Creek USFS Campground where facilities are available. The campground is a fee area.

About 5 miles farther, another point of interest is located at the turnoff to Animas Overlook, an interpretive trail and picnic area. The scenic view over Animas Valley against the backdrop of the skyscraping peaks of the San Juan Mountains to the north is worth the stop. At the overlook, the pleasant, 0.6-mile interpretive trail, with opportunities for wildlife viewing, sweeping vistas, and information boards about the geology of the Animas Valley, is a pleasant opportunity to stretch your legs.

Gaining elevation beyond the overlook, the road follows Junction Creek Canyon on its western side. The canyon is scenic with

Junction Creek Trail gains elevation as it leaves Durango

views down to Junction Creak and interesting rock formations on the opposite canyon wall.

Past the overlook, backcountry camping is allowed adjacent to the trail. At its upper reaches, the shelf road runs high above Junction Creek, and scenic and expansive views open up through breaks in the ponderosa pine, juniper, and aspen forest. The drop-off is significant, but the trail remains an easygoing and wide one-lane road, although sections that are quite corrugated will make the ride bumpy.

After traveling approximately 21 miles, a 3-rated, 1.6-mile spur trail heads off to the left and ends at a good clearing for backcountry camping and a hiking trailhead accessing the Colorado Trail. Along this spur is where the profitable Neglected Mine was once located. For a trail so close to the city, this track has quite a remote feel, a nice escape from the traffic and buzz of Durango. Beyond the spur about two miles farther, the main trail ends at a dead end.

Overall, the drive is worth the trip for the wildlife viewing and scenic overlooks that are enhanced by brilliant yellow aspens in fall. Located within Durango, this trail is a haven for all types of outdoor recreation, including fishing, white water sports, mountain biking, camping, hiking, horseback riding, 4-wheeling, hunting, and ATV and motorbike trail riding.

Current Road Information

San Juan National Forest
Columbine Ranger District (East)
PO Box 439
367 South Pearl Street
Bayfield, CO 81122
(970) 884-2512

Map References

Benchmark's *Colorado Road and Recreation Atlas*, p. 122
USFS San Juan National Forest
USGS 1:24,000 Monument Hill,
    Durango East, Durango West
    1:100,000 Durango
Maptech CD-ROM: Southwest Colorado/

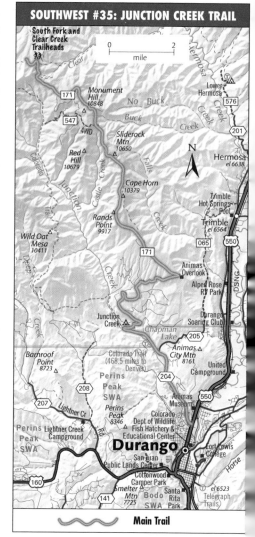

SOUTHWEST #35: JUNCTION CREEK TRAIL

Durango/Telluride
Colorado Atlas & Gazetteer, p. 86
The Roads of Colorado, pp. 138, 154

Route Directions

▼ 0.0   Trail begins at intersection of Main
         Street (US 550) and Junction Road
         (25th Street) in Durango.
         GPS: N37°17.47' W107°52.50'

▼ 0.84 SO Road becomes CR 204.
▼ 2.88 SO Intersection with CR 205 to the right.
            Follow signs to Colorado Trail and

Junction Creek Campground.
GPS: N37°19.47' W107°53.77'

▼ 3.5   SO   Cattle guard and pavement ends; then enter San Juan National Forest.
GPS: N37°19.88' W107°54.15'

▼ 4.93   SO   Junction Creek USFS Campground on left. Zero trip meter.
GPS: N37°20.24' W107°54.86'

▼ 0.0   Continue northeast on FR 171.
▼ 2.32   SO   Seasonal closure gate.
GPS: N37°21.16' W107°55.04'

▼ 2.9   SO   Track on right.
▼ 5.57   BL   Animas Overlook and interpretive trail on right. Zero trip meter.
GPS: N37°21.77' W107°52.97'

▼ 0.0   Proceed northwest on FR 171.
▼ 4.66   SO   Track on left.
GPS: N37°24.36' W107°55.17'

▼ 5.18   SO   Track on right to undeveloped campsite.
GPS: N37°24.72 W107°55.17'

▼ 6.82   SO   Track on left.
GPS: N37°25.77' W107°55.96'

▼ 7.53   SO   Track on right is narrow 0.5-mile trail to campsite with expansive views.
GPS: N37°26.27' W107°56.26'

▼ 8.39   SO   Track on left.
GPS: N37°26.70' W107°56.77'

▼ 10.6   SO   Road on right is 1.6-mile spur trail rated a 3 for difficulty. Zero trip meter.
GPS: N37°27.20' W107°58.38'

▼ 0.0   Continue northwest on FR 171.
▼ 0.89   BL   Hiking trails, gated road, and parking area on right.
GPS: N37°27.81' W107°58.48'

▼ 2.17   Trail ends at turn around.
GPS: N37°27.93' W107°59.34'

ASPEN

Aspen trees, North America's widest-spread tree species, have smooth, cream-colored bark with green, heart-shaped, deciduous leaves that turn brilliant gold in the fall. Because of the wide, flat shape of aspen leaves, the breeze nearly constantly flutters the tree's foliage, giving them the nickname "quaking aspen."

Older trees are dark at the base. Aspen

Aspen trees

grow from forty to seventy feet tall and one to two feet in diameter. They are normally found in montane and subalpine elevations up to timberline, in dry, cool places, often close to clean, flowing water. Often growing alongside Douglas firs, groves of aspen trees allow sunlight to penetrate to the forest floor, thus encouraging diverse plant growth and providing food and shelter for numerous wildlife species.

Green aspen foliage is preferred over the leaves of other trees by deer, cattle, sheep, and goats. The bark of the tree is a beaver's primary food source.

The pioneering species often quickly populates disaster-struck areas, such as after wildfires, landslides, mudslides, or avalanches. Colorado boasts the largest percentage of natural acreage of aspens in the world.

Transfer Park Road

STARTING POINT Intersection of CR 240 (Florida Road) and CR 243, 14 miles north of Durango

FINISHING POINT Weminuche Wilderness Boundary at Endlich Mesa Trailhead

TOTAL MILEAGE 20.6 miles (one-way)

UNPAVED MILEAGE 17.5 miles

DRIVING TIME 1.5 hours (one way)

ELEVATION RANGE 7,794 to 11,269 feet

USUALLY OPEN May through October

BEST TIME TO TRAVEL Mid-May through mid-October

DIFFICULTY RATING 2, 3 for the spur

SCENIC RATING 9

Special Attractions

- Scenic and historic trail ending at boundary of Weminuche Wilderness.
- Low-use Miller Creek, Florida, and Transfer Park USFS Campgrounds.
- Scenic, shady developed campsites on Florida River.
- Fishing, boating, and other water recreation on Lemon Reservoir.
- Mountain biking, ATV riding, hiking, horseback riding, fishing, and hunting access.
- Network of 4WD tracks to explore near the boundary of the Weminuche Wilderness.

History

Among the initial undertakings of the Colorado River Storage Project, the Lemon Dam and Reservoir were designed to store the waters of the 68-mile drainage area that originates on the slopes of the 13,000-foot Needle Mountains and converge in the Florida River.

At one-half mile wide and 3 miles long, Lemon Reservoir's storage capacity is 40,146 acre-feet of which 39,030 acre-feet is designated for active conservation. State lawmakers originally approved the water storage project in April 1956. The project was conceived for water conservation and to provide ample water for farmers and ranchers during the short growing season on the

Lemon Reservoir

Fishing access at Upper Lemon Day Use Area

The trail is rocky, making for a rough ride

Florida Mesa, where agriculture by white settlers developed after the Ute were relocated to reservations in 1899.

The rest of the water flowing through the Lemon Reservoir complex is designated for irrigation, and the annual irrigation supply averages 25,740 acre-feet of water. Crops are grown on a total of 14,259 acres of the Florida Mesa and include corn, oats, wheat, alfalfa and other kinds of hay, as well as irrigated pastureland for livestock.

Named for the landowner of the site at the time of the dam's construction, Charles H. Lemon, the dam and reservoir along with its irrigation facilities were completed in December 1963 at a total cost of $11.1 million.

The National Park Service also recognized the recreation value of the reservoir and in 1964, invested more than $100,000 on camping areas, roads, parking lots, and a boat launch. Overwhelmed with campers, picnickers, and other visitors after the area opened for public use, sanitation facilities were added in 1967. In July of the same year, the US Forest Service began supervising the public facilities and lands in the vicinity of Lemon Reservoir.

Not surprisingly, the scenic banks of the Florida River, which can easily be explored north of the Lemon Reservoir, were used for thousands of years before the campers, picnickers, and 4-wheelers of today. It is believed the Anasazi roamed southwest Colorado, where they farmed corn and squash, hunted, and gathered wild plants, seeds, and berries, more than 10,000 years ago.

When the group mysteriously disappeared, the Ute Indians lived off the land in much the same way. Historians date the first contact between the Ute and Spanish explores to as early as 1640 when the Ute first obtained horses from the encounters. A Spanish expedition in the early 1760s led by Juan de Rivera is credited as being the first European explorer in the vicinity. On this journey, de Rivera named the Florida River and the La Plata Mountains, along with most of the other peaks and rivers in what is today La Plata

County. Florida is Spanish for "flowery" and La Plata means "silver" in English.

Gold fever brought the first white settlers to the area as early as the 1860s. White settlement expanded with the increase of mining in the mountains, spurring the removal of the Utes from their land. The controversial process began in the 1860s and was complete by the turn of the 20th century.

During the mining boom in the late 1880s, the banks of the Florida River and the park where the Transfer Park USFS Campground is located today were used as transfer sites where mining equipment and supplies were unloaded from wagons onto pack animals and transported to the mines near the head of the Florida drainage.

Local history recounts that Logtown was one of the isolated towns to which supplies were carried from Transfer Park. However, the town was so named in the late 1950s by backpackers who discovered the abandoned settlement that was located about 40 miles northeast of Durango. At that time 20 to 30 log cabins were still standing and an extensive amount of old mining equipment littered the area.

Although the true name of the town is unknown, one well-known mine, the Pittsburg, located in this inaccessible area, produced more than $1 million in bullion in the 1880s and 1890s. Today nothing much is left at the site, which is only accessible via a strenuous 8.5-mile hike beyond City Reservoir within the Weminuche Wilderness. The Forest Service Trail is #542, City Reservoir Trail via Lime Mesa.

Description

This trail follows the length of Lemon Reservoir and climbs Miller Mountain (11,740 feet) to Endlich Mesa. Beginning at the intersection of CR 240, Florida Road, and CR 243, zero your trip meter and proceed north on CR 243. The pavement ends at the 1.6-mile point and Lemon Dam is on the left side of the road immediately after the pavement ends. Lemon Reservoir comes into view as you proceed north along the main trail. You will also notice barren trees on the

Transfer Park Trail switchbacks up Miller Mountain to Endlich Mesa

surrounding slopes, remains of the Missionary Ridge Wildfire in June 2002.

The road becomes a wide, maintained gravel road that is passable by passenger vehicle in good conditions. Potholes are the only hindrance to a smooth ride. The first section of the road travels beside private property (please do not trespass), and you soon arrive at Miller Creek USFS Campground on the banks of Lemon Reservoir. The campground has well-maintained facilities, including picnic tables, 12 camping spots, flush toilets, and fireplaces. Another advantage of all the campgrounds on this trail is that they are generally mostly vacant.

Beyond Miller Creek Campground at the north end of the reservoir is Upper Lemon Day Use Area, featuring a concrete boat launch, fishing access, and restroom facilities. Fishermen who cast a line are frequently successful because the reservoir is stocked with kokonee salmon and trout. The road narrows slightly and begins gaining elevation just beyond the day use area. Ample shade is provided by the surrounding forest of blue spruce, Douglas fir, and aspen.

After approximately 7 miles, you will arrive at the intersection of FR 597 and FR 597A. FR 597A is a 1.5 mile, two-lane gravel road that travels beside the Florida River to the Florida and Transfer Park USFS Campgrounds. Smooth and maintained, the easy track has a few potholes, corrugations, and widely disbursed embedded rock but is passable by passenger vehicle. At 0.2 mile is the large Florida USFS Campground and picnic area with shady spots right on the banks of the Florida River.

Beyond the Florida Campground, the road travels over the flat forest floor. Transfer Park USFS campground has two campsite loops and well-maintained facilities, including grill grates and picnic tables. Both lightly-used campgrounds, Transfer Park also has ample parking for a popular hiking trailhead, Burnt Timber Trail, which accesses the Weminuche Wilderness and proceeds to Lime Mesa, Mountain View Crest, the scenic City Reservoir, and historic Logtown town site.

Proceeding north on the main trail (FR 597), the road narrows, becomes eroded and rocky, and travels through forested land with limited views of the surrounding San Juan Mountains. Although the road narrows, passing oncoming vehicles is not an obstacle. Since the surrounding terrain is flat, there are plenty of pullouts and there are also plenty of good backcountry campsites that are especially popular with hunters in fall. The ride is bumpy from embedded rock, loose rock, and erosion, giving the trail its difficulty rating of 2. For 4WD vehicles, the trail is easy, although still a rough ride.

As the trail continues to climb, it becomes an easy shelf road that gently slopes on the drop-off edge. The track is consistently rough as it switchbacks up the mountain. From the higher reaches of the trail, overlooks present the scenic Florida River Canyon and the slopes of Lime Mesa blanketed with aspens, a brilliant yellow display in fall.

The turnoff to FR 597C is located after traveling approximately 8 miles. This track is just under a mile in length and is a 3-rated spur off the main trail. The road is narrow and very eroded, but its end provides a scenic overlook of Lime Mesa and the Florida River canyon to the west.

The main trail proceeds about a mile and a half to another turnoff onto FR 597D. The short track dead ends after 0.75 mile. Proceed on the main trail a short distance (0.75 mile) beyond the last turnoff to its end at the Endlich Mesa Trailhead and boundary of the Weminuche Wilderness. The trailhead has hitching rails and loading chute for horses. The view here (above 11,000 feet) is open and expansive, with Endlich Mesa to the northeast, Miller Mountain to the south, and the Florida River Canyon and Lime Mesa to the west. In spring, the colorful wildflowers in the meadow at the trail's end are a must-see.

Florida River near Florida USFS Campground

〜〜〜 **Main Trail**

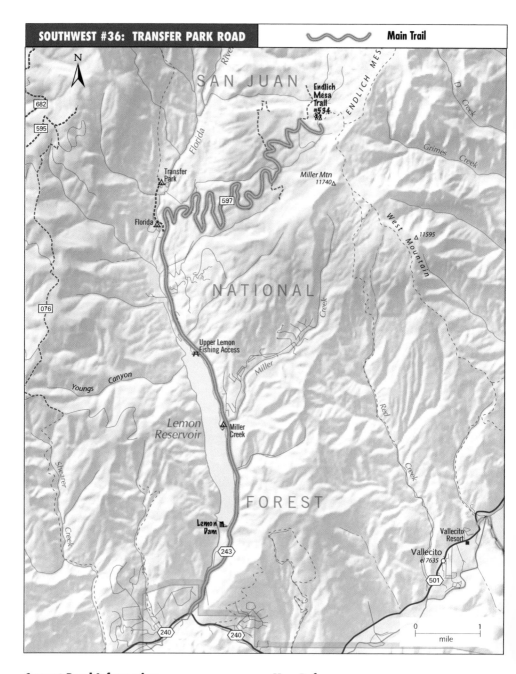

Current Road Information

San Juan National Forest
Columbine Ranger District (East)
PO Box 439
367 South Pearl Street
Bayfield, CO 81122
(970) 884-2512

Map References

Benchmark's *Colorado Road and Recreation Atlas*, p. 122
USFS   San Juan National Forest
USGS   1:24,000   Rules Hill, Lemon Reservoir
1:100,000 Durango
Maptech CD-ROM: Southwest Colorado/

Durango/Telluride
Colorado Atlas & Gazetteer, pp. 86, 87
The Roads of Colorado, pp. 139, 155
Trails Illustrated, #140 (incomplete)

Route Directions

▼0.0		Trail begins at the intersection of CR 240 (Florida Road) and CR 243, 14 miles north of Durango.
		GPS: N37°21.66' W107°40.28'
▼1.63	SO	Pavement ends and Lemon Dam on left.
▼3.44	SO	Miller Creek Campground and boat launch on left.
		GPS: N37°24.37' W107°39.64'
▼4.81	SO	Upper Lemon Day Use Area on left.
		GPS: N37°25.41' W107°40.21'
▼5.15	SO	Cattle guard.
		GPS: N37°25.62' W107°40.47'
▼6.92	SO	Cattle guard; then intersection with FR 597A to Florida Transfer Park USFS Campgrounds to the left. Zero trip meter.
▼0.0		Proceed north on FR 597.
		GPS: N37°27.10' W107°40.70'
▼7.14	SO	Cattle guard.
		GPS: N37°27.86' W107°38.78'
▼8.11	TR	Intersection with FR 597C straight ahead and FR 597 to the right. Zero trip meter.
		GPS: N37°28.22' W107°38.88'
▼0.0		Continue east on FR 597.
▼1.66	TR	Intersection with FR 597D straight ahead and FR 597 to the right. Zero trip meter.
		GPS: N37°28.69' W107°38.26'
▼0.0		Proceed southeast on FR 597.
▼0.75		Trail ends at border of Weminuche Wilderness and trail head.
		GPS: N37°28.65' W107°37.95'

Middle Mountain Trail

STARTING POINT Intersection of CR 501 and FR 724 due north of Vallecito Reservoir
FINISHING POINT Weminuche Wilderness Boundary
TOTAL MILEAGE 14.05 miles (one-way)
UNPAVED MILEAGE 14.05 miles
DRIVING TIME 1.5 hours
ELEVATION RANGE 7,686 to 11,517 miles
USUALLY OPEN Late May to October
BEST TIME TO TRAVEL June to mid-October
DIFFICULTY RATING 1 on FR 724, 5 beyond Tuckerville Historical Marker
SCENIC RATING 8

Special Attractions

- Remote-feeling, easy forest road leading to a network of more challenging 4WD trails.
- Sweeping views of Vallecito Reservoir and surrounding peaks.
- Historic Tuckerville town site.
- Cave Basin Trail for hiking and horseback riding.
- Fishing in Vallecito Reservoir and hunting in the vicinity.
- Access to Weminuche Wilderness.
- Many nearby developed USFS campgrounds.
- Wildlife viewing.

History

This remote and isolated area was probably first roamed by Indian big game hunters between 5,000 and 10,000 years ago. The Anasazi likely settled in villages until sometime around the thirteenth century. The Ute Indians lived in the region probably beginning in the sixteenth century. Juan de Rivera led the first recorded Spanish expedition through the vicinity in the 1760s, although Spanish encounters with the Ute were reported as early at the 1600s. Spanish explorers named many of the mountains, rivers, and streams in the area including the Los Pinos River and Vallecito Creek. *Pino* is

Spanish for "pine" and *vallecito* translates to "little valley" in English.

White settlers encroached in the 1800s when thousands of miners flooded the area in search of precious metals. A small-scale gold rush to the Cave Basin mining district on Middle Mountain began in 1913 when outcroppings of ore were discovered. A few optimistic prospectors arrived and settled the tiny, isolated town of Tuckerville, but limited access to the remote location combined with disappointingly low output from the mines left the area largely untouched.

Not much is known about the history of Tuckerville and nothing except an information board and a few timbers are left at the site to commemorate its presence. Mineral records show that a limited amount of mining took place during the 1900s. Between 1913 and 1928, 54 tons of ore were extracted from the mines in the area that are known collectively as the Cave Basin mining district.

Ore came primarily from the Holbrook, the Mary Murphy, and the Silver Reef mines,

the majority of which was copper, totaling 2,900 pounds. Other minerals mined include 12 ounces of gold, 237 ounces of silver, and 1,700 pounds of lead with an estimated total value of just $3,200. Another brief attempt at prospecting was made from 1934 through 1936, during which time 62 tons of ore were shipped, yielding only approximately seven pounds of gold and four ounces of silver.

The unsuccessful prospectors, which were most, turned to farming. Skirmishes between the Ute and the white intruders led to intervention by the U.S. Government. Completely relocating the Ute to reservations, the government opened most of the native Ute hunting lands to white settlement by 1899.

The Pine River Indian Agency regulated local Indian lands and filed for irrigation rights of 18,336 acres of land in 1895. White settlers who had filed earlier claims contested the claim. The controversy and resulting litigation led to the approval of the Pine River Project in 1937. In the settlement, one-sixth of the water supplied from the construction of

Pine Point USFS Campground has shady spots right on the shore of Vallecito Reservoir

Vallecito Reservoir from FR 724, viewed from nearly 11,000 feet

Scenic backcountry campsites adjacent to FR 724

the dam and reservoir was designated for the Pine River Indian Irrigation Project with the balance allotted to the Pine River Irrigation District.

Surveys located the reservoir site in 1937, and the Denver-based Weston Lumber Company started clearing trees that would yield an estimated 5 million board feet of lumber from the site in 1938. Land acquisition for the dam and reservoir was completed by 1939. Construction was completed and the dam dedicated by 1941.

Vallecito Reservoir's maximum capacity is 129,700 acre-feet of water and its surface area is 2,720 acres. The Pine River Project provides water for irrigation of 40,000 acres of privately owned farmland and more than 15,000 acres of Indian lands. Crops produced include oats, wheat, barley, and alfalfa. Project water also supports livestock ranches on an estimated 24,000 privately owned acres and 9,000 Indian-owned acres.

Vallecito Dam has also been useful for flood control, preventing an estimated $500,000 in flood damage as of September 1992. In addition, some water is diverted to the 5 megawatt Ptarmigan Resources hydroelectric power plant just downstream from the reservoir.

Description

This pleasant trail follows the east side of Vallecito Reservoir and then climbs Middle Mountain to nearly 11,000 feet beyond the old mining outpost, Tuckerville, before ending at the border of the Weminuche Wilderness. Begin at the intersection of CR 501 and CR 501A, 22 miles northeast of Durango and at the south end of Vallecito Reservoir.

Proceed east on the paved CR 501A over the concrete one-lane bridge and across Vallecito Dam where the pavement ends and the road heads north along the eastern edge of Vallecito Reservoir. Most of the length of the road beside the reservoir is a wide, well-maintained dirt and gravel road with access to five shady USFS campgrounds situated right on the banks of the reservoir. Camping outside these areas is not permitted.

This section of the trail also crosses through the Missionary Ridge burn area. The wildfire, which was apparently started from a carelessly discarded cigarette, started on June 9, 2002. The fire scorched 73,391 acres in just over one month and cost approximately $39.9 million in suppression efforts by the time it was extinguished on July 15, 2002.

Just beyond Pine Point USFS Campground, the trail narrows and descends, winding through two private campgrounds between which the trail crosses over the Los Pinos River. Exiting the private campgrounds, CR 501 continues to the north and FR 602 heads east, ending at Pine River trailhead and USFS Campground, a popular base camp and parking area for horseback riders, back-packers, and hikers into the Weminuche Wilderness. Proceed north on CR 501 and continue following the eastern edge of the reservoir.

After the pavement begins at the north-eastern edge of the reservoir, FR 724 begins and heads northeast up Middle Mountain. Exit CR 501 and proceed northeast on FR 724, a wide dirt and gravel road. The trail rapidly gains elevation, climbing through stands of lodgepole pines, engleman spruce, and apsen trees. Breaks in the trees reveal expansive views more and more frequently as the trail scales Middle Mountain. You'll see Vallecito Reservoir and the Grassy Mountains to the south, Table Mountain to the north, and The Notch to the east.

As the trail gains elevation, shady clearings adjacent to the trail make nice backcountry campsites, picnic spots, and wildlife viewing locations. Abundant wildlife in the area includes elk, deer, bears, snowshoe hares, ptarmigan, and wild turkey. The numerous aspen trees in the surrounding forest also make for good fall color viewing.

The Cave Basin Trailhead (#530) is located at mile 9.9. The hiking and equestrian trail reaches 5 miles into the Weminuche

Rugged peaks form the west wall of Vallecito Creek Canyon, part of the Weminuche Wilderness Area

Wilderness and ends at a scenic overlook of Dollar Lake and Emerald Lake.

Beyond the closure gate at 10.6 miles, the trail narrows, but is still an easygoing drive. About half-a-mile south of the closure gate are some old mines and tailings heaps from the area's short-lived mining days. On the main trail, approximately 1.7 miles beyond the gate, you arrive at the Tuckerville historical marker. Nothing remains at the site.

The road becomes a 4WD track beyond the historical marker. It narrows significantly and is eroded, rocky, rough, and steep. Avoid this section of trail in wet conditions. Vehicles could easily become bogged. Just past the Tuckerville site (0.2 mile) is a seasonal closure gate and then 0.3 mile farther, the road forks.

The two tracks ahead are fun and challenging 4WD trails that end at the boundary of the Weminuche Wilderness, about a mile farther. The two tracks are rated 5 for difficulty. Trees along the left-hand track are very close to the trail, making the navigation of this trail by drivers in full size vehicles nearly impossible. Additional challenges to consider before you proceed include ruts, potholes, boulders, mud, and steep, loose and off-camber sections of trail.

Current Road Information

San Juan National Forest
Columbine Ranger District (East)
PO Box 439
367 South Pearl Street
Bayfield, CO 81122
(970) 884-2512

Map References

Benchmark's *Colorado Road and Recreation Atlas,* p. 122
USFS   San Juan National Forest
USGS 1:24,000   Vallecito Reservoir,
   Ludwig Mtn., Columbine Pass,
   Granite Peak, Emerald Lake
   1:100,000 Durango
Maptech CD-ROM: Southwest Colorado/
   Durango/Telluride
Colorado Atlas & Gazetteer, pp. 77, 87
The Roads of Colorado, p. 139
Trails Illustrated, #140 (incomplete)

Route Directions

▼ 0.0   Trail begins at the intersection of CR 501 and CR 501A, 22 miles northeast of Durango. Zero trip meter and proceed east on paved CR 501A toward Vallecito Dam. Signed-posted to numerous campgrounds and Vallecito Reservoir.
   GPS: N37°22.92′ W107°34.79

▼ 0.3   SO Cross over concrete one-lane bridge over water outflow onto Vallecito Dam.
▼1.1   SO End of dam and pavement ends.
▼1.8   SO Old Timer USFS Campground for dispersed camping on left.
   GPS: N37°22.59′ W107°33.58′

▼2.1   SO Private driveway on right.
▼2.3   SO Seasonal closure gate.
▼3.2   SO Gated track on right.
▼3.3   SO Graham Creek USFS Campground on left.
   GPS: N37° 23.33′ W107°32.35′

▼3.6   SO North Canyon USFS Campground on left; then creek on right.
   GPS: N37°23.59′ W107°32.25′

▼3.7   SO FR 852 on right.
▼4.1   SO Pine Point USFS Campground on left. Zero trip meter.
   GPS: N37°23.98′ W107° 32.04′

▼0.0   Proceed north on CR 501A.
▼0.3   SO Seasonal closure gate.
▼0.4   SO Croll Cabins on left and gates. Then Five Branches Campground office on left and general store on right.
▼0.7   SO Bridge over Los Pinos River.
▼1.0   TR Elk Point Lodge.
▼1.05   TL Intersection with CR 501 on left and FR 602 to campground on left. Signs for Five Branches Camper Park and Elk Point lodge at intersection.
   GPS: N37°24.42′ W107°32.03′

▼1.2   SO Road on left of Middle Mountain USFS Campground.
▼2.9   SO Pull off for picnic area and fishing

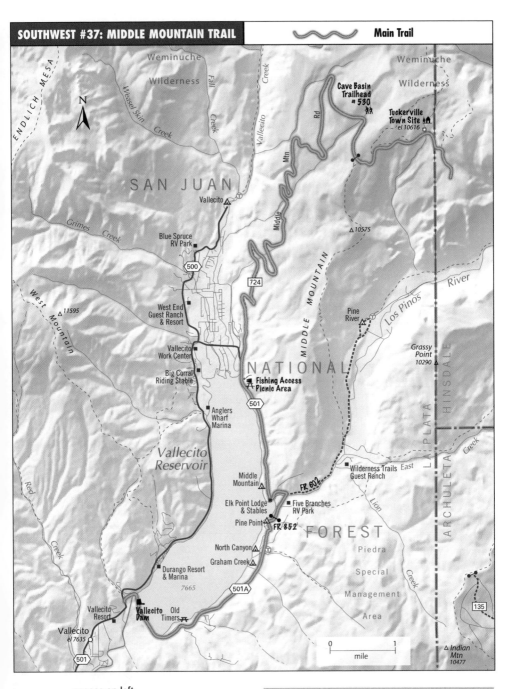

access on left.

▼3.1   SO   Wits End Ranch Trout House on left; then pavement begins for a short section.
GPS: N37°26.17' W107° 32.57'

▼3.3   TR   Onto FR 724, Middle Mountain Road.
GPS: N37°26.30' W107°32.58'

▼ 0.0   Zero trip meter and proceed north on FR 724.

▼ 0.56   SO   Cattle guard.

▼ 4.86   SO   Cattle guard.

▼ 5.92   SO   Road on right.

▼ 10.6   SO   Cattle guard and seasonal closure

gate. Zero trip meter.
GPS: N37°29.19' W107°30.40'

▼ 0.0   Continue south on FR 724.
▼ 0.10 SO Track on right.
▼ 1.70 SO Tuckerville town site on left and right and historical marker on right.
▼ 1.89 SO Seasonal closure gate.
▼ 2.25 SO Road forks. Zero trip meter.
         GPS: N37°29.29' W107°28.88'

▼ 0.0   BL On unmarked road.
▼ 0.95 TR Road forks into unmarked tracks.
         GPS: N37°29.88' W107°28.21'

▼ 1.2   Trail ends at drop off and Weminuche Wilderness Boundary.
         GPS: N37°30.02' W107°28.28'

SOUTHWEST REGION TRAIL #38

First Notch Road

STARTING POINT Intersection of US 160 and First Notch Road, 23 miles west of Pagosa Springs
FINISHING POINT Intersection of US 160 and CR 135, 32 miles west of Pagosa Springs
TOTAL MILEAGE 20.8 miles
UNPAVED MILEAGE 20.8 miles
DRIVING TIME 1.5 hours
ELEVATION RANGE 6,671 to 9,610 feet
USUALLY OPEN April through October
BEST TIME TO TRAVEL May through October
DIFFICULTY RATING 4
SCENIC RATING 9

Special Attractions
■ Trail within a network of 4WD roads.
■ Spectacular fall aspen viewing.
■ Access to trails for ATVs, motorbikes, and snowmobiles.
■ Shady and private backcountry camping sites.
■ Popular with hunters in fall season.

Description
West of Pagosa Springs 20 miles, the trail begins at the intersection of US 160 and First Notch Road (FR 620). Crossing a cattle guard, proceed north on First Notch Road (FR 620), a wide, maintained, smooth dirt and gravel road.

Initially the trail crosses through forest of low oak and willow scrub, ponderosa pines, engleman spruce, cottonwood, and aspen trees, which blocks views of the surrounding terrain. The forest recedes in sections revealing grassy parks and shady clearings for backcountry camping and picnicking.

The easygoing road passes gated tracks and grazing cattle, following power lines generally to the northwest. The smooth surface ends at a turnaround area after which the road becomes FR 620, a narrow one-lane 4WD trail. The rock-embedded, eroded track runs through a dense stand of aspen trees that are close to the road, making passing along this section impossible without backing up. The difficulty rating increases from 1 to 4 on this section due to the large embedded rock, uneven surface, and narrow width of the trail.

Sign at turnaround area before the trail becomes difficult

Potentially muddy section through aspen forest

The embedded rock and eroded surface make this section slow going. In wet conditions, this drive can be muddy and slippery, creating the likelihood of puncturing a tire or getting stuck in the mud. If you drive this trail in wet conditions, mud tires are highly recommended.

After about 8 miles, bear left at a fork in the road. This portion of trail has less embedded rock, but the rough ride continues due to potholes and ruts.

While the trail gains elevation, there are few views because of the generally dense vegetation bordering the road. When rare views present themselves, they are particularly scenic in the fall months due to the large number of aspens growing in the vicinity.

After traveling 11.5 miles, FR 620 intersects with CR 135. Turn left and head south on the wide, maintained dirt road. If scenery is your thing, take note of the broad, expansive views of the Grassy Mountains to the northwest, Indian Mountain (10,477 feet) to the north, Wickenson Mountain (8,792 feet), Severn Peak (8,178 feet), and Shaefer Mountain (8,646 feet) to the west.

Along CR 135, the difficulty rating drops back down to a 1 with more difficulty in wet and muddy conditions. Traveling 9.2 more miles, the trail ends at the intersection with US 160, approximately 32 miles west of Pagosa Springs and 27 miles east of Durango.

Current Road Information

San Juan National Forest
Columbine Ranger District (East)
PO Box 439
367 South Pearl Street
Bayfield, CO 81122
(970) 884-2512

Map References

Benchmark's *Colorado Road and Recreation Atlas,* pp. 122, 123
USFS   San Juan National Forest
USGS   1:24,000   Chimney Rock, Baldy Mtn.
1:100,000 Durango
Maptech CD-ROM: Southwest Colorado/ Durango/Telluride

Colorado Atlas & Gazetteer, p. 87
The Roads of Colorado, p. 155

Route Directions

▼ 0.0 SO 23 miles west of Pagosa Springs, the trail begins at the intersection of US 160 and First Notch Road (FR 620); then cattle guard.

6.95 ▲ SO Cattle guard; then trail ends at the intersection of First Notch Road (FR 620) and US 160 between Durango and Pagosa Springs.
GPS: N37°13.74' W107°21.46'

▼ 0.19 SO Cattle guard; then seasonal closure gate.

6.76 ▲ SO Seasonal closure gate; then cattle guard.
GPS: N37°13.90' W107°21.46'

▼ 2.58 SO Cattle guard.

4.37 ▲ SO Cattle guard.
GPS: N37°15.21' W107°23.23'

▼ 2.6 SO Corral on left.

4.4 ▲ SO Corral on right.

▼ 5.33 SO FR 133 on left.

1.62 ▲ SO FR 133 on right.
GPS: N37°16.60' W107°24.11'

▼ 6.24 SO Cattle guard.

0.71 ▲ SO Cattle guard.
GPS: N37°17.27' W107°24.50'

▼ 6.95 TR Turnaround area with FR 620 on right. Zero trip meter.

0.0 ▲   Proceed southwest on First Notch Road (not marked).
GPS: N37°17.72' W107°24.97'

▼ 0.0   Proceed northwest on FR 620 signed Moonlick Park Road.

4.61 ▲ TL Enter turnaround area with trail on left. Zero trip meter.

▼ 1.16 SO Pass through gate.

3.45 ▲ SO Pass through gate.
GPS: N37°18.70' W107°25.18'

Main Trail

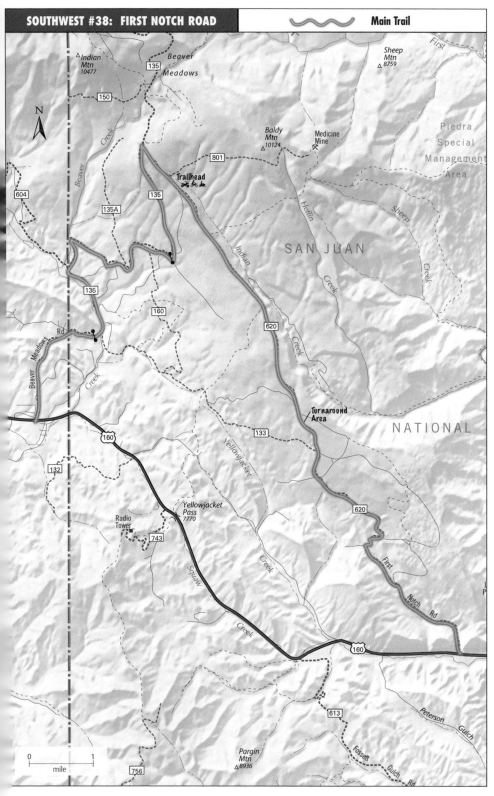

Indian Mtn
10477

Beaver Meadows

135

150

Sheep Mtn
8759

First

Piedra Special Management Area

Baldy Mtn
10124

Medicine Mine

801

604

Trailhead

135

135A

Heflin

Sheep

Creek

SAN JUAN

Beaver

Creek

Indian

135

160

620

Creek

Rd

Beaver Meadows

Creek

Turnaround Area

NATIONAL

160

133

Yellowwicker

132

Radio Tower

Yellowjacket Pass
7770

743

620

Creek

Squaw

First

Notch

Rd

160

L
P

0   1
mile

756

Pargin Mtn
8936

613

Peterson

Gulch

Fossett

Gulch

Rd

▼ 1.3   BL   Road forks with unmarked track on right.
3.31 ▲   SO   Unmarked track on left.
      GPS: N37°18.81' W107°25.24'

▼ 2.65   SO   Pass through gate.
1.96 ▲   SO   Pass through gate.
      GPS: N37°19.68' W107°26.17'

▼ 2.71   SO   Trail on right to numerous springs, open to snowmobiles, ATVs, and dirt bikes.
1.9 ▲   SO   Trail on left to numerous springs, open to snowmobiles, ATVs, and dirt bikes.
      GPS: N37°19.73' W107°26.22'

▼ 4.61   TL   Cattle guard; then T-intersection with CR 135. Zero trip meter.
0.0 ▲   Proceed northeast on FR 620; then cattle guard.
      GPS: N37°21.00' W107°27.51'

▼ 0.0   Proceed southwest on CR 135; then cattle guard.
9.21 ▲   TR   Cattle guard; then intersection with FR 620 on right.

▼ 1.95   SO   Closure gate.
7.26 ▲   SO   Closure gate.
      GPS: N37°19.44' W107°26.93'

▼ 3.26   SO   FR 135A, Beaver Slope Road on right.
5.95 ▲   SO   FR 135A, Beaver Slope Road on left.
      GPS: N37°19.33' W107°27.83'

▼ 5.26   SO   FR 604 on right.
3.95 ▲   BR   FR 604 on left.
      GPS: N37°19.20' W107°28.74'

▼ 6.66   SO   Seasonal closure gate; then cattle guard.
2.55 ▲   SO   Cattle guard; then seasonal closure gate.
      GPS: N37°18.32' W107°28.33'

▼ 7.59   SO   Private drive on right.
1.62 ▲   SO   Private drive on left.
      GPS: N37°18.28' W107°29.18'

▼ 8.84   SO   Cattle guard.
0.37 ▲   SO   Cattle guard.
      GPS: N37°17.41' W107°29.54'

▼ 9.21   SO   Trail ends at intersection of CR 135 and US 160 approximately 32 miles west of Pagosa Springs and 27 miles east of Durango.
0.0 ▲   Trail begins at intersection of US 160 and CR 135 between Durango and Pagosa Springs.
      GPS: N37°17.10' W107°29.61'

Muddy, rocky, and eroded FR 620, part of the First Notch Road

First Fork Road

STARTING POINT Intersection of US 160 and CR 166 (FR 622), 23 miles west of Pagosa Springs

FINISHING POINT First Fork Trailhead at Piedra River crossing

TOTAL MILEAGE 11.9 miles (one-way)

UNPAVED MILEAGE 11.7 miles

DRIVING TIME 45 minutes (one-way)

ELEVATION RANGE 6,518 to 7,628 feet

USUALLY OPEN April through October

BEST TIME TO TRAVEL May through October

DIFFICULTY RATING 1

SCENIC RATING 7

Special Attractions

- Scenic Piedra River in First Box Canyon.
- Access to prime fly fishing spots a short hike along Piedra River Trail (#596).
- Nearby Lower Piedra USFS Campground on the banks of the Piedra River.
- Wildlife viewing.
- Snowmobile trail in winter.

Description

First Fork Road (also marked CR 166) proceeds north from US 160, 23 miles west of Pagosa Springs. Pavement on the road ends after 0.2 mile and the dirt and gravel road is wide and well-maintained. Following the Piedra River (river is on the left) the road travels through First Box Canyon, cloaked with ponderosa pine, blue and engleman spruce forest.

The Piedra River flows alongside First Fork Road

Dubbed "River of the Rock Wall," the Piedra River's cold alpine waters flow through the narrow and steep First and Second Box Canyons. Technical Class IV and V rafting trips ride the demanding rapids from May through July. The 22-mile rafting run is normally broken into a 2-day adventure.

Abundant wildlife make this canyon home, and commonly spotted animals include elk, mule deer, black bears, and river otters. Lucky viewers may also spot peregrine falcons, which are nested at the nearby Chimney Rock Fire Lookout.

The road becomes a wide, low shelf road overlooking the scenic river valley. In sections, the canyon walls on the east side of the road are adorned by red rock formations. Use caution in wet conditions since the trail can be slippery when wet.

Gradually the shelf road climbs high above the Piedra River, creating dramatic drop-offs and overlooks above the river. Although the trail is high above the river, the road remains wide and smooth with plenty of room for passing.

Just before 12 miles on the odometer, the trail crosses the Piedra River and ends at Piedra Hunters Campground and the Piedra River Trailhead. The trailhead is marked on maps as the First Fork Trailhead. The campground is a large, dispersed camping area with a large corral for horses. The Piedra River hiking trail climbs northeast through Second Box Canyon with easy access to the river and some of the best fly fishing in the area. Commonly caught fish include rainbow, brown, and cutthroat trout.

Current Road Information

San Juan National Forest
Pagosa Ranger District
180 Second St
PO Box 310
Pagosa Springs, CO 81147
(970) 264-2268

Piedra Hunters Campground, a dispersed camping area at the end of the trail

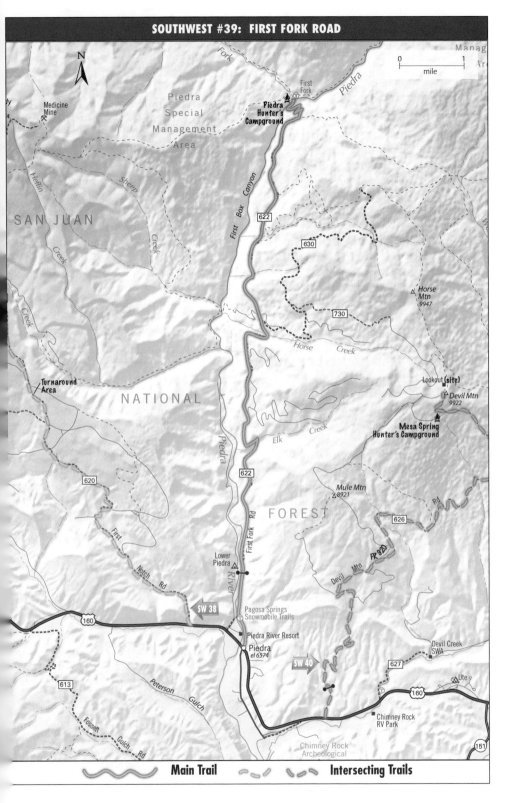

N

Manag
Ar

0   1
mile

Fork

Piedra

First
Fork

Piedra
Special
Management
Area

Medicine
Mine

Piedra
Hunter's
Campground

ly

First Box Canyon

Heflin

Sheep

Creek

SAN JUAN

622

630

Horse
Mtn
9947

730

Creek

Creek

Horse   Creek

Lookout (site)

Devil Mtn
9922

Turnaround
Area

NATIONAL

Creek

Mesa Spring
Hunter's Campground

Piedra

Elk   Creek

620

622

Mule Mtn
8921

FOREST

Rd

626

First Fork Rd

First

Rd

Devil Mtn Rd

Notch Rd

Piedra

River

Lower
Piedra

SW 38

Pagosa Springs
Snowmobile Trails

160

Piedra River Resort

Piedra
el 6374

SW 40

Devil Creek
SWA

627

Ute

160

613

Peterson   Gulch

Chimney Rock
RV Park

151

Fossett

Gulch   Rd

Chimney Rock
Archeological

〰〰〰 **Main Trail**   〰 〰 〰 〰 〰 **Intersecting Trails**

Map References

Benchmark's *Colorado Road and Recreation Atlas*, p. 123
USFS San Juan National Forest
USGS 1:24,000 Chimney Rock, Devil Mtn.
1:100,000 Durango
Maptech CD-ROM: Southwest Colorado/Durango/Telluride
Colorado Atlas & Gazetteer, p. 155
The Roads of Colorado, p. 87

Route Directions

▼ 0.0   Trail begins at the intersection of US 160 and CR 166/FR 622 west of Pagosa Springs 23 miles.
         GPS: N37°13.42' W107°20.45'

▼ 0.17   SO Pavement ends.
▼ 0.38   SO Cattle guard.
         GPS: N37°13.74' W107°20.45'

▼ 1.21   SO Seasonal closure gate.
         GPS: N37°14.45' W107°20.49'

▼ 4.64   SO Track on right.
▼ 5.9   SO Cattle guard.
         GPS: N37°17.84' W107°20.39'

▼ 6.77   SO Intersection with FR 630 on right and parking lot and trail head on left.
         GPS: N37°18.18' W107°20.15'

▼ 6.95   SO Seasonal closure gate.
         GPS: N37°18.32' W107°20.18'

▼ 7.73   SO Cattle guard.
         GPS: N37°18.82' W107°20.30'

▼ 9.0   SO Cattle guard.
         GPS: N37°19.75' W107°19.84'

▼ 11.8   SO Bridge over Piedra River; then cattle guard.
         GPS: N37°21.21' W107°19.44'

▼ 11.9   Trail ends at closure gate.
         GPS: N37°21.39' W107°19.53'

Devil Mountain Trail

STARTING POINT Intersection of US 160 and FR 626, 20 miles west of Pagosa Springs
FINISHING POINT Summit of Devil Mountain
TOTAL MILEAGE 11.3 miles, including spur (one-way)
UNPAVED MILEAGE 11.3 miles, including spur
DRIVING TIME 1.75 hours (one-way)
ELEVATION RANGE 6,532 to 9,957 feet
USUALLY OPEN April through October
BEST TIME TO TRAVEL May through mid-October
DIFFICULTY RATING 2, 4 for the spur
SCENIC RATING 8

Special Attractions

- Site of Devil Mountain Fire Lookout.
- Sweeping panoramas from the summit of Devil Mountain.
- Shady, private backcountry camp sites.
- Wildlife viewing.
- Views of Chimney Rock and the adjacent Chimney Rock Archeological Area.

History

Originally built in 1955 to assume primary lookout duties for the region, the steel-framed Devil Mountain Fire Lookout replaced the nearby Chimney Rock Fire Lookout, which is still located within the

USGS marker on Devil Mountain Trail

Rocky sections on Devil Mountain Trail

Chimney Rock Archeological Area just south of the start of Devil Mountain Trail (FR 626).

Devil Mountain Fire Lookout was sold to the Jicarilla Tribe in the 1990s and relocated from the summit of Devil Mountain to a spot on their land in New Mexico. The lookout is now known as *Atole*. The footings that remain at the summit of Devil Mountain are now used for radio equipment and a few other small structures.

The old Chimney Rock Fire Lookout can be visited from mid-May through September by guided tour. A fee is charged for access to the Chimney Rock Archeological Area. The lookout was originally built in 1940 on the site of an ancient fire pit, probably used by Chacoan Indians, who primarily lived in Chaco Canyon, 90 miles south, in what is today New Mexico.

When the Chimney Rock Lookout was decommissioned, the upper story was removed. In 1988, the structure was modified again to be used by the Chimney Rock Interpretive Association. From October to February, when the Archeological Area is closed for winter, the lookout can be viewed by walking three miles south from US 160. From March 1 to May 15, the area is closed for falcon nesting.

Located due south of Devil Mountain Trail, the geological formation known as Chimney Rock includes the two rock "towers" that stand 300-feet above the surrounding terrain. Spanish explorers referred to the formations as *La Piedra Parada*, or standing rock, and later American settlers dubbed the formation Chimney Rock. It wasn't until the 1920s that researcher Jean Jeançon named the smaller of the two rock towers Companion Rock.

Jeançon is also credited with the discovery

Views of aspen stands are particularly scenic in fall

Radio equipment at the site of Devil Mountain Fire Lookout

of the ancient structures at the base of Chimney Rock. Finally in the 1970s, archeologists excavated and reinforced the 16 structures, which include the Great Kiva, a pit house, the Ridge House, and the Great House. All these historic sites can be explored on a guided tour in the Chimney Rock Archeological Area, 4,100 acres of San Juan National Forest established in 1970.

Chocoan Indians are thought to have built these ancient structures near Chimney Rock sometime around A.D. 1,000. Historians believe Chimney Rock was sacred to the group. Suggestions of the rock's significance and function include a religious shrine, a lunar observatory, or a timber-harvesting site. Research shows the short-lived settlement burned and was abandoned around A.D. 1,100.

In more recent times, Chimney Rock and Companion Rock have been a refuge of a different sort. Companion Rock in particular is a popular nesting site for the peregrine falcon. After the use of DDT became widespread in the 1930s and 40s, populations of the falcon in the eastern United States became completely extinct and populations in the west were reduced 80 to 90 percent by the mid-1960s.

In 1970, the falcon was placed on the endangered species list. Through the efforts of reintroduction programs and the ban on the use of DDT, the U.S. Fish and Wildlife Service reclassified the status of the falcon as threatened in 1984. Falcon populations have increased and stabilized so much that the falcon was removed from both the endangered and threatened species list in August 1999. Keen wildlife observers may spot the falcon from any of the trails in the vicinity.

Only footings of Devil Mountain Fire Lookout remain at the summit of Devil Mountain, but there are still beautiful views over Devil Creek Canyon

Old outhouse at the summit of Devil Mountain

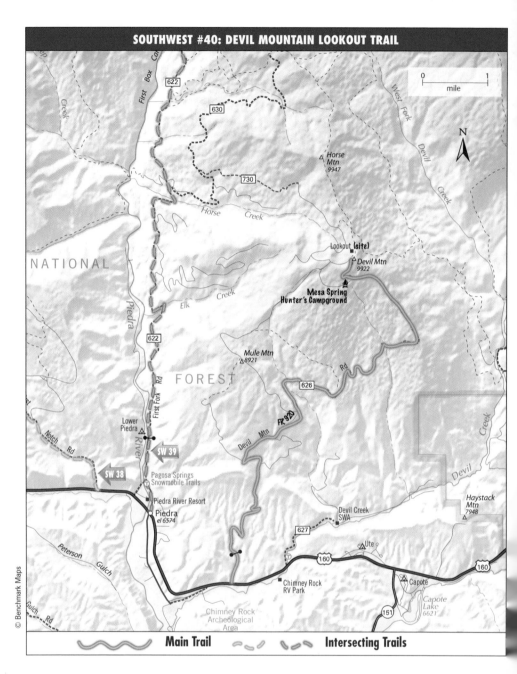

Main Trail ⌒⌒⌒ 〰〰 **Intersecting Trails**

Description

FR 626 or Devil Mountain Road begins traveling north from US 160, 20 miles west of Pagosa Springs, 21 miles east of Bayfield, and approximately 40 miles east of Durango. The unmaintained dirt road is a wide one-lane trail with room to pass oncoming vehicles. Embedded rocks and ruts make the drive rough, and the trail is best driven in dry conditions to avoid damaging the road or getting bogged. Although the ride is rough, the main trail is not difficult.

Initially the road travels through forest of scrub oak and evergreens, predominantly ponderosa and lodgepole pines. Also along the first half a mile, the track follows alongside private land. Please stay on the trail and respect private property.

Consistently rocky, the track continues to climb, snaking toward the summit of Devil Mountain (9,922 feet); overlooks from the trail become increasingly expansive through the trees. There are particularly scenic views to the south of Chimney Rock in the Chimney Rock Archeological Area. Aspen and cottonwood trees along with pinyon and juniper begin to appear in the forest surrounding the trail.

At 4.2 miles on the odometer, the trail forks and the main trail, FR 626, continues and becomes a shelf road with overlooks of aspen stands below in Devil Creek Canyon. Around this point on the trail are some clearings for shady backcountry campsites, picnic spots, or wildlife viewing locations. Elk and mule deer, along with a variety of other wildlife are commonly seen in the vicinity.

Past the short section of shelf road, just over 10 miles into the trip, the Mesa Spring Hunter's Campground is located beside the trail, not far from the summit of Devil Mountain. The dispersed camping area has grill grates, a pit toilet, and a fresh water spring. Traveling through dense stands of aspen, other clearings near the trail make ideal backcountry campsites.

About one mile farther, the trail crosses over a section of slickrock, where it forks. The remaining section of the trail is the right-hand spur to the summit of Devil Mountain and the site of Devil Mountain Fire Lookout. The spur has a difficulty rating of 4, and this point makes a convenient turnaround for travelers not wanting the extra challenge. The rough, rocky 0.3-mile trip is worth the effort for the sweeping 360° panoramas at the summit of Devil Mountain. Radio equipment and an old outhouse are all that remain at the summit.

Current Road Information

San Juan National Forest
Pagosa Ranger District
180 Second St
PO Box 310
Pagosa Springs, CO 81147
(970) 264-2268

Map References

Benchmark's *Colorado Road and Recreation Atlas,* p. 123
USFS   San Juan National Forest
USGS   1:24,000   Chimney Rock, Devil Mtn.
    1:100,000 Durango
Maptech CD-ROM: Southwest Colorado/ Durango/Telluride
Colorado Atlas & Gazetteer, p. 87
The Roads of Colorado, pp. 155, 156

Route Directions

▼ 0.0   Trail begins at intersection of US 160 and FR 626 between Durango and Pagosa Springs.
    GPS: N37°12.41' W107°18.89'

▼ 0.54 SO Seasonal closure gate.
    GPS: N37°12.88' W107°18.81'

▼ 2.23 SO Cattle guard.
    GPS: N37°13.69' W107°18.46'

▼ 4.23 BR Road forks with FR 920 on left. Zero trip meter.
▼ 0.0   Proceed east on FR 626.
    GPS: N37°14.63' W107°17.94'

▼ 0.48 SO Cattle guard.
    GPS: N37°14.86' W107°17.59'

▼ 6.61 SO Mesa Spring Hunter's Campground on left.
    GPS: N37°16.81' W107°16.68'

▼ 6.75 BR Road forks in wide solid rock clearing. Zero trip meter.
▼ 0.0   Proceed northeast toward lookout area.
    GPS: N37°16.82' W107°16.78'

▼ 0.3   Trail ends at site of lookout tower.
    GPS: N37°17.06' W107°16.57'

Summitville Ghost Town Trail

STARTING POINT Intersection of Colorado 17 and FR 250
FINISHING POINT Del Norte
TOTAL MILEAGE 68.3 miles
UNPAVED MILEAGE 57.9 miles
DRIVING TIME 4 hours
ROUTE ELEVATION 8,000 to 11,900 feet
USUALLY OPEN Early July to late October
DIFFICULTY RATING 2
SCENIC RATING 6

Special Attractions
■ The well-preserved ghost town of Summitville.
■ An easy 4WD trail that is not heavily used.

History
This route crosses Stunner Pass and skirts Elwood Pass, both of which were part of two early access roads through the area. In 1884, the LeDuc and Sanchez Toll Road Company constructed the first road over Stunner Pass as a freight route to service mines that had started activity in the early 1880s. Mining activity here was short-lived, and by the early 1890s, the area was almost deserted. However, the route has been maintained for recreational access to the area.

The U.S. army constructed a road across Elwood Pass in 1878 to connect Fort Garland and Fort Harris in Pagosa Springs. In the 1880s, mining began in the area, and significant deposits of gold and silver were found. Summitville ghost town is the best preserved of the mining camps from this period; numerous buildings still stand.

Gold was discovered in the Summitville area in 1870, and hundreds of prospectors rushed to the site. At its peak, the town had a population of more than 600, and 2,500 mining claims were staked. Summitville boomed during the 1880s and produced a fortune for Tom Bowen, who became a leading figure in Colorado politics and a great rival of Horace Tabor. The town was in decline by 1890 and deserted by 1893.

Shortly before the halfway point of the

The trail beside the Conejos River near Platoro

trail, you pass the township of Platoro, which was established after ore was discovered in 1882. It was named for the Spanish words *plata* and *oro* meaning silver and gold. Because of its inaccessibility, burros were the only means of transporting ore and supplies. In 1888, the wagon road to Summitville was completed and the town grew to a population of 300 by 1890. However, the ore in the area was of indifferent quality and the miners drifted away.

Although little is known about the township of Stunner, located a short distance northwest of Platoro, it is suspected that the first construction occurred in 1882. Both gold and silver were mined in the vicinity, but the remoteness of the camp prevented proper development. No railroad came through Stunner, but the LeDuc and Sanchez Toll Road Company built a road to the area.

Between 100 and 150 people lived in Stunner in its best days. A post office was established in 1890, but the town lasted only a few more years. Stunner's decline began because of the high costs of transporting ore from the area's mines and was speeded by the lack of good ores to justify these costs. Because nearby Summitville (on the other side of the range) offered better ore and lower transportation costs, Stunner's population began to dwindle. There is nothing left of Stunner. A U.S. Forest Service ranger station and the Stunner Campground are on the site of the old town.

Summitville, on South Mountain, at 11,200 feet, was once the highest of Colorado's major gold camps. In 1870, miner John Esmund discovered rich ore in abundance near the area that would, years later, become the Summitville mining camp. After Esmund's initial discovery, he returned to the location several times to extract ore, during which time he failed to file proper paperwork to become legal owner of the claim. When he showed up at the site in 1873, he found that someone else had established a mine on his spot. The mine, the Little Annie, became the best gold-producing mine in the district.

MOUNTAIN LION

Also referred to as cougars or pumas, these wildcats have grayish-, yellowish-, or reddish-brown fur, with buff areas on their bellies, necks, and faces. They are feline in appearance, with long, heavy legs; padded feet; retractable claws; black-tipped tails; small, round heads; short muzzles; small, rounded ears;  supple bodies; strong legs; and long tails. The females range in weight from 80 to 150 pounds, and males range from 120 to 180 pounds. Cougars are good climbers and jumpers, able to leap more than twenty feet.

Elusive and rarely seen, cougars are territorial loners who live in the wilderness throughout the mountains, foothills, and canyons. Carnivorous eaters, they thrive on large mammals such as deer and elk as well as on porcupine, mice, rabbits, and grouse. They locate prey, slink forward close to the ground, then spring onto their victims' backs, holding and biting the neck. They may bury the "leftovers" of a large kill and return one or more times to eat.

The cougars breed in pairs, and females with young move together. Each has its home range and rarely ventures outside it. Cougars breed every other year, and although there is no fixed breeding season, it often occurs in winter or early spring. Their maternity dens are lined with vegetation and may be located in caves, in thickets, under rock ledges, or in similarly concealed, protected places. Two to four spotted kittens are born in maternity dens from May to July.

By 1882, Summitville had boomed to a population of more than 1,500; the town was made up of several hotels, *The Summitville Nugget* newspaper, saloons, stores, and nine mills at which ore from the nearby mines was processed. One of the mining companies set up a pool hall to entertain the men during their free time, especially over the long winter months. The hall attracted pool sharks who came to match skills with the miners from all over the state.

Del Norte, about twenty-four miles northeast of Summitville, was an important shipping point, supply center, and stagecoach junction. One of its residents, Tom Bowen, struck it rich with his Little Ida Mine in Summitville. Suave and colorful, Bowen wore many hats; and his skill and luck were legendary. Over the course of his life, Bowen was a judge, an entrepreneur, a lawyer, governor of Idaho Territory, brigadier general for the Union army, a U.S. senator, and a very big gambler. Bowen once lost shares of a mining company in a poker game, only to have the winner decide he didn't want the shares. Bowen redeemed the stock for a nominal purchase; and the mine, the Little Ida, later made him very rich. He purchased many other mining properties, including the Little Annie.

In 1885, some of the nearby mines began having financial difficulties and even the Little Annie could not pay workers' salaries. Other mines were playing out, so the population of Summitville rapidly declined. By 1889, only about 25 residents remained in town.

There were a few short revivals in mining: one in the late 1890s and another in the late 1930s. In recent years, Galactic Resources, Ltd. re-opened operations, but they suffered heavy losses through 1991 and sold the balance of their mining interests. In 1993, Galactic filed for bankruptcy.

Although some of the ghost town's buildings have been torn down to make room for modern-day mining, a number of well-preserved buildings still stand in Summitville. It is an interesting ghost town to explore and photograph.

Chandler Mine boardinghouse, circa 1935

Description

The first section of this route, FR 250 over Stunner Pass, is a well-maintained dirt road. The pass stretches between the Alamosa River to the north and the Conejos River to the south.

It offers a peaceful journey through gentle, rolling hills, interspersed with rock formations and overlooks that provide wonderful views along the valley and across the mountains. Abundant aspen groves spangle the hillsides in gold during the fall. The area also offers many accessible campsites and hiking trails.

In good weather conditions, the Stunner Pass section (FR 250) of this route warrants a difficulty rating of only 1. The Elwood Pass section (FR 380) is more difficult and causes this route to be rated at 2; although FR 380 is higher, narrower, and rougher than FR 250, it is a relatively easy route and should provide no obstacles for a 4WD vehicle.

An extensive network of 4WD and hiking trails are located near the trail. Mining activity has continued in the Summitville area until recent times, although presently operations are restricted to an EPA-mandated cleanup of the mine remains.

Current Road Information

Rio Grande National Forest
Divide Ranger District
13308 West Hwy 160
Del Norte, CO 81132
(719) 657-3321

Rio Grande National Forest
Conejos Peak Ranger District
15571 County Road T.5
LaJara, CO 81140
(719) 274-8971

Map References

Benchmark's *Colorado Road and Recreation Atlas,* pp. 112, 124
USFS   Rio Grande National Forest
USGS   1:24,000   Del Norte, Indian Head, Horseshoe Mtn., Del Norte Peak, Summitville, Elwood Pass, Summit Peak, Platoro, Red Mtn., Spectacle

Chandler Mine boardinghouse at Summitville ghost town today

Lake, La Jara Canyon
1:100,000 Antonio, Del Norte
Colorado Atlas & Gazetteer, pp. 79, 80, 89, 90
The Roads of Colorado, pp. 141, 142, 157, 158
Trails Illustrated, #142

Route Directions

▼ 0.0   At intersection of Colorado 17 and FR 250, zero trip meter. There is a signpost for Platoro. Turn onto the unpaved road.

16.1 ▲   End at intersection of Colorado 17 and FR 250.

GPS: N 37°07.98′ W 106°21.01′

▼ 6.0   SO   Cattle guard. USFS Spectacle Lake Campground.

10.1 ▲   SO   USFS Spectacle Lake Campground. Cattle guard.

▼ 6.3   SO   USFS Conejos Campground.

9.8 ▲   SO   USFS Conejos Campground.

▼ 7.4   SO   Intersection. FR 855 on left goes to Rybold Lake and No Name Lake.

8.7 ▲   SO   Intersection. FR 855 on right goes to Rybold Lake and No Name Lake.

▼ 8.8   SO   Cattle guard.

7.3 ▲   SO   Cattle guard.

▼ 10.8   SO   Southfork Trailhead.

5.3 ▲   SO   Southfork Trailhead.

▼ 11.1   SO   Intersection. Track on left for fishing access. Public restrooms.

5.0 ▲   SO   Intersection. Track on right for fishing access. Public restrooms.

▼ 11.8   SO   Cattle guard.

4.3 ▲   SO   Cattle guard.

▼ 13.2   SO   Valdez Creek Campground.

2.9 ▲   SO   Valdez Creek Campground.

▼ 13.8   SO   Trail Creek backcountry camping area.

2.3 ▲   SO   Trail Creek backcountry camping area.

▼ 13.9   SO   Track on right.

2.2 ▲   SO   Track on left.

▼ 14.2   SO   Cattle guard.

1.9 ▲   SO   Cattle guard.

▼ 16.1   SO   Track on left is FR 100 to Lake Fork Ranch. Zero trip meter.

Stunner in 1913

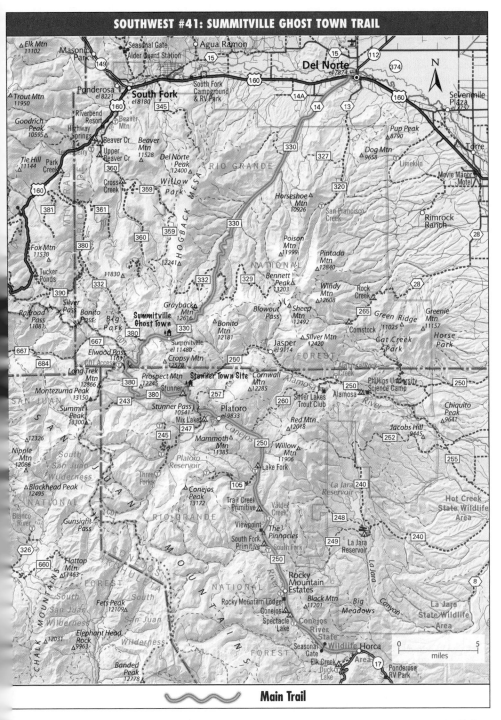

Main Trail

0.0 ▲	Proceed along main road.	
	GPS: N 37°17.87' W 106°28.63'	
▼ 0.0	Proceed along main road.	

12.0 ▲	SO	Track on right is FR 100 to Lake Fork Ranch. Zero trip meter.
▼ 0.6	SO	Cattle guard.

11.4 ▲ SO Cattle guard.

▼ 0.8 SO USFS Lake Fork Campground.
11.2 ▲ SO USFS Lake Fork Campground.

▼ 1.6 SO Beaver Lake Trailhead.
10.4 ▲ SO Beaver Lake Trailhead.

▼ 3.5 SO Fisher Gulch.
8.5 ▲ SO Fisher Gulch.

▼ 4.1 SO Track on right is FR 260 to Robinson
Gulch.
7.9 ▲ SO Track on left is FR 260 to Robinson
Gulch.

▼ 4.7 SO Cattle guard.
7.3 ▲ SO Cattle guard.

▼ 6.1 SO Intersection. Platoro on left.
5.9 ▲ SO Intersection. Platoro on right.
GPS: N 37°21.25′ W 106°31.72′

▼ 6.5 SO Track on left to Mix Lake Campground.
5.5 ▲ SO Track on right to Mix Lake Campground.

▼ 7.6 TR T-intersection. Left goes to Mix Lake
and Platoro Reservoir.
4.4 ▲ TL Intersection.

▼ 8.6 BL Stunner Pass (unmarked). FR 257 on
right goes to Lilly Pond and Kerr Lake.
3.4 ▲ BR FR 257 on left goes to Lilly Pond and
Kerr Lake. Stunner Pass (unmarked).
GPS: N 37°21.73′ W 106°33.44′

▼ 11.7 SO Bridge over Alamosa River. Campsites.
0.3 ▲ SO Campsites. Bridge over Alamosa River.

▼ 12.0 UT Intersection. Straight on goes to Monte
Vista. Zero trip meter.
0.0 ▲ Continue on FR 380.
GPS: N 37°23.04′ W 106°33.95′

▼ 0.0 Continue on FR 380.
11.7 ▲ UT Intersection. Straight on goes to Monte
Vista. Zero trip meter.

▼ 0.3 SO USFS Stunner Campground on left. Old
cabin on right is part of Stunner town site.

11.4 ▲ SO Old cabin on left is part of Stunner town
site. USFS Stunner Campground on right.
GPS: N 37°22.88′ W 106°34.21′

▼ 0.9 SO Cattle guard.
10.8 ▲ SO Cattle guard.

▼ 1.1 SO Drainage ford.
10.6 ▲ SO Drainage ford.

▼ 2.1 SO Track on right.
9.6 ▲ SO Track on left.

▼ 2.4 SO Track on right.
9.3 ▲ SO Track on left.

▼ 4.0 SO Lake DeNelda on left (private property).
7.7 ▲ SO Lake DeNelda on right (private property).

▼ 4.1 BR Intersection. Dolores Canyon Road,
Treasure Creek Road, and Lake Annella
are straight ahead. Turn toward
Summitville and US 160.
7.6 ▲ TL Intersection. Dolores Canyon Road and
Treasure Creek Road are to the right.
Proceed toward Platoro.

▼ 4.6 SO Cattle guard.
7.1 ▲ SO Cattle guard.

▼ 6.5 SO Track on right.
5.2 ▲ SO Track on left.

▼ 7.7 SO Crater Lake hiking trail on left.
4.0 ▲ SO Crater Lake hiking trail on right.

▼ 8.4 SO Intersection. Track and Continental
Divide Trail on left. Elwood Pass is a
short distance along it. Straight ahead
is South Fork sign.
3.3 ▲ SO Intersection. Track and Continental
Divide Trail on right. Elwood Pass is a
short distance along it.

▼ 8.7 SO Elwood Cabin on right. Track FR 3802A
on left.
3.0 ▲ SO Elwood Cabin on left. Track FR 3802A
on right.

▼ 9.6 SO Track on right.

2.1 ▲ SO Track on left.

▼ 9.8 SO Cattle guard.
1.9 ▲ SO Cattle guard.

▼ 11.7 TR Intersection. Summitville ghost town
to the right. Southfork to the left.
Zero trip meter.
0.0 ▲ Proceed toward Platoro.
GPS: N 37°25.75' W 106°37.70'

▼ 0.0 Proceed toward Summitville.
2.5 ▲ TL Intersection. Southfork to the right.
Platoro to the left. Zero trip meter.

▼ 2.0 SO Summitville Historic Mining Town sign.
0.5 ▲ SO Summitville Historic Mining Town sign.

▼ 2.5 BL Summitville visitor information board.
Zero trip meter.
0.0 ▲ Continue on route.
GPS: N 37°25.93' W 106°35.94'

▼ 0.0 Continue on route.
26.5 ▲ BR Summitville visitor information board.
Zero trip meter.

▼ 0.1 TL Turn onto FR 330.
26.4 ▲ TR Intersection with FR 244.

▼ 0.3 SO Intersection. Go toward Del Norte.
Wightman Fork is to the right and
forks off from the mining entrance.
26.2 ▲ SO Intersection.

▼ 0.6 SO Track on right.
25.9 ▲ SO Track on left.

▼ 1.7 SO Track on left.
24.8 ▲ SO Track on right.

▼ 2.7 SO Track on left.
23.8 ▲ SO Track on right.

▼ 7.8 TR Intersection. Crystal Lakes and South
Fork to the left. Follow toward Del Norte.
18.7 ▲ BL Intersection. Crystal Lakes and South
Fork to the right.
GPS: N 37°29.31' W 106°32.81'

▼ 9.3 TL Cattle guard. Intersection. Fuches
Reservoir and Blowout Pass to the
right. Follow road to Del Norte (FR 14).
17.2 ▲ TR Intersection. Fuches Reservoir and
Blowout Pass straight on. Follow
FR 330. Cattle guard.

▼ 11.0 SO Road on left.
15.5 ▲ SO Road on right.

▼ 11.2 SO Cattle guard.
15.3 ▲ SO Cattle guard.

▼ 12.3 SO Track on right to campsite.
14.2 ▲ SO Track on left to campsite.

▼ 13.0 SO Track on left is FR 331 to Bear Creek.
13.5 ▲ SO Track on right is FR 331 to Bear Creek.

▼ 14.0 SO Track on right.
12.5 ▲ SO Track on left.

▼ 14.3 SO Track on right.
12.2 ▲ SO Track on left.

▼ 14.4 SO Track on right.
12.1 ▲ SO Track on left.

▼ 15.1 SO Seasonal gate.
11.4 ▲ SO Seasonal gate.

▼ 15.2 SO Cattle guard.
11.3 ▲ SO Cattle guard.

▼ 15.6 SO Pavement begins. Bridge.
10.9 ▲ SO Bridge. Unpaved.

▼ 24.4 SO Road 14A forks off on left.
2.1 ▲ SO Road 14A on right.

▼ 26.5 End at intersection of FR 14 and US
160 in Del Norte.
0.0 ▲ At intersection of FR 14 and US 160 in
Del Norte, zero trip meter and proceed
along FR 14. Sign reads "National
Forest Access, Pinos Creek Rd,
Summitville."
GPS: N 37°40.75' W 106°21.66'

Owl Creek and Chimney Rock Trail

STARTING POINT Intersection US 550 and County 10 near Ridgway

FINISHING POINT Intersection County 858 and US 50

TOTAL MILEAGE 40.9 miles

UNPAVED MILEAGE 40.9 miles

DRIVING TIME 2 hours

ROUTE ELEVATION 7,000 to 10,200 feet

USUALLY OPEN May to November

DIFFICULTY RATING 1

SCENIC RATING 8

Special Attractions

- An easy trail that provides a more interesting, alternate route to the paved road between Ouray and Gunnison.
- Views of Chimney Peak and Courthouse Mountain.
- Scenic Silver Jack Reservoir.
- Access to good hiking, fishing, and backcountry camping.

Description

This route, on maintained gravel roads across mainly gentle grades, starts just north of Ridgway at the intersection of US 550 and County 10. Initially, the road travels through ranch land before crossing Cimarron Ridge at Owl Creek Pass, and then it continues through Uncompahgre National Forest.

The route offers many good views of the conspicuous rock peaks known as Chimney Rock and Courthouse Mountain. Many large stands of aspen line the route, providing wonderful fall scenery for photographers or for those who just enjoy the bright yellow panorama typical of fall in Colorado.

The road continues its gentle course past Silver Jack Reservoir and on to US 50.

Current Road Information

Grand Mesa, Uncompahgre and Gunnison National Forests
Ouray Ranger District
2505 South Townsend Avenue
Montrose, CO 81401
(970) 240-5300

Map References

Benchmark's *Colorado Road and Recreation*

A stand of aspen and a rock outcrop near Silver Jack Reservoir

Atlas, p. 96
USFS Uncompahgre National Forest
USGS 1:24,000 Cimarron, Washboard
      Rock, Courthouse Mtn., Dallas
      1:100,000 Montrose
The Roads of Colorado, pp. 107, 123
Colorado Atlas & Gazetteer, pp. 66, 67
Trails Illustrated, #141 (incomplete)

Route Directions

▼ 0.0   From US 550 (1.7 miles north of the
           junction with Colorado 62 in Ridgway
           and approximately 26 miles south of

Montrose), zero trip meter and proceed
east along County Road 10. This turnoff is marked with a National Forest
Access sign to Owl Creek Pass.

8.6 ▲   End at intersection with US 550. This
          intersection is 12 miles north of Ouray.
          GPS: N 38°10.44′ W 107°44.47′

▼ 0.8 BL Road forks.
7.7 ▲ BR Intersection.

▼ 2.5 BL Cow Creek goes to the right.
6.1 ▲ BR Cow Creek goes to the left.

Chimney Rock

Easygoing trail through aspen forest

▼ 3.9 BR County 8 enters on left.
4.7 ▲ BL Remain on County Road 10 toward
           Ridgway and US 550.

▼ 4.9 SO Bridge over creek.
3.7 ▲ SO Bridge over creek.

▼ 5.3 BL Road forks. Turn onto County 8 toward
           Owl Creek Pass.
3.3 ▲ BR Onto County Road 10.

▼ 5.6 SO Cattle guard.
3.0 ▲ SO Cattle guard.

▼ 6.1 SO Cattle guard.
2.5 ▲ SO Cattle guard.

▼ 6.8 SO Cattle guard. Road narrows.
1.8 ▲ SO Cattle guard.

▼ 7.7 SO Cattle guard. Enter Uncompahgre
           National Forest. Name of road
           becomes FR 858.
0.9 ▲ SO Leave Uncompahgre National Forest,
           then cross cattle guard.

▼ 8.6 BL Vista Point scenic overlook on right.
           Zero trip meter.
0.0 ▲   Continue toward Ridgway.
           GPS: N 38°11.21′ W 107°37.74′

▼ 0.0   Continue toward Owl Creek Pass.
6.6 ▲ BR Vista Point scenic overlook on left.
           Zero trip meter.

▼ 0.3 SO Road on right.
6.3 ▲ SO Road on left.

▼ 2.7 SO Track on left.
3.8 ▲ SO Track on right.

▼ 3.4 SO Cattle guard.
3.2 ▲ SO Cattle guard.

▼ 4.0 BL Track on right dead-ends in short
           distance.
2.5 ▲ BR Track on left dead-ends in short
           distance.

▼ 5.9 SO Cross over Nate Creek Ditch.

0.6 ▲ SO Cross over Nate Creek Ditch.

▼ 6.6 SO Cattle guard; then Owl Creek Pass.
           Track on left goes to parking bay.
           Zero trip meter at summit.
0.0 ▲   Continue along main road toward
           Ridgway.
           GPS: N 38°09.45′ W 107°33.71′

▼ 0.0   Continue along FR 858.
6.6 ▲ SO Owl Creek Pass. Track on right goes to
           a small parking area. Zero trip meter at
           the summit and cross over cattle guard.

▼ 0.3 BL Track on right is FR 860, which offers
           several viewing areas for Chimney Rock.
6.3 ▲ BR Track on left is FR 860. Remain on FR
           858 toward Owl Creek Pass.

▼ 0.8 SO Cattle guard.
5.8 ▲ SO Cattle guard.

▼2.9   SO Cross over bridge.
3.7 ▲ SO Cross over bridge.

▼ 5.0 SO Cattle guard.
1.6 ▲ SO Cattle guard.

▼ 6.3 SO Cimarron Fork track on left.
0.3 ▲ SO Track to Cimarron Fork on right.

▼ 6.4 SO Cross over bridge.
0.2 ▲ SO Cross over bridge.

▼ 6.5 SO Track on right to Middle Fork (FR 861.1)
           Trailhead. Cross over bridge.
0.1 ▲ SO Cross over bridge. Track on left goes
           to Middle Fork Trailhead.

▼ 6.6 TL Follow FR 858 toward Cimarron and
           Silver Jack Reservoir. Right goes to
           East Fork Trailhead. Zero trip meter.
0.0 ▲   Continue toward Owl Creek Pass.
           GPS: N 38°12.32′ W 107°30.92′

▼ 0.0   Continue along FR 858.
19.1 ▲ TR Straight goes to East Fork Trailhead.
           Zero trip meter.

▼ 0.8 SO Cross cattle guard with fishing access

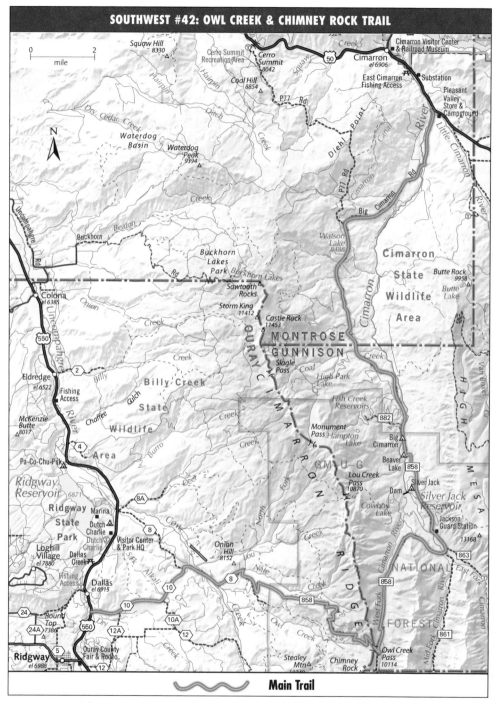

~~~~~~~~ **Main Trail**

on left.

18.3 ▲ SO Fishing access on right. Cross cattle
            guard.

▼ 1.7 SO Alpine Trailhead on right.

17.4 ▲ SO Alpine Trailhead on left.

▼ 2.3 SO FR 838 on right and Silver Jack
            Reservoir overlook on left.

16.8 ▲ SO Overlook to Silver Jack Reservoir on

right and FR 838 on left.

▼ 2.6   SO USFS Silver Jack Campground on left.
16.5 ▲ SO USFS Silver Jack Campground on right.

▼ 3.9   SO USFS Beaver Lake Campground on left.
15.2 ▲ SO USFS Beaver Lake Campground on right.

▼ 4.6   SO USFS Big Cimarron Campground on
              left. Paddock on right; then cattle
              guard. Cross bridge and leave the
              Uncompahgre National Forest. Road is
              now County 858.
14.5 ▲ SO Enter Uncompahgre National Forest
              and road becomes FR 858. Cross
              bridge and cattle guard. USFS Big
              Cimarron Campground on right.

▼ 5.4   SO Cross over bridge.
13.7 ▲ SO Cross over bridge.

▼ 9.0   SO Cross over bridge.
10.1 ▲ SO Cross over bridge.

▼ 10.7 SO Cross over bridge.
8.4 ▲   SO Cross over bridge.

▼ 11.4 SO Cross over bridge.
7.7 ▲   SO Cross over bridge.

▼ 13.4 SO County Road P 77 on left.
5.7 ▲   SO County Road P 77 on right.

▼ 17.2 SO Cross over bridge.
1.9 ▲   SO Cross over bridge.

▼ 19.1   End at intersection with US 50.
0.0 ▲   From US 50 (approximately 40 miles
              west of Gunnison) at the National
              Forest Access sign to Cimarron Road
              and Silver Jack Reservoir, zero trip
              meter and proceed southbound along
              Cimarron Road (County Road 858).
              GPS: N 38°24.86′ W 107°31.57′

RIDGWAY

Ridgway was founded in 1890 as a transportation center, named for R. M. Ridgway, a railroad official.

The Denver & Rio Grande's railway line ran between Ouray and Montrose, with Ridgway located between them. The Rio Grande Southern's Telluride route also passed by Ridgway.

The town attracted swarms of gamblers and con men. Swindlers encouraged bets on fixed horse races and lion hunts. Reportedly, an unfortunate mountain lion was kept tied behind one of Ridgway's saloons. Once a week the lion was released as the subject of a hunt, in which he would be captured and promptly hauled back to the saloon—only to be tethered and forced to await the next week's hunt.

Ridgway became a prosperous town; attractive stone and brick buildings, Victorian-style houses, stores, saloons, and pool halls adorned its streets. Its post office was established in the year the town

The Galloping Goose

was founded and still exists.

Bank president C. M. Stanwood pulled off a noteworthy fraud in Ridgway in 1931. He "borrowed" the deposits and contents of customers' security boxes and invested them in the stock market; but the market dropped and most everything was lost. The bank's patrons were wiped out. Some depositors were able to recoup some of their money, but those who lost their securities were unable to retrieve them.

When mining tapered off, the railroad began to suffer economic problems, although it continued to operate. In an effort to cut costs, the railroad introduced the Galloping Goose, a relatively inexpensive construction—part car, part train, with a cowcatcher on the front. The Galloping Goose operated until the early 1950s, and then the train and tracks were disposed of for scrap.

Much of the John Wayne movie *True Grit* was filmed in locations around Ridgway.

Ridgway is alive and well today. The town now consists of a number of homes, modern stores, and other businesses.

Uncompahgre Plateau Trail

STARTING POINT Intersection of US 550 and Jay Jay Road, north of Montrose
FINISHING POINT Intersection of Colorado 141 and County 26.10 (FR 402)
TOTAL MILEAGE 90.3 miles
UNPAVED MILEAGE 85.6 miles
DRIVING TIME 4 hours
ROUTE ELEVATION 5,597 to 9,120 feet
USUALLY OPEN Mid-June to late November
DIFFICULTY RATING 2
SCENIC RATING 7

Special Attractions
- Expansive views from the Uncompahgre Plateau, particularly from Windy Point.
- An extensive network of 4WD trails.
- Good backcountry camping.

History
Columbine Pass was named for Colorado's state flower, which once grew in abundance here. The pass is located on Uncompahgre Plateau. The Hayden Survey expedition noted and used the pass in the mid-1870s. The plateau was also an important summer hunting ground for the Ute for thousands of years prior to the Washington Treaty of 1880, in which they ceded the entire area and were relocated to reservations.

Description
This route starts at the intersection of US 550 and Jay Jay Road, 4.7 miles northwest of the National Forest office in Montrose (2505 S. Townsend). The next five miles involve a considerable number of intersections, so care is necessary to navigate correctly. At the end of this section of the route, you should turn onto Rim Road. There are more direct routes from Montrose, but this route offers the more varied and interesting views.

Initially, Rim Road is a well-maintained, wide 2WD road with some good views over the local ranch land and the San Juan Mountains in the distance to the south.

There are also numerous small side roads: stay on the main road in each case. Farther along the road, there are some sections that are rocky, but they will not pose any problems. The road travels along the rim of a canyon and provides good views of the terrain below.

After turning on to FR 402 (Divide Road), you will pass numerous campsites, which are heavily used in hunting season, and an extensive network of 4WD side roads, many of which can be very muddy. FR 402 is wide and well-maintained and suitable for passenger vehicles in dry conditions. The views to the west, down into the valley below, are particularly scenic.

As you descend from Uncompahgre Plateau, the scenery transforms over to the red rock walls of Jacks Canyon before connecting with Colorado 141 in the vast Unaweep Canyon. From here, the road travels along the path of East Creek before crossing the Gunnison River and joining US 50. Gunnison is approximately 24 miles from the intersection with Colorado 141, at the start of the paved road.

Current Road Information
Grand Mesa, Uncompahgre and Gunnison National Forests
Grand Valley Ranger District
2777 Crossroads Blvd, Suite 1
Grand Junction, CO 81506
(970) 242-8211

Colorado Bureau of Land Management
Uncompahgre Field Office
2465 South Townsend Avenue
Montrose, CO 81401
(970) 240-5300

Map References
Benchmark's *Colorado Road and Recreation Atlas*, pp. 82, 94, 95
BLM Montrose, Nucla, Delta
USFS Uncompahgre National Forest
USGS 1:24,000 Jacks Canyon, Uncompahgre Butte, Snipe Mtn., Windy Point, Starvation Point, Moore Mesa, Ute, Antone Spring,

Jacks Canyon

Pryor Creek, Dry Creek Basin,
Hoovers Corner, Olathe
1:100,000 Montrose, Nucla, Delta
Maptech CD-ROM: Grand Junction/
Western Slope
The Roads of Colorado, pp. 105, 105, 122
Colorado Atlas & Gazetteer, pp. 54, 55, 65, 66

Route Directions

▼ 0.0   At intersection of US 550 and Jay Jay
Road, turn west (left, if coming from
Montrose).
5.0 ▲   End at intersection with US 550.
       GPS: N 38°31.91′ W 107°56.19′

▼ 0.1   SO   Cross railroad tracks. Name of road
changes to Menoken Road.
4.9 ▲   SO   Cross railroad tracks.

▼ 1.4   SO   Cross over bridge and then a second
bridge.
3.6 ▲   SO   Cross over two bridges.

▼ 1.6   BL   Fork in road; go left onto South River Road.
3.4 ▲   BR   At fork in the road.

▼ 2.0   BR   County 5975 is on the left.
3.0 ▲   BL   County 5975 is on the right.

▼ 2.9   BL   Intersection. Remain on paved road.
2.1 ▲   BR   Intersection.

▼ 3.5   TL   Stop sign at intersection. Turn onto
County 5850.
1.5 ▲   TR   Intersection. Turn onto South River Road.
       GPS: N 38°31.56′ W 107°59.68′

▼ 3.9   TR   Onto Kiowa Road.
1.1 ▲   TL   Onto County 5850.

▼ 4.7   BL   Bear left, then cross bridge. Bear left
again onto unpaved road named
Shavano Valley Road.
0.2 ▲   BR   Onto Kiowa Road. Then cross bridge
and bear left again.

▼ 5.0   TR   Onto Rim Road. Zero trip meter.
0.0 ▲   Continue to the left.
       GPS: N 38°30.92′ W 108°00.54′

▼ 0.0   Proceed along Rim Road.
13.1 ▲   TL   Intersection. Zero trip meter.

▼ 1.7   SO   Track crosses road.
11.4 ▲   SO   Track crosses road.

▼ 2.2   SO   Track on right.
10.9 ▲   SO   Track on left.

▼ 2.5   SO   Track on right. Note: From this point,
there will be numerous side tracks,
but remain on Rim Road.
10.7 ▲   SO   Track on left.

▼ 3.0   SO   Track on right goes into canyon.
10.2 ▲   SO   Track on left goes into canyon. Note:
From this point, there will be numerous
side tracks, but remain on Rim Road.
       GPS: N 38°29.14′ W 108°02.50′

▼ 5.7   SO   Cross under high voltage wires and
cross cattle guard.
7.5 ▲   SO   Cattle guard. Cross under high
voltage wires.

▼ 9.7   BL   Cattleyards on left, then fork in road.
3.5 ▲   BR   Fork in the road, then cattleyards on right.

▼ 12.2   SO   Cattleyards on left, then cattle guard.
0.9 ▲   SO   Cattle guard, then cattleyards on right.
       GPS: N 38°24.43′ W 108°04.21′

▼ 13.1   TR   T-intersection with Old Highway 90.
Turn right and go through seasonal
closure gate. Zero trip meter.
0.0 ▲   Turn onto Rim Road.
       GPS: N 38°21.79′ W 108°02.94′

▼ 0.0   Proceed along Old Highway 90.
23.6 ▲   TL   Intersection. Zero trip meter.

▼ 0.4   SO   Cross over East Fork of Dry Creek.
23.2 ▲   SO   Cross over East Fork of Dry Creek.

▼ 5.8   SO   USFS Silesca Ranger Station on left.
17.8 ▲   SO   USFS Silesca Ranger Station on right.

▼ 7.9   SO   FR 402 on left (Dave Wood Road and
Norwood).

15.7 ▲ SO FR 402 on right.
GPS: N 38°19.02' W 108°09.21'

▼ 8.3 SO USFS Iron Springs Campground on left.
15.2 ▲ SO USFS Iron Springs Campground on right.

▼ 8.5 BR Old Highway 90 turns left.
15.0 ▲ BL Intersection: Old Highway 90.

▼ 8.8 SO FR 527 on right.
14.7 ▲ SO FR 527 on left.

▼ 9.5 SO Road on right is Transfer Road/FR 508 to Olathe.
14.0 ▲ SO FR 508 on left.

▼ 10.9 SO West Antone Spring on left.
12.7 ▲ SO West Antone Spring on right.

▼ 11.9 SO Road to Pool Creek on right.
11.6 ▲ SO Road to Pool Creek on left.

▼ 13.7 SO Pool Creek Trailhead on right.
9.9 ▲ SO Pool Creek Trailhead on left.

▼ 14.0 SO West Pool Creek on right.
9.5 ▲ SO West Pool Creek on left.

▼ 15.2 SO FR 546 on right.
8.3 ▲ SO FR 546 on left.

▼ 16.3 SO FR 545 on right.

View from Rim Road into Dry Creek Basin

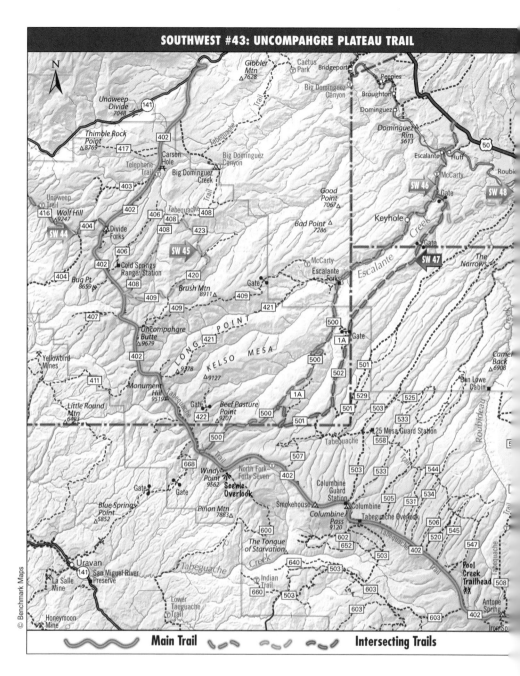

© Benchmark Maps

Main Trail 〜〜〜 ᶜᵒᵒ ᶜᵒᵒ **Intersecting Trails**

7.3 ▲	SO	FR 545 on left.

▼ 17.5	SO	FR 520 on right to Long Creek.
6.0 ▲	SO	FR 520 on left to Long Creek.

▼ 18.2	SO	FR 506 on right to Payne Mesa.
5.4 ▲	SO	FR 506 on left to Payne Mesa.

▼ 18.7	SO	Cattleyards on left. FR 534 on right.
4.9 ▲	SO	FR 534 on left. Cattleyards on right.

▼ 19.7	SO	FR 531 to Moore Mesa on right.
3.9 ▲	SO	FR 531 to Moore Mesa on left.

▼ 21.2	SO	FR 505 on right.
2.4 ▲	SO	FR 505 on left.

▼ 0.0   Continue on FR 402 to the right.

33.6 ▲   BL   Columbine Pass. FR 503 and cattleyards are on left. Zero trip meter.

▼ 0.3   SO   FR 533 to Monitor Mesa on the right.

33.2 ▲   SO   FR 533 to Monitor Mesa on the left.

▼ 0.7   SO   USFS Columbine Campground on left.

32.9 ▲   SO   USFS Columbine Campground on right.

▼ 0.9   TL   Cattle guard, then cross through creek to intersection. Follow FR 402 toward Windy Point. To the right is FR 503, Delta-Nucla Road.

32.7 ▲   TR   Intersection. FR 503 to Delta-Nucla is to the left. Turn right toward Columbine Pass. Cross creek, then cattle guard.

▼ 2.4   SO   Track on right.

31.1 ▲   SO   Track on left.

▼ 3.1   SO   FR 529 to Sawmill Mesa on right.

30.5 ▲   SO   FR 529 to Sawmill Mesa on left.

▼ 6.5   SO   FR 507, Lockhart on right.

27.1 ▲   SO   FR 507, Lockhart on left.

▼ 10.9   SO   FR 600 on left.

22.7 ▲   SO   FR 600 on right.

▼ 11.1   SO   Windy Point (great views!) on left.

22.5 ▲   SO   Windy Point (great views!) on right.

▼ 13.3   SO   FR 500 on right.

20.3 ▲   SO   FR 500 on left.

▼ 14.3   SO   Cattleyards on right.

19.3 ▲   SO   Cattleyards on left.

▼ 16.4   SO   Track on left.

17.2 ▲   SO   Track on right.

▼ 17.8   SO   Monument Hill on right.

15.7 ▲   SO   Monument Hill on left.

▼ 19.5   SO   Long Point and FR 421 on right.

14.0 ▲   SO   Long Point and FR 421 on left.

▼ 22.8   SO   USFS Tabeguache scenic overlook on left.

0.7 ▲   SO   USFS Tabeguache scenic overlook on right.

▼ 23.6   BR   Columbine Pass. FR 503 and cattleyards are on left. Zero trip meter.

0.0 ▲   Continue on FR 402 to the left.

▼ 21.3 SO FR 411 on left, then cattle guard.
12.3 ▲ SO Cattle guard, then FR 411 on right.

▼ 21.6 SO Short track on right.
12.0 ▲ SO Short track on left.

▼ 23.0 SO Uncompahgre Butte on right.
10.5 ▲ SO Uncompahgre Butte on left.

▼ 24.2 SO Track on right.
9.3 ▲ SO Track on left.

▼ 25.0 SO 3 H on left.
8.6 ▲ SO 3 H on right.

▼ 25.8 SO Mesa Creek FR 407 on left.
7.8 ▲ SO Mesa Creek FR 407 on right.

▼ 27.3 SO FR 408 on right.
6.3 ▲ SO FR 408 on left.

▼ 28.2 SO 3 J on right dead-ends.
5.4 ▲ SO 3 J on left dead-ends.

▼ 29.2 SO FR 410 on left dead-ends.
4.4 ▲ SO FR 410 on right dead-ends.

▼ 29.4 SO Track on right to USFS Cold Springs
             Work Center.
4.2 ▲ SO Track on left to USFS Cold Springs
             Work Center.

▼ 31.0 SO Track and cattleyards on left.
2.5 ▲ SO Cattleyards and track on right.

▼ 33.4 SO USFS Divide Forks Campground on left.
0.2 ▲ SO USFS Divide Forks Campground on right.

▼ 33.6 SO FR 404 Uranium Road on left.
             Zero trip meter.
0.0 ▲   Continue along FR 402.
             GPS: N 38°41.21' W 108°41.18'

▼ 0.0   Continue along FR 402.
15.0 ▲ SO FR 404 Uranium Road on right.
             Zero trip meter.

▼ 2.9   SO Cattle guard.
12.1 ▲ SO Cattle guard.

▼ 5.4   SO FR 403 to Big Creek Reservoir on left.
9.6 ▲ SO FR 403 to Big Creek Reservoir on right.

▼ 7.0   SO Cattle guard.
8.0 ▲ SO Cattle guard.

▼ 8.8   SO USFS Uncompahgre information board,
             seasonal closure gate, and cattle guard.
6.2 ▲ SO Cattle guard. Seasonal closure gate and
             USFS Uncompahgre information board.

▼ 9.2   SO Dominquez State Wildlife area on right and
             road to Dominquez BLM campground.
5.8 ▲ SO Dominquez State Wildlife area on left
             and road to Dominquez BLM
             campground.

▼ 12.9 SO Cattle guard.
2.1 ▲ SO Cattle guard.

▼ 15.0   Cattle guard. End at intersection with
             Colorado 141.
0.0 ▲   At intersection of County 90 and
             Colorado 141, zero trip meter and
             proceed along County 90. Cross
             cattle guard.
             GPS: N 38°50.26' W 108°34.45'

Far Pond Trail

STARTING POINT Intersection of Southwest
  #43: Uncompahgre Plateau Trail (FR
  402) and FR 404
FINISHING POINT Overlook of Unaweep
  Canyon
TOTAL MILEAGE 9.2 miles (one-way)
UNPAVED MILEAGE 9.2 miles
DRIVING TIME 1.25 hours (one-way)
ELEVATION RANGE 8,706 to 9,429 feet
USUALLY OPEN Year-round
BEST TIME TO TRAVEL Mid-April through
  mid-October
DIFFICULTY RATING 5
SCENIC RATING 8

Special Attractions

- Fun, remote-feeling 4WD trail.
- Access to Divide Forks ATV Complex, a network of trails for ATVs, motorbikes, and mountain bikes as well as access to trailheads for hikers and horseback riders only.
- Spectacular fall color aspen viewing.
- Wildlife viewing.

Description

Toward the north end of Southwest #43: Uncompahgre Plateau Trail is the intersection with FR 404. Zero your trip meter and proceed southwest on FR 404 toward Divide Forks USFS Campground to begin the trail. The wide one-lane dirt trail begins as a well-maintained road traveling along the aspen, ponderosa pine, and evergreen forest floor. In fall, the majority of the length of this trail is shaded by a beautiful yellow canopy of fall aspen foliage.

Divide Forks Campground is a no-fee dis-persed camping area with fire grates and picnic tables. No water or toilet facilities are available at the site and there is no trash pick up.

Proceed on FR 404 until the intersection with FR 416 at 2.8 miles on the odometer. After turning right onto FR 416, you will see a sign for the Divide Forks ATV Complex. In this vicinity is a shady picnic area and a sign showing a map of all the trails within the ATV complex. The network contains as many as 15 trails, several of which intersect with the main trail.

At this point the road narrows and becomes more challenging due to both embedded and loose rock. The difficulty rating of the trail is a 5 for the track after the turn off onto FR 416. Do not attempt this drive in wet conditions. The trail's surface is composed almost exclusively of dirt, making it a certainty vehicles will get stuck in the mud when the road is wet. Other obstacles to consider before navigating the remainder of the trail include large rocks, large ruts,

One in a series of ponds toward the end of Far Pond Trail

downed trees, and sections of slickrock.

Clearings in the forest near the trail make for shady backcountry campsites, picnic sites, or wildlife viewing locations. Readily spotted wildlife include mule deer, elk, and ducks among other flora and fauna. In sections the aspens grow quite close to the trail, minimizing passing ability. The track alternately travels over short sections of solid rock, forest, and grassy meadows.

At approximately 5.5 miles, cross through a gate making sure to leave it in the state you found it. Beyond the gate there are a series of ponds, Big Pond, Rim Pond, Middle Pond, and Far Pond. Approximately 0.5 mile past Far Pond, the trail ends at a picturesque overlook of Unaweep Canyon near some radio equipment.

Current Road Information

Grand Mesa, Uncompahgre and Gunnison National Forests
Grand Valley Ranger District
2777 Crossroads Blvd, Suite 1
Grand Junction, CO 81506
(970) 242-8211

Map References

Benchmark's *Colorado Road and Recreation Atlas,* pp. 82, 94
USFS   Uncompahgre National Forest
USGS 1:24,000   Casto Reservoir, Pine Mtn.
1:100,000 Delta
Maptech CD-ROM: Grand Junction/ Western Slope
Colorado Atlas & Gazetteer, p. 54
The Roads of Colorado, pp. 104, 105

Route Directions

▼ 0.0   Trail begins at the intersection of Southwest #43: Uncompahgre Plateau Trail (FR 402) and FR 404. Proceed southwest on FR 404.
GPS: N38°41.21' W108°41.22'

▼ 1.15 SO FR 637 on right, open for all uses.
▼ 2.55 SO FR 404 1A on right.
GPS: N38°40.95' W108°43.54'

▼ 2.62 SO Cattle guard.
▼ 2.84 TR FR 416 on right, signed to Wolf Hill

Section of slickrock on Far Pond Trail

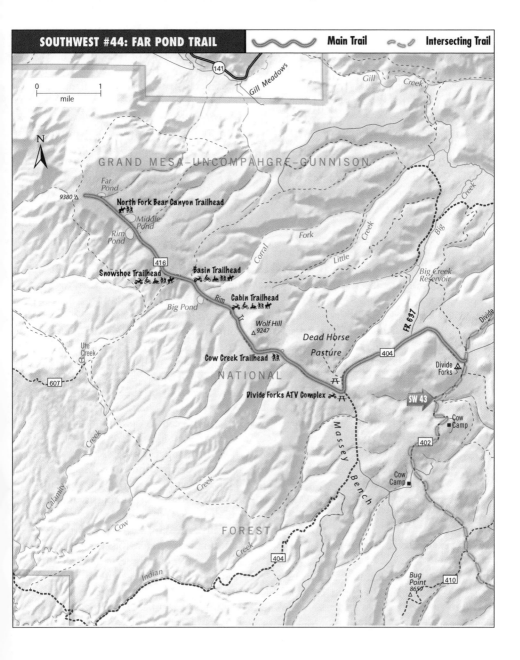

and Big Pond. Zero trip meter.
GPS: N38°40.71' W108°43.50'

on right.
GPS: N38°41.30' W108°44.74'

▼ 0.0   Continue west on FR 416.

▼ 1.0   SO   FR 416 1A on left.
GPS: N38°41.08' W108°44.43'

▼ 1.69   SO   Fence line on left and right.

▼ 2.70   TL   Gate.
GPS: N38°41.91' W108°45.67'

▼ 1.34   SO   Cow Creek Trail #611 on left for hiking and horseback riding only; then pond

▼ 3.33   SO   Big Pond on left.
GPS: N38°' W108°46.27'

▼ 3.63 SO Gate.

▼ 3.75 BL Intersection with Basin Trail #603, open for all uses.
GPS: N38°42.36' W108°46.58'

▼ 3.84 SO Snowshoe Trail #607 on left, open for all uses except 4WD vehicles.

▼ 4.51 SO Pond on left.
GPS: N38°42.77' W108°47.19'

▼ 5.0 TR Follow track around to the right of Rim Pond on left.
GPS: N38°43.00' W108°47.59'

▼ 5.30 SO Mid Pond on right.
GPS: N38°43.22' W108°47.67'

▼ 5.48 SO North Fork Bear Canyon Trail #653 on right for hikers and horseback riders only.

▼ 5.87 BL Far Pond on right.
GPS: N38°43.52' W108°48.10'

▼ 6.39 Trail ends at communications equipment and overlook of Unaweep Canyon.
GPS: N38°43.50' W108°48.58'

SOUTHWEST REGION TRAIL #45

Dominguez Ridge Loop

STARTING POINT Intersection of Southwest #43: Uncompahgre Plateau Trail and FR 408

FINISHING POINT Intersection of Southwest #43: Uncompahgre Plateau Trail and FR 408

TOTAL MILEAGE 21.3 miles

UNPAVED MILEAGE 21.3 miles

DRIVING TIME 1.75 hours

ELEVATION RANGE 7,840 to 9,069 feet

USUALLY OPEN Year-round

BEST TIME TO TRAVEL May through October

DIFFICULTY RATING 2

SCENIC RATING 7

Special Attractions

■ Expansive views of Grand Mesa.
■ Remote, low traffic trail.
■ Backcountry camping opportunities.

Description

The trail begins in a wide open meadow at the intersection of Southwest #43: Uncompahgre Plateau Trail and FR 408. Zero your trip meter and proceed east on FR 408. For nearly a mile after the trail commences, it travels through private ranch land. The high elevation (more than 9,000 feet) open range is clearly a prime location for grazing cattle, so be alert for cows in the road. The trail also crosses a number of cattle guards and near several corrals.

With few trees near the trail, expansive views of Grand Mesa to the northeast are common. Scenic in the fall when the few aspens glow yellow, the low pinyon and juniper pines and sagebrush growing on the undulating landscape give the feeling of being a cowboy on the open range before the West was won. The trail is dusty in dry conditions and can be quite muddy when wet.

At the intersection of FR 408 and FR 423, turn right onto FR 423. The trail becomes narrow and rutted due to erosion. This section gives the trail its difficulty rating of 2, although the majority is an easygoing difficulty rating of 1.

The pleasant trail undulates over Dominguez Ridge, following both Keith Creek and Dominguez Creek at different points. At the intersection with FR 420, leave FR 423 and proceed on FR 420 for just under 4.9 miles. Traveling over the open range and alternately through scrub oak and stands of aspens, there are many good backcountry camping opportunities along the entire length of this trail.

The last leg of the trail is a 3.7 mile section of FR 409 (Brush Ridge Trail), which completes the loop back to FR 408 near where the trail began.

Current Road Information

Grand Mesa, Uncompahgre and Gunnison National Forests

Dominguez Ridge Loop with Grand Mesa in the background

Easygoing Dominguez Ridge Loop

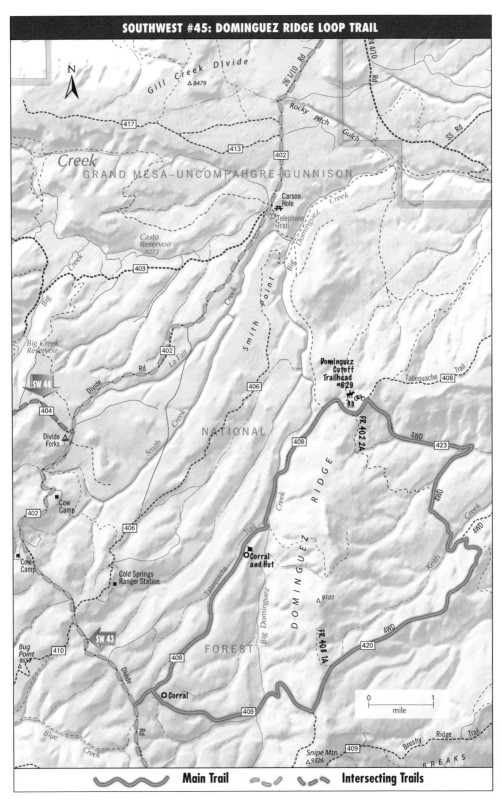

N

Gill Creek Divide
△ 8479

26 1/10 Rd

24 4/10 Rd

Rocky Pitch

SS. Rd

Gulch

417

413

402

Creek

GRAND MESA–UNCOMPAHGRE–GUNNISON

Carson Hole

Telephone Trail

Creek

Casto Reservoir 8073

Big Dominguez

403

Creek

Big

Big Creek Reservoir

402

La Fair

Rd

Smith Point

Dominguez Cutoff Trailhead #629

Tabeguache Trail 408

SW 44

Divide

406

Smith Creek

NATIONAL

FR 40 2A

4WD

423

404

Divide Forks △

408

RIDGE

4WD

Cow Camp

402

406

Creek

Keith

4WD

Creek

Cow Camp

Cold Springs Ranger Station

Corral and Hut

Tabeguache Trail

DOMINGUEZ

△ 9101

4WD

SW 43

Big Dominguez

FR 408 1A

420

Bug Point 8650 △

410

Divide

FOREST

408

Rd

0   1
mile

Corral

409

Blue Creek

Snipe Mtn △ 9326

409

Brushy Ridge Trail

BREAKS

Main Trail   〰   **Intersecting Trails**

Grand Valley Ranger District
2777 Crossroads Blvd, Suite 1
Grand Junction, CO 81506
(970) 242-8211

Map References

Benchmark's *Colorado Road and Recreation
  Atlas*, p. 94
USFS Uncompahgre National Forest
USGS 1:24,000 Casto Reservoir, Keith
  Creek, Snipe Mtn., Uncompahgre
  Butte
  1:100,000 Delta
Maptech CD-ROM: Grand Junction/
  Western Slope
Colorado Atlas & Gazetteer, pp. 54, 55
The Roads of Colorado, p. 105

Route Directions

▼ 0.0   Trail begins at intersection of Southwest
           #43: Uncompahgre Plateau Trail

(FR 402) and FR 408. Proceed east
on FR 408.

7.38 ▲   Trail ends at intersection with
           Southwest #43: Uncompahgre
           Plateau Trail (FR 402).
           GPS: N38°37.24' W108°40.02'

▼ 0.38 SO FR 409 on right; then cattle guard.
7.0 ▲   SO FR 409 on left; then cattle guard.
            GPS: N38°37.48' W108°39.73'

▼ 1.01 SO Closed track on right; then cattle guard.
            Enter private property for the next 0.75 mile.
6.37 ▲ SO Cattle guard and exit private property;
            then track on left.

▼ 1.22 SO Corral and hut on right on private property.
6.16 ▲ SO Corral and hut on left on private property.
            GPS: N38°38.00' W108°39.15'

▼ 1.32 SO Private road on right.
6.06 ▲ SO Private road on left.

Narrow section of Dominguez Ridge Loop

▼ 1.43 SO Stock pond on left.
5.95 ▲ SO Stock pond on right.

▼ 1.93 SO Cattle guard and old zigzag pattern
            fence line.
5.45 ▲ SO Old zigzag fence line and cattle guard.
            GPS: N38°38.44' W108°38.61'

▼ 3.97 SO Road on right.
3.41 ▲ SO Road on left.
            GPS: N38°39.82' W108°37.52'

▼ 4.08 SO Cross through wash.
3.3 ▲   SO Cross through wash.

▼4.86   SO Cross through creek.
2.52 ▲ SO Cross through creek.
            GPS: N38°40.54' W108°37.33'

▼ 5.75 SO Gate.
1.63 ▲ SO Gate.
            GPS: N38°41.09' W108°36.81'

▼ 6.32 SO FR 418 on right.
1.06 ▲ SO FR 418 on left.
            GPS: N38°41.50' W108°36.45'

▼ 6.68 SO FR 629, Dominguez Cutoff, on left for
            hikers, horseback riders, and mountain
            bikers only.
0.70 ▲ SO FR 629, Dominguez Cutoff, on right for
            hikers, horseback riders, and mountain
            bikers only.
            GPS: N38°41.56' W108°36.11'

▼ 7.00 BL FR 408 2A on right.
0.38 ▲ BR FR 408 2A on left.
            GPS: N38°41.38' W108°35.83'

▼ 7.38 TR FR 423 on right. Zero trip meter.
0.0 ▲   Proceed southwest on FR 423.
            GPS: N38°41.65' W108°35.61'

▼ 0.0   Proceed southeast on FR 423.
4.95 ▲ TL FR 423 on left. Zero trip meter.

▼ 0.67 SO Stock pond on left.
4.28 ▲ SO Stock pond on right.

▼ 0.83 SO Stock pond on left.
4.12 ▲ SO Stock pond on right.

▼ 2.01 SO Gate.
2.94 ▲ SO Gate.
            GPS: N38°40.95' W108°33.92'

▼ 2.32 TR FR 635, Bad Land, on left for hikers
            and horseback riders only. Stock pond
            on right. Proceed across dam.
2.63 ▲ TL Cross dam and stock pond on left. FR
            635, Bad Land, on right for hikers and
            horseback riders only.
            GPS: N38°40.98' W108°33.60'

▼ 2.4   SO Gate.
2.55 ▲ SO Gate.

▼ 3.40 SO FR 408 2A on right.
1.55 ▲ SO FR 408 2A on left.
            GPS: N38°40.34' W108°34.35'

▼ 4.95 SO Intersection with FR 420. Zero trip meter.
0.0 ▲   SO Proceed southwest on FR 423.
            GPS: N38°39.56' W108°33.92'

▼ 0.0   Proceed southeast on FR 42.
4.89 ▲ SO Intersection with FR 423. Zero trip meter.

▼ 0.60 BR Track on left.
3.31 ▲ BL Track on right.
            GPS: N38°39.46' W108°33.45'

▼ 1.86 SO Gate.
3.03 ▲ SO Gate.
            GPS: N38°38.63' W108°34.16'

▼ 3.9   TL/SO Road on left and gate. Proceed
               through gate then track on left.
               Continue straight on FR 420.
1.0 ▲   SO/TR Pass track on right then proceed
               through gate and turn right on road
               on right.
            GPS: N38°37.92' W108°36.15'

▼ 4.14 BL FR 408 1A on right.
0.75 ▲ BR FR 408 1A on left.
            GPS: N38°37.77' W108°36.32'

▼ 4.60 BR Track on left.

0.29 ▲	BL	Track on right.

▼ 4.89	TR	Intersection with FR 409. Zero trip meter.
0.0 ▲		Proceed west on FR 409.

GPS: N38°37.21' W108°36.67'

▼ 0.0		Proceed northwest on FR 409.
3.72 ▲	TL	FR 420 on left and FR 409 straight on. Zero trip meter.

▼ 0.20	BL	Track on right.
3.52 ▲	SO	Track on left.

▼ 0.43	SO	Cattle guard.
3.29 ▲	SO	Cattle guard.

▼ 0.85	SO	Track on right.
2.87 ▲	SO	Track on left.

GPS: N38°37.61' W108°37.30'

▼ 1.14	SO	Cross through wash.
2.58 ▲	SO	Cross through wash.

▼ 2.53	SO	Private access road to cabin on right.
1.19 ▲	BL	Private access road to cabin on left.

▼ 3.33	SO	Corral on right then cattle guard.
0.39 ▲	SO	Cattle guard then corral on left.

GPS: N38°37.25' W108°39.41'

▼ 3.72	TL	T-intersection with FR 408. Zero trip meter.
0.0 ▲		Proceed southeast on FR 409.

GPS: N38°37.48' W108°39.73'

▼ 0.0		Proceed southwest on FR 408.
0.38 ▲	TR	FR 409 on right. Zero trip meter.

▼ 0.38	SO	Trail ends at intersection with Southwest #43: Uncompahgre Plateau Trail.
0.0 ▲		Trail begins at intersection with Southwest #43: Uncompahgre Plateau Trail and FR 408.

GPS: N38°37.24' W108°40.02'

Escalante Canyon Road

STARTING POINT Intersection of US 50 and Road 650 (Escalante Canyon Road), 12 miles northwest of Delta

FINISHING POINT Intersection of Southwest #34: Uncompahgre Plateau Trail

TOTAL MILEAGE 38.3 miles

UNPAVED MILEAGE 38.2 miles

DRIVING TIME 2.5 hours

ELEVATION RANGE 4,809 to 9,665 feet

USUALLY OPEN Year-round

BEST TIME TO TRAVEL April through October

DIFFICULTY RATING 2

SCENIC RATING 8

Special Attractions

- Historic trail through a scenic red rock canyon.
- Walker Cabin and Palmer Smith Cabin.
- Gunnison River boat and raft launch.
- Access to a network of 4WD trails.

History

Escalante Canyon was formed over 600 million years as Escalante Creek carved the 1,300-foot deep gorge. Named for the two Spanish priests, Escalante and Dominguez, who explored the region (though never set foot in the actual canyon) in 1776, Escalante Canyon has a long history of human occupation. The Ute Indians for years had made the North Fork of the Escalante River their winter home. Early settlers, attracted by the year-long water supply and sheltering cliffs, soon pushed the Indians off the land.

Many cattle outfits began using the canyon as their winter quarters. In 1886, John Musser took up residence in one of the first homesteads in the canyon where he operated the Musser Cattle Company. Over the years the company has acquired ranch after ranch so that now most of the grazing paddocks along the canyon's entire length are consolidated under Musser Cattle. Not only is the cattle company the oldest and the largest in the area, it still uses some of its original ranching tech-

Walker Cabin

niques, moving cattle on horseback.

John Musser chose Escalante Forks as the site of his original homestead. Where the branches of the Escalante join, this strategic location gave his cattle ready access to various grazing pastures.

The infamous Colorado Sheep War centered around cattlemen protecting their grazing land from flocks of hungry sheep. In the early 1900s, an unwritten code existed which relegated sheep to one side of the Gunnison River. When Howard Lathrop hung a swinging bridge across the river and brought his sheep to graze on "cattle" land, the cattlemen retaliated by shooting hundreds of his sheep under the cover of darkness. Eventually Lathrop fled unscathed with the rest of his sheep back across the divide. Two residents of the canyon, Cash Sampson and Ben Lowe, however, died in a shootout supposedly instigated by a quarrel stemming from the Sheep War.

Most people in the canyon managed to live peaceably with one another. One man, Henry Walker and his large family lived in

Escalante Canyon where his skillfully crafted brick cabin still stands. The well-built structure is a testament to Walker's bricklaying ability. Built in 1911, the family was unable to afford cement for the mortar between the bricks, so Henry and his four sons laid the bricks using mud dug from a hole in the yard. The cement that exists on the cabin today is a thin coating, applied later after the family earned enough money to buy the materials. The Colorado Division of Wildlife owns the historic building today and visitors are welcome to explore the cabin.

Another resident, Captain Henry A Smith, was particularly sociable. When Smith was 65, the small but spunky man packed up and left his lifelong home of Joliet Indiana to serve in the Civil War. Though he only served a month in the war as acting captain, he became "Captain" for life.

A tombstone carver by trade, Cap, as he was known, laid three rock walls against an upright stone slab and hollowed a bed and gun-niche for himself out of the stone. Reportedly he intended the hollowed-out bed alcove to be his crypt after his death. Ironically, he died while on a trip to California where he was buried instead.

Above the stone house, high on the cliff, he inscribed his initials as well as the name of a friend, R. Bowen, who was a blacksmith in Delta. The two played cards during their visits. Located beneath Bowen's name is the symbol of his blacksmith shop, carved by Captain Smith. A talented carver, cemeteries throughout western Colorado had tombstones Cap had adorned with beautiful sentimental messages, roses, leaf arrangements, and ivy.

A convenient stopover between the mountain and town, fellow area residents often stopped to visit over dinner or even stay overnight. To accommodate all his visitors, Cap later built a second rock house for all of his guests, complete with beds below and in the loft. The back wall of his cabin has a set of hinged shelves, which conceals the secret room where he supposedly used to hide his meat supply. The house is now state owned, but remains open to visitors. The Colorado Division of Wildlife maintains the site and has added a picnic table and fire grate—perhaps carrying on Cap's tradition of the stone cabin as being the most visited location in Escalante Canyon.

Description

Escalante Canyon Trail commences at the intersection of US 50 and Road 650 (Escalante Canyon Road). The intersection is 12 miles northwest of Delta and is easily identified by the Escalante Canyon historical marker and rest area.

Zeroing your trip meter, proceed southwest on the wide, graded gravel road. The road is flat and easygoing and surrounded by desert vegetation of pinyon and juniper,

Escalante Creek flowing through Escalante Canyon

Cottonwoods growing on the banks of Escalante Creek

thistle, rabbit brush, and various cacti. Winding down into Escalante Canyon, the road follows a dry creek bed. The canyon begins to take shape as scenic rock buttes rise up from the rocky landscape. Red rock formations adjacent to the road create a maze of nooks and crannies that are interesting to explore.

At approximately 2.6 miles on the odometer, the road briefly becomes paved as it crosses Southern Pacific railroad tracks and the Gunnison River. Large cottonwood trees with colorful fall foliage grow on the banks of the river, and a boat launch that is frequently used for rafting trips is situated at the crossing.

At the river crossing and beyond, the road travels through private property. Please be respectful and stay on the trail. The trail follows alongside Escalante Creek after crossing the Gunnison River, and the next major point of interest, old Walker Cabin, is located beside the road. Henry Walker's well-crafted cabin makes a great place to stop and take photos. Beyond the cabin, the red rock canyon walls rise higher above the trail. The creek below is an oasis where wildlife is abundant among the rocky terrain.

Palmer Smith cabin is located 3.8 miles farther along the trail. Worth exploring, several structures remain at the site where Captain Smith carved his initials on the face of the red rock canyon wall. Please be respectful of the historical sites in the vicinity and leave them as you found them for future generations to enjoy.

Along the trail are sites for backcountry camping. Low vegetation provides some privacy, but sites within the canyon will have little if any shade. Be sure you are not on private property before setting up camp.

Along the section of trail between Palmer Canyon and Escalante Forks, the canyon widens, allowing more trees to grow around the trail. On this section of the trail is the

olorful rock formations in Escalante Canyon

Captain Smith's cabins in Escalante Canyon

Cap's bed alcove and gun niche inside the main cabin

Escalante Potholes Recreation Area. You will also cross numerous washes on the trail (not all are noted in the route directions). Some corrugations are the only obstacles to a smooth drive, and most of the length of the trail is graded and well-maintained.

Passing several tracks off the main trail and privately owned grazing paddocks, Escalante Forks is located 16.7 miles into the trail. About a mile farther there is a shallow ford through the North Fork of Escalante Creek.

Beyond the ford, the road becomes rougher with some embedded rock and erosion, but the difficulty rating does not increase. Use caution in this area in wet conditions as the road can become boggy.

After entering Uncompahgre National Forest the trail becomes signed FR 500. Beyond another creek crossing, the road traverses the canyon and switchbacks up the canyon wall onto Love Mesa. The short section of shelf road that climbs steeply out of the canyon provides dramatic overlooks of Escalante Canyon. For a short time the road rides along the rim of the canyon delivering more sweeping vistas of the surrounding terrain.

The road follows the desert-like Love Mesa over open range. Use caution as cattle pay little attention to where they graze (in the road). Gradually gaining elevation and traveling through canopies of aspen and ponderosa pine, private and shady back-country camp sites are more readily located.

Many of the tracks and side roads off the main trail are not marked on the Forest Service map, so stay on the main trail and follow the route directions carefully to avoid going off track. On the last several miles of this trail, high clearance is preferred to best navigate the rocky and eroded sections, which increases the trail's difficulty rating to a 2. Through breaks in the aspen and conifer forest along the higher reaches of the trail near its end, expansive views over Uncompahgre Plateau are worth commemorating with a photograph, especially in the fall before the aspens lose their bright yellow leaves.

Current Road Information

Colorado Bureau of Land Management
Uncompahgre Field Office
2465 South Townsend Avenue
Montrose, CO 81401
(970) 240-5300

The tombstone engraver carved his initials in the stone rock wall near his cabins

Fording Escalante Creek

Grand Mesa, Uncompahgre and Gunnison
National Forests
Grand Valley Ranger District
2777 Crossroads Blvd, Suite 1
Grand Junction, CO 81506
(970) 242-8211

Map References

Benchmark's *Colorado Road and Recreation
    Atlas*, pp. 83, 94, 95
BLM   Delta
USFS Uncompahgre National Forest
USGS 1:24,000 Windy Point, Snipe
    Mtn., Point Creek, Good Point,

    Escalante Forks, Kelso Point
    1:100,000 Delta, Nucla
Maptech CD-ROM: Grand Junction/
    Western Slope
Colorado Atlas & Gazetteer, p. 55
The Roads of Colorado, pp. 105, 106

Route Directions

▼ 0.0   Trail begins at intersection of US 50
        and Road 650, 12 miles northwest of
        Delta. Rest area and historical marker
        on left; then proceed southwest on
        Road 650.

The trail winds through scenic Escalante Canyon

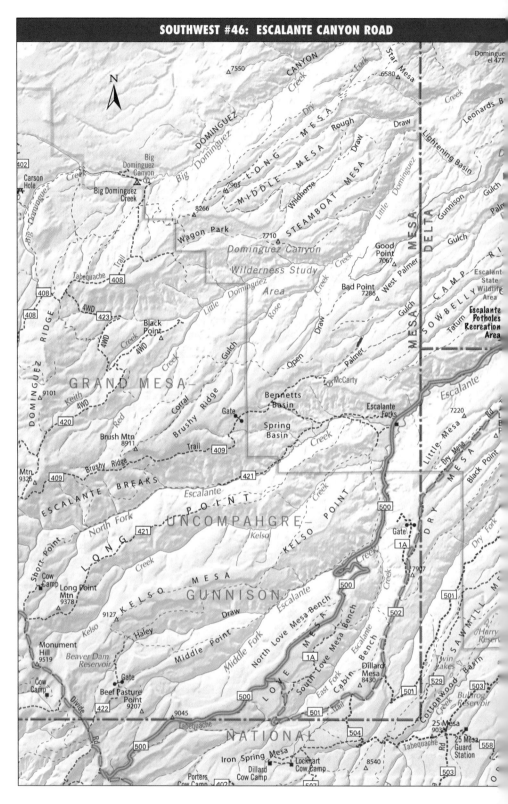

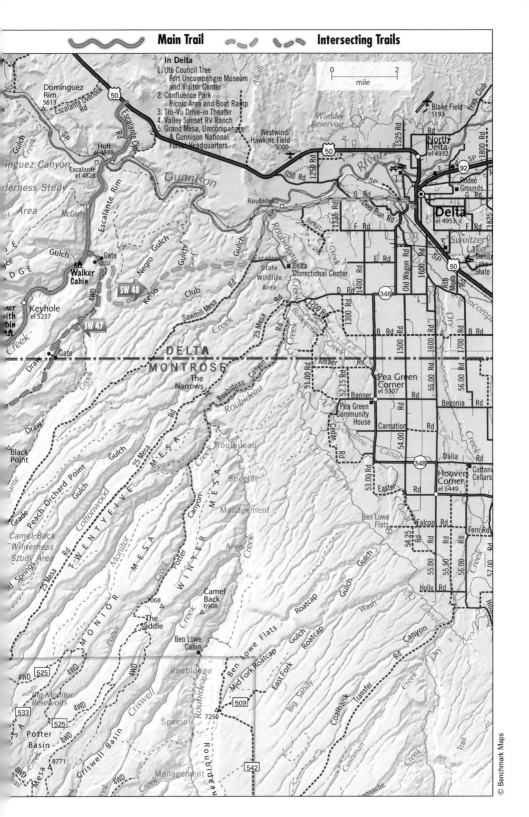

Main Trail   Intersecting Trails

In Delta
1. Ute Council Tree
   Fort Uncompahgre Museum
   and Visitor Center
2. Confluence Park
   Picnic Area and Boat Ramp
3. Tru-Vu Drive-in Theater
4. Valley Sunset RV Ranch
5. Grand Mesa, Umcompahgre
   & Gunnison National
   Forest Headquarters

0 _____ 2
mile

Dominguez
Rim
5613

Blake Field
5193

Trap Club

Alkali

Winkler
Reservoir

North
Delta
el 4932

92

Escalante Overlook Rd

50

Huff
el 4838

Escalante
el 4828

Escalante Cut

Westwind/
Hawkins Field
5000

50

1525 Rd

1800 Rd

Escalante Rim Rd

Gunnison

G50 Rd

1250 Rd

Rodeo
Grounds

SP

River

Delta
el 4953

McCarty

Roubideau

G Rd

Deer Run Rd

Sweitzer
Lake

DGE

Gulch

Negro Gulch

Gulch

Gate

Escalante
State
Wildlife
Area

Delta
Correctional Center

1325 Rd

F Rd

E Rd

Old Wagon Rd

1600 Rd

Sweitzer
Lake
State

Walker
Cabin

SW 48

Kelso

Club

Gulch

1400 Rd

348

50

Keyhole
el 5237

SW 47

4WD

Sawmill Mesa

25 Mesa

D Rd

1300 Rd

1500 Rd

1600 Rd

B Rd

Ash Mesa Rd

Uncompahgre

Rd

B Rd

B Rd

Draw

Gate

DELTA
MONTROSE

The
Narrows

Roubideau Canyon Rd

Roubideau

Amber Rd

1200 Rd

51 50 Rd

52.15 Rd

Banner

Buttermilk

Pea Green
Corner
el 5307

54.00

55.00 Rd

56.00 Rd

Begonia Rd

Black
Point

Draw

25 Mesa

MESA

Roubideau

Creek

Roubideau

Special

Management

Area

Pea Green
Community
House

Carnation

Rd

Cedar Rd

Ironstone Canal

348

Dalia Rd

Peach Orchard Point

Gulch

Gulch

Cottonwood

TWENTY FIVE

MONITOR MESA

Camel Back
Wilderness
Study Area

25 Mesa Rd

Potter

Monitor

Creek

WINTER MESA

Canyon

Creek

Hoovers
Corner
el 5449

Easter Rd

53.00 Rd

CR Lateral

Ben Lowe
Flats

Falcon Rd

54.25 Rd

Fern Rd

Cottony
Cellars

Hot Springs Rd

7068

The
Saddle

Camel
Back
6908

Ben Lowe
Cabin

Roubideau

Ben Lowe Flats

Mid Fork Roatcap

Roatcap Gulch

Gulch

East Fork

Roatcap

Big Sandy

Wash

Gulch

Holly Rd

55.00

55.50

56.00

57.00

Canyon

Dry

525

533

Big Monitor
Reservoirs

4WD

525

4WD

Criswell

Roubideau

Special

509

7250

Mid Fork

Coalbank Transfer Rd

Cushman

Creek

Trail

Potter
Basin

8771

Mesa

4WD

Criswell Basin

Creek

4WD

Management

Roubideau Creek

542

Uncompahgre

2.67 ▲ Trail ends at intersection with US 650 at rest area and historical marker. Turn right for Delta and left for Grand Junction.
GPS: N38°47.08' W108°14.81'

▼ 0.45 SO Tracks on right and left.
2.22 ▲ SO Tracks on left and right.

▼ 0.55 SO Cross over creek.
2.12 ▲ SO Cross over creek.

▼ 1.11 SO Two tracks on right.
1.56 ▲ SO Two tracks on left.

▼ 2.6 SO Pavement begins.
0.07 ▲ SO Pavement ends.

▼ 2.67 SO Cross railroad tracks; then boat launch on right and cross bridge over Gunnison River. Pavement ends. Zero trip meter.
0.0 ▲ Continue northeast on Road 650.
GPS: N38°45.49' W108°15.44'

▼ 0.0 Proceed southwest on Road 650.
3.55 ▲ SO Pavement begins. Cross bridge over Gunnison River; then boat launch on left and cross railroad tracks. Zero trip meter.

▼ 0.13 SO Cattle guard; then cross one-lane bridge over creek.
3.42 ▲ SO Cross one-lane bridge over creek; then cattle guard.

▼ 0.25 BL Private driveway on right.
3.3 ▲ BR Private driveway on left.

▼ 2.10 SO McCarty Trail for hikers only on right.
1.45 ▲ SO McCarty Trail for hikers only on left.
GPS: N38°44.24' W108°16.05'

▼ 2.55 SO Cattle guard.
1.0 ▲ SO Cattle guard.

▼ 3.55 SO Intersection Southwest #47: Dry Mesa Jeep Road (Road E23) on left. Signed to Escalante Rim Road and Dry Mesa Road and straight on to Escalante Forks and Palmer Gulch Road. Zero trip meter.
0.0 ▲ Continue northeast on Road 650.

GPS: N38°43.06' W108°16.15'

▼ 0.0 Continue southwest on Road 650.
12.2 ▲ SO Intersection with Southwest #47: Dry Mesa Jeep Road (Road E23) on right. Zero trip meter.

▼ 0.38 SO Cross through wash.
11.82 ▲ SO Cross through wash.
GPS: N38°42.81' W108°16.42'

▼ 0.51 SO Walker Cabin on left.
11.69 ▲ SO Walker Cabin on right.
GPS: N38°42.71' W108°16.48'

▼ 0.62 SO Pavement begins.
11.58 ▲ SO Pavement ends.

▼ 0.72 SO Pavement ends.
11.48 ▲ SO Pavement begins.

▼ 3.17 SO Cabin and corral on right on private property.
9.03 ▲ SO Cabin and corral on left on private property.

▼ 4.32 SO Palmer Smith Cabin and picnic area on right.
7.88 ▲ SO Palmer Smith Cabin and picnic area on left.
GPS: N38°40.83' W108°18.73'

▼ 4.35 SO Cross through wash.
7.85 ▲ SO Cross through wash.

▼ 4.58 SO Cattle guard.
7.62 ▲ SO Cattle guard.

▼ 5.24 SO Cross through wash.
6.96 ▲ SO Cross through wash.

▼ 5.50 SO Road on left to parking area for Escalante Potholes Recreation Area.
6.7 ▲ SO Road on right to parking area for Escalante Potholes Recreation Area.

▼ 5.77 SO Enter Montrose County; leave Delta County.
6.43 ▲ SO Enter Delta County; leave Montrose County.

▼ 6.22 SO Cross through wash.
5.98 ▲ SO Cross through wash.

▼ 7.1 SO Cross through wash.
5.1 ▲ SO Cross through wash.

▼ 7.41 SO Track on left.
4.79 ▲ SO Track on right.
     GPS: N38°39.39' W108°21.27'

▼ 8.47 SO Cross over creek.
3.73 ▲ SO Cross over creek.
     GPS: N38°39.22' W108°22.25'

▼ 9.1 SO Cross over creek.
3.1 ▲ SO Cross over creek.

▼ 9.19 SO Enter Mesa County; leave
           Montrose County.
3.01 ▲ SO Enter Montrose County; leave
           Mesa County.

 9.42 SO Track on right.
2.78 ▲ SO Track on left.
     GPS: N38°38.62' W108°22.80'

▼ 10.3 SO Cattle guard.
1.9 ▲ SO Cattle guard.

▼ 10.5 SO Escalante Forks; then bridge over creek.
1.7 ▲ SO Bridge over creek; then Escalante Forks.
     GPS: N38°38.02' W108°23.68'

▼ 10.8 SO Cattle guard.
1.4 ▲ SO Cattle guard.

▼ 11.0 SO Ford through creek.
1.2 ▲ SO Ford through creek.
     GPS: N38°37.61' W108°23.75'

▼ 11.2 SO Cross through large wash.
1.0 ▲ SO Cross through large wash.

▼ 11.5 SO Cattle guard.
0.7 ▲ SO Cattle guard.

▼ 11.9 SO Cross through washes.
0.3 ▲ SO Cross through washes.

▼ 12.2 BL Intersection with FR 421 on right and
           FR 500 to left, signed to Love Mesa
           and Divide Road. Zero trip meter.
0.0 ▲   Continue north on Road 650.
     GPS: N38°36.73' W108°24.00'

▼ 0.0   Continue south on FR 500.
8.57 ▲ BR Intersection with FR 421 to left and FR
           500 on right. Zero trip meter.

▼ 0.36 SO Cross through wash.
8.21 ▲ SO Cross through wash.

▼ 1.10 SO Cross through wash.
7.47 ▲ SO Cross through wash.

▼ 2.70 SO Cattle guard; then enter state land.
5.87 ▲ SO Exit state land; then cattle guard.

▼ 2.91 SO Cross through creek.
5.66 ▲ SO Cross through creek.
     GPS: N38°34.86' W108°24.30'

▼ 3.19 BR Road on left.
5.38 ▲ BL Road on right.
     GPS: N38°34.73' W108°24.43'

▼ 3.58 SO Cattle guard and exit state land.
4.99 ▲ SO Cattle guard and enter state land.

▼ 4.2 BL Road on right to undeveloped campsites.
4.37 ▲ SO Road on left to undeveloped campsites.
     GPS: N38°34.32' W108°24.43'

▼ 5.6 SO Gate.
2.97 ▲ SO Gate.

▼ 8.31 BL Track on right.
0.26▼ BR Track on left.
     GPS: N38°33.29' W108°25.55'

▼ 8.51 SO Track on left.
0.06 ▲ BL Track on right.
     GPS: N38°33.11' W108°25.59'

▼ 8.57 SO Intersection of FR 500 and FR 501 1A.
           Zero trip meter.
0.0 ▲   Continue northeast on FR 500.
     GPS: N38°33.07' W108°25.62'

▼ 0.0   Continue southwest on FR 500.
3.6 ▲   SO   Intersection with FR 501 1A.
               Zero trip meter.

▼ 1.6   SO   Cattle guard.
2.00 ▲   SO   Cattle guard.

▼ 2.50   SO   Track on left.
1.10 ▲   SO   Track on right.

▼ 2.8   SO   Track on right.
0.80 ▲   SO   Track on left.
               GPS: N38°31.55' W108°'

▼ 3.6   SO   Intersection with Southwest #47: Dry
               Mesa Jeep Road (FR 501). Zero trip meter.
0.0 ▲   SO   Continue north on FR 500.
               GPS: N38°' W108°27.74'

▼ 0.0   Continue south on FR 500.
4.58 ▲   SO   Intersection with Southwest #47: Dry
               Mesa Jeep Road (FR 501). Zero trip meter.

▼ 1.06   SO   Unmarked road on left and right.
3.52 ▲   SO   Unmarked road on left and right.
               GPS: N38°30.62' W108°28.99'

▼ 1.12   SO   Road on right.
3.46 ▲   SO   Road on left.
               GPS: N38°30.58' W108°29.04'

▼ 3.47   SO   Cattle guard.
1.11 ▲   SO   Cattle guard.

▼ 4.58   SO   Road on left is FR 500 1A.
               Zero trip meter.
0.0 ▲   Proceed southwest on FR 500.
               GPS: N38°29.74' W108°32.11'

▼ 0.0   Continue northeast on FR 500.
3.09 ▲   SO   FR 500 1A on right. Zero trip meter.

▼ 2.53   SO   Cattle guard.
0.56 ▲   SO   Cattle guard.

▼ 2.87   SO   Cattle guard.
0.22 ▲   SO   Cattle guard.

▼ 3.09   Trail ends at intersection with
               Southwest #43: Uncompahgre Plateau

Trail (FR 402).
0.0 ▲   Trail commences at intersection of
               Southwest #43: Uncompahgre
               Plateau (FR 402) and FR 500. Proceed
               north on FR 500.
               GPS: N38°28.53' W108°34.14'

SOUTHWEST REGION TRAIL #47

Dry Mesa Jeep Road

STARTING POINT   Intersection with Southwest #46: Escalante Canyon Road and FR 501

FINISHING POINT   Intersection with Southwest #46: Escalante Canyon Road and FR 501

TOTAL MILEAGE   24.3 miles

UNPAVED MILEAGE   24.3 miles

DRIVING TIME   1.75 hours

ELEVATION RANGE   5,031 to 8,606 feet

USUALLY OPEN   Year-round

BEST TIME TO TRAVEL   April through October

DIFFICULTY RATING   4

SCENIC RATING   8

Special Attractions

- Ute Petroglyphs.
- Exciting, rocky descent into Esclante Canyon.
- One in a large network of 4WD trails.

Indian petroglyphs near Dry Mesa Jeep Road

History

Humans have occupied the Escalante Canyon as early as 12,000 years ago during the Paleo-Indian Era, which is generally defined as the period from which the first signs of human presence can be found until the time agriculture and other signs of permanent settlement were detected.

As a result, researchers have found hundreds of unique sites that are evidence of the earliest inhabitants of the Escalante Canyon and the Uncompahgre Plateau. Particularly striking are the carvings in the stone canyon walls, or petroglyph sites. Ranging in age from 7,000 B.C. to as recent as the 1800s, these historical records are believed to depict maps, hunting stories, histories, clan information, religious ceremonies, and shamanic themes.

Signs that the early inhabitants began farming and living off the land have also been located in Escalante Canyon and on Uncompahgre Plateau in the stone structures and caves they bore into the plateau slopes and canyon walls. It has not yet been established that these early artifacts can be linked to the amazing Anasazi cliff dwellings in Mesa Verde National Park, but no doubt historians will continue their fieldwork to determine the origins.

Arid Dry Mesa

The trail descends steeply into Escalante Canyon

However, evidence can be directly linked to the subsequent Native American inhabitants, the Ute, who left behind scarred trees, Bear Dance rock art, teepee rings, and wickiups. The Tabeguache and Uncompahgre bands of Ute lived here from approximately the fifteenth century until their forcible relocation by white settlers in 1881.

The Spanish explored the area in the 1600s and 1700s. Their explorations provided the origins of many of the names of geographical features in the area, such as Escalante, who was a Spanish priest that passed near the area in 1776. By 1828, many fur traders had passed through the area, and Antoine Roubidoux constructed Fort Uncompahgre on the Gunnison River as a trading post in what is today the city of Delta. In the following years miners, farmers, ranchers, and loggers arrived, and they all left their mark on the land.

In fact, on the land managed by the Uncompahgre Field Office of the Bureau of Land Management, more than 4,600 sites with artifacts have been recorded to date. Undoubtedly thousands more remain to be discovered because only 17% of this land has been formally surveyed for artifacts.

Dry Mesa Jeep Road itself is a part of the history of settlement in the canyon. It was constructed in 1926 as an improvement to the original road into Escalante Canyon. The road was extremely narrow and steep with large rocks making travel over it extremely treacherous for the horse-pulled buggies and wagons entering and exiting the canyon. Apparently it took four horses to pull one buggy and six horses to pull a wagon up the road.

Although Dry Mesa Jeep Road made canyon access easier, it also had a negative effect. The road's proximity to the Indian petroglyph made it readily accessible to vandals. Originally the petroglyph depicted chiefs riding horses, which were acquired after the Pueblo uprisings in 1680, but graffiti has all but decimated the original inscriptions. Viewing these historic artifacts is an amazing opportunity, so please treat all sites with respect so we can preserve this history for future generations.

Description

This historic trail runs from the aspen and conifer forests of the Uncompahgre Plateau and along Dry Mesa and descends the colorful eastern rock wall of Escalante Canyon. At the intersection of Southwest

#46: Escalante Canyon Road (FR 500), approximately 7.5 miles northeast of Southwest #43: Uncompahgre Plateau Trail, zero your trip meter and proceed east on FR 501, a wide dirt road with some embedded rock in sections. Initially traveling through aspen, ponderosa pine, and scrub oak forest, this section has beautiful fall color aspen viewing. Between breaks in the forest vegetation are overlooks of extensive aspen stands.

At the intersection with FR 501 1A, the surface of the road becomes gravel, and the track runs through sections of open meadows with good views of Escalante Canyon to the north. Beyond the intersection with FR 504, the road widens, and a lot of backcountry camping opportunities exist near the trail. Such sites are popular with hunters in the fall.

After approximately 2.7 miles, the road's gravel surface becomes primarily dirt, and it is rutted and eroded in places. Past the Dinosaur Quarry, the trail crosses through gates. Be sure to leave the gates as you found them, closing them if you had to open them to pass through.

Running alternately along the edge and the middle of Dry Mesa, the trail is a wide shelf road at times. It is recommended to avoid this trail when it is wet. The six- and seven-inch deep wheel ruts that remain imprinted on the road's dry surface are a testament to how muddy the road can be, and how easily vehicles can get bogged. Also on this part of the trail, a few sections of slickrock create a stair effect that makes for a bumpy ride.

After approximately 10 miles, the trail begins to steeply descend the eastern wall of Escalante Canyon, and a sign warns of a section of rough, 4WD road ahead. This exciting section of the narrow shelf trail, which switchbacks over a rocky surface into the canyon, increases the difficulty rating from a 2 to a 4, mainly for its steep aspect. This section may be more difficult or the road may even become impassible due to rockslides and washouts. In addition to being exciting, the descent is also quite scenic as the trail progresses through a rock garden of boulders, some of which are larger than a jeep!

After descending into Escalante Canyon, the trail travels toward Escalante Creek then follows it for a time, crossing through it numerous times. The crossings are most exciting in wet months. The road through this narrow and very scenic section of the canyon is rocky and lined with cottonwoods and sage.

Just before the intersection with Southwest #48: Escalante Rim Trail, you can walk over to view what remains of the Indian Petroglyphs that date back to as early as the 1680s. The artifacts have been extensively vandalized, making it difficult to locate the original inscriptions. Please respect historic sites to preserve them for future generations. The trail ends just under a mile beyond the petroglyph site at the intersection with Southwest #46: Escalante Canyon Road approximately 3.5 miles south of US 50.

Current Road Information

Colorado Bureau of Land Management
Uncompahgre Field Office
2465 South Townsend Avenue
Montrose, CO 81401
(970) 240-5300

Grand Mesa, Uncompahgre and Gunnison National Forests
Grand Valley Ranger District
2777 Crossroads Blvd, Suite 1
Grand Junction, CO 81506
(970) 242-8211

Map References

Benchmark's *Colorado Road and Recreation Atlas,* p. 95
BLM Delta
USFS Uncompahgre National Forest
USGS 1:24,000 Good Point, Cottonwood Basin, Kelso Point, Starvation Point
1:100,000 Delta, Nucla
Maptech CD-ROM: Grand Junction/ Western Slope
Colorado Atlas & Gazetteer, p. 55
The Roads of Colorado, pp. 105, 106

Route Directions

▼ 0.0   Trail begins at the intersection of Southwest #46: Escalante Canyon Road and FR 501. Proceed east on FR 501.

1.2 ▲   Trail ends at intersection with Southwest #46: Escalante Canyon Road (FR 500)
GPS: N38°31.05' W108°28.26'

▼ 0.62 SO Cattle guard.
0.58 ▲ SO Cattle guard.

▼ 1.2 BR Intersection of FR 501 1A on left. Zero trip meter.
0.0 ▲ Continue north on FR 501.
GPS: N38°30.48' W108°27.61'

▼ 0.0 Continue south on FR 501.
3.7 ▲ BL Intersection with FR 501 1A on right. Zero trip meter.

▼ 0.41 SO Track on right.
3.29 ▲ SO Track on left.
GPS: N38°30.17' W108°27.80'

▼ 0.55 SO Cattle guard.
3.15 ▲ SO Cattle guard.

▼ 0.73 SO Track on right.
2.97 ▲ SO Track on left.
GPS: N38°29.97' W108°28.06'

▼ 0.81 SO Cross over creek.
2.89 ▲ SO Cross over creek.
GPS: N38°29.95' W108°28.12'

▼ 1.09 SO Cattle guard.
2.61 ▲ SO Cattle guard.

▼ 2.1 SO Cross over creek.
3.29 ▲ SO Cross over creek.

▼ 3.7 TL Cattle guard; then intersection with FR 501 to the left and FR 504 to the right. Zero trip meter.
0.0 ▲ Continue southwest on FR 501.
GPS: N38°30.64' W108°25.42'

▼ 0.0 Continue northeast on FR 501.
1.8 ▲ TR Intersection with FR 501 to the right and FR 504 to the left; then cattle

Loose, rocky switchback section of Dry Mesa Jeep Road

Main Trail | **Intersecting Trails**

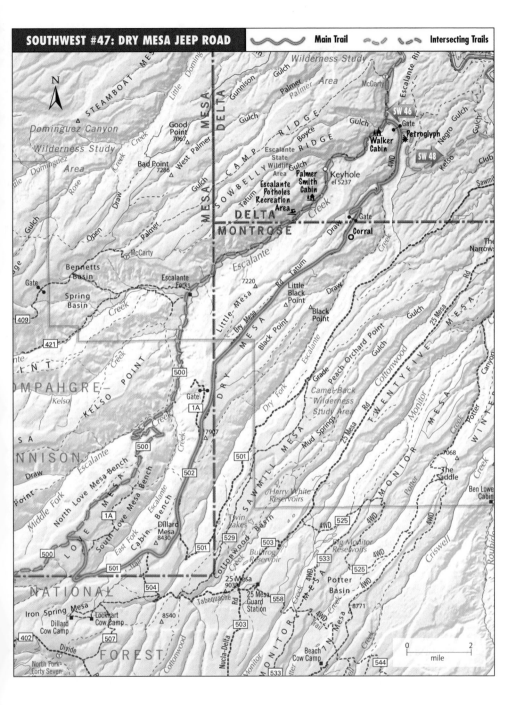

guard. Zero trip meter.

▼ 0.11   BR   Track on left.
1.69 ▲   SO   Track on right.
      GPS: N38º30.66' W108º25.30'

▼ 1.08   SO   Cattle guard.
0.72 ▲   SO   Cattle guard.

▼ 1.8   TL   Intersection with FR 502 on left.
                 Zero trip meter.
0.0 ▲   Continue south on FR 501.

Dry Mesa Jeep Road in Escalante Canyon

GPS: N38°31.18' W108°23.96'

▼ 0.0   Continue north on FR 502.
3.38 ▲   TR   Intersection with FR 501 on right. Zero trip meter.

▼ 0.18   SO   Cross over creek.
3.2 ▲   SO   Cross over creek.

▼ 1.5   SO   Track on left; then cattle guard.
1.88 ▲   SO   Cattle guard; then track on right.

▼ 2.66   SO   Track on right.
0.72 ▲   SO   Track on left.
       GPS: N38°33.27' W108°23.51'

▼ 3.33   SO   Gate.
0.05 ▲   SO   Gate.
       GPS: N38°33.77' W108°23.18'

▼ 3.38   BR   Intersection with FR 502 1A on left to Dinosaur Quarry. Zero trip meter.
0.0 ▲   Continue south on FR 502.
       GPS: N38°' W108°'

▼ 0.0   Continue north on FR 502 toward Dry Mesa.

10.2 ▲   BL   Intersection with FR 502 1A on right to Dinosaur Quarry. Zero trip meter.

▼ 1.0   SO   Track on right.
9.2 ▲   SO   Track on left.
       GPS: N38°34.55' W108°22.99'

▼ 1.9   SO   Track on right.
8.30 ▲   SO   Track on left.

▼ 3.89   SO   Cattle guard; then road on left.
6.31 ▲   SO   Road on right; then cattle guard.
       GPS: N38°36.76' W108°21.92'

▼ 5.65   SO   Old corral on right.
4.55 ▲   SO   Old corral on left.

▼ 5.94   SO   BLM water catchment and tanks on left; then gate.
4.26 ▲   SO   Gate; then BLM water catchment and tanks on right.

▼ 7.52   SO   Track on left.
2.68 ▲   SO   Track on right.

▼ 8.47 SO Track on right.
1.73 ▲ SO Track on left.
         GPS: N38°39.23' W108°18.10'

▼ 8.95 SO Old corral on right.
1.25 ▲ SO Old corral on left.

▼ 9.98 SO Advisory sign posted. Steep rough trail
            ahead. 4WD suggested.
0.22 ▲ SO Sign. Standard of road improves.

▼ 10.2 SO Gate. Zero trip meter.
0.0 ▲   SO Continue southwest on FR 502.

▼ 0.0   SO Continue northeast on FR 502; then
            stock pond on right.
5.24 ▲ SO Stock pond on left; then gate.
            Zero trip meter.

▼ 2.37 SO Cross through rocky wash.
2.87 ▲ SO Cross through rocky wash.
         GPS: N38°41.17' W108°16.28'

▼ 2.44 SO Cross through wash.
2.8 ▲   SO Cross through wash.

▼ 2.66 SO Cross through wash.
2.58 ▲ SO Cross through wash.
         GPS: N38°41.35' W108°16.07'

▼ 2.80 SO Gate; then cross through creek.
2.44 ▲ SO Cross through creek; then gate.
         GPS: N38°41.46' W108°15.96'

▼ 2.93 SO Cross through creek.
2.31 ▲ SO Cross through creek.

▼ 3.02 SO Cross through creek.
2.22 ▲ SO Cross through creek.

▼ 3.40 SO Cross through muddy section of creek.
1.84 ▲ SO Cross through muddy section of creek.
         GPS: N38°41.87' W108°15.76'

▼ 3.46 SO Cross through creek.
1.78 ▲ SO Cross through creek.

▼ 3.59 SO Cross through creek.
1.65 ▲ SO Cross through creek.

▼ 3.67 SO Cross through creek.
1.37 ▲ SO Cross through creek.

▼ 3.87 SO Gate.
1.37 ▲ SO Gate.

▼ 3.92 SO Cross through creek.
1.32 ▲ SO Cross through creek.

▼ 3.97 SO Cross through creek.
1.27 ▲ SO Cross through creek.

▼ 4.13 SO Cross through creek.
1.11 ▲ SO Cross through creek.
         GPS: N38°42.41' W108°15.48'

▼ 4.19 SO Cross through creek.
1.05 ▲ SO Cross through creek.

▼ 4.24 SO Cross through creek.
1.0 ▲   SO Cross through creek.

▼ 4.42 SO Indian Petroglyphs on left; then cross
            through creek.
0.82 ▲ SO Cross through creek; then Indian
            Petroglyphs on right.
         GPS: N38°42.62' W108°15.53'

▼ 4.68 SO Intersection with Southwest #48:
            Escalante Rim Trail on right.
0.56 ▲ BR Intersection with Southwest #48:
            Escalante Rim Trail on left.
         GPS: N38°42.77' W108°15.72'

▼ 4.72 SO Cattle guard; then cross through creek.
0.52 ▲ SO Cross through creek; then cattle guard.

▼ 4.90 SO Cross through creek.
0.34 ▲ SO Cross through creek.

▼ 5.18 O   Cross through creek.
0.06 ▲ SO Cross through creek.

▼ 5.24   Trail ends at intersection with FR 500
            Southwest #46: Escalante Canyon Road.
0.0 ▲   Trail begins at the intersection of FR
            500 Southwest #46: Escalante
            Canyon Road and FR 502.
         GPS: N38°43.05' W108°16.15'

Escalante Rim Trail

STARTING POINT Intersection of 6th and Main Streets in downtown Delta
FINISHING POINT Southwest #46: Escalante Canyon Road
TOTAL MILEAGE 14.29 miles
UNPAVED MILEAGE 14.29 miles
DRIVING TIME 1 hour
ELEVATION RANGE 4,876 to 5,855 feet
USUALLY OPEN Year-round
BEST TIME TO TRAVEL April through October
DIFFICULTY RATING 3
SCENIC RATING 9

Special Attractions

- Scenic shelf road along Escalante Canyon rim.
- Trail begins in downtown Delta.
- Town site of Roubideau.

History

After the Spanish explored the area in the 1600s and 1700s, many white European fur traders passed through the area on alternate routes off of the California and Santa Fe Trails. The enterprising French fur trader, Antoine Roubidoux, established trade lines through the area and constructed a permanent outpost nearby in 1828. In all likelihood, the Ute helped him locate the strategic position for his trading post, Fort Uncompahgre, on the Gunnison River in what is today the city of Delta.

In the following years miners, farmers, ranchers, loggers, and eventually the railroad arrived and settled the region. The town of Roubideau, named for the colorful French fur trader, was established by the Denver & Rio Grande Railroad sometime in 1881 after Indians were relocated to reservations. After the D&RG arrived in the Uncompahgre Valley and established the end of its line at Roubideau, the settlement developed as a prime ranching location, and cowboys and cattle quickly flooded the area.

Not surprisingly, the cattle town's main

structures included unloading ramps, loading chutes, corrals, and stockyards, although one resident recalls as many as five houses, a post office, a schoolhouse, a general store, and a dance hall. The dance hall and the saloons occupied the numerous cowboys during their time off—and probably accounts for why the schoolhouse was located on a hillside well away from the main street.

Gradually the numbers of incoming livestock dwindled as herds living on the surrounding plateaus and mesas multiplied. Most of the activity became rounding up cattle and shipping them off from Roubideau. Today the railroad spur that

Escalante Rim Trail crosses through Escalante Creek

created the town still exists as a Southern Pacific line, but all that remains to commemorate the existence of the town is an information board at the site.

Description

Beginning in downtown Delta, this incredibly scenic trail passes the town site of Roubideau and descends into Escalante Canyon, traveling along its rim and providing fantastic views.

At the intersection of West 6th Street and Main Street, signed Public Lands Access Uncompahgre Plateau, proceed east on West 6th Street. Navigating the city streets heading west out of town, the trail crosses the railroad tracks and the Uncompahgre River before arriving at what remains of the town of Roubideau.

The trail runs out a paved two-lane road to the intersection with dirt E23 Road, a wide, graded gravel road with a few characteristics of a 4WD road. Proceeding west on E23 Road the trail becomes rocky with some embedded rocks and crosses through a canyon and under power lines. The surrounding desert-like landscape is barren and rocky with sparse, low vegetation of cacti, rabbit brush, scrub grass, and pinyon and juniper pines.

Escalante Rim Trail is a shelf carved in the wall of Escalante Canyon

As the road climbs approaching the Escalante Canyon, there are 360° views of the surrounding countryside. Numerous tracks head off from the main trail in all directions with too many to note in the Route Directions below. Navigation is easy, though, proceeding east on the wide, maintained dirt road.

Suddenly Escalante Canyon opens up before you and the trail begins to navigate down the canyon wall. The trail becomes a shelf road from which you can see down into the canyon and easily locate Escalante Creek, lined with cottonwoods and other vegetation. Views of the rocky surroundings are spectacular. In addition to the sheer drop-offs, the shelf is steep and narrow in sections with a moderately loose surface, all features that give the trail a 3-rating for difficulty. It is no obstacle for a high clearance 4WD. The trail ends after a short but scenic 14 miles at the intersection with Southwest #47: Dry Mesa Jeep Road (FR 502).

Current Road Information

Colorado Bureau of Land Management
Uncompahgre Field Office
2465 South Townsend Avenue
Montrose, CO 81401
(970) 240-5300

Map References

Benchmark's *Colorado Road and Recreation Atlas,* pp. 83, 95
BLM   Delta
USGS 1:24,000   Roubideau, Delta
      1:100,000 Delta
Maptech CD-ROM: Grand Junction/ Western Slope
Colorado Atlas & Gazetteer, pp. 55, 56
The Roads of Colorado, p. 106

Expansive view of Escalante Canyon from the trail

Main Trail ～～ ～～ Intersecting Trails

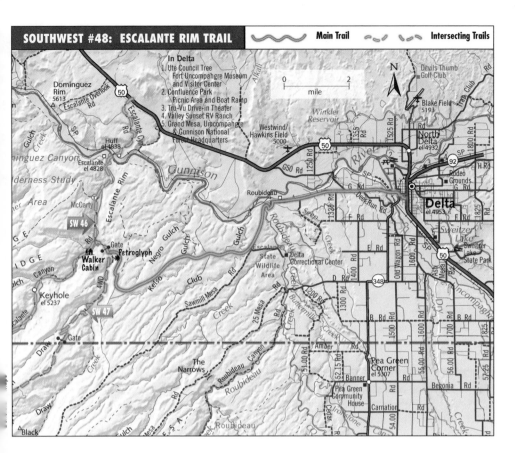

Route Directions

▼ 0.0   Trail begins at intersection of 6th and Main Streets in Delta, signed Public Lands Access to Uncompahgre Plateau. Proceed west down West 6th Street.

6.63 ▲   Trail ends at intersection with Main Street in downtown Delta.

GPS: N38°44.35' W108°04.26'

▼ 0.13   TR   Intersection with Dodge Street.

6.5 ▲   TL   Intersection with 6th Street.

▼ 0.21   TL   Intersection with 5th Street.

6.42 ▲   TR   Intersection with Dodge Street.

▼ 0.40   SO   Cross railroad tracks.

6.05 ▲   SO   Cross railroad tracks.

▼ 0.58   SO   Cross bridge over Uncompahgre River.

6.05 ▲   SO   Cross bridge over Uncompahgre River

GPS: N38°44.43' W108°04.84'

▼ 0.69   SO   Cross railroad tracks.

5.94 ▲   SO   Cross railroad tracks.

▼ 4.33   SO   Historical marker for town of Roubideau on right.

2.3 ▲   SO   Historical marker for town of Roubideau on left.

▼ 5.08   SO   Cross bridge over Roubideau Creek.

1.55 ▲   SO   Cross bridge over Roubideau Creek.

▼ 6.63   BR   Pavement ends and intersection with Road E23 and G Roads. Zero trip meter.

0.0 ▲   Continue northeast on G Road.

GPS: N38°42.83' W108°10.17'

▼ 0.0   Continue southwest on Road E23.

6.06 ▲   BL   Pavement begins and Road E23 intersects with G Road. Zero trip meter.

▼ 0.26   SO   Fence line on left and right.

5.8 ▲   SO Fence line on left and right.

▼ 0.35 SO Cross through wash.
5.71 ▲   SO Cross through wash.

▼ 0.96 SO Cattle guard.
5.1 ▲   SO Cattle guard.

▼ 1.58 BL Track on right.
4.48 ▲   BR Track on left.

▼ 1.65 BR Track on left.
4.41 ▲   BL Track on right.
             GPS: N38°42.63' W108°11.74'

▼ 2.35 SO Cross through wash.
3.71 ▲   SO Cross through wash.

▼ 2.54 SO Track on left.
3.52 ▲   SO Track on right.

▼ 2.83 SO Track on left.
3.23 ▲   BL Track on right.
             GPS: N38°42.60' W108°12.76'

▼ 3.44 SO Track on left; then track on right.

2.62 ▲   BL Track on left; then track on right.

▼ 3.98 SO Short section of pavement crosses
             rocky area; then road on left.
2.08 ▲   SO Road on right; then short section of
             pavement crosses rocky area.

▼ 6.06 BL Cattle guard; then track on right.
             Zero trip meter.
0.0 ▲   Continue southeast on Escalante Rim
             Road (Road E23).
             GPS: N38°42.04' W108°15.31'

▼ 0.0   Continue northwest on Escalante Rim
             Road (Road E23).
1.6 ▲   BR Track on left; then cattle guard.

▼ 1.6   Trail ends at intersection with Southwest
             #47: Dry Mesa Jeep Road (FR 502).
0.0 ▲   Trail begins at intersection of
             Southwest #47: Dry Mesa Jeep Road
             (FR 502) and Road E23 or Escalante
             Rim Road.
             GPS: N38°42.77' W108°15.71'

Cottonwoods line Escalante Creek

ATV riders on Escalante Rim Trail

Selected Further Reading

Abbott, Carl, Stephen J. Leonard, and David McComb. *Colorado: A History of the Centennial State.* Niwot, Colo.: University Press of Colorado, 1994.

Aldrich, John K. *Ghosts of the Eastern San Juans.* Lakewood, Colo.: Centennial Graphics, 1987.

Aldrich, John K. *Ghosts of the Western San Juans.* Vols. 1 and 2. Lakewood, Colo.: Centennial Graphics, 1991.

Bancroft, Caroline. *Colorful Colorado.* Boulder, Colo.: Johnson Books, 1987.

Bancroft, Caroline. *Unique Ghost Towns and Mountain Spots.* Boulder, Colo.: Johnson Books, 1961.

Bauer, Carolyn. *Colorado Ghost Towns—Colorado Traveler Guidebooks.* Frederick, Colo.: Renaissance House, 1987.

Beckner, Raymond M. *Along the Colorado Trail.* Pueblo, Colo.: O'Brien Printing & Stationery, 1975.

Benham, Jack. *Ouray.* Ouray, Colo.: Bear Creek Publishing, 1976.

Boyd, Leanne C. and H. Glenn Carson. *Atlas of Colorado Ghost Towns.* Vols. 1 and 2. Deming, N.M.: Carson Enterprises, Ltd., 1984.

Bright, William. *Colorado Place Names.* Boulder, Colo.: Johnson Books, 1993.

Brown, Robert L. *Colorado Ghost Towns Past & Present.* Caldwell, Idaho: Caxton Printers, Ltd., 1972.

———. *Ghost Towns of the Colorado Rockies.* Caldwell, Idaho: Caxton Printers, Ltd., 1990.

———. *Jeep Trails to Colorado Ghost Towns.* Caldwell, Idaho: Caxton Printers, Ltd., 1995.

Bueler, Gladys R. *Colorado's Colorful Characters.* Boulder, Colo.: Pruett Publishing, 1981.

Carver, Jack, Jerry Vondergeest, Dallas Boyd, and Tom Pade. *Land of Legend.* Denver, Colo.: Caravon Press, 1959.

Colorado Trail Foundation. *The Colorado Trail: The Official Guidebook.* 6th ed. Golden, Colo: Colorado Mountain Club Press, 2002.

Crofutt, George A. *Crofutt's Grip-Sack Guide of Colorado.* Omaha: Overland Publishing, 1885. Reprinted, Boulder, Colo.: Johnson Books, 1981.

Cromie, Alice. *A Tour Guide to the Old West.* Nashville, Tenn.: Rutledge Hill Press, 1990.

Crutchfield, James A. *It Happened in Colorado.* Helena & Billings, Mont.: Falcon Press Publishing, 1993.

Dallas, Sandra. *Colorado Ghost Towns and Mining Camps.* Norman, Okla.: University of Oklahoma Press, 1985.

DeLong, Brad. *4-Wheel Freedom.* Boulder, Colo.: Paladin Press, 1996.

Dorset, Phyllis Flanders. *The New Eldorado: The Story of Colorado's Gold & Silver Rushes.* New York: Macmillan, 1970.

Eberhart, Perry. *Guide to the Colorado Ghost Towns and Mining Camps.* 4th ed. Chicago, Ill.: Swallow Press, 1995.

Fisher, Vardis, and Opal Laurel Holmes. *Gold Rushes and*

Mining Camps of the Early American West. Caldwell, Idaho: Caxton Printers, Ltd., 1968.

Florin, Lambert. *Ghost Towns of the West.* New York: Promontory Press, 1993.

Foster, Mike. *Strange Genius: The Life of Ferdinand Vandeveer Hayden.* Niwot, Colo.: Roberts Rinehart Publishers, 1994.

Green, Stewart M. *Bureau of Land Management Back Country Byways.* Helena, Mont.: Falcon Press, 1995.

Gregory, Lee. *Colorado Scenic Guide: Southern Region.* Boulder, Colo.: Johnson Books, 1990.

Gregory, Marvin, and P. David Smith. *The Million Dollar Highway, Colorado's Most Spectacular Seventy Miles.* Ouray, Colo: Western Reflections, 1997.

Haynes, Patrick E., and Paul F. Hlava. "Minerology of Tuckers Tunnel, Tuckerville, Hinsdale County, Colorado." *Rocks & Minerals* Sept. 1998.

Heck, Larry E. *4-Wheel Drive Roads & Ghost Towns of the San Juans.* Aurora, Colo.: Pass Patrol, 1995.

Helmuth, Ed and Gloria. *The Passes of Colorado.* Boulder, Colo.: Pruett Publishing, 1994.

Hilton, George W. *American Narrow Gauge Railroads.* Stanford: Stanford University Press.

Jessen, Ken. *Colorado Gunsmoke: True Stories of Outlaws and Lawmen on the Colorado Frontier.* Loveland, Colo.: J. V. Publications, 1986.

Koch, Don. *The Colorado Pass Book.* 2nd ed. Boulder, Colo.: Pruett Publishing, 1992.

La Plata Mineral Belt. Map. Ouray, Colo: Jack Benham.

Marshall, Muriel. *Uncompahgre: A Guide to the Uncompahgre Plateau.* Ouray, Colo.: Western Reflections, 1998.

McTighe, James. *Roadside History of Colorado.* Boulder, Colo.: Johnson Books, 1984.

Noel, Thomas J., Paul F. Mahoney, and Richard E. Stevens. *Historical Atlas of Colorado.* Norman, Okla.: University of Oklahoma Press, 1994.

Norton, Boyd and Barbara. *Backroads of Colorado.* Stillwater, Minn: Voyageur Press, 1995.

Ormes, Robert M. *Railroads and the Rockies.* Denver, Colo.: Sage Books, 1963.

———. *Tracking Ghost Railroads in Colorado.* Colorado Springs, Colo.: Green Light Graphics, 1992.

O'Rourke, Paul M. *Frontier in Transition: A History of Southwestern Colorado.* Denver, Colo.: Bureau of Land Management, 1980.

Parker, Ben H., Jr. *Gold Panning and Placering in Colorado.* Denver, Colo.: U.S. Geological Survey, Department of Natural Resources, 1992.

Pettem, Silvia. *Colorado Mountains & Passes—Colorado Traveler Guidebooks.* Frederick, Colo.: Renaissance House, 1991.

Pettit, Jan. *Utes: The Mountain People.* Boulder, Colo.: Johnson Books, 1994.

Pritchard, Sandra F. *Men, Mining & Machines.* Dillon, Colo.: Summit County Historical Society, 1996.

Reidhead, Darlene A. *Tour the San Juans. Vols. 1 and 2.* Cortez, Colo.: Southwest Printing.

Reyher, Ken. *Antoine Robidoux and Fort Uncompahgre: The Story of a Western Colorado Fur Trader.* Ouray, Colo.: Western Reflections, 1998.

Sagstetter, Beth and Bill. *The Mining Camps Speak.* Denver, Colo.: BenchMark Publishing of Colorado, 1998.

Sinnotte, Barbara. *Colorado: A Guide to the State & National Parks.* Edison, N.J.: Hunter, 1996.

Smith, Duane A. *Colorado Mining: A Photographic History.* Albuquerque, N.M.: University of New Mexico Press, 1977.

Southworth, Dave. *Colorado Mining Camps.* Wild Horse, 1997.

———. *Gunfighters of the Old West.* Wild Horse, 1997.

Taylor, Colin F. *The Plains Indians.* New York: Barnes & Noble Books and Salamander Books, 1997.

Thompson, Ian. *A Historical Touring Guide to the San Juan Skyway.* Durango, Colo.: Fort Lewis College, 1994.

Ubbelohde, Carl, Maxine Benson, and Duane A. Smith. *A Colorado History.* Boulder, Colo.: Pruett Publishing, 1995.

Waldman, Carl. *Encyclopedia of Native American Tribes.* New York: Facts on File, 1988.

Wilkins, Tivis E. *Colorado Railroads Chronological Development.* Boulder, Colo.: Pruett Publishing, 1974.

Wilson, Ray D. *Colorado Historical Tour Guide.* Carpentersville, Ill.: Crossroads Communications, 1990.

Wolle, Muriel Sibell. *The Bonanza Trail.* Chicago, Ill.: The Swallow Press, 1953.

Selected Web sources

Animas Museum, http://animasmuseum.org

Chimney Rock Archeological Area, http://chimneyrockco.org

Colorado State Parks, http://parks.state.co.us

Durango Telegraph, http://durangotelegraph.com

Forest Fire Lookout Association, Colorado and Utah Chapter, http://coloradolookouts.com

Fort Lewis College, Center of Southwest Studies, http://swcenter.fortlewis.edu

Fort Tours, http://forttours.com

GORP.com, http://gorp.away.com

La Plata County, http://co.laplata.co.us

Mancos Chamber of Commerce, http://manosvalley.com

Minerology Database, http://mindat.org

Mountain Studies Institute, http://moutainstudies.org

National Center for Disease Control: Hantavirus Pulmonary Syndrome, http://cdc.gov/ncidad/diseases/hanta/hps/

San Juan Public Lands Center, http://fs.fed.us/r2/sanjuan or http://co.blm.gov/sjra/index.htm

U.S. Bureau of Land Management, Colorado, http://blm.gov/co

U.S. Department of the Interior, Bureau of Reclamation, http://usbr.gov

U.S. Fish & Wildlife Service, http://fws.gov

U.S. Forest Service, http://www.fs.fed.us/r5/forests.html

White Water Rafting in North America, http://e-raft.com/regions/Colorado/colorado.asp

Photo Credits

more colorado trails
backroad guides

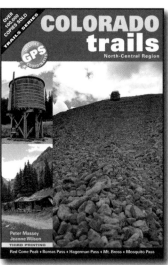

Colorado Trails–North-Central
This guidebook is composed of comprehensive statistics and descriptions of 28 trails, including 8 trails additional to those profiled in the Adventures Colorado book, around Breckenridge, Central City, Fraser, Dillon, Vail, Leadville, Georgetown, and Aspen.
ISBN 978-1-930193-11-6; Price $19.95

Colorado Trails–South-Central
This edition of our Trails series includes meticulous trail details for 30 off-road routes located near the towns of Gunnison, Salida, Crested Butte, Buena Vista, Aspen, and the Sand Dunes National Monument.
ISBN 978-1-930193-29-1; Price $19.95

to order
call 800-660-5107 or
visit 4WDbooks.com

utah trails
backroad guides

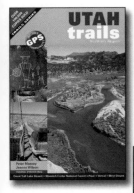

Utah Trails–Northern
This field guide includes meticulous trail details for 35 off-road routes near the towns of Vernal, Logan, Salt Lake City, Price, Wendover, Beaver, and Milford.
ISBN 978-1-930193-30-7; Price $19.95

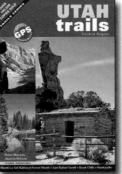

Utah Trails–Central
This volume is composed of comprehensive trail statistics for 34 trails near the towns of Green River, Richfield, Hanksville, Crescent Junction, and Castle Dale.
ISBN 978-1-930193-31-4; Price $19.95

Utah Trails–Moab
This guidebook contains detailed trail information for 57 trails in and around Moab, Monticello, Canyonlands National Park, Arches National Park, Green River, Mexican Hat, Bluff, and Blanding.
ISBN 978-1-930193-09-3; Price $24.95

Utah Trails–Southwest
This travel guide outlines detailed trail information for 49 off-road routes in the Four Corners region and around the towns of Escalante, St. George, Kanab, Boulder, Bryce Canyon, Hurricane, and Ticaboo.
ISBN 978-1-930193-10-9; Price $24.95

to order
call 800-660-5107 or
visit 4WDbooks.com

4WDBOOKS.COM

arizona trails
backroad guides

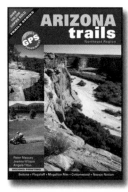

Arizona Trails–Northeast

This guidebook consists of meticulous details and directions for 47 trails located near the towns of Flagstaff, Williams, Prescott (northeast), Winslow, Fort Defiance and Window Rock.

ISBN 978-1-930193-02-4; Price $24.95

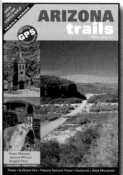

Arizona Trails–West

This volume consists of comprehensive statistics and descriptions for 33 trails located near the towns of Bullhead City, Lake Havasu City, Parker, Kingman, Prescott (west), and Quartzsite (north).

ISBN 978-1-930193-00-0; Price $24.95

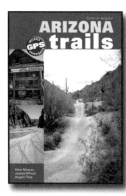

Arizona Trails–Central

This field guide includes meticulous trail details for 44 off-road routes located near the towns of Phoenix, Wickenburg, Quartzsite (south), Payson, Superior, Globe and Yuma (north).

ISBN 978-1-930193-01-7; Price $19.95

Arizona Trails–South

This handbook is composed of comprehensive statistics and descriptions for 33 trails located near the towns of Tucson, Douglas, Mammoth, Reddington, Stafford, Yuma (southeast), Ajo and Nogales.

ISBN 978-1-930193-03-1; Price $24.95

to order
call 800-660-5107 or
visit 4WDbooks.com

california trails
backroad guides

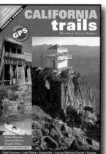
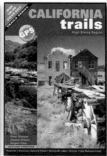

California Trails–Northern Sierra

This book outlines detailed trail information for 55 off-road routes located near the towns of Sacramento (east), Red Bluff (east), Truckee, South Lake Tahoe, Sonora, Susanville, Chico, Oroville, Yuba City, Placerville, Stockton (east), Jackson, and Sonora.

ISBN 978-1-930193-23-9; Price $24.95

California Trails–High Sierra

This guidebook navigates and describes 50 trails located near the towns of Fresno (north), Oakhurst, Lone Pine, Bishop, Bridgeport, Coulterville, Mariposa, and Mammoth Lakes.

ISBN 978-1-930193-21-5; Price $24.95

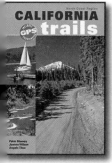

California Trails–North Coast

This guide meticulously describes and rates 47 off-road routes located near the towns of Sacramento, Redding (west), Red Bluff, Clear Lake, McCloud, Mount Shasta, Yreka, Crescent City, and Fort Bidwell.

ISBN 978-1-930193-22-2; Price $19.95

California Trails–Central Mountains

This guide is comprised of painstaking detail and descriptions for 52 trails located near the towns of Big Sur, Fresno, San Luis Obispo, Santa Barbara, Bakersfield, Mojave, and Maricopa.

ISBN 978-1-930193-19-2; Price $24.95

California Trails–South Coast

This field guide includes meticulous trail details for 50 trails located near the towns of Los Angeles, San Bernardino, San Diego, Salton Sea, Indio, Borrego Springs, Ocotillo and Palo Verde.

ISBN 978-1-930193-24-6; Price $19.95

California Trails–Desert

This edition of our Trails series contains detailed trail information for 51 off-road routes located near the towns of Lone Pine (east), Panamint Springs, Death Valley area, Ridgecrest, Barstow, Baker and Blythe.

ISBN 978-1-930193-20-8; Price $24.95

to order
call 800-660-5107 or
visit 4WDbooks.com

backcountry adventures
guides

Each book in the award-winning *Adventures* series listed below is a beautifully crafted, high-quality, sewn, 4-color guidebook. In addition to meticulously detailed backcountry trail directions and maps of every trail and region, extensive information on the history of towns, ghost towns, and regional history is included. The guides provide wildlife information and photographs to help readers identify the great variety of native birds, plants, and animals they are likely to see. This series appeals to everyone who enjoys the backcountry: campers, anglers, four-wheelers, hikers, mountain bikers, snowmobilers, amateur prospectors, sightseers, and more...

Backcountry Adventures Northern California

Backcountry Adventures Northern California takes readers along 2,653 miles of backroads from the rugged peaks of the Sierra Nevada, through volcanic regions of the Modoc Plateau, to majestic coastal redwood forests. Trail history comes to life through accounts of outlaws like Black Bart; explorers like Ewing Young and James Beckwourth; and the biggest mass migration in America's history—the Gold Rush. Contains 152 trails, 640 pages, and 679 photos.
ISBN 978-1-930193-25-3
Price, $39.95.

Backcountry Adventures Southern California

Backcountry Adventures Southern California provides 2,970 miles of routes that travel through the beautiful mountain regions of Big Sur, across the arid Mojave Desert, and straight into the heart of the aptly named Death Valley. Trail history comes alive through the accounts of Spanish missionaries; eager prospectors looking to cash in during California's gold rush; and legends of lost mines. Contains 153 trails, 640 pages, and 645 photos.
ISBN 978-1-930193-26-0
Price, $39.95.

to order
call 800-660-5107 or
visit 4WDbooks.com

backcountry adventures
guides

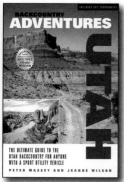

Backcountry Adventures Utah

Backcountry Adventures Utah navigates 3,721 miles through the spectacular Canyonlands region, to the top of the Uinta Range, across vast salt flats, and along trails unchanged since the riders of the Pony Express sped from station to station and daring young outlaws wreaked havoc on newly established stage lines, railroads, and frontier towns. Trail history comes to life through the accounts of outlaws like Butch Cassidy; explorers and mountain men; and early Mormon settlers. Contains 175 trails, 544 pages, and 532 photos.

ISBN 978-1-930193-27-7

Price, $39.95.

Backcountry Adventures Arizona

Backcountry Adventures Arizona guides readers along 2,671 miles of the state's most remote and scenic backroads, from the lowlands of the Yuma Desert to the high plains of the Kaibab Plateau. Trail history is colorized through the accounts of Indian warriors like Cochise and Geronimo; trailblazers; and the famous lawman Wyatt Earp. Contains 157 trails, 576 pages, and 524 photos.

ISBN 978-1-930193-28-4

Price, $39.95.

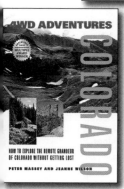

4WD Adventures Colorado

4WD Adventures Colorado takes readers to the Crystal River or over America's highest pass road, Mosquito Pass. This book identifies numerous lost ghost towns that speckle Colorado's mountains. Trail history is brought to life through the accounts of sheriffs and gunslingers like Bat Masterson and Doc Holliday; millionaires like Horace Tabor; and American Indian warriors like Chief Ouray. Contains 71 trails, 232 pages, and 209 photos.

ISBN 978-0-9665675-5-7.

Price, $29.95.

to order
call 800-660-5107 or
visit 4WDbooks.com

other
colorado outdoors
guides

Colorado 4-Wheel Drive Roads

Whether you are a novice out for the first time or an expert well-versed in off-road driving, there is something in this book for you. Full of detailed maps, directions, and vital information, this guide takes you off the paved roads and into Colorado's scenic backcountry.

ISBN 978-0-930657-40-6; Price $19.95

Colorado Fishing Guide & Atlas

This top-selling guide is the ultimate for any angler looking for new fishing spots in Colorado. It is packed with extensive information on hot spots in Colorado's public lands. It includes directions, detailed maps, information about governing agencies, and insightful comments.

ISBN 978-0-930657-41-3; Price $24.95

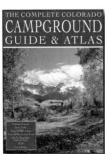

The Complete Colorado Campground Guide & Atlas

This guide is packed with information about more than 500 campgrounds in Colorado's public lands. It includes directions, regulations and restrictions, fee information, detailed maps, and more. New fully revised eleventh edition.

ISBN 978-0-930657-23-9; Price $19.95

Colorado Biking Trails

From urban bike paths to scenic mountain roads, challenging single-track rides to manicured trails, this bike guide has something for everyone. It includes directions to trailheads, maps, trail length, elevation gain, and difficulty for more than 77 trails throughout Colorado.

ISBN, 978-0-930657-28-4; Price $14.95

Fishing Close to Home

This book is for anglers who want to spend their time reeling in the big one rather than spending hours on the road. It provides directions, fishing information, lake size, and more for hot spots near metro Denver, Boulder and Clear Creek Counties.

ISBN, 978-0-930657-51-2; Price $14.95

to order
call 800-660-5107 or
visit 4WDbooks.com

other
colorado outdoors
guides

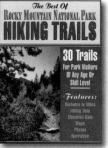

Colorado's Guide to Hunting

Colorado's backcountry is habitat for all sorts of game animals. This guide contains land regulations, permits needed, detailed directions and maps for the best places to hunt.

ISBN 978-0-930657-42-0; Price $14.95

Best of Rocky Mountain National Park Hiking Trails

Contains 30 trails for hikers of all skill levels from short, easy hikes to more difficult trails. It includes camping information, estimated hiking time, trail narratives, directions, maps, trail length, elevation gains, and difficulty.

ISBN 978-0-930657-39-0; Price $9.95

Best of Northern Colorado Hiking Trails

Contains 77 trails from short, easy day hikes to difficult backpacking adventures. This book covers Arapaho, Roosevelt, White River, and Routt National Forests. It includes directions, maps, trail length, elevation gains, and difficulty.

ISBN 978-0-930657-18-5; Price $12.95

**Colorado Lakes & Reservoirs:
Fishing and Boating Guide**

Colorado is home to hundreds of natural and man-made lakes. This book provides information about 150 of them. Included are driving directions, maps, fishing regulations, lake size, fish species, boating ramps, camping facilities, and contact information.

ISBN 978-0-930657-00-0; Price $14.95

Best of Western Colorado Hiking Trails

Contains 50 trails from short, easy day hikes to difficult backpacking adventures. This book covers White River and Gunnison National Forests. It includes directions, maps, trail length, elevation gains, and difficulty.

ISBN 978-0-930657-17-8; Price $9.95

to order
call 800-660-5107 or
visit 4WDbooks.com

benchmark maps
road & recreation atlases

Arizona
Detailed maps pinpoint thousands of miles of backcountry roads, trailheads, campgrounds, and hundreds of points of interest. Public lands maps show hunting units and a recreation guide includes the latest information on campgrounds, RV parks, golf, and boating. Contains 112 pages.
ISBN 978-0-929591-97-1; Retail: $22.95

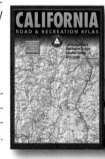

California
With this marvelous atlas, travelers will discover the geographical diversity and natural beauty of California. A comprehensive recreation guide and accompanying maps are the perfect resource for planning the ultimate California adventure. Contains 144 pages.
ISBN 978-0-929591-80-3; Retail: $24.95

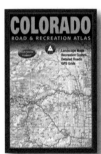

Colorado
No other publication can convey the entrancing scenery and abundant outdoor activities of Colorado's mountains and plains with more precision than Benchmark's new Colorado Road & Recreation Atlas. Contains 144 pages.
ISBN 978-0-929591-94-0; Retail: $24.95

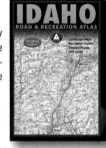

Idaho
Idaho's boundless recreation opportunities and varied scenery is skillfully captured in this atlas. Landscape maps illustrate the full range of topography: from the forest stands of the panhandle, and the mountainous backlands of central Idaho, to the plains and prairies in the south. Contains 96 pages.
ISBN 978-0-929591-82-7; Retail: $22.95

Nevada
Nevada is known as the wildest adventure state in the lower 48. Finally all of Nevada's outdoor assets are captured in one publication. Thorough field checking and local research have made this atlas an essential resource for both urban and backcountry locations. A recreation guide features maps with hunting unit and public land boundaries and emphasizes historic trails and points of interest. Contains 96 pages.
ISBN 978-0-929591-95-7; Retail: $22.95

to order
call 800-660-5107 or
visit 4WDbooks.com

Adler Publishing distributes the full series of Benchmark Road & Recreation Atlases. This award-winning series is distinguished by the exclusive Benchmark Landscape Maps, which combine vivid gradient color tints with 3-D terrain shading to reveal landforms with impressive clarity and detail. Page-to-page overlap, large type, and field-checked accuracy set the Benchmark series apart and make them standouts among state road atlases. Each saddle stitched, 15³⁄₈" x 10³⁄₄" book includes United States, regional, and state maps for orientation, as well as "Metro Maps," enlarged for navigating urban areas.

New Mexico
For the 10th Anniversary Edition, Benchmark has drafted completely new landscape maps and public lands maps, both at larger scales, with far more field-checked information. This edition also includes a new, recreation guide. Contains 96 pages.
ISBN 978-0-929591-87-2; Retail: $22.95

Oregon
Oregonians love their state and they love this atlas. It's no wonder since it clearly shows the roads—all of them—not to mention its accuracy, page overlap, and cleary illustrated landmarks. A hunting and fishing section has been added, and the recreation information and index listings have been updated. Contains 112 pages.
ISBN 978-0-929591-88-9; Retail: $22.95

Utah
Utah, with its flat-topped mountains, deep-gouged canyons and salt deserts, deserves an atlas that matches its dynamic scenery. Landscape maps show all passable Utah roads, classed by surface and purpose, and thousands of campgrounds and other destinations. Contains 96 pages.
ISBN 978-0-929591-93-3; Retail: $22.95

Washington
This atlas has the latest, most accurate maps and reliable recreation information. Its large-scale landscape maps are perfect for either freeway travel or remote backroads. Includes complete public land ownership and game management unit boundaries. Contains 128 pages.
ISBN 978-0-929591-83-4; Retail: $22.95

Wyoming
Wyoming is the heart of the American West. Experience the spirit of the West with Benchmark's new Wyoming Road & Recreation Atlas. Landscape maps clearly depict the terrain and pinpoint Wyoming's backroads and urban corridors as well as its outstanding recreation destinations with field-checked accuracy. Contains 96 pages.
ISBN 978-0-929591-96-4; Retail: $22.95

to order
call 800-660-5107 or
visit 4WDbooks.com